SHADOW NETWORK

BY THE SAME AUTHOR

Murder Under Two Flags: The U.S., Puerto Rico, and the Cerro Maravilla Cover-Up

The Guys: A Play

Red Orchestra: The Story of the Berlin Underground and the Circle of Friends Who Resisted Hitler

Suzanne's Children: A Daring Rescue in Nazi Paris

SHADOW NETWORK

MEDIA, MONEY, AND THE SECRET HUB OF THE RADICAL RIGHT

ANNE NELSON

BLOOMSBURY PUBLISHING
NEW YORK • LONDON • OXFORD • NEW DELHI • SYDNEY

BLOOMSBURY PUBLISHING
Bloomsbury Publishing Inc.
1385 Broadway, New York, NY 10018, USA

First published in the United States 2019

ISBN: HB: 978-1-63557-319-0; eBook: 978-1-63557-320-6

LIBRARY OF CONGRESS CATALOGING-IN-PUBLICATION DATA IS AVAILABLE

2 4 6 8 10 9 7 5 3 1

Typeset by Westchester Publishing Services
Printed and bound in the U.S.A. by Berryville Graphics Inc., Berryville, Virginia

For my friends, and for our country.

CONTENTS

DRAMATIS PERSONAE

*A * denotes a member of the Council for National Policy, past or present. The following is not a complete roster of CNP membership.*

THE FUNDAMENTALISTS

***Paul Pressler III**: Texas lawyer and later judge; helped launch the Southern Baptist Convention's Conservative Resurgence.

***Paige Patterson**: Southern Baptist pastor; helped launch the Conservative Resurgence. Later president of the Southwestern Baptist Theological Seminary in Fort Worth.

***Tony Perkins**: president, Family Research Council; president (as of 2016) of the Council for National Policy.

***Richard Land**: president, Southern Evangelical Seminary; former president, Ethics and Religious Liberty Commission of the Southern Baptist Convention; co-author, Family Research Council iVoterGuide; member, President Donald Trump's Evangelical Advisory Council.

***Tim LaHaye**: California pastor; first president of the Council for National Policy; co-author of bestselling *Left Behind* series of novels about the Rapture.

***Beverly LaHaye**: Tim's wife; founder of Concerned Women for America.

***James Dobson**: fundamentalist psychologist; founder of Focus on the Family and its media empire, as well as the Family Research Council.

Mike Pence: Vice President of the United States.

THE POLITICAL OPERATIVES

***Edwin Meese III**: counselor to President Ronald Reagan; U.S. attorney general (1985–1988); president, CNP, 1996.
***Paul Weyrich**: conservative visionary, co-founder of the Heritage Foundation, the American Legislative Exchange Council, among others.
***Richard Viguerie**: chairman, American Target Advertising; pioneer in the use of direct mail in political campaigns.
***Morton Blackwell**: founder and president of the Leadership Institute, which trains candidates and activists in campaign technology.
***Paul Teller**: former executive director of the House Republican Study Committee; special assistant to President Donald Trump for legislative affairs.
***Kellyanne Conway**: pollster and political consultant; former secretary/treasurer of CNP; counselor to President Donald Trump.
***Ralph Reed**: former director of the Christian Coalition; chairman of the Faith & Freedom Coalition; key figure in the United in Purpose initiative.
***Bill Dallas**: director, United in Purpose coalition, created to register and engage evangelical voting blocs through data mining and canvassing.
George Barna: fundamentalist pollster; co-founder of the Barna Group; executive director of the American Culture & Faith Institute, a division of United in Purpose.

THE MEDIA

***Stuart W. Epperson**: co-founder and chairman, Salem Communications; former president, Council for National Policy (2012).
***Edward G. Atsinger**: co-founder and CEO, Salem Communications.
***Richard P. Bott Sr.**: founder and chairman, Bott Radio Network; ***Richard P. Bott II** is president and CEO.
***Donald Wildmon**: Mississippi minister who founded the American Family Association and American Family Radio; current president of the AFA is Wildmon's son ***Tim Wildmon**.
***Neil Patel**: co-founder and publisher, the *Daily Caller*.
***Steve Bannon**: former executive chairman of Breitbart News; former senior counselor to President Donald Trump.

***Todd Starnes**: Fox News Radio host and Fox News commentator.
James O'Keefe: founder and president, Project Veritas; graduate of Morton Blackwell's Leadership Institute.

THE MONEY

***Richard DeVos Sr.**: co-founder, Amway; ***Richard DeVos Jr.**: former CEO, Amway.
***Edgar Prince**: founder, Prince Corporation; ***Elsa Prince Broekhuizen**, chairman, EDP Management (widow).
Elizabeth "Betsy" DeVos: daughter of Edgar and Elsa Prince; married to Richard DeVos Jr.; Secretary of Education.
***Erik Prince**: son of Edgar and Elsa Prince; former Navy SEAL; founder and former CEO of Blackwater security company (now called Academi).
***Foster Friess**: former manager of the Brandywine Fund; co-founder and president, Friess Family Foundation.
***Robert Mercer**: former co-CEO of Renaissance Technologies, and daughter ***Rebekah Mercer**; investor in Cambridge Analytica.
Charles Koch: CEO of Koch Industries, and **David Koch**, executive vice president, Koch Industries.

HEADS OF ORGANIZATIONS

***Wayne LaPierre**: CEO, National Rifle Association.
***Marjorie Dannenfelser**: President, Susan B. Anthony List.
***Penny Nance**: President and CEO, Concerned Women for America
***Jenny Beth Martin**: founder and CEO, Tea Party Patriots.
***Kristan Hawkins**: president, Students for Life of America.
***Lila Rose**: founder and president, Live Action.
***Jay Sekulow**: chief counsel, American Center for Law & Justice; key attorney for Donald Trump.
***Leonard Leo**: executive vice president, Federalist Society.
***Tim Phillips**: president, Americans for Prosperity, funded by the Koch Brothers.
Charlie Kirk: founder and president of Turning Point USA, youth organization.

TECHNOLOGY STRATEGISTS

Thomas Peters: founder and CEO of uCampaign political app platform, and RumbleUp text messaging platform.

Chris Wilson: CEO, WPA Intelligence; former director of research, analytics and strategy for Ted Cruz campaign, early client of the uCampaign app.

PROLOGUE

One day in August 2004, as I drove down the street in my hometown of Stillwater, Oklahoma, I tuned the radio dial to a new station. I settled on a random call-in show and sat back to listen. The host was denouncing the candidacy of John Kerry in terms that went something like this. "He legalized gay marriage in Massachusetts," he said. "That's exactly what he'll do all over the country if he gets elected president of the United States."

An anxious elderly woman called in. "I've been married to my husband more than forty years—are you saying my marriage would be in danger?"

"That's right," he answered. "John Kerry is threatening the sanctity of marriage, including yours. So you better get out and vote."

When I arrived at my destination, I parked in the driveway to listen to the rest, just to make sure I'd gotten it right. I'd heard debates about same-sex marriage in New York, but none of them suggested that it would challenge the legitimacy of heterosexual marriage. But I dismissed the broadcast as a regional curiosity. After all, I was in a middling town in a deep-red state, and I thought the influence of a radio preacher was unlikely to reach beyond a local audience.

The following years brought historic milestones, including the inauguration of our first African American president, environmental protections, and the legalization of same-sex marriage. But the same period witnessed a social and political backlash that took aim at the very institutions of American government, leading to the rise of the Tea Party, obstructionist Republican majorities in Congress, and the stunning election of Donald Trump in 2016.

America's national news media were caught off guard, and experts scrambled to find an explanation. The *New York Times* turned to Fox News. Trump voters "don't believe what anyone in the news media is telling them, except for maybe Fox News," stated one op-ed.[1] The *New Yorker* named *The Apprentice* as "the show that made [Trump's] Presidency possible."[2] A report from Harvard's Berkman Klein Center pointed to news platforms, making a case that conservatives shunned professional online media organizations in favor of "pro-Trump, highly partisan media outlets" such as *Breitbart News*.[3]

Each of those factors played an important role. But as someone who has shuttled between the East Coast and the Midwest over the past four decades, I saw mounting evidence of a larger force at work. Through my research, I discovered the rapidly evolving ties connecting the manpower and media of the Christian right with the finances of Western plutocrats and the strategy of right-wing Republican political operatives. Many of their connections were made through a secretive organization called the Council for National Policy, which, as one member has said, brings together the "donors and the doers."

The CNP was founded in 1981 by a small group of archconservatives who realized that the tides of history had turned against them. They represented an American past dominated by white Protestant male property owners. They dreamed of restoring a nineteenth-century patriarchy that limited the civil rights of women, minorities, immigrants, and workers, with no income tax to vex the rich or social safety net to aid the poor. Now they faced a future in which minorities, women, gays, and atheists were gaining in number, rights, and political influence. If the country abided by a clear-cut democratic process, these constituencies, leaning Democratic, would consolidate their power based on majority rule.

So the CNP decided to change the rules. This task would require developing a long-range strategy to target critical districts and activate previously unengaged voting blocs. But, as author David Daley has pointed out, the conservatives faced a deadline: once Democratic-leaning youth and minorities reached a decisive majority—which could be as early as 2031—there might be no turning back.[4]

The CNP spent decades building a framework to advance its agenda. One pillar has been its ability to master the basic rules of media and write new ones.

I began my research by examining how the massive disruption of the news media has contributed to the fractured state of our politics. Middle America has been a victim of a colony collapse in journalism, triggered in part by the headlong rush for profits in the news industry in the late twentieth century. I found that as local and regional newspapers collapsed over the early 2000s, media owned by CNP members rushed to fill the vacuum. They developed a sophisticated strategy, starting with local radio, an old-fashioned but powerful medium that had been written off too soon by the CNP's opposition.

I discovered hundreds of broadcast outlets, such as the radio station I heard back in 2004, that belong to members of the CNP. Three key players dominate this landscape: Salem Media Group, Bott Radio Network, and the American Family Radio networks. Over the years they have connected their holdings to a cohort of pastors, politicians, and tycoons, creating an armada of radio stations and news outlets loyal to the CNP's political agenda, and selling millions of Americans on its harsh combination of plutocracy and theocracy.

Their programming is not uniform, but it harmonizes. In Detroit, Salem Media's WDTK ("The Patriot") stokes the ire of disaffected Rust Belt listeners with complaints about the economy and immigration.[5] The same network offers its audience in Little Rock its "first FM commercial Christian Talk and Teach station . . . Our partnership with national programmers and local churches, ministries and businesses ensures that our listeners will receive solid teaching and informative talk."[6] American Family Radio preaches the dangers of modern science and "moral decay": "The complete absence of transitional fossils disprove evolution," it tells listeners, and reports that "God agrees . . . that homosexuality should be against the law."[7]

Because these stations' audiences have lost or abandoned professional news outlets—and because their interests had been ignored by major national media—they are more vulnerable than ever. Over time, the media empire has expanded its reach into Fox News operations and grown to include fundamentalist television broadcasting, digital platforms, book publishing, and feature-film production.

The "wallpaper effect" of wraparound media can have a powerful impact. Abraham Hamilton III, host of American Family Radio's *Hamilton Corner*, described the October 1, 2017, mass shooting in Las Vegas as "Satan's work," immune to legislation. The Democrats, he complained, were "exploiting" the victims by calling for hearings on gun control. This charge was repeated, often in the same language, by other CNP-affiliated political and media figures across platforms, including the *Daily Signal*, the *Hillsdale Collegian*, and Fox News' *Todd Starnes Show*.[8] The cumulative effect is the creation of a parallel universe of information. The results have been devastating to American democracy, as two parts of our country constantly talk past each other.

CNP strategists showed an astute grasp of electoral politics, finding hidden pockets of evangelical voters and identifying the issues that could drive them to the polls. They displayed a special talent for pinpointing the districts and swing states that could win them critical victories. The intricate mechanics of the Electoral College and redistricting presented a narrow window to circumvent the popular vote, and they seized the opportunity.

The CNP and its allies spent years building party machines at a state level. The Republican control of statehouses supported their gerrymandering efforts, and powerful donors helped them tackle labor unions in Wisconsin, Michigan, and other former Democratic strongholds. When unions lost the right to collective bargaining in the Rust Belt, it crippled their ability to represent their members in the political process.

The statehouse stratagem also allowed the CNP and its allies to use state governments as staging grounds for aspirants to national office. One such state was Michigan, the home of Trump's secretary of education, Betsy DeVos, and her powerful clan; another was vice president Mike Pence's Indiana.

I learned that the CNP originated in the "Conservative Resurgence" of the Southern Baptist Convention in the 1970s and early '80s, which reversed a trend toward liberalization and purged moderates from church institutions. The movement learned from this success and replicated it, developing an impressive capacity to co-opt existing organizations and draw them into its web. One example is the National Rifle Association, a former gentlemen's marksmanship club that has been weaponized for political purpose. The CNP set its sights on the Republican Party, conducting a decades-long crusade to promote right-wing extremists and drive moderates out of office.

One of the most surprising elements of this story is the coalition's fusion of digital campaign tools to its grassroots organizations and media. Stung by Obama's successful digital strategy in 2008, the movement turned to the Koch Brothers' state-of-the-art i360 data platform, linking data and ground troops to a new generation of networked apps. This marriage was designed to reach targeted populations, creating discreet communications channels that were hardly visible to opponents and national news media. As Democratic strategists note, their party has sophistical digital tools, but a less cohesive organizational structure. Meanwhile, groups run by CNP members and their favored candidates benefit from a subsidized, turnkey digital package. Their coordinated apps collaborate across platforms and weave seemingly independent groups into tightly networked operations.

These measures played a significant role in the 2016 surprise and continue to affect the electoral landscape today. The CNP's preferred Republican candidate that year was Senator Ted Cruz, but when Donald Trump won the nomination, the movement turned on a dime, delivering its national network of media and manpower to carry his message, in return for his promise to advance its policy objectives. The impact of this network was borne out again in key races in the 2018 midterm elections, and can be anticipated for 2020.

Digital tools are unlikely to be effective if they are not rooted in social relationships. The movement has benefited from the gradual decline of mainline Protestant denominations and the rapid growth of the evangelical population over the past half century. Pastors have been wooed, pressured, and sometimes bullied to adopt increasingly political stands.

The movement has also appropriated a vocabulary that it redeploys with Orwellian flair. "Family" is a code word for homophobic, and "defense of marriage" means prohibition of same-sex unions. "Fairness" and "justice" mean lowering taxes for the wealthy and corporations. "Values" means conservative evangelical ideology. "Right to work" means depriving unions of the benefits of collective bargaining. The movement's brand of "religious freedom" often disparages other beliefs, and would allow fundamentalist churches to support political campaigns while retaining their tax-exempt status. And in the lexicon of Betsy DeVos, crown princess of the movement, "educational reform" means redirecting public school funding to religious schools, charter schools, and homeschooling. All of these euphemisms promote policies that victimize low-income and minority populations.

My reporting in this book builds on decades of invaluable work by scholars and journalists such as Frederick Clarkson, Lee Fang, Frances FitzGerald, Dan Gilgoff, Jane Mayer, Adam Piore, Jeff Sharlet, Theda Skocpol, Katherine Stewart, and too many others to list here. (A Recommended Reading section is provided at the end of this book, for those who wish to explore further.)

Shadow Network adds new findings on the strategy and mechanics of the operation. As I pursued my research, I spent long hours tracing webs of funding and digital platforms. I also spent time among the partisans of the movement, attending their meetings, their church services, and their rallies. I listened hard and found virtues as well as failings. I spent long hours of time listening to fundamentalist radio shows and watching videos to learn their perspective, and I heard valid points, ingenious strategies, and outright lies.

I've also acquired a stronger grasp of regional resentments. One marker is my struggle to label the vast region of the United States that lies between the coasts and increasingly functions as a political unit. It is often dismissed as "flyover country"—as though that's a clever summation of a large and complex population that is often overlooked. (Another dismissive term is "the noncoastal area.") I've seen glaring examples of the way national news media and the Democratic Party have taken these populations for granted, at a cost for all concerned. As these regions lose representation in the media sphere, they are all the more determined to claim it elsewhere.

The CNP understood this. Its roots lie in the oil-producing states of Texas, Louisiana, and Oklahoma. One outcome has been the sudden prominence of individuals from those states under the Trump administration, in federal agencies, advisory bodies, and the cabinet. Oklahoma, in particular, has served as an incubator state for the CNP's political and social vision; my home state appears again and again as a breeding ground for the movement's policies and advocates. My friends and family have watched with sorrow as environmental regulations have been suspended, public education has been gutted, and public health indicators have plummeted. Under the Trump administration, the same model is being promoted at a federal level.

At the heart of the debate is climate. In a world where the options for preserving our environment are rapidly diminishing, advocates of sustainable growth face a movement set on accelerating the damage in the interests of short-term profit. Health, education, and welfare are also under attack. The rights of women, gays, minorities, and immigrants are at stake. On the economic front, a shell game is taking place. It's no secret that the electorate can be seduced by deceptive economic upticks, based on slashed entitlements and historic levels of debt. Members of the Council for National Policy have worked in concert with affiliates of the Koch network to advance these goals, at a mounting cost to the polity.

The CNP has labored in the shadows, but not in utter darkness. Some leading members made headlines in past decades, including Tim LaHaye, Jerry Falwell, Paul Weyrich, and Richard Viguerie. Others may be less familiar to readers, including Stuart Epperson and Edward Atsinger III of Salem Communications, Richard P. Bott Sr. and Jr. of the Bott Radio Network, and the Wildmon family of the American Family Association. Vice President Mike Pence emerges, not as a meek sidekick, but as an indispensable bridge to power.

Here you will find the myriad ways that money, media, and mobilization have been synchronized in the pursuit of power and profit. The story is peopled by shrewd, remarkable and sometimes unscrupulous characters, and rife with unexpected connections and synchronicities. The larger picture is one that the American public needs to understand. We must ask ourselves whether the country the CNP has planned for us is one we can accept for ourselves and our children.

CHAPTER 1

IN THE BEGINNING: TEXAS

The endless analyses of the current crisis in American politics have pinpointed everything from the influence of social media to white male rage. But as valid as these points may be, few of them fully explore the deep historical roots of Protestant fundamentalism and the ways it has been mobilized in the modern era.

Protestantism dominated American society for two centuries, informing the values that made history. American Protestantism existed in many variations and experienced waves of transformation, but its most conservative bastions held fast to the notion of God-given exceptionalism—the United States as the "City upon a Hill." In the Civil War, both sides claimed the Almighty's blessing. In the final brutal year of the conflict, the U.S. Treasury began to imprint "In God We Trust" on coins—at the same time the South argued its God-given entitlement to slavery and states' rights.

Waves of immigration brought new religions and new ways of thinking to the country, but the pervasive spirit of American Protestantism remained. In 1954 a Presbyterian minister convinced President Eisenhower to add a clause to the Pledge of Allegiance. "To omit the words 'under God' from the Pledge of Allegiance is to omit the definitive factor in the American way of life," the Scottish-born pastor said. "If you deny the Christian ethic, you fall short of the American ideal of life."[1]

That notion came under increasing challenge. By the time Donald Trump was elected in 2016, Americans had multiplied, urbanized, diversified, and secularized. This had a profound influence on the American way of life. The population had tripled over the course of the previous century. Sixty percent of Americans lived in rural areas in 1900, but by 2016 over 80 percent lived in cities, heavily concentrated on the coasts.[2] A century earlier the U.S. population was close to 90 percent non-Hispanic white, but by 2016 that figure dropped to 60 percent and was falling steadily. In 1972 Protestants made up two-thirds of the U.S. population, but by 2012 they had dropped to less than half.[3] Nonetheless, a sizable contingent of fundamentalists believed that God had chosen them to impose His will on the nation. The mores of the new America created an unbearable tension. These demographic trends—and the anxiety they provoked—contributed to the forces that brought Trump to power.

The figures who would create the Council for National Policy had a fierce allegiance to the white Protestant culture of the past, and presumed it would prevail forever. But the shifting electorate challenged that notion. As the power of the federal government expanded, its courts and agencies reflected national trends and imposed change on regions that had long lived as semiautonomous enclaves.

In the late 1960s these tensions came to a head in a bedrock of American Protestantism: the Southern Baptist Convention. This conflict was an essential prologue to the story of the Council for National Policy. It was a key proving ground for some of the council's founders; it would shape the group's core and inform its tactics over the next half century. At the conflict's heart was a belief in authoritarian principles, linking "biblical inerrancy" to theocracy. This approach extended to the tenet of strict constructionism, which upheld a literal interpretation of the Constitution and other laws, restricting their meaning to their supposed intent at the time they were written.[4]

The key players learned how to achieve minority rule through long-term strategies, which they would soon apply to the country as a whole, manipulating the electoral process and reshaping the judiciary. They would achieve astonishing success.

THE COUNTERCULTURE CALLED the 1960s the "Age of Aquarius," but Southern fundamentalists feared the decade as the eve of the apocalypse. They were rattled by the disturbing images the network news broadcasts brought into their living rooms. Nineteen sixty-seven was the year of reckoning. Southern society was based on segregation, but in June the Supreme Court struck down all state laws banning interracial marriage, and that October the court installed its first African American justice. Southerners were steeped in military tradition, but that month they watched almost one hundred thousand protesters march on the Pentagon. The South was still the land of church socials and sock hops, but that year *Hair* opened off Broadway, celebrating LSD and nudity onstage. Even the Bible was under scrutiny, as a new generation of theologians reviewed the scientific record and suggested that the Good Book was a profound work of literature, not a chronicle of historical fact. The conservative wing of the Southern Baptist Convention was profoundly shaken.

It wasn't their first encounter with existential crisis. The denomination was born of a split in 1845, in the heat of the national debate over slavery. When the Baptist church barred slave owners from serving as missionaries, the southern brethren seceded. In the ensuing conflict, the Southern Baptists backed the Confederacy with money, soldiers, and chaplains. Their support was ideological as well as material. Historian M. F. Fiegel wrote, "Coinciding with propaganda designed to arouse fear and hatred of the Union, the Baptists made an effort to portray the war as a holy struggle . . . They tended to think of themselves as God's chosen people. Therefore, it was easy for them to combine politics, patriotism, and religion."[5]

In this spirit, the Southern Baptist Convention drew up a set of resolutions in 1861, asserting that "the Union, constituted by our forefathers, was one of co-equal sovereign States. The fanatical spirit of the North has long been seeking to deprive us of rights and franchises guaranteed by the Constitution." They had no doubt of the Confederacy's sacred calling: "We beseech the churches to cherish the spirit, and imitate the example of this noble army of saints and heroes."[6] This language of state sovereignty and holy war would resonate far into the future.

Other Protestant denominations split during the war as well, but for the most part they mended fences afterward. The Baptists remained divided. The (predominantly African American) National Baptist Convention and the American Baptist Churches identified with mainline Protestant churches and joined them in the National Council of Churches. The Southern Baptist Convention remained apart, consolidating its position as a religious powerhouse in the South, with a far larger membership than its two counterparts. Southern Baptists were heavily concentrated in the states of the former Confederacy. As of 1980 there were more than 2.6 million Southern Baptists in Texas, almost a sixth of the state's population.[7] Southern Baptists represented over a quarter of all Alabamans, but they were scarce in New England.[8] There were affiliated churches in forty-one states as of 2019, but the denomination remains a predominantly southern institution.

Allegiance to states' rights continued to be part of the church's birthright, and it represented another principle under threat amid the social changes of the 1960s. One of its tenets was the believers' right to conduct certain religious practices in the public square. For generations Southern Baptists and other Christians had taken it for granted that public institutions should double as religious venues. Public school days and sports events began with Christian devotions. High school football teams joined the Fellowship of Christian Athletes to pray for victory in the locker room, and county employees installed Christmas crèches on the courthouse lawn. These practices went unquestioned, and for generations few religious minorities or public atheists were around to object. For many communities in Middle America, Protestantism was the organizing principle for society, its various denominations serving as silent markers for tribes, class, and ethnicity. Churches were where housewives displayed their finery and teenagers courted under the watchful eyes of adults. Congregations served as nonstate social agencies, helping the needy and lending a hand to members in trouble. As long as communities were uniformly Christian and the nation's values were shaped by their ethos, these phenomena were an accepted way of life.

But as America changed, the courts changed with it. They began to respond to the growing population of atheists and adherents of minority religions, who argued that state institutions should not be used to promote one religion over other beliefs. In 1962 the Supreme Court ended public school prayer. The following year it ended devotional Bible study in public schools. The fundamentalists were outraged.

Southerners resented the federal courts' intrusion into their local affairs. In the same way antebellum Southern Baptists refused to be governed by their northern counterparts, Southerners rejected the imposition of national norms on their society. It was another holy war: they considered the line between their church and their concept of the state to be next to invisible.

The spirit of the 1960s reached the Southern Baptist seminaries, where theologians reconsidered the tenets of their faith. In 1961, for example, the Southern Baptist Broadman Press published a book called *The Message of Genesis*. Its author, Old Testament scholar Ralph Elliott, wrote that the Bible could be considered spiritually true even if it was not historically accurate. Adam and Eve were not historical figures, he posited; Noah's flood did not cover the entire earth, and Sodom and Gomorrah suffered a natural disaster, not divine wrath. Church conservatives immediately objected.

The debate over biblical inerrancy had broader implications. Questioning the literal truth of the Bible could open the door to teaching evolution, environmentalism, and cultural relativism. But Broadman Press was unrepentant.

For a Baptist seminarian named Paige Patterson, it was all too much. By 1967 the young Texan feared that his church, and by extension his country, were headed for the abyss. Patterson was pursuing a degree at the New Orleans Baptist Theological Seminary. He belonged to the same generation as the antiwar protesters and free-love advocates, but culturally he was miles away. A stocky twenty-five-year-old with wiry red hair and the flat face of a boxer, Patterson had begun preaching in his teens and continued at his tiny Baptist college in Abilene.[9]

A mutual friend suggested that Patterson should meet a like-minded fellow Texan, Herman Paul Pressler III. Pressler was Houston aristocracy, descended from a long line of lawyers and judges; his father and grandfather represented the Humble Oil and Refining Company, which would later become ExxonMobil. A graduate of Phillips Exeter and Princeton, Pressler cut an urbane figure with square black glasses and a ready smile, but he was at least as fierce as Patterson in defense of the fundamentals.

The two men first met in March 1967 at the Café du Monde in New Orleans, an event that has gone down in Southern Baptist history. Pressler recalled that the two men simply "shared concerns" about their church's alarming lurch toward liberalism. How could they stem the tide? The Southern Baptist Convention consisted of tens of thousands of independent congregations, without bishops or similar church hierarchy. Power resided in the annual gatherings attended by tens of thousands of delegates, called "messengers." These members elected the representatives who set church policy, in coordination with the powerful presidents of six Southern Baptist seminaries spread across the South.

Patterson and Pressler formulated a sophisticated strategy, informed by intelligence from a church employee familiar with the convention's inner workings. They saw no need to persuade moderates through reasoning or debate; rather, they would outmaneuver them with a Baptist version of get-out-the-vote tactics, mobilizing previously unengaged members to elect their chosen candidates at the annual meeting. Once they installed a series of like-minded conservative presidents, they could leverage their powers of appointment to take over the church's various divisions. Inerrancy of the Bible would be their core issue. Patterson and Pressler called their movement the Conservative Resurgence, but unhappy moderates would call it a fundamentalist takeover.

The two men remained in touch as they advanced their respective careers. Their crusade began in earnest in 1979, with a churchwide get-out-the-vote campaign. Volunteers from fifteen states were recruited to attend the convention in Houston, where they voted as a bloc to elect conservative Florida-born pastor Adrian Rogers as president.

The following year Pressler declared his intent to install a conservative president every year for the next decade using the same tactics. "I remember one family from South Bend, Indiana," he recalled. "They had five children and drove non-stop to Los Angeles to the Southern Baptist Convention in 1981. They voted and drove non-stop back, eating peanut butter and jelly sandwiches. They didn't spend a night in a motel because they didn't have the money."[10]

A moderate Baptist pastor named Will Campbell described the outcome. "Year after year thousands of messengers poured into Dallas, Miami, St. Louis, Atlanta, San Antonio, Las Vegas for the annual gathering. They came in cars, church buses, recreation vehicles, airplanes, and on trains to cast their ballots. Each year the Pressler-Patterson faction won. The mission was accomplished."[11]

The appointments followed. The church's boards, agencies, and charities of the denomination were reconstituted year by year, until they were uniformly conservative. Dissent was quelled.

The two leaders developed other tactics as well, later revealed in the *Texas Observer* in an article by Michael Erard about a young protégé of Patterson's named Ben Cole. "Patterson became a father figure, Cole recalls, offering counsel, calling him in his dorm room, bringing him to functions, telling him secrets. Admitted to the inner circle, Cole began to learn political tactics: reserving blocks of rooms in conference hotels to enfranchise sympathizers, building communication networks, enlisting the media in disinformation campaigns, and spying on enemies."[12] Cole rebelled against his mentor and went on to become a dissident pastor and blogger.

Paul Pressler called these stratagems "going for the jugular." Similar tactics would be deployed against moderate Republican congressmen in the years to come.

The issue of biblical inerrancy remained an internal theological matter. At the same time, Southern Baptists prepared to enter the political arena to do battle over homosexuality and abortion rights. The new policies on these issues represented a backlash against the church's previous positions. In 1971 the Southern Baptists had passed a resolution liberalizing its stance on abortion, accepting it in cases of severe fetal abnormalities and where the "emotional, mental, and physical health of the mother" was at stake.

Social issues were key to organizing the Southern Baptist messengers, but the fundamentalist leaders were equally determined to expand their role in the public sphere. At the core of their political mission was the demand for "religious freedom" to enhance their political influence, using the church as a tax-exempt power base.

The Southern Baptists' activism benefited from a decline among their competitors. Only a few decades earlier the Methodists had been the largest Protestant church in America, but they, like other mainline Protestant congregations, lost membership in the late twentieth century. (Some observers believed that their milder theology mitigated their followers' fear of damnation.) Over the same period, Southern Baptist membership exploded from just over 7 million in 1950 to 13.6 million in 1980, overtaking the Methodists.

Patterson and Pressler's next step was to extend their strategy from church to state. Their plan was rooted in the concept of theocracy: the belief that government should be conducted through divine guidance, by officials who are chosen by God. The fundamentalists believed that this concept was written into the country's founding principles: after all, they said, the Declaration of Independence held that all men are "endowed by their Creator" with inalienable rights.

The historical record wasn't so clear. The Declaration of Independence was signed by adherents of various denominations: Anglicans, Calvinists, Quakers, Unitarians, and a Catholic. They were keenly aware of the religious wars that had shattered Europe, and took pains not to impose one sect over others. The framers of the Constitution broke with the European tradition of a national state church; in the early days of the Republic most states supported "established churches" (mostly Congregational in the North and Episcopalian in the South), but they all suspended this practice by the mid-nineteenth century. Thomas Jefferson pointedly wrote his Virginia Statute for Religious Freedom on behalf of "the Jew and the gentile, the Christian and the Mahometan, the Hindu and the infidel of every denomination."

The Founding Fathers were overwhelmingly Protestant, but they stipulated that no religious test would be allowed for federal office holders. The First Amendment proclaimed: "Congress shall make no law respecting the establishment of religion, or prohibiting the free exercise thereof." (The constitutions of eight states still prohibit atheists from holding state office, but a 1961 Supreme Court decision rendered such articles unenforceable.) That said, a tacit ethos held. Forty-one of the forty-five presidents of the United States have been Protestant. (Kennedy was Catholic, and Thomas Jefferson, Abraham Lincoln, and Andrew Johnson were described as unaffiliated.)

But as American Protestants began to lose their social dominance, U.S. courts increasingly ruled to secularize the public sphere. There was an inevitable backlash, especially among evangelicals, a term that covered a wide range of beliefs. It included fundamentalists, among them the Southern Baptists, who were distinguished by their literal interpretation of the Bible and their strict social codes. It also included charismatic Pentecostals and Seventh-Day Adventists, who embraced prophecy and faith healing, as well as those mainline Protestants who identified as "born again."

Some conservative evangelicals adhered to a philosophy called Dominionism. In his book *The Changing of the Guard: Biblical Principles for Political Action*, Texas pastor George Grant wrote, "Christians have an obligation, a mission, a holy responsibility to reclaim the land for Jesus Christ—to have dominion in civil structures, just as in every other aspect of life . . . of men, families, institutions, bureaucracies, courts and governments for the Kingdom of Christ."[13] One variant, "Seven Mountains Dominionism," aimed to "bring Godly change to a nation by reaching its seven spheres, or mountains, of societal influence . . . religion, family, education, government, media, arts and entertainment, and business."[14] Seven Mountains Dominionism had followers from various conservative sects, including Southern Baptists, and its intense will to power would inform the vision of the Council for National Policy.

Patterson and Pressler's strategies dovetailed neatly with a movement led by a Southern Baptist preacher named Jerry Falwell, taking shape across the country. The son of a Virginia bootlegger, Falwell fueled his clerical career with the drive of an entrepreneur. His *Old-Time Gospel Hour* broadcast, launched in 1956, generated tens of millions of dollars. As a son of the Old South, Falwell opposed Martin Luther King Jr. and condemned the 1964 Civil Rights Act as "Civil Wrongs." In 1967 he answered the challenge by founding a segregated academy in his hometown of Lynchburg, Virginia. A few years later President Nixon ordered the IRS to deny tax exemptions to all segregated schools in the United States, and Falwell's academy was in its sights. With his tax-exempt empire at stake, he looked for a way to strike back.

* * *

IN 1979 FALWELL convened a meeting with some fellow pastors, inviting a Republican powerbroker named Paul Weyrich, who would become one of the architects of the Council for National Policy. Weyrich didn't look the part of a Machiavelli. In his youth his pink cheeks, blond forelock, and engaging smile gave him an innocent air; he was described as "cherubic" with a "pugnacious temperament."[15] He came to the Southern Baptists as a strategist, not a coreligionist. Born into a German immigrant family in Wisconsin, Weyrich was raised a Catholic, but he rejected the liberal reforms of Vatican II and converted to a conservative Eastern Orthodox sect. After college he went to work on Capitol Hill, in the thick of the political upheaval of the 1960s.

According to journalist David Grann's account in the *New Republic*, Weyrich's idea for a conservative network arose in Washington one day in 1969. Weyrich snuck into a meeting for a liberal coalition, where he beheld congressional aides, political analysts, and Democratic activists, all coordinating press outreach and demonstrations in support of a housing bill. Liberals and Democrats, Weyrich observed, enjoyed long-standing structural advantages. Their policy prescriptions were informed by think tanks such as the Brookings Institution, founded in 1916. Their campaigns were grounded in powerful labor unions, whose membership rolls were still robust at that point. The Democrats' urban coalition included well-established groups like the NAACP, as well as new activists like the National Organization for Women (NOW). Progressive clergy were stirring change in their Catholic, Protestant, and Jewish congregations.

In contrast, the popular image of the typical Republican was of a well-heeled businessman and his neatly coiffed wife, relaxing at the country club and complaining about taxes. The Democrats' organizations stirred their members to march, lobby, and vote. Weyrich wondered why the right couldn't do the same.

Weyrich's starting point was Richard Nixon's resounding defeat of George McGovern in 1972. Over the following year, in what must be acknowledged as a stunning achievement, Weyrich cofounded three institutions that became crucial building blocks of the radical right (and, eventually, of the Council for National Policy). One was the Heritage Foundation, intended as a counterweight to Brookings and other liberal think tanks, with major funding from beer scion Joseph Coors and Mellon heir Richard Scaife. Weyrich became its first president. Weyrich also cofounded the Republican Study Committee (RSC) to counter the Democratic Study Group, founded in 1959. The RSC would advance the interests of the conservative wing of the Republican Party in Congress, to the detriment of party moderates. Finally, Weyrich founded an influential Republican lunch club on Capitol Hill, with the help of two youngsters named George Will and Trent Lott. The Weyrich Lunch would become a Washington institution.[17]

Weyrich was not content with creating parallel institutions; he also devised resources the Democrats lacked. He saw untapped potential in state-level politics. The Democrats controlled more state legislatures than the Republicans, but there was little coordination among them. Weyrich cofounded the American Legislative Exchange Council, or ALEC, as a way for the Republican minority to gain the upper hand. Republican state legislators and their spouses were invited to junkets at luxury hotels and resorts, organized and financed by hundreds of lobbyists and corporations. There the lawmakers studied "model" legislation, drafted by the corporations they purported to regulate. The bills were often introduced in states with favorable conditions, such as West Virginia, Oklahoma, and Mississippi.[18] There they were validated in state courts, then leveraged to other states, bringing the advantage of a legal precedent. Extractive industries, Big Pharma, tobacco companies, and others flocked to ALEC conferences, paid their dues, and emerged with their reward. (It would take the Democrats four decades to launch the State Innovation Exchange as a tactical response.)

Weyrich and his allies knew that the Democrats enjoyed a mounting demographic advantage. The coming generations of voters, newly enfranchised minorities, and energized women all leaned Democratic. Much of the national news media also skewed liberal, especially in the era of Watergate and the Vietnam War. The Democrats benefited from support at many universities, and student protests against the Nixon administration were a frequent occurrence.

But Weyrich saw other trends playing in his favor. The nation's population was on the move. As the economy suffered in Rust Belt states, millions of Americans made their way to the Sun Belt. Many southern states were hostile to labor unions. Over the 1940s and '50s many had passed right-to-work laws limiting collective bargaining, which hampered unions' organizing abilities on behalf of their Democratic allies.

The New South offered Republicans the potential for a new well of untapped voters, and Weyrich embarked on a search for the partners who could turn his dreams of a conservative coalition into a reality. The resurgent Southern Baptists were a logical starting point.

Weyrich and Falwell's circle found common ground at their 1979 gathering, and the pastors began to explore a partnership with Weyrich and his team of Washington operatives. These included Howard Phillips, a Boston-born Jewish convert to evangelical Christianity. Phillips had joined the Nixon administration and used his positions at federal agencies to defund social programs launched in the 1960s. Another member was Richard Viguerie, a marketing wizard who started out working for a Tulsa radio evangelist, building a valuable bridge to the fundamentalists.

Southern Baptist pastor Richard Grant complained that Weyrich's squad was a "sham . . . controlled by three Catholics and a Jew." (Aside from Weyrich, Viguerie and their colleague Terry Dolan had been raised as Catholics.) Nonetheless, Weyrich's team would engineer the Southern Baptists' foray into politics.

Weyrich and company offered the Southern Baptists a path to theocracy through the electoral process. They drew on a recent poll reporting that 70 percent of evangelical and fundamentalist Christians, estimated at fifty to sixty million people, had sat out the 1976 elections. Jimmy Carter had won the presidency by less than two million votes. If religious conservatives could be mobilized, their votes could turn the tide. Falwell envisioned an army of 72,000 clergy—"Jews, Catholics, Protestants and Mormons"—whose mission would be political, not religious. Paul Weyrich came up with a name for the movement: "The Moral Majority."

That year a controversy arose in Dallas, offering the new movement a useful platform. The instigator was a thirty-six-year-old Southern Baptist preacher named James Robison, who had made local headlines with his homophobic broadcasts on the local ABC affiliate. One Sunday in 1979 he took his statements even farther, claiming homosexuals were prone to molesting and murdering young boys. He added that the assassination of gay San Francisco elected official Harvey Milk was a sign of God's judgment against them.[19]

Gay activists in Dallas objected. Under the FCC fairness doctrine in force at the time, they claimed equal time to contest Robison's slander. Rather than adjudicate the dispute, the Dallas station canceled his broadcast.[20] Robison staged a mass rally that obliged the station to restore the broadcast, attracting the attention of Jerry Falwell and his associates.

A year later, Weyrich's Washington crew joined forces with the Moral Majority and the Texas Baptists in Dallas. The occasion was a mass rally held in the Reunion Arena, a vast new sports stadium shaped like a flying saucer. Only a few weeks earlier the venue had featured rock concerts by the Who and Queen. Now it was handed over to Ed McAteer, a Southern Baptist activist and Colgate-Palmolive salesman, working on behalf of a group of fundamentalist pastors called the Religious Roundtable. The two-day event began on August 21, 1980, in sweltering heat; the next day reached 105 degrees. The *Washington Post* reported that at its height, the crowd reached fifteen thousand, including several thousand pastors from forty-one states. Much of the $450,000 bill was covered by a Fort Worth oil baron.[21]

The rally represented a watershed, in both religious and political terms. The speakers included the pastors and politicos who would come to be known as the New Right, among them Weyrich, Pat Robertson, Jerry Falwell, Tim LaHaye, and James Robison.[22] Many Old Guard evangelicals stayed away. The event was billed as nonpartisan, in keeping with IRS regulations, but Ronald Reagan was the only candidate to accept an invitation to attend, and his staff carefully briefed him on the fundamentalists' concerns.

James Robison was a popular host. At thirty-nine, he had parlayed his dark good looks and fire-and-brimstone oratory into media celebrity. He scheduled his own remarks immediately before Reagan, the last speaker of the day, and his message was clear: "Not voting is a sin against Almighty God!"

Before he spoke, Robison took the candidate aside to explain that he would not be endorsed at the rally. "I suggested to Mr. Reagan that because it was a bipartisan [event] that it would be in his best interest, since we could not and would not endorse him as a body," he told W. Scott Lamb of the *Washington Times*.[23] "But it would probably be wise if his opening comment would be 'I know this is nonpartisan so you can't endorse me. But I want you to know—I endorse you and what you're doing.'"[24] Reagan delivered his lines to perfection, and the masses leaped to their feet.

The throng included men who would guide the movement for decades to come. Mike Huckabee, Robison's assistant, was in charge of logistics. Meeting Reagan for the first time showed the twenty-four-year-old Arkansan how religion and media could be channeled into political power. "No one had ever given so much attention to, or paid respect for the evangelicals," Huckabee told the *Washington Times*. "It was magic, and [the evangelicals were] a major force in Reagan winning."[25]

Another supporter was Rafael Cruz, a Cuban exile who would become an influential Dominionist pastor. Cruz had spent the year steeping his nine-year-old son, Ted, in the doctrine.[26]

The Southern Baptists were well represented. Judge Pressler traveled up from Houston at the urging of some friends. He arrived with low expectations, but once he met Reagan, he immediately grasped his potential to build out their base.

Weyrich had labored for two decades to expand the conservative footprint in Washington, networking among right-wing congressional offices, lobbyists, and associations, but he had yet to tap into a mass base. In Dallas he offered a glimpse of his plan: "We are talking about Christianizing America. We are talking about simply spreading the gospel in a political context."[27]

This meant a new approach to get-out-the-vote tactics, mirroring Patterson and Pressler's tactics. It wasn't about representational democracy. "I don't want everybody to vote," Weyrich told his audience. "Elections are not won by a majority of people. They never have been from the beginning of our country, and they are not now. As a matter of fact, our leverage in the elections, quite candidly, goes up as the voting populace goes down."

In other words, suppressing opposition voters was as critical as engaging supporters.

Ronald Reagan assessed the crowd and quickly adopted its vocabulary. "I was asked once in a press interview what book I would choose if I were shipwrecked on an island and could have only one book for the rest of my life," he told them. "I replied that I knew of only one book that could be read, and reread, and continue to be a challenge: the Bible . . . Indeed, it is an incontrovertible fact that all the complex and horrendous questions confronting us at home and worldwide have their answer in that single book."[28]

Only four years earlier, the fundamentalists had embraced Jimmy Carter: a Southern Baptist Sunday school teacher, decorated navy officer, and devoted husband and father. Reagan, on the other hand, was a sometime Presbyterian who had spent his wartime military service doing public relations; worst of all, he was divorced.

But Carter had infuriated the fundamentalists by supporting the Equal Rights Amendment and abortion rights, as well as allowing the IRS to conduct its ongoing audits of segregated institutions. The fundamentalists might do better cutting a deal with a questionable Reagan, they reasoned, than relying on a righteous Carter.

The leading pastors at the Dallas rally recognized the possible new opening. After the event they invited Paul Weyrich to meet with them in a small room in the arena. The group included Jerry Falwell and Adrian Rogers, Patterson and Pressler's chosen president of the Southern Baptist Convention. Another important attendee was Oklahoma-born W. A. Criswell, the pastor of the First Baptist Church of Dallas, a Southern Baptist juggernaut.

Dan Gilgoff described the scene in *The Jesus Machine*: the pastors asked Paul Weyrich how they could leverage the rally into a political movement, given their limitations. Weyrich understood their concerns. "You don't think your congregations will tolerate your involvement in public policy," he told them. "Amen—that's right," they answered.[29] Many churchgoers believed the church should attend to spiritual life, and render politics "unto Caesar." There was a lot at stake: evangelism had become big business, and millions of dollars hung in the balance.

Weyrich had an answer. His entourage included Lance Tarrance, a young Republican pollster who had conducted an exhaustive survey of Texas voting precincts a few years earlier. The group commissioned Tarrance to conduct a poll asking their congregations first whether they would support their pastors' active involvement in politics, and second, whether they would help pay for it—without cutting back on their usual tithing.[30] The result was affirmative on both counts. Weyrich and the preachers had a deal.

The Dallas rally ignited political mobilization across the map of the South. Bill Moyers, a journalist and former Southern Baptist pastor, reported, "In Dallas, the religious right and the political right formally wed . . . By the mid-1980s, Southern Baptist annual conventions began to look like precinct meetings of the Republican Party."[31]

The harvest of votes was potentially massive. Falwell had noted that only 55 percent of evangelicals were registered to vote, compared to the national average of 72 percent. His movement set up tables in church lobbies and parking lots with the mantra, "Number one, get people saved. Number two, get them baptized. Number three, get them registered to vote." Falwell claimed his supporters registered 8.5 million voters over the next five years.[32]

Party affiliation tilted across the South. In his memoirs Paul Pressler cited surveys showing that from 1980 to 1984, the percentage of Southern Baptist clergymen who described themselves as Republican rose from 29 to 66, while those identifying as Democrats fell from 41 to 25 percent.[33] Many of their congregants followed. Southern Democrats lost their footing, and a powerful new voting bloc emerged.

Some of the new movement's adherents showed a troublesome penchant for bigotry, which made them hard to wrangle from a public relations standpoint. The Moral Majority was officially ecumenical, and its leadership urged its members to skirt controversy. But Oklahoma pastor Bailey Smith told the Dallas rally, "With all due respect for those dear people, my friend, God Almighty does not hear the prayer of a Jew, for how in the world can God hear the prayer of a man who says Jesus Christ is not the true Messiah?" The following year Bailey Smith succeeded Adrian Rogers as Southern Baptist Convention president.

Some liberal circles were alarmed. People for the American Way documented the early days of the movement in a 1982 documentary called *Life and Liberty . . . for All Who Believe* (the title taken from the "Pledge of Allegiance to the Christian Flag"). The film included clips from the Dallas rally and other settings. The narration quoted Jerry Falwell's declaration, "The church should be a disciplined charging army. Christians, like slaves and soldiers, ask no questions. We are fighting a holy war." In another clip, the

Moral Majority's national secretary, Dr. Greg Dixon, objected to an Indiana law against child abuse. He condemned the state's "Gestapo agencies" for removing children from homes that practice "normal biblical discipline"—his term for corporal punishment. Another protester quoted Proverbs 20:30 in praise of child beating: "The blueness of a wound cleanseth away evil."

Dean Wycoff, a California spokesman for the Moral Majority, was even more alarming: "I agree with capital punishment, and I believe homosexuality is one of those that could be coupled with murder and other sins."

The documentary did highlight extremists from the Moral Majority, and some of its most radical voices soon left or were ushered out of the movement. But the radical nature of its philosophy remained.

Paul Pressler expressed his ultimate goal in his autobiography, *A Hill on Which to Die*: "An unanticipated effect of the conservative movement and the Southern Baptist Convention could possibly be a long-term change in the political climate and the public policy thinking of some Americans. During the preceding thirty years, the religion of secular humanism had been promoted with great effectiveness by the media and many secular and religious elites. Now the establishment of the religion of secular humanism possibly can be destroyed and true freedom of religion can be restored to America."[34]

There was a basic philosophical difference, Pressler wrote, between fundamentalists and their political adversaries; the fundamentalists "believe in the sinfulness of each person . . . the consistent liberal, on the other hand, believes in the basic goodness of human beings."[35]

The theocracy envisioned by Pressler began to take shape, with his home state as a laboratory. Texas had already enacted some of harshest antigay policies in the country.[36] In 1973 the state had passed the sweeping Penal Code Section 21.06, designating any sexual relations between two people of the same sex as a misdemeanor punishable by a fine of up to $500. The law could be used to fire gay teachers from public schools or to reject applicants for jobs in law enforcement as criminals.[37] Repression of homosexuality became a linchpin of the movement.

The leaders of the Conservative Resurgence refined their other policy priorities. They wanted to impose severe legal restraints on the right to abortion wherever possible, limiting it to cases in which the life of the mother was at stake. This reversed the more liberal position the Southern Baptists had adopted in 1971. They also sought to eliminate IRS restrictions on using their churches to pursue their political agenda while maintaining their tax-exempt status.

All of these goals could be blocked by court rulings and federal regulations, so they focused on the mechanics of government: limiting the power of the federal government, strengthening state government, and installing sympathetic judges to the federal courts.

Expanding their influence beyond Southern Baptist strongholds would require money, media, and manpower. But the Texas Baptists had already created a template by deploying Patterson's three-way tactics of "building communication networks, enlisting the media in disinformation campaigns, and spying on enemies," in combination with Pressler's will to "go for the jugular." In Paul Weyrich they found the man who could implement their plan.

Weyrich needed the Southern Baptists as much as they needed him. Author Dan Gilgoff wrote that it was Weyrich who had the "vision for launching the Christian Right, and for constructing a nationwide evangelical political machine."[38] Gazing out at the Dallas rally, Weyrich beheld an army of Southern Baptists who could serve as foot soldiers and an electoral base to fulfill his political agenda. But the Southern Baptists—13.7 million of the U.S. population of 226 million—couldn't do it alone. The previous year Weyrich told Jerry Falwell of his vision of tens of millions of evangelicals, fundamentalists, Catholics, Mormons, and certain mainline Protestants, who put aside their religious divisions to form a massive voting bloc.[39]

Implementing this vision would require registering, indoctrinating, and mobilizing a broad sector of this population—a daunting but not impossible task. Religious divisions were not a light matter; the churchgoers' ancestors had slaughtered each other for generations over theological fine points.

Another issue lay in identifying common ground. Blue-collar Catholics and rural Pentecostals led vastly different lives, and many of their interests diverged. The old approach involved polling and reporting to learn what mattered to the constituents, then packaging their concerns into political platforms. Weyrich and his comrades understood they would need to go further, and shape their base's opinions through direct messaging.

By 1980 Weyrich's complex machine was under construction, with the Heritage Foundation to program policy, the Republican Study Committee to wrangle congressional votes, ALEC to draft state-level legislation, and the Moral Majority to mobilize the masses.

Now the movement needed money. For this Weyrich looked to the business sector. He had already recruited Joseph Coors and Richard Scaife to back the Heritage Foundation, but there were many more fortunes to be mined. The nation's vast business community brimmed with magnates who chafed at corporate taxes, oil barons who resented environmental regulations, and entrepreneurs who wanted to pursue risky ventures without pesky investigations.

These individuals sought to curtail the power of the federal government and reassign it to more easily managed statehouses. Weyrich's political machine was an investment that promised massive returns.

Weyrich's larger vision called for the creation of a new organization capable of channeling the money into shaping the message and rousing the manpower. That entity would be the Council for National Policy.

CHAPTER 2

THE BIRTH OF THE CNP: WASHINGTON

Judge Pressler's will to power would have been familiar to John Calvin, the austere sixteenth-century French lawyer who became a leading architect of Protestantism. Calvin prepared for the Roman Catholic priesthood as a youth, but he was swept away by a conversion experience that convinced him of the corruption of Catholicism and its opulent trappings. Since God was all-powerful, he reasoned, all of history was foreordained. Salvation and damnation were predestined on an individual basis, and those lucky souls who were destined for heaven, known as "the elect," were also chosen to govern on earth. French Catholics took violent exception to Calvin's ideas, and he fled to Geneva. There he succeeded in establishing a theocracy governed by and for "the elect."

A counsel of pastors and elders imposed "God's law" according to Calvin's interpretation, dispensing harsh punishment to libertines and dissidents. Their reforms banned theater, dancing, profanity, and gambling. Citizens were barred from celebrating holidays. Governing councils enforced the restrictions and dispatched spies and inspectors to monitor compliance. Calvin established schools, but their first order of business was "the instruction of the faithful in true doctrine."[1] The Spanish physician Michael

Servetus and Calvin carried out an extensive correspondence until Servetus publicly disagreed with him on matters of theology. With Calvin's blessing, Servetus was executed—burned alive on a pyre of his own books.

There were social benefits to Calvin's teachings. When he replaced the spectacle of Catholicism with reverence for "the Word," he encouraged a surge of literacy. The Gutenberg revolution placed the Bible in the hands of the common man, and Calvinists were committed to reading it for themselves. Their churches dismissed the notion of priests as God's intermediaries and replaced them with learned pastors governed by councils of elders. These practices served as a foundation of American democracy.[2]

The New England Puritans followed in Calvin's footsteps, stressing the terrors of damnation and the need to impose a strict moral order, but over time their rigor gave way to moderating influences. Institutions that once promoted Calvinist theology—including Harvard, Yale, and Princeton—evolved into secular entities.[3]

With or without the Puritans, the new Americans still loved to convene. Alexis de Tocqueville observed that their organizations performed functions that were the purviews of the aristocracy, the church, and the state in European societies. He asked, "But what political power would ever be in a state to suffice for the innumerable multitude of small undertakings that American citizens execute every day with the aid of an association?"[4]

Paul Weyrich's new movement needed associations too. If the Texas fundamentalists and their Washington allies were going to make national inroads, they had to appeal to nonfundamentalists in other regions of the country, based on a new network of seemingly secular organizations. Paul Weyrich had replicated Democratic institutions in a conservative mold. He and his supporters revisited Democratic institutions, seeking new models.

In the 1930s the New Deal coalition united urban ward heelers with farmers battered by the Great Depression. Reformers joined their ranks to promote the rights of African Americans, women, and Jews. The New Deal benefited from their support, even if it did not always advance their causes.

Weyrich's colleague Richard Viguerie studied their success. The creation of effective coalitions, he stated, "takes two things: It takes things to get real bad very quickly, and there has to be some political machinery there to take advantage of that opportunity."[5] The New Deal was the perfect example.

Over the 1930s things got "real bad very quickly," and FDR's crack team of advisors assembled the political machinery to consolidate the Democrats' advantage.

The New Deal coalition held firm through World War II, but as Americans settled back into a peacetime existence, the coalition developed fissures. By the time Weyrich mounted his challenge in the late 1970s, those fractures had become chasms.

The Democrats had long depended on the votes of the "Solid South," made up of the former Confederate and border states. But Harry Truman threatened that support with his determination to add a major civil rights plank to the Democratic Party platform. There was an immediate backlash: thirteen Southern states boycotted the 1948 Democratic convention in Philadelphia, and six thousand delegates mounted a rival convention in Birmingham. There they founded the States' Rights Democratic Party, popularly known as the Dixiecrats.

Their presidential nominee, Strom Thurmond, used states' rights as the basis for his argument against integration. He denounced Truman for trying to "dominate this country by force and to put into effect these uncalled-for and these damnable proposals he has recommended under the guise of so-called civil rights. And I tell you, the American people, from one side or the other, had better wake up and oppose such a program. And if they don't, the next thing will be a totalitarian state in these United States."[6]

The party's platform, proclaimed in Oklahoma City on August 14, based its arguments on "strict adherence" to the Constitution, foreshadowing language that would be used by the Council for National Policy in the future. It opposed any legal measures that served to support integration, bolster labor unions, or advance affirmative action. This laid the conceptual groundwork for future measures restricting LGBT rights:

> We stand for the segregation of the races and the racial integrity of each race; the constitutional right to choose one's associates; to accept private employment without governmental interference, and to earn one's living in any lawful way. We oppose the elimination of segregation, the repeal of miscegenation statutes, the control of private employment by Federal bureaucrats called for by the

> misnamed civil rights program. We favor home-rule, local self-government and a minimum interference with individual rights.[7]

The split in the Democratic Party persisted through the national election, and many believed that it would hand the victory to Truman's Republican rival, John Dewey. But Truman squeaked through, and the States' Rights Democratic Party dissolved soon after.

The Democratic Party continued to promote a national civil rights agenda—and the southerners continued to resist. Many responded to school desegregation by creating so-called segregation academies, private schools that claimed tax-exempt status as nonprofit institutions. One leader in the movement was Bob Jones Sr., son of a Confederate soldier and founder of segregated Bob Jones University. Jones claimed that by maintaining segregation he was merely adhering to a biblical mandate from Acts 17:26: "And He [God] made from one man every nation of mankind to live on all the face of the earth, having determined allotted periods and the boundaries of their dwelling place."[8]

Jones and his colleagues had skin in the game. They reaped healthy revenues from their Christian academies, which were promoted as an alternative to the forced integration of secular society. Jerry Falwell saw his schools' tax-exempt status as a matter of "religious freedom."[9]

But the fundamentalists faced increasing challenges, some from within their own ranks. Over the 1950s Billy Graham began to show support for the civil rights movement, integrating his audiences and inviting Martin Luther King Jr. to join him at the pulpit of his New York City crusade. In 1960 Graham returned from a trip to Africa and denounced segregation in the United States.[10] (Notably, Graham would be one of the Old Guard clergy who declined to attend the 1980 watershed rally in Dallas.[11])

Bob Jones responded to Graham's denunciation with a bizarre radio address titled "Is Segregation Scriptural?"[12] There were no superior or inferior races, he argued, "but all men have mortal bodies, and God fixed the boundaries of the races of the world." The trouble today, he continued, "is a Satanic agitation striking back at God's established order."

In the eyes of the fundamentalists, things got "real bad very quickly." Tensions mounted, and civil rights protesters marched across southern cities, met by fire hoses and police dogs. The national print and broadcast media, much of it concentrated in the Northeast, covered the story in force—often dwelling on the legal segregation in the South while ignoring systemic segregation in the North.

In June 1963, John F. Kennedy proposed sweeping legislation to promote civil rights, which was bitterly opposed by many congressmen from the South. On July 2, 1964, Lyndon Johnson signed the Civil Rights Act, the most extensive civil rights legislation since Reconstruction, barring discrimination in schools and the workplace. This energized the backlash in the South, spurring the Christian academy movement and driving a wedge through the Democrats' Solid South. Richard Viguerie observed these events with care, spotting an opportunity to profit from the Democrats' discord.

The first chance arrived with the 1964 Republican candidate, Barry Goldwater of Arizona. Goldwater had not opposed civil rights initiatives in the past, but his campaign advisors explored the benefits of using coded language like "states' rights" to court the segregationist vote in the South. Goldwater went down in epic defeat, but his campaign recruited the farm team that would launch the Council for National Policy in the future.

AT THIRTY-THREE, RICHARD Viguerie was a bantam Texas Cajun, the son of a Shell Oil man, with thinning hair and a toothy grin. His politics were shaped by his early career working for Oklahoma radio evangelist Billy James Hargis, an enthusiastic supporter of the John Birch Society.[13] Viguerie started out marketing Hargis's books, such as *The Negro Question: The Communist Civil War Policy*, which described segregation as "one of God's natural laws." As recounted by Tulsa journalist Lee Roy Chapman, Hargis's long career was plagued with scandal.[14] The IRS investigated his operations for using his tax-exempt religious status to pursue political activities.[15] In later years he was accused of acting as a sexual predator and deflowering both male and female students from his Tulsa Bible college.[16] Hargis denied the charges but resigned as president of the college.

As Hargis's aide, Viguerie chafed at mainstream news organizations' disdain for his boss's racist rants and the John Birch Society's anti-Communist screeds. Direct mail, he observed, was a way to circumvent the gatekeepers by bringing the material directly to the public's mailbox. It was also a highly effective fund-raising tool.

Viguerie continued on to the Goldwater campaign. He was an ardent supporter, perceiving the Arizona senator as a genuine conservative alternative to moderate Republicans such as Nelson Rockefeller. Viguerie and his associates were crushed by Goldwater's humiliating defeat, but the rout sowed the seeds of a new movement.[17] By law, a list of everyone who contributed $50 or more to a presidential campaign had to be filed with the clerk of the U.S. House of Representatives. Viguerie was inspired to use Goldwater's list as a marketing tool.

"I sat in the clerk's office," Viguerie recalled, "copying Goldwater donor names and addresses and building a list of those who would oppose Johnson's program when he was elected. I soon realized that working by myself was getting me nowhere fast, and I hired six women, who produced 12,500 three-by-five index cards with the names and addresses of Goldwater donors. Eventually, I went around the country doing the same thing in state capitals where the rules were favorable."[18]

In January 1965 Viguerie launched American Target Advertising, creating an opportunity to thwart the elected administration's goals long after the election was past.[19]

Viguerie prepared to take on the Republican establishment. His list not only anchored an impressive fund-raising operation, it also offered a way to bypass the national news media. "We couldn't get our candidates on the evening news or our issues talked about," he stated.[20] Direct mail allowed him to expand the influence of candidates who were otherwise written off.

Weyrich's vision required a grassroots strategist, and he found him in a young Louisiana Republican named Morton Blackwell. At twenty-five, Blackwell had served as the youngest elected delegate for Goldwater at the 1964 Republican Convention, and moved to Washington to run the national College Republicans.[21] In 1968 he met Paul Weyrich; four years later he met Viguerie, and the three joined forces to pursue their common goal.[22] Blackwell was all about mastering the rules—Republican Party rules, congressional rules of order, election laws—in order to bend them. Viguerie soon hired Blackwell to help him design a new conservative movement. The two spent long hours analyzing the lessons of the left, exploring how it had won so many victories over conservatives.[23] Goldwater's failure, they decided, was written into his campaign slogan: "In your heart you know he's right."

The young southerners reached three sweeping conclusions. First, they determined that "being right" was irrelevant to political victory. "Unfortunately the real world doesn't work that way," Blackwell observed. "The side that's right doesn't necessarily win."[24]

Second, they decided that the winner of an election is "determined by the number and the effectiveness of the activists and leaders on the respective side."

Third, they declared that "the number and effectiveness of the activists and leaders . . . is determined by the political technology used by that side."[25]

These three principles would shape the strategy of Council for National Policy for decades to come: first, dispense with the need to "be right"; second, emphasize the recruitment and training of activists; and third, make sure political technology is integrated into the organizational framework.

Their understanding was sophisticated from the start. "Political technology can be roughly divided into communication technology and organization technology," Blackwell wrote, "with no neat line of separation between communication and organization." This principle would lead to the movement's most striking electoral victories.

But a list of donors did not constitute an organizational network, and creating one was a complex undertaking. Weyrich was the ideal architect. Like Blackwell and Viguerie, the young congressional staffer was a bitter survivor of the Goldwater campaign. ("We weren't high enough in the campaign to know each other, but our involvement with Goldwater credentialed us for each other," Blackwell later told Randolph-Macon professor Richard Meagher.[26]) When the three joined forces in 1972, Weyrich shared his vision of a matrix of interlocking (but seemingly independent) organizations, mirroring groups on the left, but with a far higher degree of coordination. Weyrich, Viguerie, and Blackwell's supporters soon labeled them "three chieftains of the emerging New Right."[27]

In 1974 the three men experimented with their concepts at the first Conservative Political Action Conference (CPAC). They hoped the event would generate more energy than previous conservative conferences, which had been largely social affairs. But the attendees struggled against the enveloping gloom of Nixon's imploding administration and the Watergate scandal.

The three chieftains set about scattering the gloom. Blackwell argued that debating ideas wasn't enough; the young conservative recruits needed practical skills. As a result, the first CPAC offered panels on direct mail fund-raising and campaign techniques to its four hundred attendees. The inaugural keynote was delivered by California's then governor, Ronald Reagan.[28]

IN 1977 PAUL Weyrich told *Newsweek*, "Conservatives have been led by an intellectual movement but not a practical movement up to now."[29] He addressed the problem by bringing Anita Bryant and Phyllis Schlafly into the fold to sow grassroots social movements. Bryant, a Southern Baptist beauty queen from Oklahoma, launched a new campaign against gay rights. She had made a fortune promoting Florida citrus products with the slogan "Breakfast without orange juice is like a day without sunshine." Her new campaign, endorsed by Jerry Falwell, proclaimed, "If gays are given rights, next we'll have to give rights to prostitutes and to people who sleep with St. Bernards and to nail biters."[30]

Phyllis Schlafly, a constitutional lawyer from St. Louis, used her legal training to restrict the rights of working women. A veteran of the John Birch Society and the Goldwater campaign, Schlafly organized a successful national movement to derail the Equal Rights Amendment in 1977. She sowed panic among her followers by warning, misleadingly, that the ERA would cost widows their Social Security benefits and deprive divorced mothers of custody of their children.[31]

Paul Weyrich recognized second-wave feminism as another cultural disconnect, ripe for political exploitation. As Middle America puzzled over news images of women trashing their bras in Atlantic City and moving into coed dorms at Oberlin, the activists took as much pleasure in shocking conservatives as in building their movements.

Another wave of the antifeminist movement was led by Beverly LaHaye, a soft-spoken matron with tight blonde curls. Beverly's husband was Tim

LaHaye, a fiery Southern Baptist preacher who would be described by *Time* magazine as "one of the shrillest of the fundamentalist ideologues in Washington."[32] The couple were both graduates of Bob Jones University. LaHaye began his career with modest postings; he served as a pastor in Pumpkintown, South Carolina, before he was eventually transferred to greener Baptist pastures in Southern California.

One evening in the fall of 1978, Beverly LaHaye sat in her San Diego living room watching a Barbara Walters interview. The subject was Betty Friedan, the outspoken feminist and founder of the National Organization for Women. LaHaye was horrified by Betty Friedan's remarks, and reacted by founding Concerned Women for America (CWA). The group began in Southern California and soon spread across the country. It claimed to have recruited half a million members (though these numbers are hard to verify), all ready to lobby their congressmen in opposition to the ERA, abortion, and gay rights—as well as rock music.[33]

Paul Weyrich was pleased to see conservative women establishing a beachhead against feminists and gay rights activists, who tended to support Democrats. Richard Viguerie gave Schlafly credit for putting his movement on solid footing: "When [Phyllis Schlafly] and I were involved in politics back in the fifties and sixties, the conservative movement rested on a two-legged stool," he recalled. "The two-legged stool was national defense, which really meant anticommunism, and economic issues. We'd win forty, forty-five, sometimes forty-seven percent of the vote. Very seldom would we ever get fifty-one percent." But under the leadership of Schlafly, Weyrich, and Falwell, "conservatives began to reach out and bring into the conservative movement social issues."[34]

In 1978 the three chieftains threw their weight behind the midterm elections. Their fund-raising and direct mail prowess helped to win the Republicans a net gain of three seats in the Senate and twelve in the House, raising the New Right's profile and their credibility within the party.[35]

In 1979 Morton Blackwell added an essential component by founding the Leadership Academy, another pillar of the movement. This institute recruited conservative activists across the country to learn Blackwell's brand of "political technology." There was a pool of potential activists among the Concerned Women for America and Falwell's fundamentalists—but they would be of limited utility without training and networking. Blackwell's project would span decades, networking candidates, operatives, and activists, and teaching the latest developments in modern political technology.

Blackwell was ever attentive to lessons from the left: "How you design a piece of political literature, how you raise funds, how you organize a precinct, how you attract a crowd to a political event, how you communicate to a mass audience online—those techniques can work for anybody," he wrote.[36] In the process, the Leadership Institute imbued generations of right-wing candidates and their campaign managers with a common ideology, vocabulary, and method.

Viguerie did his part to stymie the Carter administration. One day in 1979, *Washington Post* reporter David Broder asked him why the administration, equipped with a Democratic Congress, was having such a hard time promoting its agenda. Viguerie took some credit—his company was sending out a hundred million pieces of direct mail a year, asking recipients to write and call their congressmen to oppose them.[37]

By the time the pastors assembled in the Dallas arena, Weyrich, Viguerie, and Blackwell had laid the foundations of their political edifice. Now they needed a facade and a roof. In July 1980, with the anointment of Ronald Reagan, their movement acquired its public face. Fundamentalists and political operatives gave Reagan their full support. He ran for office on the slogan "Let's Make America Great Again," and won.

Now Blackwell, Weyrich, and Viguerie were ready to consolidate their gains. On May 19, 1981, Viguerie gathered more than fifty conservatives at his handsome brick home in McLean, Virginia, to found the Council for National Policy.[38]

Viguerie had created an informal version of the group six years earlier, a counterpart to the Weyrich Lunch. Viguerie later recalled, "We of . . . the 'New Right' believed that having a plan and coordinating our efforts on the conservative agenda was the only way to achieve success. We soon formalized a breakfast meeting every Wednesday from 8:00 am to 10:00 am. To the extent that Hillary Clinton's vast right-wing conspiracy ever existed, it met at Elaine's and my home in McLean from 1975 until 1984."[39] Half of Viguerie's breakfast club would be members of the CNP's new board of governors a year later.[40]

Weyrich and Blackwell—by then special assistant to President Reagan in the Office of Public Liaison—were founding members. So was Southern Baptist pastor Tim LaHaye, Texas oilman Nelson Bunker Hunt, and beer magnate Joseph Coors, who had helped Weyrich launch the Heritage Foundation. Phyllis Schlafly and Ed McAteer, the Colgate-Palmolive salesman who organized the 1980 Dallas rally, were in attendance. As president the group chose Tim LaHaye, who left the pulpit to take up political activism the same year he assumed the helm of the CNP.[41] LaHaye would win renown as the co-author of twelve novels known as the *Left Behind* series, launched in 1995. Their common theme was "the Rapture," in which millions of Christians were evaporated into heaven against a backdrop of Communist villainy and potboiler romance. The series sold more than 65 million copies.[42]

For executive director, the founders chose Louis Elwood "Woody" Jenkins, a young Louisiana state legislator, who held that position for the next four years. The organization based its initial headquarters in Jenkins's hometown of Baton Rouge, where Morton Blackwell had served as Young Republican state chairman. Jenkins opened CNP offices at Great Oaks, a twentieth-century copy of an antebellum mansion.[43] Great Oaks wasn't the organization's only echo of the Old South. The 1982 Executive Committee included Richard Shoff, former state secretary of the Indiana Ku Klux Klan.[44]

The CNP took a strong interest in international affairs, starting with Central America. One of the early objectives of the Reagan Administration was to bring down the Sandinista regime in Nicaragua, a project that met with considerable opposition among the reigning Democrats in the House, led by House Speaker Tip O'Neill.

The Reagan Administration tapped retired Army General John Singlaub, a founding member of the CNP's board of governors, to raise money and purchase arms for the Contra forces waging guerrilla warfare against the Sandinistas. The CNP had its eye on Marine Colonel Oliver North, a deputy director at the National Security Council. North engineered the secret Iran–Contra deal to funnel money from weapons sales to Iran to the Nicaraguan rebels. The CNP gave North a special award "for national defense" in 1984, and invited him to speak on Central America at its meetings in 1985 and 1986; he was a member of the organization as of 1998.[45]

Under the 1982 Boland Amendment, Congress had prohibited "the use of [government] funds for the purpose of overthrowing the government of Nicaragua." Oliver North took charge of raising third-party and private donations to bypass the legislation.[46] Woody Jenkins and the CNP were eager to help. Jenkins raised millions of dollars for Friends of the Americas, which sent aid on military aircraft for the Contras' families, explaining, "Soldiers will not fight if their families are dying of disease or starvation." The CNP's Pat Robertson and James Dobson raised more money for the Contra cause on their broadcasts. The CNP beer mogul Joseph Coors donated $65,000 for a Contra aircraft at North's behest.[47]

The CNP's interests in Central America were revealed by Ron Akers, Jenkins's brother-in-law and onetime CNP staff member. Akers had parted ways with Jenkins and was ready to talk. He told the Baton Rouge *State-Times* that the CNP invited the notorious Salvadoran leader Roberto D'Aubuisson to address a 1984 meeting at the Homestead in Hot Springs, Virginia, a popular spa for American tycoons and presidents.[48] Akers reported that a CNP member flew Roberto D'Aubuisson to the resort on his private jet.

D'Aubuisson's homicidal record was already well-known. In 1993 a United Nations–backed Truth Commission confirmed that D'Aubuisson was the mastermind behind the murder of Archbishop Oscar Romero as he said Mass in 1980. (Romero was canonized in 2018.)

In 1981 the CIA submitted a memorandum to Vice President George Bush, stating, "D'Aubuisson has served as principal henchman for wealthy landowners and as a coordinator of the right-wing death squads that have murdered several thousand suspected leftists and leftist sympathizers during the past year."[49] As a young reporter in El Salvador, I was an arm's length away from D'Aubuisson at a 1981 press conference in San Salvador where he announced that it would be necessary to kill a quarter of a million people to pacify the country.

On December 5, 1984, D'Aubuisson was the guest of honor at a dinner at the Capitol Hill Club. The hosts included a number of CNP partners, among them the Viguerie Co., Weyrich's Free Congress Foundation, and Falwell's Moral Majority. One young activist told the *Washington Post* that D'Aubuisson "hasn't had a fair shake" in the media. "Death squads have a very negative connotation."[50]

Oliver North's plans to support the Contras fell apart under Congressional scrutiny. In 1988 he was convicted for his role in the scandal after admitting that he had lied to Congress, but the conviction was later reversed on a technicality.[51] North went on to become a host for Fox News and president of the National Rifle Association.

The founding fathers of the CNP set their sights high. Woody Jenkins told the Baton Rouge *State-Times*, "It is no secret that the Council for National Policy was modeled after the Council on Foreign Relations. Despite its wrong-headed philosophy, the CFR is the most influential single private organization in America today. Our greatest challenge is to have an even larger influence on public policy than has the CFR."

Jenkins continued, "To do this, our members must do two things: First they must have an enormous amount of economic, political and intellectual power. Second, we must learn to wield that power effectively. I predict that one day before the end of this century, the Council will be so influential that no President, regardless of party or philosophy, will be able to ignore us or our concerns or shut us out of the highest levels of government."[52]

There had been fundamentalist organizations, conferences, and coalitions before, but this was something new. The *New York Times* quoted Richard Viguerie as saying "We have never had, up to now, any kind of broad, all-inclusive organization of conservative-thinking people, people who have a lot of leverage."[53] The Council for National Policy made no pretense of bipartisanship. One of the group's first acts was to present an award to Reagan official David Stockman for his efforts to cut the federal budget and defund the left.

The conveners often compared the new group to the Council on Foreign Relations. The name was strikingly—even confusingly—similar. But the Council on Foreign Relations had enviable qualities beyond its august name and prestigious reputation: it was also tax-exempt, assigned 501(c)(3) status as an educational institution by the IRS. This gave the CFR an advantage in fund-raising and financing its programs.

The term "tax code" may seem opaque, but its impact can be surprisingly powerful. American churches have enjoyed tax relief since the founding of the Republic, and the status was later extended to charitable and educational institutions. But the political role of such institutions has been hotly debated. Unsurprisingly, some advocacy organizations made a practice of publicly supporting bills and politicians who endorsed their positions. In 1934 Congress tried to impose limits by revoking tax-exempt status for groups that were "carrying on propaganda or otherwise attempting to influence legislation."

In 1954 then senator Lyndon Johnson took the matter further. Stung by the use of two nonprofit groups to campaign for his opponent in Texas, he proposed the Johnson Amendment to the tax code.[54] This became a plague to the fundamentalist movement. It limited tax-exempt status to groups whose activity "does not participate in, or intervene in (including the publishing or distributing of statements), any political campaign on behalf of (or in opposition to) any candidate for public office." The Revenue Code further ruled that groups could engage in voter education so long as it was "conducted in a non-partisan manner"—but not if it favored one candidate over another.[55] This wording applied to churches as well. Critics noted that Lyndon Johnson slipped his amendment into the bill without debate.[56]

Daily life in the United States has been dramatically shaped by the existence of 501(c)(3) status. It has been the hidden state subsidy for art museums and opera companies, whose donors can write off their contributions. It has allowed churches to amass vast real estate holdings and universities to build up huge endowments and fund critical research.

The Council on Foreign Relations justified its 501(c)(3) status by serving as a leading think tank on foreign policy.[57] As an educational institution, it offered a portfolio of publications, starting with its journal, *Foreign Affairs*, as well as numerous online resources and academic partnerships. Its membership was a matter of public record. Most of its frequent meetings were closed, but others were open to the press. The Council on Foreign Relations became a routine stop for every presidential candidate from a major party. The members' politics ranged from archconservative to extremely liberal, making it a venue for spirited debate.

Soon after the Council for National Policy was founded in 1981, its leaders applied to the Internal Revenue Service for 501(c)(3) status, arguing their group's similarity to the Council on Foreign Relations. They pointed to *Foreign Affairs*, claiming that they would produce similar educational materials, and the IRS granted their request.

The CNP's 501(c)(3) status benefited the network's financial strategy. But unlike the Council on Foreign Relations, the CNP and its partners did not promote bipartisan discussion or open-ended policy debates. They functioned to promote the right wing of the Republican Party, skirting the IRS restrictions against partisan campaigning with the airiest of pretenses. Many organizations in its network, such as Concerned Women for America, claimed 501(c)(3) status as well, with similar goals.

The radical right was not alone in this practice. Experts in tax law point out that the IRS has been leery of cracking down on violators of tax-exempt status, in part because American churches have engaged in political activity for generations—including African American churches that have traditionally supported Democrats. When the IRS has attempted to enforce the Johnson Amendment, it has come under political attack. The newborn Council for National Policy was depending on America's blurry line between church and state, and it was a safe gamble.

The Council for National Policy would meet two or three times a year in posh hotel settings. (The *Washington Post* reported that the CNP told the IRS it needed to hold meetings in opulent surroundings because that's what its members were used to.[58]) Its membership was secret, as were most of its proceedings, and its publications were sporadic and hard to come by. There was no pretense of bipartisanship. The CNP was designed to serve as the engine for a radical political agenda. Everything else was window dressing.

CHAPTER 3

LORDS OF THE AIR: THE CNP'S MEDIA EMPIRE

The founders of the CNP exulted in Reagan's election. They considered the traditional Republican Party to be controlled by the East Coast elite, and saw Ronald Reagan as a true conservative. They had encouraged him to run, supported his campaign, and played an important role in his victory: white evangelicals had voted in equal numbers for Carter and Ford in 1976, but they voted two to one for Reagan, and the Republicans took control of the Senate for the first time in twenty-six years. "The men who recruited Reagan were all men of the New West," Richard Viguerie wrote. "They had no ties to the old Republican establishment."[1]

Reagan's landslide victory energized the movement. In 1981 Viguerie told *People* magazine that he had grown his original mailing list of 12,500 into a computerized roster of 4.5 million potential Republican donors. He stated that he planned to "double his list by 1984 and pour the donations into a massive conservative media blitz . . . in the forefront of a revolution being fought with 20-cent stamps."[2] He would be called "the funding father of the conservative movement."[3] Under Viguerie's influence, Jerry Falwell and the Moral Majority invested $6 million in a massive direct mail campaign aimed at registering and engaging additional fundamentalist voters.

But the founders of the CNP understood that their ultimate victory depended on a fully integrated strategy that controlled their messaging from creation to distribution. Viguerie's experiments in direct mail showed them the impact of targeting an audience. Now they followed Viguerie's lead in bypassing the national news media and started building a media empire composed of sympathetic outlets. They started expanding to new platforms—cable, satellite, internet, mobile—as the regulatory environment and technology evolved.

The history of U.S. media tends to focus on East Coast institutions: the great urban newspapers and magazines, public broadcasting, and the three major networks. The networks made a point of hiring announcers with midwestern and southwestern accents, but they answered to the Boston-Washington corridor.

In the hinterlands, a parallel universe of media bloomed. Thousands of daily newspapers served communities with hometown news, public notices, and local advertising. The same was true of local broadcasting outlets. During World War II, Middle Americans turned to outlets such as *Life* magazine and CBS for reports from the front, but they found their hometown heroes in the local paper.

Radio played a different role in rural America from its role in the coastal cities. It was affordable, accessible, and easy to integrate into everyday life. People who couldn't afford magazine subscriptions gathered around the radio to hear the news. Most stations were locally owned and locally oriented. Announcers read the national news off the wires, but they were sure to include high school football scores.

In my father's hometown of Clay Center, Nebraska, broadcasting arrived with Old Trusty, a company that manufactured copper incubators for hatching chicks. In 1926 Old Trusty's founder, Manander M. Johnson, "The Incubator Man," launched KMMJ, the local radio station bearing his initials, to market his products to farmers across the region. It was one of the first commercial radio stations in the area.

Performers from local schools and churches filled the airtime. My Swedish great-grandfather's gospel quartet sang favorites like "Telephone to Glory" and "There Is a Fountain Filled with Blood." "Johnson's Radio

Visitor Monthly" offered listeners photos of local artists "Emmett Kinney, Harmonica" and "Ralph Snoddy, Xylophone."[4] In 1939, battered by the Great Depression, the station was sold and moved to Nebraska's "Third City" of Grand Island, just in time for the war years, when everyone hungered for news from overseas.

But times changed, and the radio market changed with it. Like many other stations, KMMJ joined the fundamentalist choir. In 2008 it was acquired by the Praise Network, adopting the motto "Keeping your Mind on the Message of Jesus," and reverting to gospel music. Its talk shows featured CNP affiliates David Barton, a Christian nationalist; and David Jeremiah, the fire-and-brimstone preacher who succeeded Tim LaHaye as pastor at his California church. Of Nebraska's 220 radio stations, at least 50 are religious, and many belong to members of the CNP. By comparison, the state has only eleven NPR stations. Crossing the Great Plains, a driver can go for miles without a public radio signal, but he'll never be far from fundamentalist broadcasting—or messaging inspired by the CNP.

Media played a critical role in the CNP agenda. It was well and good for Weyrich, Viguerie, and Blackwell to recruit millions of evangelical voters. But they needed a way to reach them that complemented their pastors' sermons, not encroached on them.

THE MOVEMENT'S MEDIA saga began in 1972, in the CNP's prehistory, when two future members acquired a radio station in Bakersfield, California, two hours north of Los Angeles. It was a fitting birthplace for their empire, reflecting the life of the migrants from Texas, Louisiana, and Oklahoma who began arriving in the 1880s to work in the oil fields. Bakersfield was the site of multiple lynchings in the late nineteenth century, and the Ku Klux Klan took over the city government in the 1920s.

In *The Grapes of Wrath* the Joad family, fleeing the Dust Bowl from Sallisaw, Oklahoma, buried Granma and tangled with vigilantes in Bakersfield. Nearby Oildale was called "Little Oklahoma"—the birthplace of Merle Haggard, the son of Okies from Checotah. Haggard's hit "Okie from Muskogee" was based on a secondhand memory.

Stuart Epperson wasn't an Okie, but he knew the tunes. He grew up on a tobacco farm in Ararat, Virginia, where his grandmother worked as midwife and his father moonlighted as an undertaker.[5] He got his start in broadcasting as a ten-year-old, reading Bible verses on a radio station set up by his brother who worked for the Naval Research Station during World War II on walkie-talkie and radar technology.[6] As a teenager Stuart Epperson drove a jalopy for his brother's moonshine business, but once his brother was sent to prison, Epperson got religion.[7] He studied broadcasting at Bob Jones University, and following graduation he married the sister of his fellow Bob Jones graduate Edward Atsinger III. Not long after, Epperson and his new wife joined Atsinger in California.[8]

The brothers-in-law brought a creative solution to a nagging problem. The radio business was in a state of flux, as popular music genres wildly multiplied and stations swapped out formats in search of a winning formula. Among the losers were ministers who paid local stations to broadcast their services, usually landing at the outer reaches of the AM dial. Epperson believed in the future of FM, a relatively new platform that was still scarce in the South and the West.

In 1973 Epperson and Atsinger launched a small FM radio station in Oxnard, northwest of Los Angeles, basing it on a new business model. They sold the local clergy on their station as a fundamentalist alternative to the secular noise on the rest of the dial. They oriented their programming to fundamentalist audiences, with sermons, call-in shows, and religious music, charging their religious customers substantial fees to carry their message to larger FM markets.[9]

In 1977 Epperson and Atsinger went for broke, mortgaging their houses and unloading their nonreligious stations to acquire stations in big-city markets from San Francisco to Staten Island. They named their company Salem, in reference to a biblical name for Jerusalem.

They had a social agenda as well as a profit motive. Epperson explained that Salem Radio was designed to counter "secular humanism" by building "a platform for the best communicators to communicate biblical truth."[10] "Biblical values" became the rallying cry for an entire movement, which divided the world into a Manichean cosmology. "Good" applied to those who adhered to a literal interpretation of the Bible and rejected homosexuality, abortion, and feminism. "Evil" was anyone who disagreed on principle. Everyone else was a candidate for proselytization. Broadcasting was the most powerful tool to date. It's not clear exactly when Epperson and Atsinger joined the Council for National Policy, but by 2014 Epperson was president and Atsinger was a member of the board of governors.[11] Salem became a linchpin of the CNP's media outreach.

Epperson and Atsinger benefited from the religious dynamics of the 1970s.[12] As rural Americans migrated to cities, they flocked to the congregations of traditional churches like First Baptist Dallas and Southern California's Saddleback Church. Many of these mushroomed into megachurches (defined as Protestant churches with a weekly attendance of over two thousand). Their preachers, whose predecessors once thundered their sermons in tent revivals, now turned to mass media.

Megachurches existed across the country, but they were largely a southern and southwestern phenomenon; of the twenty-five largest churches in America, the vast majority are in the Sun Belt and the Old South.[13] They also provided important platforms for Southern Baptists and other fundamentalist denominations. The megachurches did not speak with one voice. The largest cohort were nondenominational: some of these were unaffiliated Pentecostal congregations, and many were proponents of the "Prosperity Gospel." This creed held that godliness, in the form of giving money to the church, led to financial gain on earth. The second largest cluster of megachurches corresponded to the Southern Baptists. Other fundamentalist sects accounted for the rest.

The megachurch phenomenon aroused some criticism. Author James B. Twitchell wrote, "Clearly, they have done to churching what Wal-Mart did to merchandising. They are the low-cost deliverer of salvation."[14] But megachurches also served an important purpose, offering mobile Americans an instant form of community. At the same time they created a seedbed for conservative activists.

Conservatives, evangelicals, and media: it was a perfect convergence of interests. The architects of the Council for National Policy, Paul Weyrich and Richard Viguerie, wanted to activate millions of unengaged evangelical voters to advance their takeover of the Republican Party. Pastors sought ways to increase their followers, their influence, and their revenues. The broadcasters pursued profits by selling airtime to their fundamentalist clientele and leveraging political interests.

Richard Viguerie developed a formula for candidates that he called "the Four Horsemen of Marketing: 1. Position (find a hole in the marketplace). 2. Differentiation 3. Benefit. 4. Brand (it's what makes you singular or unique)."[15] Conveniently, Salem's broadcasting business also met Viguerie's marketing requirements at the same time it provided an important platform for his agenda.

Salem found a new way to monetize religion. Other radio outlets depended on advertising for 95 percent of their revenue, subject to the state of the economy. Less than half of Salem's revenue came from traditional advertising; most of it came from selling blocks of time to scores of religious organizations that solicited contributions from the listenership.[16] Over time, the definition of "religious" customers evolved to encompass partisan organizations tied to the Council for National Policy.

One of Salem's earliest and most durable partnerships was with another early member of the CNP, the fundamentalist psychologist James Dobson, who hosted a radio program called *Focus on the Family*. A Louisiana native, Dobson was the scion of ministers from the Church of the Nazarene, a small Pentecostal sect that spun off in the early twentieth century. He was a true son of the Bible Belt, born in Louisiana and educated in Oklahoma, Texas, and Southern California.

Evangelicals tended to distrust psychology, but Dobson embraced the field as his calling, earning his doctorate from the University of Southern California. Visitors to pediatricians' offices in the Southwest can find racks of Dobson's publications in the waiting room, covering topics ranging from the dangers of working mothers to the benefits of "discipline." The only question regarding corporal punishment, Dobson wrote, was whether a parent uses a hand or an object when he strikes his child. "The reason I suggest a switch or a paddle," he argued, "is because the hand should be seen as an object of love—to hold, pat, hug or caress." He added that "the spanking should be of sufficient magnitude to cause the child to cry genuinely."

Dobson took similarly harsh stands against homosexuality, abortion, and pornography, clinging to positions that were increasingly discredited by the medical establishment. He claimed that "no credible scientific research has substantiated the claim that homosexuality is genetic or innate." Instead, he held that it was usually the result of "a home where the mother is dominating, overprotective, and possessive while the father rejects or ridicules the child."[17]

Dobson was no fan of feminism. "A good part of my professional life," he noted, "has been devoted to trying to straighten out some of the feminist distortions about marriage and parenting and to address the relationships between men and our women in our society." His radio program invited Dorothy Patterson—wife of the Conservative Resurgence leader Paige Patterson—to support his case. "A wife was created from the beginning to be a helper to her husband," she told his listeners. "That functional role . . . is one of subjection, it is one of submission."[18]

Dobson founded his flagship organization and launched his broadcasts, both named Focus on the Family, in 1977. By 1982 his programs had expanded to a half hour daily and were carried by almost two hundred stations.[19]

Dobson sported metal aviator glasses and thinning ginger hair draped in a long comb-over, the image of a social engineering nerd. His nostrums, delivered in a folksy drawl, urged parents to exercise the same authoritarian principles at home that they heard from the pulpit. Dobson's show was especially popular with homemakers struggling with marriage and parenting, who called in and wrote in epic numbers. Dobson hired a staff of Christian therapists to make sure every question received a sympathetic response. There was no charge for these services, but donations were gratefully accepted. Focus on the Family became a multimedia empire. Dobson published a series of bestselling marriage and parenting manuals, and his broadcasts reached audiences across the country on fundamentalist radio stations.

But Dobson aspired to more than counseling; he was also interested in politics. He had grown close to Paul Weyrich in the late 1970s, and the two men looked for ways to leverage his influence.

The 1980 elections amounted to a declaration of war between fundamentalists and liberals in the United States. Ronald Reagan was the standard-bearer not just of the fundamentalists but also of hawks on defense and fiscal conservatives. Over the early years of his presidency, advocacy organizations proliferated on both sides. In 1981 television producer Norman

Lear, Texas civil rights leader Barbara Jordan, and a group of their associates cofounded People for the American Way specifically to oppose the fundamentalist movement.

In 1983 James Dobson cofounded a new organization called the Family Research Council. This group, despite its anodyne title, served as the policy arm for Dobson's agenda, in partnership with the Council for National Policy. "Family" was a loaded term from the start; it became the movement's code for its militant opposition to same-sex marriage. Dobson's programs kept homosexuals in the line of fire, cherry-picking, inflating, and inventing bogus "research" to suggest their pernicious influence in society, and ignoring legitimate studies that demonstrated their success in partnerships and parenting.

Communities in Middle America, like the ones where I grew up, were ripe for manipulation. In my hometown in Oklahoma in the 1970s and '80s, no one came out of the closet. I'd never knowingly seen or heard of a gay person until I left for college. Years later I heard that one of my Sunday school classmates—a kind, quiet boy with freckles—had moved to San Francisco after college, come out, and died by suicide. It's painful to think of the burden of secrecy and opprobrium he must have endured in our town.

Radio offered an obvious advantage for the fundamentalist strategists. Over the postwar period, the American landscape was covered by an interstate highway system. Americans commuted in their cars, ate in their cars, courted in their cars—often with the radio on. Epperson and Atsinger systematically expanded the Salem network across the country, station by station.

But radio wasn't the fundamentalists' only platform; television also played an essential role. Richard Viguerie's patron Billy James Hargis was one forerunner; Jerry Falwell was another. Both men purchased time on local stations, and fund-raising went hand in hand with audience engagement. In one mailing, dated August 13, 1981, Falwell urged his followers to send him money because his broadcast was "one of the few major ministries in America crying out against militant homosexuals . . . They do want to transform America into a modern Sodom and Gomorrah."[20]

Falwell staged *The Old Time Gospel Hour* from his Baptist megachurch in Lynchburg, Virginia. At its height in the 1980s, his program was carried on nearly four hundred U.S. television stations and nearly five hundred radio stations, and he claimed an audience of fifty million monthly viewers. (By comparison, the combined audiences for ABC, CBS, and NBC network news in 1980 was around forty-two million.[21])

But the true pioneer was Pat Robertson, the son of a U.S. senator from Virginia. Robertson graduated with high marks from Yale Law School, but inexplicably failed the bar exam. He dealt with the trauma by becoming a Southern Baptist pastor. In 1960 the Federal Communications Commission opened up a new world of opportunity for fundamentalist preachers, giving commercial broadcasters the right to sell airtime they had previously given to traditional churches as a public service. The new ruling allowed fundamentalists the chance to compete in the marketplace and develop telemarketing as a profit center.

That year the thirty-year-old Robertson founded the Christian Broadcasting Network (CBN), with the vision of owning his own network rather than simply purchasing time on existing stations. His flagship program was called the 700 Club, named after the seven hundred donors who initially kept it afloat. CBN would become a major force among fundamentalist media, as well as a platform for Robertson's political ambitions. Robertson was an early member of the Council for National Policy's board of governors.

Robertson's initiative was emulated by the enterprising California pastor Paul Crouch and his wife Jan, who founded the Trinity Broadcasting Network (originally Trinity Broadcasting Systems) in 1973. CBN and TBN attracted vast audiences in Middle America with highly politicized programming, yet they were almost invisible to the national press corps. Following Reagan's election, Richard Viguerie was invited to a press breakfast in Washington. "We had a political earthquake last Tuesday," a puzzled journalist said. "Nobody saw it coming. What happened?" Viguerie, amused, responded by asking how many of the two dozen or so journalists had ever heard of Pat Robertson. Only two or three raised their hands.[22]

But the *Christian Science Monitor* noted that while Pat Robertson's broadcasts didn't endorse specific candidates, they could (and did) "insinuate" endorsements on the air. Fundamentalist media was becoming a political force. The *Monitor* reported that Christian broadcasters ran around 1,300 radio stations in the United States (one out of every seven); a third of commercial publishing was evangelical, and that the outcome of the election "may ultimately depend on the impact of the so-called 'electronic church,' the far-reaching Christian broadcast networks." Viguerie predicted that born-again evangelicals could become "the strongest force in American politics in the next few years."[23]

The CNP leadership was disappointed by the early days of the Reagan administration. His cabinet appointments favored moderates, such as chief of staff James Baker, and the traditional Republican congressional leadership showed an unwelcome spirit of compromise with the Democrats across the aisle. The fundamentalists had expected Reagan to show his gratitude by moving full steam ahead on their social issues, ending abortion and quashing IRS challenges to their tax-exempt status. Instead, the White House emphasized economic policy and put the fundamentalists' issues on the back burner.

But they had a strong ally in California Republican Ed Meese, counselor to the president. It's not clear when Meese joined the CNP, but he served on the executive committee as of 1994 and as president in 1996.

In Reagan's second term, his administration handed the fundamentalists a gift that would galvanize their media and leverage it into an even more powerful political tool: its ruling on the Fairness Doctrine. The doctrine had been in effect since 1949, and required any radio or television broadcaster seeking a license to devote a certain amount of airtime to controversial matters of public interest and to offer opposing views on critical issues.

The doctrine also dealt with two other contingencies. If a station aired personal attacks on an individual involved in public issues, it was obliged to notify the party in question and offer a chance to respond. If a station endorsed a candidate, it had to provide other qualified candidates the opportunity to respond over its airwaves.

In 1985 the Federal Communications Commission's chairman (who had served as a Reagan campaign advisor) released a report arguing that the Fairness Doctrine violated First Amendment rights. The ensuing debate broke down along sharp party lines: the Democrat-controlled Congress passed legislation that codified the Fairness Doctrine into law, and Reagan vetoed the measure. In August 1987 the four FCC commissioners—all Reagan or Nixon appointees—abolished the doctrine unanimously.

Critics argued that the Fairness Doctrine had stopped making sense when cable television burst upon the scene with the birth of CNN in 1980. Television and radio transmissions were no longer captive to "scarce frequencies." Cable channels (which were not covered by the Fairness Doctrine) proliferated, representing diverse points of view.

The advent of cable television—combined with the demise of the Fairness Doctrine—represented a bonanza for the radical right. Many critics have focused on Fox News, launched in 1996, but the fundamentalist broadcasters benefited far earlier. Cable allowed them to both target and grow their audiences on a national level. The traditional networks employed huge teams of professional reporters, gatekeeping editors who checked facts, and vice presidents to enforce standards and practices, but the newly liberated cable broadcasters were unencumbered. Not only did they find ways to "insinuate" their endorsements of candidates, skirting the Johnson Amendment, they also launched an attack on professional news outlets.

North Carolina State professor Jason Bivens wrote in *Pacific Standard* magazine that fundamentalist broadcasting was politicized over the Reagan era: "Pat Robertson's longstanding talk show 'The 700 Club' . . . and others began to address what was happening in the news from a biblical perspective. They claimed they were providing viewers with 'real' explanations that media and liberal politicians covered up. These shows also reinforced conservative talking points as objective facts."

Fundamentalist broadcasting, Bivens added, "authorizes a particular, often conspiratorial way of viewing the world. It denounces neutrality or accountability to multiple constituencies as burdensome or even hostile to the Christian faith."[24] These rallying cries to tribalism and paranoia, echoing across the South and the West, would cleave a rift in Americans' political perceptions that persists to this day.

The disruption of the American media landscape didn't end with the birth of cable; it had just begun. Technology would shake up American journalism many times over the next few decades. The previous era had represented the apogee of legacy media. The national news media—especially New York based—had played an important role in supporting the civil rights movement, providing a platform for Martin Luther King Jr. and shaming southern states for their brutal police tactics. The *New York Times* and the *Washington Post* rode high on the Pentagon Papers and Watergate, where the power of the press triumphed over government lies and misdeeds. When Walter Cronkite, the most trusted man in television, declared that the Vietnam War was unwinnable, President Johnson responded, "If I've lost Cronkite, I've lost Middle America."[25]

I traveled across the national fault line. When I graduated from my high school in Oklahoma in 1972, my hometown newspaper's front page was dominated by national and international stories from the Associated Press and United Press International. Our family subscribed to *Newsweek* and *Life*, and dinner was accompanied by the six o'clock network news. When I left for Yale, I'd never seen the *New York Times* or the *Village Voice*, but my classmates and I shared the same reference points for current events. American journalism was a national institution, and it was thriving.

But the ground rules for broadcasting had been transformed, and the demise of the Fairness Doctrine paved the way for the expansion of companies like Salem. There was no more right of reply. "The last thing a religious broadcaster wanted to do was eat up airtime with liberals 'promoting' abortion and homosexuality," wrote Adam Piore in *Mother Jones*. "But when the FCC repealed the fairness doctrine, the shackles that had forced Salem to tiptoe cautiously around the society's great cultural fault lines fell away."[26] The repeal gave Salem and other fundamentalist media new opportunities to widen the fault line across a regional as well as a cultural divide.

Other CNP members ran additional broadcasting operations, and the events of the late 1980s gave them a chance to grow. One important player was Donald Wildmon, a Methodist minister from Tupelo, Mississippi. Wildmon's crusade began one evening in 1976 as he watched television sitcoms with his family and was shocked by what he beheld: curse words and an extramarital love scene. Wildmon assigned his congregation to monitor network television and emerged with a list of programs to boycott—including *Three's Company*, *Love Boat*, and *Charlie's Angels* (in which an attentive monitor counted twenty-three "jiggle scenes").[27] Wildmon resigned from his pastorate and founded a group to organize pickets and boycotts against the networks.

In 1982 Wildmon was appointed to the board of governors of the Council for National Policy, and in 1988 he changed the name of his group to the American Family Association. Three years later he launched American Family Radio. It would expand into scores of stations across the South and the Midwest, providing a platform for Wildmon and other CNP stalwarts, including James Dobson.[28]

Dobson was also reviewing his strategy. His Family Research Council had begun to run short of funds and lose steam. In 1989 Dobson merged Focus on the Family and the Family Research Council, and ramped up the Family Research Council's radio programming, with an emphasis on influencing policy. That same year he brought on a new president, Gary Bauer, a diminutive Southern Baptist from Covington, Kentucky. Bauer's credentials were ideal: he had worked in opposition research for the Republican National Committee, in government relations for the Direct Mail Marketing Association, and as an advisor on domestic policy for the Reagan administration. Bauer and Dobson began planting Family Policy Councils, state-based organizations with a mandate to lobby legislatures for "profamily" (i.e., anti-LGBT) laws.

But the movement experienced some setbacks. Over 1987 and 1988, a series of sex scandals broke involving prominent televangelists with connections to the movement. One was Pentecostal preacher Jim Bakker, who began his broadcasting career at Pat Robertson's Christian Broadcasting Network. A 1987 investigation revealed that Bakker had defrauded his contributors, in part to fund a $279,000 payoff to a young assistant who accused him of rape. Bakker was sentenced to forty-five years in prison. (His term was later reduced to eight years, and he was freed in 1994.) Next came Louisiana Pentecostal preacher Jimmy Swaggart (a cousin to rockabilly star Jerry Lee Lewis), who was exposed for patronizing prostitutes.

CNP member Jerry Falwell denounced Bakker as "the greatest scab and cancer on the face of Christianity in 2,000 years of church history." Falwell—whose own broadcast lost fifty stations in the fallout—took the program over himself, but the damage was done.[29]

Televangelism had grown exponentially in the South and the West, but it was regarded as a regional curiosity by the mainstream news media. When televangelism made the headlines, it was often in the worst possible way, identified with conspiracy, fraud, and rape.

The movement was further fractured when Robertson decided to run for president in 1988, only to have Falwell endorse George Bush instead. Robertson brought fervent supporters and a sizable war chest to his campaign, second only to Vice President Bush's, but it sputtered out before the end of the primaries.

Once again, CNP regulars were disappointed; Bush's establishment Republican, Episcopalian credentials were not to their liking. In the face of political division and financial setbacks, Falwell disbanded the Moral Majority. But he put a brave face on it, proclaiming, "Our goal has been achieved . . . The religious right is solidly in place and . . . religious conservatives are now in for the duration."

But here Falwell had gotten ahead of himself. He and his colleagues at the CNP chose to depict Bush's election as a favorable development. Their members had launched important media initiatives that would exert influence in the future, especially in swing states in the South and the Midwest. But media and churches were only two legs of this stool. There was considerable work to be done, connecting media and churches to the active electorate, and turning sermons into votes.

CHAPTER 4

THE NEWS HOLE IN THE HEART OF AMERICA

The architects of the radical right studied the art of the "soft coup d'etat"—not just to take over the Republican Party but to weaken various public institutions that challenged their "biblical values." These included public schools that taught evolution, universities that advanced climate science, and businesses that supported equal rights for the LGBT community.

They also disapproved of the professional news media, which seemed to bear every trait they spurned: urban, liberal, and more secular by the minute.[1] They resolved to break its hold on the nation's psyche.

On the eve of the Reagan era, this goal seemed unlikely. The prestige of American journalism was at its apex; journalists had just brought down a president with the Watergate investigation and challenged a war with the Pentagon Papers.

James Squires summarized the role of the press in American history in his 1993 book *Read All About It! The Corporate Takeover of American Newspapers*. His assessment is worth quoting at length:

> It fell to the press to stir the colonies to revolution in the first place. A hundred years later, it was the newspaper voices of abolition that

> ultimately propelled the nation to the twin brinks of destruction and greatness over the slavery question—the Civil War. Another century later, it was dramatic press accounts of oppression in the South that produced desegregation across the land, as well as a public rebuke of the war in Vietnam.

Squires had come to praise journalism, not to bury it. But his paean inadvertently listed the original sins of American journalism as they were perceived by the fundamentalists. The Southern Baptist Convention had been established in defense of slavery; it was the meddling northern press that fanned the flames of abolition. A century later, segregationists thought the South was doing fine until northern newspapermen arrived to tell them it wasn't. (One frequently cited turning point was the arrival of Harrison Salisbury from the *New York Times* to cover the Birmingham protests, which ignited a national debate on the civil rights movement.[2])

Squires continued,

> Between 1960 and 1974, the press played a vital role in an unprecedented empowerment of the citizenry—the extension of participatory rights to minorities in new civil rights legislation and a similar enhancement of the roles of women and youth by the feminist and peace movements.
>
> In such a system, it is the reporting of unfettered truth about how things are and ideas of how they might be made better that motivates a citizenry to act and educates it to courses of action. People cannot govern what they cannot see. And whatever its imperfections, the unquestioned purpose of the old business of journalism was to provide America with an accurate reflection of itself and the understanding necessary to preserve freedom.[3]

The 1946 Hutchins Commission report defined news as "a truthful, comprehensive, and intelligent account of the day's events in a context which gives them meaning." James Squires paid homage to the concept of fact-based reporting, but the CNP's Morton Blackwell stressed that "being right" was less important than winning.[4] The power and influence of the national media were mighty, and the fundamentalist challenge might have come to naught, if the "old business of journalism" had not decayed from within.

Modern American journalism is a surprisingly recent phenomenon. Nineteenth-century newspapers were generally openly partisan party organs (as reflected by the names like the *Arkansas Democrat-Gazette* and the *Waterbury Republican*). In the Civil War, Confederate reports were often written by army officers who exaggerated their victories; while many northern correspondents moonlighted working for the government.[5]

Professional journalism evolved over the next century, along with journalism schools, associations, and prizes to uphold its values. Nonetheless, while American journalists benefited from an unusual degree of political freedom and legal protection, their outlets were still answerable to business interests and advertising revenues. The twentieth century brought massive growth in the newspaper and magazine industries, as well as the birth of broadcasting. Media companies were founded and run by business people—in Squires' words, "men of wealth, power, politics and eccentricity."[6]

World War II served as a great unifier, as the press became an important component of the war effort. Broadcasters expanded their news divisions as a public service, shielding them from the need to turn a profit, and reaped national prestige in return. The spirit of public service lingered. In 1962 William Paley told CBS correspondents, "You guys cover the news; I've got Jack Benny to make money for me."[7] News organizations proliferated across the country, most with local ownership. In 1940 there were 1,878 newspapers in the United States; as of 1946, there were a dozen large magazine companies and competing newspapers in 117 American cities.[8]

Metropolitan dailies assumed an outsize role. If the *New York Times* ran with a major story, other media had to follow suit. If it passed on a story, other outlets were less likely to follow up. The perspective of midtown Manhattan could be radically different from that of other parts of the country, and no matter how diligently news organizations pursued fact-based reporting, they could lose sight of their own subjectivity.

Print and broadcast journalism continued to grow in influence and revenue. Newspaper penetration peaked between roughly 1970 and 1990, when the ratio of circulation to American households approached one to one.[9] Network news, launched in the 1940s, reached an apex around the same time, and the evening news expanded from fifteen minutes to half an hour in the early 1960s. By 1980, 75 percent of American households were tuned to network news programs over the dinner hour.[10]

But this news ecosystem, as some journalism professors called it, was already in trouble. Newspapers were advertising-rich, producing returns of 10 to 20 percent, outstripping most investments in the manufacturing sector.[11] But family-owned newspapers paid a price for their success; when the patriarchs died, their descendants faced inheritance taxes of up to 70 percent, prompting many to cash out by selling their papers to corporations. Family owners were answerable to their communities and their peers, but corporations responded to shareholders who were more interested in quarterly earnings than Pulitzer Prizes. By the early 2000s, the new news business was implementing massive cost-saving measures: firing thousands of reporters, slashing circulations in underserved communities with commercially unattractive demographics, and refusing to invest in the vital new technologies that were transforming the culture. The new corporate owners squeezed every last penny from their newspapers, in many cases using their revenues to float their debt.

The result was devastating. Local voices were silenced, local populations abandoned. Newspaper ownership was increasingly concentrated in fewer and fewer hands. By 1990 just fourteen companies controlled half of the sixteen hundred daily papers, and the concentration of ownership would increase.[12]

Newspapers were losing ground to television, but network news divisions were also troubled. Over the late twentieth century networks were acquired by increasingly diversified corporations. CBS's Viacom, NBC's General Electric, and ABC's Disney saw no need to subsidize news divisions, directing them to turn a profit like other divisions. Television news reporting slid into softer stories, shorter soundbites, and more reporting tied to entertainment and human interest. Over the next few decades, the management closed both international and domestic bureaus and laid off legions of reporters. Cable and public broadcasting filled some of the information gaps, but cable channels tended to emphasize opinion, debate, and sensationalism over traditional reporting and cultivated like-minded niche audiences. Public television was worthy but chronically underfunded.

Over the decades the American appetite for news declined, especially among younger people. For much of the twentieth century the broader American public had largely been working off the same page, relying on the network evening news and newspapers that followed the wires and the *New York Times'* lead on major national and international stories, but that accord weakened under economic pressure. And the worst was yet to come.

The digital revolution was gathering steam. News organizations warily adopted the use of email and online search functions in their newsrooms, but publishers were fatally slow to understand how the upheaval would affect their business model and innovate in response. Display and classified advertising made up their core income; subscriptions were a minimal source of revenue.

In 1995 a newcomer to San Francisco named Craig Newmark launched a digital service that would turn into Craigslist, a direct competitor to classified advertising. It took a few years for the impact to hit, but then it was catastrophic. Newspaper advertising revenues, which peaked in 2000, utterly collapsed. More digital assaults were underway. Over the 1990s, digital entrepreneurs experimented with advertising approaches that took advantage of their ability to direct advertising to the users who were most likely to respond. The public moved online, and digital advertising was waiting for them: on their searches, in their emails, on their phones.

Classifieds weren't the only problem; display advertising revenues took a massive hit as well. Derek Thompson described the collapse in the *Atlantic*: "Between 2000 and 2015, print newspaper advertising revenue fell from about $60 billion to about $20 billion, wiping out the gains of the previous 50 years."[13]

In 2013, the struggling *Washington Post* would be sold to Jeff Bezos for $250 million, which would cover the cost of a middling superyacht. In 2016 the *Tampa Tribune* went for a paltry $9.5 million, the same price paid for a racehorse named Songbird the following year. The *Tribune* was subsumed into its rival, the *Tampa Bay Times*. Since 2004, almost 1,800 U.S. newspapers have disappeared altogether, and hundreds of communities have become "news deserts," without a single local news organization.[14] These are disproportionately communities of older, lower-income residents without college educations.

The classified and display advertising that had paid journalists' salaries migrated online, but the erratic business model that underwrote professional reporting did not. By 2018, Forbes estimated that the worth of Craigslist had grown to nearly $4 billion.[15] It was fairly easy for news organizations to place their news content online, making it easier to update, navigate, and personalize. But digital ads sold for a tiny fraction of the cost of print ads, and once readers got used to free online content, it was hard to build revenues from paid subscriptions.

The catastrophe was less visible from the Boston-Washington corridor, where the *New York Times*, the *Wall Street Journal*, and the *Washington Post* built online readerships and began to transition toward a new digital business model—even if the future was far from secure. The rest of the country's newspaper culture suffered a colony collapse. One of the most significant casualties was statehouse reporting, the traditional purview of midsize newspapers in Middle America. Pew Research reported that between 2003 and 2014, the number of full-time statehouse reporters dropped 35 percent.[16] The press corps in many statehouses dwindled, allowing state lawmakers to go about rewriting laws with less scrutiny.

All of this must have been music to the ears of the Council for National Policy. The ongoing disruption of the traditional news industry created a vacuum, and they were systematically building a stable of media partners prepared to fill it. The regulatory environment was working in their favor.

The gutting of the Fairness Doctrine had opened the door for Salem and other CNP media partners' highly politicized, one-sided broadcasts. One beneficiary was American Family Radio, founded by CNP member Donald Wildmon, Tupelo's scourge of the sitcoms. AFR expanded into a network of almost two hundred stations in thirty-five states, with three different programming streams designed for its various markets: AFR Talk, AFR Hybrid, and Urban Family Talk, which employed an African American staff to target an African American audience. All three adhered to the same statement of faith: "The American Family Association believes that God has communicated absolute truth to mankind, and that all people are subject to the authority of God's Word at all times. Therefore AFA believes that a culture based on biblical truth best serves the well-being of our nation and our families, in accordance with the vision of our founding documents."

The organization's action statement spurred followers to "promote virtue by upholding in culture that which is right, true and good according to Scripture." Its overtly political goal was to "motivate people to take a stand on cultural and moral issues at the local, state, and national levels."[17]

CNP members ran other broadcasting operations as well. The Bott Radio Network was founded in 1962 by the CNP's Dick Bott, a former child evangelist, and his wife, Sherley. Bott quickly recognized the potential of commercial religious broadcasting, and his radio network grew to over a hundred stations in fifteen states, heavily concentrated in the Bible Belt.[18] States like Kansas and Missouri had plenty of news deserts without a daily newspaper, but they were blanketed by Bott radio signals carrying the programs of CNP stalwarts such as James Dobson and Gary Bauer.[19]

Together, Salem's Epperson and Atsinger, American Family Radio's Donald Wildmon, and Bott Radio's Dick Bott—all members of the CNP—built overlapping radio empires that were all but invisible to the urban Northeast. But it was hard to drive very far across the Plains without running into their signals and their increasingly virulent rhetoric.

Wildmon's American Family Radio network, for example, produced segments with titles like "Infanticide Adopted by Democrats" and "Homosexuality is the Dividing Line between Light and Darkness."[20] One considered the question of how Christians should respond to a Muslim call to prayer, and answered, "They should take the call to prayer as a call to arms, to go to war in the Spirit against the demon-god Allah and the spiritual deception of Islam."[21]

The Salem Radio Network was especially aggressive in acquiring new stations. Atsinger and Epperson developed a successful strategy of purchasing leveraged stations in urban markets. But they ran into an obstacle with the Federal Communications Commission, which prohibited a broadcaster from owning too many stations in one market. Epperson and Atsinger—by now members of the CNP board of governors— joined other broadcasters to lobby against the regulations; Salem contributed $74,000 to key legislators. The Telecommunications Act of 1996 was written by industry lobbyists, promoted by Newt Gingrich, and signed into law by Bill Clinton.[22] It eased the ownership regulations, to the benefit of Salem and other large companies. Salem went on an acquisition binge and created a system of station "clusters" to cut costs.

In 1999 *Forbes* magazine reported that Salem Communications (as it was now called) owned fifty-seven stations. This made it the eighth-largest broadcaster and the largest religious broadcaster in the country, with at least one station in nineteen of the biggest twenty-five markets. "Christian radio" had become the third-most-popular format in the United States, following country music and talk.[23]

In July 1999 Salem issued an initial public offering. The company was booming. It still reaped half of its revenues—nearly $78 million—from the sale of block programming, but advertising accounted for a third, and it was growing. The IPO's influx of capital allowed the company to acquire more stations.

Salem's reach extended beyond religious programming; it also rode the wave of conservative talk radio. Local radio stations, like hometown newspapers, had traditionally been owned by—and answerable to—members of the community. In the wake of deregulation, over a quarter of the nation's radio stations were sold, many passing from local to corporate owners, while new satellite technology facilitated national programming.

Eventually the Salem, Bott, and American Family Radio empires extended to at least forty-six states. (As of January 2019, they owned stations in every state except Idaho, Nevada, Utah, and Alaska.) Their programming, including political content produced by CNP members, was utilized by other radio networks, including the Christian Satellite Network and Family Life Radio. In combination with their affiliates, the CNP radio broadcasters covered the entire nation; California and Texas hosted all three. ABC, NBC, and CBS began to dump their radio stations, especially in small and midsize markets, and their news programs disappeared. The Great American News Desert grew drier by the year.

National Public Radio, founded in 1970, did much to fill in the gap. Serving more than a thousand public radio stations, NPR offered traditional journalism and newscasts that presented multiple perspectives on public issues. Listeners could turn to NPR for detailed, thoughtful interviews with leaders from the leading political parties. Nonetheless, many conservatives in Middle America distrusted NPR as a smugly liberal voice with little interest in their issues, a maddening focus on identity politics, and a propensity for promoting the Democrats' agenda.

NPR tilted urban and coastal for obvious reasons. Its stations, its listeners—and its listener contributions—were concentrated in urban areas, suburbs, and college towns. NPR's weekly listenership would reach 28.5 million by 2017—but that was still less than 10 percent of the national population. Public broadcasting was founded with federal support, but the ongoing assault by Republican administrations whittled that funding down to almost nothing over the years. NPR responded by basing its budgets on listener contributions. But that meant that urban NPR stations—especially major stations in New York, Washington, and San Francisco—had outsize budgets and programming capacity. Stations in conservative, rural areas—the news deserts that needed them most—got by on a fraction of the funding, with part-time employees and spotty local coverage.

Many public radio stations are low-budget operations based on college campuses that broadcast from translator stations whose signals vanish a few miles out of town. Those who can't afford to pay for all of the syndicated news and information programs often substitute light musical offerings.

Oklahoma, for example, has six NPR stations, mostly in cities and college towns, while Bott and American Family Radio have a combined twenty stations blanketing the state.[24] And radio matters: it remains an important part of daily life for millions of Americans, whether in the home, the workplace, or the car.

Salem Communications developed three principal formats for its stations: Christian (fundamentalist) talk, contemporary Christian music, and conservative news and talk.[25] The company created a syndication service that distributed talk programs and a twenty-four-hour news service to over two thousand affiliates nationwide. It billed its programs as "Christian Radio's Definitive Source for News," breaking "the ivory tower approach of the traditional networks."[26] This was not news about Christianity, it was current events filtered through a highly partisan fundamentalist lens.

Salem's "Christian journalism" was a new genre, unhampered by professional practices of multisourced reporting, fact-checking, and corrections.

The Salem, Bott, and American Family Radio networks averted the crisis in business models that afflicted the rest of the industry, buoyed by blocks of airtime sold to fundamentalist churches and advertising sold to CNP affiliates such as the Family Research Council.

Further revenues resulted from the Dietary Supplement Health and Education Act of 1994 (DSHEA, pronounced "D-shay"), promoted by Senator Orrin Hatch. Hatch and his family had extensive involvement in the nutritional supplements industry, which is based in Hatch's home state of Utah. DSHEA prevented the FDA from regulating harmful or fraudulent supplements before they hit the market. The *Los Angeles Times* concluded, "The harvest [of DSHEA] has been a public health disaster."[27] It also created an advertising revenue stream for online and broadcast outlets of various persuasions. Bott and American Family Radio run ads for vitamins and medical and dietary supplements, many of them directed at the elderly. (Other ads promote organizations such as the Institute for Creation Research, which argues that "Birds didn't evolve from dinosaurs because they can fly.") Salem's online outlet RedState rented its email lists to the Health Sciences Institute, which used it to promote a product that supposedly "vaporizes cancer in six weeks."[28]

Salem's stations took a regional approach. In Irving, Texas, The Word 100.7 FM was overtly religious. Focus on the Family and related programming offered advice from a fundamentalist perspective for listeners' daily problems of marriage infidelity, alcoholism, and depression, and condemned abortion and homosexuality. CNP member and attorney Jay Sekulow's programs expounded on policy issues from a fundamentalist perspective.

Beyond the South, Salem's conservative-news-and-talk format built on the success of talk radio's secular "shock jocks" like Rush Limbaugh, promoting hosts such as Hugh Hewitt, Sean Hannity, and the ubiquitous Sekulow. Salem's Detroit station, The Patriot WDTK, focused on the anxieties of the Rust Belt: "politics, pop culture, the war on terror, education, immigration, and much more."[29]

Atsinger and Epperson expanded their political footprint along with their radio empire. In 2005 journalist Adam Piore published a detailed history of Salem's strategy called "A Higher Frequency" in *Mother Jones* magazine. Piore reported that between 1998 and 2004, Atsinger, Epperson, and their company offered $423,000 in federal campaign contributions, 96 percent of it to Republicans. This rendered them the sixth largest donor in the industry.[30] In 2000 Atsinger, Epperson, and a colleague donated $780,000 toward a California state ballot initiative to oppose gay marriage.

Conservative and fundamentalist talk radio served as both the training grounds and the meeting place for a new generation of leadership. One beneficiary was a young Indiana lawyer named Mike Pence. Pence, a Catholic who converted to fundamentalist Christianity in college, made two unsuccessful runs for a congressional seat in 1988 and 1990. In 1991 he accepted a position as president of the Indiana Policy Review Foundation. This was the Indiana affiliate of the State Policy Network, whose members were described as a "mini-Heritage Foundation in each state," concentrating on influencing state legislation. The State Policy Network funds its state affiliates, and is heavily funded by the Charles Koch Foundation and the Donors Trust and Donors Capital Fund, whose major backers include the Koch brothers and the CNP's DeVos family.[31]

From 1994 to 1999 Pence worked as a host for conservative radio programs, many of them syndicated across the state. Pence used the job to hone his public speaking skills, build a following, and promote his image as a self-described "Rush Limbaugh on decaf." His smooth baritone was well suited for radio, and his youthful face, prematurely white hair, and aw-shucks manner sold him as a "safe" baby boomer who respected his elders and drank milk for a nightcap. But he was a stalwart opponent to abortion, Planned Parenthood, and same-sex marriage.[32] His mild exterior belied a bigoted streak. While he was president of the Indiana Policy Review, it published an article called "Military Necessity and Homosexuality," stating, "The homosexuals are not as a group able-bodied. They are known to carry extremely high rates of disease brought on because of the nature of their sexual practices and the promiscuity which is a hallmark of their lifestyle."[33]

Mike Pence met a new ally named Tony Perkins around 1998, when the thirty-five-year-old Louisiana state legislator reportedly appeared on his radio show. Perkins had come to Indianapolis to testify before the state legislature on the "covenant marriage" law he had drafted in Louisiana, which created a voluntary marriage contract restricting the right to divorce. Like Pence, Perkins was a fierce opponent of gay marriage and abortion. He was also one of nine Louisianans who belonged to the Council on National Policy.[34] It was a beautiful friendship. Perkins and Pence shared a talent for broadcasting and a thirst for power, though it wasn't initially clear had who would pursue each path.

Perkins had left his tiny hometown of Cleveland, Oklahoma, to serve in the Marine Corps. He moved to Baton Rouge, where he joined the police force. Then he got a job reporting for the television station run by Woody Jenkins, the founding executive director of the CNP. Along the way Perkins attended Jerry Falwell's Liberty University, though he didn't graduate until he was nearly thirty.

In 1995 Perkins ran successfully for the Louisiana state legislature, and was reelected four years later. The CNP's Richard Viguerie was one of his campaign fund-raisers.[35] Perkins also managed the unsuccessful Senate campaign of former CNP director Woody Jenkins.

There were bumps along the way. A 1999 federal investigation revealed that Perkins, on behalf of the Jenkins campaign, had contracted the services of a media company partially owned by Ku Klux Klan Grand Wizard David Duke. Perkins later reported that he was "profoundly grieved" to learn of the association.[36] In 2001 Perkins gave a speech to the Baton Rouge chapter of the Council of Conservative Citizens (an organization the future Supreme Court Justice Thurgood Marshall labeled the "uptown Klan").[37] Dobson was undeterred by the negative press. Such events set a pattern that would be played out in the future. The Council for National Policy and its affiliates would be revealed to associate with unsavory characters, and they would be shocked that such nice folk could harbor such nasty ideology.

In 2003 a conclave calling itself the Arlington Group reconvened in Virginia, assembling such CNP stalwarts as Paul Weyrich, Donald Wildmon, Gary Bauer, Richard Bott, and James Dobson. Worried they were losing ground, the group focused on three issues: abortion, gay marriage, and gun rights. Polling showed that the topic where they could get the most traction was same-sex marriage.[38]

James Dobson, nearing seventy, was slowing down, and he was ready to bring in some new blood. He turned to Tony Perkins: youthful and honey-voiced at forty, with a southern variant of Mike Pence's aw-shucks manner.

As soon as Perkins was hired by the Family Research Council, he launched a new radio program, broadcast on Bott Radio and the American Family Radio network. In the past, the Family Research Council had tried to maintain cordial relations with Democrats, but Perkins' *Washington Watch* was unabashedly political, celebrating conservative Republicans and excoriating their Democratic opponents. For all practical purposes, the CNP had anointed the Family Research Council as its public lobbying and organizational front.

Nonetheless, the IRS assigned tax-exempt, 501(c)(3) status to both the Family Research Council and American Family Radio—in keeping with the FRC's stated mission to advance "faith, family and freedom in government and culture from a Christian worldview," and the American Family Radio's calling as an "educational organization" devoted to "spiritual development."[39]

As for Pence, he had run in 2000 for Congress again, and this time he had won. His radio expertise made him a hot commodity among Republicans on Capitol Hill, and his reactionary position on social issues won him favor with the CNP.

CHAPTER 5

MONEY PEOPLE

The founding fathers of the Council for National Policy understood that their vision would require money—lots of it. There were institutions to be founded, polling to be conducted, meetings to hold. The new organization acquired some funds from membership fees, and more from the surcharge for members of the executive committee, whose elevated status granted them the right to select officers.

Tracing the details of the CNP is a challenge. The CNP has stressed secrecy throughout its existence, but at certain times names of some members have been disclosed, and its annual directory has been leaked on several occasions. Other sources of information include issues of the CNP newsletter and public letters the members sign on policy issues. A copy of the 1998 directory was published by the Institute for First Amendment Studies. This document specified that the location of meetings and their participants should not be disclosed to the press. It listed a forty-eight-member board of governors, who paid $6,000 a year in dues. Premium "Gold Circle" members paid $10,000, while regular members paid $1,750, and those under thirty paid $100.[1] Years later, the Southern Poverty Law Center published the 2014 directory on its website, providing additional information on the CNP's members and the organizations they oversaw.[2]

The CNP's goals required far greater investments than its dues could provide. The Council for National Policy would be a private club for donors as well as a network of strategists. "As one member described it," the *Baton Rouge State-Times* reported, "the Council was a vehicle for people who needed resources to meet others who could provide those resources."[3]

The 1998 directory's roster of CNP leadership combined those who needed and those who could provide: Tim LaHaye, Pat Robertson, and Paul Pressler spoke for the fundamentalists; Paul Weyrich, Richard Viguerie, and Morton Blackwell represented the political operatives. Salem's Atsinger and Epperson brought media to the mix. The money men included Wyoming financier Foster Friess, two members of the Colorado Coors dynasty, and an outlying Michigander named Rich DeVos. Texans were active from the start. The 1980 Dallas rally brought oilmen like Cullen Davis into the CNP fold, and Nelson Bunker Hunt served as CNP president from 1983 to 1984.[4]

While the movement's public platform preached a return to Judeo-Christian values and regressive social policies, the underlying economic issues were equally critical. Many of these concerned environmental regulations. The Environmental Protection Agency had been founded in 1970 under the Nixon administration, in reaction to a run of national emergencies. In November 1966, a three-day blanket of smog covered New York City, leading to over 150 deaths.[5] A 1969 blowout at an offshore oil platform released an estimated three million barrels of crude oil off Santa Monica, killing thousands of birds, fish, and other marine wildlife.[6] Later that year, an oil slick on Ohio's Cuyahoga River caught fire.[7] But these were just the events that made the headlines.

In Texas and Oklahoma, runoff from abandoned oil wells had been quietly poisoning farmland and drinking water for decades.[8] In 1969 DuPont opened a chloroprene plant among the petrochemical facilities on an eighty-five-mile stretch of the Mississippi River in Louisiana that would be dubbed the Chemical Corridor. A 2014 assessment by the EPA found that the five census tracts around the plant had the nation's highest cancer risk in the country.[9]

But the extractive industries treated the Clean Air Act (1963), the Clean Water Act (1972), and the EPA (1970) as existential threats. It didn't take an oracle to see that environmental regulations would take a bite out of oil, coal, and mining profits, and could promote a culture of alternative energy that could end the fossil fuel era. A battle ensued between environmental activists, affiliated with the Democratic Party and liberal Republicans, and their adversaries, the extractive industries and their allies.

The conflict was defined by cultural and geographical loyalties as well as economic interests. It was no coincidence that Richard Viguerie described fellow Republican Theodore Roosevelt as an ancient enemy. Following in the conservationist president's footsteps, patrician Republicans prized the epic landscapes of the Northeast and the Far West, supported national parks, and created vast land reserves (often to the benefit of their country houses and trout streams).

The Southwest was a different story. In 1870, as New York City was gliding into the Gilded Age, Dallas was still a dusty cow town of three thousand. Oklahoma was Indian territory, home to the native populations of the Southeast who had fallen victim to Andrew Jackson's ethnic cleansing. Pioneers regarded nature as a brutal adversary. Farmers coaxed their crops from stubborn soil, clawing into grasslands and red clay—only to be wiped out by plagues of insects and drought. The weather was capricious at best. Oklahoma baked you in August, froze you in March, and dust-whipped you in between. It could just as easily ambush you with a day of glorious weather in any month it chose. Many traditional crops understandably balked at these conditions.

Oil changed everything. In the nineteenth century, settlers stumbled upon the first signs of the great Midcontinent oil field, a vast region of oil and gas deposits concentrated beneath Kansas, Oklahoma, Texas, and Louisiana. Serious prospecting began in the early twentieth century, in step with America's automotive revolution. Vast fortunes were made overnight, and Tulsa, Oklahoma City, Houston, and Dallas were transformed into boomtowns. Opportunists swarmed the countryside, piercing the earth and throwing up shards of shale and toxic brine. When I was a teenager, oil companies operated rigs on the very grounds of the Oklahoma state capitol.

There was little talk of preserving the environment; indeed, theology was right on hand to justify the pillage. Nature existed to be conquered and exhausted. The Dominionists cited Genesis 1:26: "And God said, Let us make man in our image, after our likeness: and let them have dominion over the fish of the sea, and over the fowl of the air, and over the cattle, and over all the earth, and over every creeping thing that creepeth upon the earth." The oil industry of Texas, Oklahoma, and Louisiana was a natural habitat for Dominionist theology.

Big Oil rained down its blessings. Oil interests had propelled Oklahoma into statehood in 1907 and controlled the state government for most of its history. For Louisiana, one of the poorest states in the Union, the oil and gas industry became an economic lifeline—and a major contributor to state politicians. Texas is the number-one oil producer in the country, accounting for 40 percent of U.S. production. The Texan economy is the second largest in the country, after California, as well as the nation's top exporter, accounting for nearly 20 percent of the total.

The oil and gas industry's might wasn't limited to these states; it also altered the national balance of power. Southern traditionalists saw this as restitution. In the past, the nation's economic elite had been concentrated in the slaveholding states; South Carolina, Georgia, Alabama, and Mississippi were the wealthiest states in the country, and Louisiana sugar planters occupied a top echelon of American society.[10] When the Confederates surrendered, they lost their status as well as their autonomy.

Confederate roots ran deep in the oil belt. After the war Confederate veterans poured into the underpopulated regions of Texas and Oklahoma, seeking a fresh start and imprinting the states with their politics and their culture. There was also an economic legacy. On a Facebook group called Sons of Confederate Veterans Oklahoma Division, a member offered his perspective on the roots of the conflict: "Y'all are partly right, but it was mostly about the Federal government's overreach in the south, extra taxes and tariffs put on them. Sort of what's been happening with all the socialist were voting for office today. You will not recognize it, you have been conditioned to accept it thru over 50 years of public school. Live free while you can."[11]

Regional tensions were transposed into the battle over the environment. Environmentalists warned that the future of the earth depended on reducing fossil fuel emissions. Oil and gas boosters told their fellow citizens that their future depended on the fossil fuel economy. There was little common ground. The battle raged on, but the overwhelming scientific consensus came to be that fossil fuel emissions and other contaminants were causing severe damage to the environment, affecting human health, and leading to devastating climate change.

The oil industry marshaled a vast public relations army, seconded from the tobacco industry's campaign to deny the harmful effects of smoking and coordinated by a purported think tank called the Heartland Institute. The CNP network was in evidence; the "endorsement" passage on Heartland's website reads, in its entirety, "The Heartland Institute is endorsed by some of the top scholars, thinkers, and politicians in the world—including many members of congress and state elected officials and the leaders of other conservative and libertarian think tanks such as Americans for Tax Reform's Grover Norquist, The Leadership Institute's Morton Blackwell, The Heritage Foundation's Jim DeMint, and many more."[12] Norquist and DeMint were longtime members of the CNP, and Blackwell, of course, was a cofounder. In 2016 Blackwell received the Heartland Foundation's Heartland Liberty Prize as a reward for supporting the foundation's campaigns over the years.[13]

The Council for National Policy's moneymen were concentrated in the Sun Belt, an arc of territory sweeping down from the Carolinas through the South and Southwest and into Southern California. But there were outposts farther afield. One was Wyoming, where the quixotic stock picker Foster Friess managed his half-billion-dollar earnings.

Friess, who served as president of the CNP from 1997 to 1998, was born in tiny Rice Lake, Wisconsin, the son of humble transplants from Texas. After graduating from the University of Wisconsin, he served as an intelligence officer for the First Guided Missile Brigade in El Paso. In 1974 he founded Friess Associates with his wife, Lynn, and the investment firm eventually took off. Friess acquired a massive property in Jackson Hole, Wyoming, along with a florid sunburn, a ten-gallon hat, and a cowboy affect. Friess wedded his born-again Christianity to political ambition and free market ideology. His website declared, "Private individuals are called to carry others' burdens—rather than relying on the government to do so."[14]

Through his massive donations, Friess was called to carry the burdens of the Council for National Policy, the Family Research Council, and a range of other conservative causes and candidates (as well as some traditional charities).[15]

Another energy center was Colorado, James Dobson's home base, which yielded a cohort of businessmen and investors. Joseph Coors, an heir to the Golden, Colorado, beer business, had backed the Heritage Foundation and the John Birch Society as well as the CNP. Coors appreciated the organizations' anti-union stance. He had fought a long battle with striking employees in the 1970s, which he finally resolved by ending union representation at his company.[16]

Some CNP donors swore on the Bible but tangled with the law. The most spectacular case involved Texas oil heir Cullen Davis, who had bankrolled the 1980 rally in Dallas and served on the board of governors of the CNP. One August night in 1976, Davis's estranged wife and her boyfriend were returning home when they were fired upon by a gunman. Her daughter from a previous marriage was found dead in the house, and the boyfriend died in the attack. Cullen's wife and another friend were wounded. The trial was a sensation; three eyewitnesses—one of them Davis's wife—testified that he was the gunman, disguised with a wig. But Davis's celebrated lawyer, Richard "Racehorse" Haynes, won an acquittal. In 1978 a friend of Cullen's told the FBI that Davis had asked him to find a hit man to kill his wife and the judge in his divorce proceedings. The FBI set up an elaborate sting operation and recorded Davis confirming his request. Once again, his lawyer got him off. After the trials, Davis chose a spiritual advisor in the form of James Robison, whose homophobic broadcasts had sparked the Dallas rally. In 1982 Davis donated $1 million in rare Asian jade, ivory, and gold religious artifacts to Robison's ministry. Robison rejected the gift on the grounds that they were "graven images." The two men proceeded to smash the collection with a hammer in Davis's driveway.[17]

No one was ever convicted of the Davis murders. Cullen Davis claimed that the legal fees wiped out his fortune, but he kept his place on the CNP rolls, billed as a "salesman and consultant."[18]

Other CNP members' financial affairs played out in different arenas. Founding member Nelson Bunker Hunt was once in the running to be the richest man in the world, but in the 1970s he was shaken by disruptions in his oil business and fundamentalist concerns that the apocalypse was near. He and his brother Herbert set out to corner the world's silver market. Their actions prompted a frenzy of speculation, and then a crash. Hunt served as CNP president from 1983 to 1984—at the same time he was under congressional investigation—and declared bankruptcy in 1986.[19] The Federal Reserve intervened to stabilize the market. In 1988 a federal grand jury found the Hunt brothers guilty of conspiracy, imposing massive fines and back taxes. Nelson Bunker Hunt was still a CNP member as of 1998.[20]

Hunt's favorite venture was a 1979 fundamentalist biblical docudrama. Hunt put up $3.5 million for the film, which purportedly reached an audience in the hundreds of millions (some said billions). "The best investment I ever made was the JESUS film," he told a pastor in his later years. "It cost me 11 cents a soul."[21] Hunt died in 2014.

A common theme emerged from Texans of the CNP: the belief that God was on their side, and that their fortunes placed them above the law.

THE TEXAS DRAMAS played out on an epic scale, but they were ultimately upstaged by the Michigan outlier.

Richard DeVos was a long-standing member of the Council for National Policy, and the ruling patriarch of an economic and political dynasty. The DeVos and Prince families—united through the marriage of Richard's son and Betsy Prince—built two vast fortunes through a range of unusual business practices. They have used their massive wealth to erode the state's power and impose their rigid theology on society. The CNP was central to their mission, and they have served as a cornerstone for it.

The two families sprang from Dutch enclaves in Michigan and the Christian Reformed Church.[22] Their communities had their roots in religious extremism. In the nineteenth century the Dutch government decided to liberalize the laws concerning the state Dutch Reformed Church. A small group of conservative farmers resisted and immigrated to America, cleaving to their old ways through the Reformed Church in America. The

"Seceders" represented only 2 percent of the Dutch population, but they made up almost 50 percent of the Dutch immigrants to America before 1850.[23]

In 1858 a third of the Dutch immigrants in Michigan decided that their American church had succumbed to "moral decay" and theological liberalism, and founded the Christian Reformed Church.[24] They blamed the Enlightenment for "idoliz[ing] human reason at the expense of Bible-based faith" and set out to contest the government's role in public education and labor relations.[25] Education should be the purview of the family and the church, not the government, they argued, and trade unions and collective bargaining undermined divine authority.

The Dominionist spirit was ever present. The website for one Christian Reformed congregation describes the denomination's mandate: "Believers were not only called to maintain holy lives in relation to God and each other, they were also called to extend God's kingdom into the society in which they lived. Believers were to look beyond the hard, wooden pews and their family altars to take on the world for Christ—using Christian schools, institutions, and organizations to make God's redemptive and recreating work a reality in the marketplace, city hall, and factory."[26]

The regulation of the Princes' Calvinist enclave of Holland, Michigan, is less dire, but it's tidy by decree. Ordinances prohibit whistling between 11:00 p.m. and 7:00 a.m., as well as selling merchandise on the street.[27] The website for Grand Rapids's Calvin College states that it "seeks to be a community where lesbian, gay, bisexual, and transgender persons are treated with respect, justice, grace and understanding," but "we also affirm that physical sexual intimacy has its proper place in the context of heterosexual marriage."[28]

Edgar Prince, patriarch of the Prince family, was an engineer and inventor who made a fortune in the auto industry. One big success among the many gizmos Prince developed was the lighted vanity mirror on flip-up sun visors—the automotive equivalent of putting wheels on a suitcase. The Texas oil barons fueled America's mad passion for cars; Prince accessorized it.

Prince and his wife, Elsa, were fervent members of the Christian Reformed Church. Their four children included son Erik and daughter Elizabeth ("Betsy"), who attended the local Holland Christian Schools and graduated from her mother's alma mater, Calvin College—both founded by the Christian Reformed Church.[29] Betsy, a slender blonde, married Dick DeVos in 1979, when she was twenty-one.

Twenty years earlier Dick's father, Richard DeVos Sr., had cofounded Amway, which grew into a multibillion-dollar global enterprise, and in 1991 he added the NBA basketball team Orlando Magic to his portfolio. Federal investigators took a keen interest in DeVos's business practices. In 1969 the Federal Trade Commission launched an investigation to establish whether Amway was a Ponzi scheme. The FTC found that Amway made "false and misleading claims" but closed the investigation without charges after six years, finding that the company did not meet the definition of a pyramid scheme.[30] But Amway's Asian operations came under further scrutiny, and the company was found guilty in the United States and Canada of price-fixing and fraud.

Described as a multilevel marketing company, Amway sold cleaning products, cosmetics, and nutritional supplements, engaging individuals to flog their products to friends and family at the same time as they absorbed the company's conservative politics and fundamentalist values. Amway also built religious networks. "Good old Amway," recalled one former Baptist minister. "There were a number of efforts to recruit me . . . They really went after pastors and church members to sell their soap."[31] Charles Stanley, pastor of the First Baptist Church in Atlanta and a past president of the Southern Baptist Convention, was a major distributor. He was rewarded with a glowing blurb from Dick DeVos for his book *Success God's Way*.[32]

Amway products had their fans, but some consumers complained they were overpriced, and disaffected dropouts called their sales force a "cult."[33] Nonetheless, Amway martialed a vast network of indoctrinated distributors and customers that could be mobilized for political as well as commercial purposes.

The dynasty spent a king's ransom on political operations. As fundamentalists they invested in campaigns against gay marriage and abortion rights. As businesspeople, they resented the federal government, especially its power to regulate business practices and carry out consumer protections. As donors, they contributed massive amounts to political campaigns, candidates, and organizations that advanced their agenda.

The clan constituted CNP royalty. Founding member Richard DeVos Sr. served twice as president, from 1986 to 1987 and from 1990 to 1993. His son Dick was also a member. Betsy DeVos's father, Edgar Prince, was an early member, and her mother, Elsa, joined the board of governors after Edgar's death. The clan funded the CNP (and a host of other right-wing organizations) through its tax-exempt "charitable foundations": the Edgar and Elsa Prince Foundation, the Richard and Helen DeVos Foundation, and the Dick and Betsy DeVos Family Foundation, as well as a number of dark money donor funds and pass-through organizations.

The DeVoses and Princes shared an abhorrence of homosexuality and abortion rights, which made them natural allies of James Dobson. In 1983 Edgar Prince became one of the founding donors of Dobson's Family Research Council, and his family would go on to play a leading role throughout the organization's history. Prince's support was especially crucial in its early years, as the FRC struggled to find its feet. Dobson brought Gary Bauer in as president in 1988, with instructions to raise its profile and increase its funding. Between 1990 and 2000 the staff quintupled from twenty to one hundred, outgrowing their Washington headquarters.

Edgar Prince stepped forward with funds to construct a new building, and brought the clan with him. Additional donations arrived from Dick and Betsy DeVos, and Prince's wife, Elsa. In 1996 FRC moved into a new six-story office building with the slogan "Faith, Family, Freedom" inscribed in Gothic lettering over the doorway, across the street from the Chinatown metro stop. It shared its new quarters with the Alliance Defending Freedom, another CNP partner. In 1998 the FRC reported that it had increased its contributions by over $14 million from the previous year; the staff grew up to a hundred and twenty, and the mailing list to half a million.[34]

The DeVos and Prince families' tax filings showed that between 1999 and 2001, the Dick and Betsy DeVos Family Foundation gave $275,000 to James Dobson's Focus on the Family. The Prince Foundation donated $5.2 million between 2001 and 2013, and $6.2 million to the FRC. All in all, the DeVoses donated nearly $100 million and the Princes $70 million between 2000 and 2014. *Mother Jones* reporter Kristina Rizga noted that the families had also contributed large amounts to hospitals, medical research, and arts institutions, but "these records show an overwhelming emphasis on funding

Christian schools, evangelical missions, and conservative, free-market think tanks . . . that want to shrink the public sector in every sphere, including education."[35]

The DeVoses ran their extended family like the government of a small country. Richard DeVos Sr. explained the system in his 2014 "definitive autobiography," *Simply Rich*:

> We formed the DeVos Family Council, which is made up of our children and their spouses and meets four times a year. The Family Council just approved a family constitution that essentially captures our family mission and values . . . The Family Council also articulates how the family will work together in managing our shared financial interests and our philanthropy.
>
> We also have the Family Assembly, which involves all three generations—Helen and I, our children and their spouses, and some of our grandchildren—and meets once a year, with all family members expected to attend.[36]

In other words, the DeVos family featured a senate called the Council and a lower house called the Assembly, with its own constitution and combined resources of over $5 billion at its disposal—slightly more than the national budget of Paraguay. The Prince family were eager partners of equal grandiosity. When Edgar Prince died in 1995, Family Research Council president Gary Bauer declared, "Ed Prince was not an empire builder. He was a kingdom builder."[37] A year later, Prince's heirs sold his company for $1.35 billion in cash.

The DeVos-Prince domain assigned family members quasi-ministerial portfolios. Betsy DeVos's brother, Erik Prince, was clearly minister of defense. Prince had been a young intern at the Family Research Council in its early days, and a former Navy SEAL. In 1997 he founded a private security services firm called Blackwater, which was widely accused of conducting paramilitary responses to conflict, both at home and abroad. In 2007 Blackwater employees fired into a crowd in Baghdad, killing seventeen civilians. An FBI review ruled that the killings were unjustified.[38] After a lengthy legal process, one guard pleaded guilty to manslaughter, and another was convicted of murder. Blackwater was barred from operating in Iraq, then sold and renamed.[39] But Erik Prince continued his crusade to privatize military operations.

Betsy DeVos served as the family's minister of public education—or rather, against public education. She had worked her way up the Republican Party ladder, primarily as a fund-raiser, to become a member of the Republican National Committee. On her home turf, she labored tirelessly to promote charter schools and school vouchers as ways to divert tax dollars from public schools to private religious schools. In Detroit, as in other Michigan locales, small charter schools sprang up across the city based on her policies. The charter schools brought "diversity of choice," but the Detroit public schools—troubled as they were—produced better test scores. At the Allen Academy charter school, only 7 percent of third-graders performed at grade level in English in 2016, and the school was closed. *Detroit Free Press* editor Stephen Henderson called DeVos's efforts "an ideological lobby that has zealously championed free-market education reform for decades, with little regard for the outcome"—and that outcome was "a deeply dysfunctional educational landscape."[40]

The family, as usual, pulled together. In 2000 Betsy and her husband Dick oversaw a Michigan ballot initiative to allow public financing of private schools. The DeVos and Prince families collectively contributed almost $500,000 to a petition-gathering campaign (which lost nonetheless).[41]

Dick and Betsy DeVos often worked as a team. With her husband, father, mother, and brother as leading members of the Council for National Policy, Betsy could scarcely escape its influence. In 2001 the couple jointly addressed the Gathering, an annual conference of fundamentalist donors, committed to each making grants of at least $200,000 a year.[42] The couple finished each other's sentences, each lavishing praise on the other's devotion to theocracy. Dick, speaking on behalf of his wife's portfolio, advocated installing the church, instead of public schools, at the center of public life:

> The church has sadly retrenched from its center role in our community to where now we look at many communities in our country, the

> church, which ought to be in our view far more central to the life of the community, has been displaced by the public school as the center for activity, the center for what goes on in the community . . .
>
> We just can think of no better way to rebuild our families and our communities than to have that circle of church and school and family much more tightly focused and being built on a consistent world view.[43]

Betsy, speaking from her perspective as a Republican Party fund-raiser, was asked whether she encouraged other fundamentalists to engage in politics. "I would say yes," she replied. "There have been a number of people with whom I have worked over the years who are in positions of influence, either in elected office or in key staff positions with elected officials . . . If they have an interest in and an obvious gift to be involved politically, I have certainly tried wherever possible to encourage them to pursue politics, to pursue public policy life, because you are right, we do need more believers involved in it."[44]

Dick DeVos Jr. was still refining his role. He became the president and CEO of Amway after his father's retirement in 1992. In 2006 he ran for governor of Michigan, spending $35 million of his family money on the campaign, but went down in humiliating defeat to Democratic incumbent Jennifer Granholm.[45]

DeVos Jr.'s campaign had collided with the Michigan Democrats' not-so-secret weapon: labor unions. Some 20 percent of Michigan's workers were represented by unions, and they played a major role in keeping Michigan blue.[46] The Rust Belt states were some of the last holdouts from organized labor's glory days. U.S. union membership peaked in 1954, when nearly 35 percent of all U.S. wage and salary workers were unionized.

By 2014, union membership had fallen to just over 11 percent.[47] There were many reasons for this decline, among them automation and manufacturers' decisions to move factories overseas—as well as decades of Republican assaults on unions' bargaining power.

Labor unions had been instrumental in achieving major reforms: abolishing child labor, advancing occupational safety, raising the standard of living. But they were not immune from corruption, and in some areas they inspired resentment by fostering a two-tier labor market that favored friends and family of members, and winning benefits denied to the self-employed and other workers.

Unions have been closely allied to the Democratic Party, and Republicans have responded by promoting so-called right-to-work legislation on a state level. These laws weaken unions by permitting workers to benefit from a union's collective bargaining process without paying union dues. Workers have less incentive to join the union, and unions lose the funds and manpower they need to participate in the political arena.

A 2018 study published by Boston and Columbia Universities and the Brookings Institution demonstrated the critical political impact of right-to-work legislation on a state level. As the study put it, "Labor unions play a central role in the Democratic party coalition, providing candidates with voters, volunteers, and contributions, as well as lobbying policymakers . . . Right-to-work laws reduce Democratic Presidential vote shares by 3.5 percentage points. We find similar effects in U.S. Senate, U.S. House, and Gubernatorial races, as well as on state legislative control. Turnout is also 2 to 3 percentage points lower in right-to-work counties after those laws pass."[48]

At the dawn of the twenty-first century, union strongholds included New York, Hawaii, Alaska—and Michigan. Although union membership in the private sector continued to decline, public sector unions grew rapidly, especially at the local level. In 2009 their membership overtook that of private sector unions for the first time.[49] Police, firefighters, and teachers' unions remained a potent political force.

Betsy DeVos had already declared war on the teachers' unions, cofounding a group called the American Federation for Children, another tax-exempt organization that lobbied to divert funding from public schools, with a name that taunted the American Federation of Teachers.

Her husband Dick's animosity toward unions ran broader and deeper. The Democrats' union support—and its delivery of some 3.5 percent of the vote state by state—brought in crucial returns from the Rust Belt time after time. In 2004, during the presidential election preceding DeVos's run for governor, three of those winner-take-all states—Pennsylvania, Ohio, and Michigan—accounted for 58 electoral college votes out of 538. Thanks to their support, John Kerry lost the electoral college to George W. Bush by only thirty-five votes—but he won the popular vote in all three Rust Belt states by a margin of less than 4 percent. This made them highly vulnerable to a potential 3.5 percent right-to-work penalty.[50]

Dick DeVos embraced the challenge in the DeVos family assembly. Just as his wife had assumed the post of minister of public education, he volunteered as minister of organized labor. He started with his home state of Michigan, where his vendetta was personal; his friends at the Council for National Policy would leverage the national campaign. (Ironically, the new FRC headquarters that the DeVos family so lavishly funded had been the site of the American Federation of Labor headquarters in the early twentieth century.)

It all went back to Paul Weyrich's formula for winning elections: build up your grassroots organizations, and erode theirs. The New Deal coalition was already weakened by decades of the Democrats' dissension and neglect. The coup de grace required only money, media, and strategy. These the CNP had in ample supply.

CHAPTER 6

FISHERS OF MEN: ELECTORAL STRATAGEMS

The takeover of the Southern Baptist Convention wasn't unique; the convention was only one of many institutions captured by the radical right. Consider an organization that was cofounded by William Conant Church, the very model of a nineteenth-century gentleman journalist. An outspoken young man with a bold gaze and a luxuriant beard, Church became the publisher of the *New York Sun* when he was only twenty-four, and the Washington correspondent for the *New York Times* the following year. When the Civil War broke out, he enlisted in the Union Army, combining his military service with his reporting for the *Times* (an accepted practice in that era). He was shot in the leg and left the army, but his year of service qualified him for a lifetime career as an expert on all things military.[1] Church's illustrious postwar record included cofounding the Metropolitan Museum of Art, directing the New York Zoological Society, and joining the Union League Club and the Century Association.

But he may be best remembered for an initiative he launched in 1871. Church came back from the front alarmed by the Union soldiers' poor marksmanship; the records showed that a thousand rounds were fired for every Confederate hit. Church and his friend General George Wingate decided that the country needed an organization to improve the marksmanship of future soldiers. They launched it in New York City's fire department headquarters at 155 Mercer Street (now a Dolce & Gabbana boutique), and named it the National Rifle Association.[2]

For its first century the NRA concentrated on hosting target practice at shooting ranges and promoting gun safety. These were useful lessons. The West was young, and settlers relied on guns to hunt game and kill the predators raiding their poultry and livestock. Rifles and shotguns were standard items in the farmers' toolkit, and lessons in firearm safety counted as a vital public service. The NRA worked closely with the National Guard and supported U.S. military training efforts in World War II. After the war, the NRA returned to educating hunters on safety and conservation measures.[3]

But things changed. As the country urbanized, the rate of violent crime rose, more than doubling between 1960 and 1970.[4] In 1963 the nation was stunned by the assassination of John F. Kennedy, committed with a weapon purchased by mail from an advertisement in *American Rifleman*, the NRA magazine.[5] Five years later Americans were shaken by the shootings of Martin Luther King Jr. and Robert F. Kennedy.

Congress responded by passing the Gun Control Act of 1968, which limited the sale of weapons to felons and minors, barred mail-order purchases, and required new firearms to bear a traceable serial number. The NRA's vice president wrote in *American Rifleman* that while he saw parts of the bill as "unduly restrictive, the measure as a whole appears to be one that the sportsmen of America can live with."[6] The NRA and the nation were still on the same page.[7]

But there was dissension in the ranks, and it erupted at the NRA's annual meeting on May 21, 1977, an event that came to be known as the Cincinnati Revolt. As the organization's genteel old guard presided from the dais, a squad of insurgents invaded the floor, wearing orange hunting caps and conferring on walkie-talkies as they lobbied the thirty thousand delegates.[8] It was over in a matter of hours. In a move that paralleled the takeover of the Southern Baptist Convention, the radicals deposed the reigning executive vice president, who had supported a ban on the cheap handguns known as Saturday Night specials, and installed Harlon Carter.

Carter was a native of Granbury, Texas, a small town just south of Fort Worth. He joined the NRA when he was sixteen; a year later he shot and killed a Mexican teenager suspected of stealing the family car after the youth pulled a knife on him. Carter served two years in prison for the crime, but his conviction was later overturned on a technicality.[9] When Carter emerged from prison, he changed the spelling of his name from "Harlan" to "Harlon" and joined the U.S. Border Patrol. In 1950 he was promoted to head the entire organization. Carter joined the national board of the NRA a year later. In 1975, equipped with a formidable government Rolodex, he became the founding director of the Institute for Legislative Action (NRA-ILA), the NRA's new lobbying arm.[10]

Carter used his position to pioneer a new style of lobbying. He orchestrated national opposition to a 1975 bill that sought to restrict the purchase of handgun ammunition under the Federal Hazardous Substances Act, generating more than three hundred thousand letters from gun owners to congressmen, some of which included petitions bearing thousands of signatures. The letters supporting the limits, in contrast, numbered four hundred.[11] Carter's campaign was successful, and the limits on handgun ammunition were defeated. Congressmen took heed of the NRA's new muscle; the NRA-ILA built out its mailing lists and began to deploy them on state and local campaigns as well as national ones.

Carter's comrade in arms was Neal Knox, born in the hamlet of Rush Springs, Oklahoma, and raised in Texas.[12] After Carter ascended to the executive vice presidency of the NRA, Knox took his place at the NRA-ILA.[13] Together, Knox and Carter, known as Second Amendment absolutists, transformed the organization from a civic-minded hunting club to a political dynamo. Under their leadership, NRA membership mushroomed from 980,000 in 1977 to 1,900,000 in 1981.[14] Their assets grew in step with the membership, since fees and contributions provided the lion's share of the organization's revenues. The NRA was exempt from federal income tax as a 501(c)(4) organization, defined as one operating "exclusively for the promotion of social welfare . . . the net earnings of which are devoted exclusively to charitable, educational, or recreational purposes."[15]

In 2006 Jeffery A. Sierpien, a Marine Corps captain working toward a postgraduate degree, wrote a paper called "Frontline Strategies of the National Rifle Association." He won access to senior NRA officials and produced a detailed, admiring account of the "political influences and victories the NRA has accomplished in the US over the past 30 years." Sierpien's interviews offered a rare glimpse into the inner workings of the NRA's political operations.[16] One watershed was the battle over California's Proposition 15 in 1982. This measure called for limiting handgun ownership through a number of measures, including a registration process and a ban on mail-order purchases. Supporters of the proposition were sanguine, based on the polls.

The NRA swung into action, with a budget of over $5 million.[17] It martialed an estimated 30,000 volunteers to distribute flyers and make phone calls, and convinced some 250,000 Californians to register to vote, just to oppose the proposition.[18] The NRA crushed the measure by a two-to-one vote. The *New York Times* suggested that the campaign not only defeated the gun control measure but also may have helped a Republican win the governorship on its coattails. The Democrats had been counting on votes from African Africans, Asian Americans, and Hispanics, but their turnout was lower than expected, while the NRA constituency's turnout was higher. Tom Bradley, the popular African American Democratic mayor of Los Angeles, lost his bid to become governor by less than 100,000 votes—a fraction of the NRA's hidden pool of 250,000 new voters.

The Weyrich formula was expanded. The new model was: identify an invisible, disengaged group of potential voters. Find a hot-button issue to activate them. Keep them riled up with targeted media and direct mail. Facilitate their interactions in gathering places they frequent, to reinforce their commitment with groupthink. Follow up with onsite voter registration and transportation to the polls on Election Day. This tactic would be adopted by various CNP partners and reinforced with digital tools, to serve as a model for elections to come.[19]

In the early 1980s the NRA hired the Oklahoma City public relations firm Ackerman McQueen to transform its brand, and in 1991 it elected Wayne LaPierre to the leadership position of executive vice president. LaPierre, a professional lobbyist, brought a new emphasis on advertising and marketing to the job. Membership, which was claimed to be 2.5 million when LaPierre came into office, rose to 3.4 million by 1994.[20]

LaPierre faced his first major test shortly after. With Bill Clinton's election in 1992, the anti-gun lobby moved swiftly to introduce the Brady Handgun Violence Prevention Act, named after James Brady, the White House press secretary who was gravely wounded in the 1981 assassination attempt on Ronald Reagan. The bill was signed into law in 1993, the first such legislation passed since 1968. LaPierre produced commercials claiming that criminals, not guns, were to blame for the rise in crime, but the networks rejected them. The NRA turned back to its grassroots supporters, this time harnessing them to a national electoral strategy. In 1994 the NRA drew up a list of twenty-four congressional supporters of the Brady Bill and went to work. On election night, nineteen of the twenty-four went down in defeat, and the Republicans won control of the House for the first time in forty years. Clinton blamed the NRA.[21]

Ackerman McQueen gave LaPierre the NRA makeover, turning the mild-mannered lobbyist into a demagogue. The advertising firm became an integral part of the operation, and from 1993 to 1995 the NRA funneled $23.6 million in contracts. The Oklahoma agency even recruited Charlton Heston as celebrity spokesman and wrote his most legendary lines. Challenging presidential candidate Al Gore's calls for gun control after the Columbine massacre, Heston appeared at a 2000 rally, hoisting a rifle and shouting, "From my cold, dead hands!"[22]

According to the *Washington Post*, "By 2000, the NRA had become even more closely aligned with the Republican Party and worked strenuously to keep Al Gore from becoming president."[23] The following year, *Fortune* magazine reported that the NRA had assumed the leading position in its Power 25 survey of lobbying organizations, outstripping the mammoth American Association of Retired People for the first time.[24]

The new NRA fulfilled many of Weyrich's requirements for a politically expedient association. It united a population of potential voters in a common crusade, combining pleasurable social interaction (hunting, target practice) with a sense of imminent threat from the gun control advocates it reviled as coastal elites.

Gun ownership was pervasive in sparsely populated states with disproportionate representation in the Senate, including Wyoming, Idaho, and Montana, and it was robust in the future swing states of Colorado, Iowa, and Wisconsin.[25]

On the level of the national popular vote, NRA members were unlikely to have much impact. Membership ranged between (a possibly inflated) 2.5 and 4.5 million between 1993 and 2013, tending to spike after school shooting incidents.[26] But properly managed and networked, the politically energized NRA could sway both the Senate and the Electoral College, and provide a template for mobilizing other organizations.

Demographically, gun owners tended to be older white males in rural areas of the South, Midwest, and West, and were more than twice as likely to be Republicans as Democrats.[27] Furthermore, white evangelicals were more likely than other religious groups to own a gun and to support the NRA.[28] The opportunities for networking were obvious.

THE NRA'S POLITICAL inroads did not pass unnoticed at the Council for National Policy. Soon the NRA became one of the CNP's most potent affiliates. Wayne LaPierre was a member by 2014, though it is not clear when he joined.

CNP partners had learned how to identify previously untapped blocs of voters and grasped how to reach them, but they didn't always control the process. This was apparent in 1988. Reagan had benefited from the fundamentalists' support over the previous two elections, and when his vice president, George Bush, ran for the presidency, he was determined not to lose the advantage. Bush faced challenges from congressman Jack Kemp and Christian broadcaster Pat Robertson. His team regarded Kemp as the greater threat, so it quietly advanced Robertson's campaign. Bush retained a fundamentalist politician from Arizona, Doug Wead, to coach him on his approach. Wead later described his scheme to religion professor Mark Silk, who published the account over the Religion News Service.

The primaries in Iowa, a fundamentalist-heavy state, offered a major opportunity, Silk reported: "The technique of the Robertson campaign was to make caucus attendance a church activity. Tables would be set up for congregants to sign on to caucus for Robertson, and when the day came they showed up en masse. Indeed, the strategy worked so well that it propelled Robertson to a second-place finish ahead not only of Kemp but also of Bush himself."[29]

Bush's Episcopalian background was a disadvantage, but Wead coached him on the art of fundamentalist fudging. Bush soft-pedaled the Episcopalian tradition of infant baptism; fundamentalists preferred adult baptism, and Southern Baptists insisted on immersion.[30] He learned the language of the conversion experience, at least well enough to sow division. "Methodically," Silk added, "[Bush's] people had taken Bush to call on leading Southern pastors, whom the transplanted Yankee convinced that yes, he too was a Christian who had been born again. Meanwhile, when the tables for Robertson began to go up in churches across Dixie, prominent congregants would go to the pastors and ask to set up their own tables for Bush. In church after church, the decision was made not to do tables and risk splitting the congregation politically."

Doug Wead instructed Bush senior to "signal early, signal often" to the evangelical community. He noted that the national media was hostile to the fundamentalists, so relations were best established early in the campaign before the coverage intensified. Wead prepared memos on fundamentalists on a state-by-state basis, naming the influential preachers, describing their doctrines, and rating their popularity.

The strategy worked. The fundamentalist machinery of the CNP and its allies swung into action. "In 1988," Wead recalled,

> hundreds and hundreds of evangelical organizations spent millions of dollars promoting George Bush Sr. for president. We were tracking it . . .
>
> Those are the unions of the Republican Party. They put out so much literature that we have big loose-leaf notebooks filled with the various types of literature. Some of them, as many as 20 million pieces [in] one mailing, and that covered two or three library shelves in my office. These were materials that we didn't pay for or authorize or know until they went out, that they had gone out, that were being produced for us by evangelicals, rallying their own people.[31]

The evangelicals' union equivalents in the Republican Party were gathering steam, at the same time the Democrats' actual labor unions were going off the rails. Between 1980 and 1990, U.S. union membership dropped by almost a third, to only 16 percent of the workforce. Over the same period, the number of Americans identifying as "evangelical" and "born again" rose to about a third of the population.[32] As the radical right dedicated ever more money and attention to its grassroots organizations, the Democrats were curiously detached about defending their own, sitting out the opportunity to support unions, even when they had the muscle to do so.[33]

One beneficiary was George Herbert Walker Bush. Wead reported, "We won the [election] in 1988 with the largest percentage of evangelical support ever in American history."[34] But the Bush campaign proved the power of the fundamentalist vote by duping it, and it didn't take the CNP leadership long to notice. Once in office, Bush, like Reagan before him, appointed moderates to key positions and focused on economic and foreign policy.

"We won three landslide presidential elections in the 1980s, but . . . we were still burdened by the dead wood of the business-as-usual Republican Party," fumed the CNP's master marketer, Richard Viguerie. "The failure of Republican president George W. Bush to deliver on his promise of conservative governance, coupled with the excesses and corruption of the Republican Congress, have so alienated conservative voters that they began to look outside the Republican establishment for new leaders and for a new vehicle to translate their anger and outrage into political action."[35]

The assembly of the "new vehicle" didn't start with the Bush era. The architects of the CNP had started building out a parallel universe of organizations before the group was formed; it was an integral part of their strategy. "Political technology can be roughly divided into communication technology and organization technology," Morton Blackwell wrote, "with no neat line of separation between communication and organization."[36]

Organizations and communications: they both proliferated over the 1990s. The virulently homophobic American Family Association had been founded in 1977 by Donald Wildmon, a founding member of the CNP's board of governors. In 1991 he added the American Family Radio network. Concerned Women for America had been founded in 1979 by Beverly

LaHaye, wife of CNP cofounder Tim LaHaye. By the early 1990s she was using her platform to produce a stream of direct mail, radio talk shows, and books with titles such as *The Hidden Homosexual Agenda* and *The Homosexual Deception: Making Sin a Civil Right.*[37] James Dobson's Family Research Council, founded in 1983, was soon harnessed to Dobson's vast publications and radio empire. The FRC became a hub and engine for other groups.

The CNP partners understood the importance of state-level organizations, over a period when the Democrats had all but abandoned the idea. In 1988 Dobson had started planting state-level affiliates called Family Policy Councils. By 2019 there were councils in forty states, armed with a mandate to "work with state legislators, local government officials, and community leaders to encourage and initiate pro-family policies." Working in concert with the Family Research Council, they lobbied to instill "common core beliefs in the sanctity of human life and in the institution of marriage"—in other words, antiabortion and anti-same-sex-marriage policies.[38]

One of the most active state-level organizations was the Florida Family Policy Council. Like other state councils, it was registered as a tax-exempt 501(c)(3) organization, declaring that its "primary purpose is to EDUCATE." But it spun off Florida Family Action, whose 501(c)(4) status allowed it to lobby, as well as the Florida Family Action PAC, designed to "engage in ELECTIONEERING or direct political advocacy for or against state legislative candidates."[39] All three organizations were headed by the same individual and headquartered in the same Orlando office building; the distinction between them was not always apparent.

Imitation is the best form of flattery. In 1992 a young antiabortion activist named Rachel MacNair learned of Emily's List, a feminist organization that raised money for pro-choice Democratic female candidates. MacNair responded by establishing an antiabortion counterpart called the Susan B. Anthony List, based on a claim that the nineteenth-century suffragette had publicly condemned abortion, a notion that has been refuted by leading Anthony scholars.[40] Within a year, a congressional aide named Marjorie Dannenfelser was recruited as president. Dannenfelser widened the group's field to include antiabortion male candidates and turned it into a vehicle for the Republican Party, targeting even pro-life Democrats. By 2012 the organization expected to spend $11 million on the election.[41] Dannenfelser would join the CNP's board of governors and convert her organization into a force to be reckoned with, networked with other CNP partners.

Minors were not exempt. In 1993 the Girl Scouts of America, in the interest of inclusiveness, decided to allow members reciting the Girl Scout Promise "to substitute for the word 'God' in accordance with their own spiritual beliefs."[42] Two years later an Ohio mother founded the rival American Heritage Girls as a "Christ-centered organization" that required troop leaders to make a statement of faith. This organization was cross-promoted by Concerned Women for America, and received a ringing endorsement from James Dobson.[43] Girls as young as six to nine ("Tenderheart") were recruited for antiabortion marches.[44] In 2015 the organization introduced a "Respect Life" badge with a big red valentine heart, earned by going to marches or joining prayer vigils at abortion clinics.[45]

The parallel universe extended to professional organizations. In 1974 the mainstream American Academy of Pediatrics ended its stigmatizing practice of describing homosexuality as a mental disorder.[46] In 2002 the American College of Pediatricians was founded—with a strikingly similar name—to promote gay conversion therapy and oppose transgender rights and adoption by same-sex couples.

Many of these groups were described as "grassroots organizations"—in 2013, the Susan B. Anthony List was honored as "Grassroots Organization of the Year" at the Weyrich awards dinner for the second time in three years, "thanks to our more than 365,000 members across the country."[47] But this description didn't do justice to the keen strategy and intensive networking that drove them.

The key element was a high degree of centralized coordination—or, as the military would say, "command and control." The groundwork was laid by Morton Blackwell, indefatigable founder and president of the Leadership Institute, which recruited, trained, and motivated the activists and candidates of the movement. He brought some muscle to the job, based on his three years as the Reagan White House's liaison to American conservative organizations.[48]

Blackwell doubled as the executive director of the Council for National Policy over a critical period, spanning at least the years between 1992 and 2000.[49] This placed him in the ideal position to coordinate CNP strategy.

He had an easy commute: as of 1998, the two organizations occupied adjoining buildings on a corner of Clarendon Boulevard in Arlington, Virginia.

The mechanics were mastered by Blackwell's associate Robert Arnakis, senior director of domestic and international programs at the Leadership Institute. A stocky man with a jovial manner, Arnakis joined the organization in 2004. In 2017 he addressed a Family Research Council Action session, detailing the lessons from the 1964 and 1980 campaigns:

> They found out that the most effective groups and organizations are the ones that are able to connect directly with the person about the issue they're most passionate about. So for instance, if you were a Second Amendment advocate, Gun Owners of America would be most effective talking to you, rather than the Heritage Foundation.
>
> If you're most concerned about life and family, the group that was most effective in communication to you would be Focus on the Family or Family Research Council, or perhaps one of your state policy networkers. And so you had the rise of single-issue groups, and as those groups came to prominence, they achieved more and more membership to the point where we're at today.[50]

Arnakis emphasized the importance of "framing" an issue through language that would excite the emotions. (Berkeley cognitive linguistics professor George Lakoff parsed this concept for the Democrats.) Arnakis reported that one watershed moment occurred in 1995, with the introduction of the term "partial birth abortion" for late-term procedures.

> We were discussing the abortion bill, and what we had was "late-term abortions." It went from "late-term abortions" to a "partial birth abortion ban." We started talking about "partial-birth abortions" . . . and the left, when they originally started discussing the issue . . . it was cold and it was callous, and they described it as a procedure called "dilation and extraction" . . . So we kept hammering on this idea of "partial birth, partial birth" . . .
>
> And how we knew we were winning that argument ended up being because the terminology we were using, the media started

> using. And eventually our opposition started using that terminology. And I would ask you today, when you heard the word "partial birth," what image do you think of? You see, I think of a child, I think of a young child. And that's a powerful, powerful image. When we can use images to tell stories, when we can use images to convey emotions, we begin winning the debate in public policy.[51]

The coining of the term "partial birth abortion" has been attributed to the National Right to Life Committee in 1995.[52] Its associate executive director, Darla St. Martin, was a member of the Council for National Policy as of 1998.[53] The campaign did not achieve immediate success, but the movement pressed on. The term would prove to have staying power long after it was rejected as misleading and inaccurate by the medical community.

Ads on the Bott Radio Network, owned by the CNP elite, proclaimed, "Christians running for political office have a moral obligation to learn how to win."[54] Listeners could fulfill that obligation, the ads continued, by signing up for Robert Arnakis's workshops at the Leadership Institute.

The Council for National Policy's ostensibly independent "grassroots organizations" organized the masses. Radio stations owned by CNP members aired commercials recruiting them for the Leadership Institute. The Leadership Institute trained them to run for office. Winning candidates responded to CNP lobbying efforts and passed laws governing the masses. Elegantly, the plan came full circle.

CNP members' organizations focused on narrow bands of issues, but the network was a large, complex organism that achieved an impressive economy of scale. The Leadership Institute's vital role was described in a 2018 promotional video on YouTube. Mike Pence, a graduate, provided the endorsement: "No one has done more to inspire and train young conservatives than Morton Blackwell and the Leadership Institute."[55]

The video went on to quantify the claim:

> Since 1979, the Leadership Institute has trained more than 185,000 activists, operatives, and elected officials. Right now, 36 Leadership Institute graduates are serving as members U.S. Congress [*sic*]. In

> State Legislatures across the U.S., Leadership Institute graduates hold more than 500 seats. This is what grassroots looks like.
>
> Founded in 1979 by its president, Morton C. Blackwell, LI provides training in campaigns, fundraising, grassroots organizing, youth politics, and communications. The Institute teaches conservatives of all ages how to succeed in politics, government, and the media.[56]

The Leadership Institute—another tax-exempt 501(c)(3) "charity"—also served as a virtual employment agency. Its website stated, "The Leadership Institute actively supports the entire conservative movement . . . LI information is used by other conservative organizations as a source of participants for their valuable programs, saving them countless hours of recruitment. LI information-sharing benefits the entire conservative movement and connects conservatives into a nationwide conservative network and a lifetime of civic involvement. Virtually all significant conservative organizations across America now employ Institute graduates."[57]

The Leadership Institute's early curriculum focused on traditional political tasks: speechwriting, media coaching, fund-raising. But America was about to be transformed by a wave of digital technology, and Morton Blackwell would help meet the challenge by creating a curriculum in networked digital campaign tools.

The coalition also benefited from the insights of pollster George Barna. In 1984 he and his wife, Nancy Nelson Barna, had founded the Barna Research Group, and he eventually attached his operations to the Family Research Council and other CNP partners.[58] Barna specialized in polling, market research, and strategy, all in the service of the fundamentalist right. (*Christianity Today* described him as the George Gallup of evangelicals.[59]) Although he was raised a Catholic in New York, he embraced fundamentalism and served as a minister for several congregations. Barna believed that God gave him a calling "to serve as a catalyst for moral and spiritual revolution in America," and he was tireless in its pursuit.[60] Barna published dozens of books, mixing fundamentalist theology and astute statistical analysis. He was good at his job, focusing on regions and demographics other pollsters missed, and identifying sweet spots in the electorate for the movement to cultivate.

He was especially adept at finding hidden pools of evangelical voters, and ran focus groups to determine which issues could move them to action.

Barna was fond of coining acronyms; one of his favorites was SAGE Cons ("Spiritually Active, Governance Engaged Conservative Christians"), a key demographic on the electoral map. These were largely older white Protestants in Middle America who revered the past and feared the future. They voted in large numbers and took on special importance in swing states. Barna noted that, unlike most Americans, the vast majority of SAGE Cons held the "biblical worldview" so popular among the CNP membership, subscribing to what they held to be a literal interpretation of the Bible.[61]

Barna took a dim view of mainline Protestants (most Methodists, Episcopalians and so on), calling them "notional" Christians who "do not take their faith seriously and generally fail to integrate biblical principles into their lifestyles."

"Notionals are kind of like jellyfish, lacking a backbone, able to see and argue both sides of any issue," he wrote. He dismissed the belief in the "social gospel" (in support of aid to the poor and civil rights) as a flawed interpretation of Christ's teachings; biblical inerrancy and fundamentalist issues were his litmus tests.[62]

The coalition's strategists continued with their experiments. Many of these were launched by the Christian Coalition of America, which was founded by CNP member Pat Robertson in the wake of his failed presidential campaign. The executive director was Ralph Reed, a young activist with a slender build and an elfin grin. Reed had come to Washington to intern at the College Republican National Committee, where he quickly joined forces with two other young activists, Jack Abramoff and Grover Norquist (a Leadership Institute graduate); all three would join the CNP. Reed, who had not been particularly religious, had a conversion experience in the unlikely venue of a Capitol Hill bar called Bullfeathers.[63] Not only did Reed find his way to fundamentalism, he found fundamentalism's path to Republican victory. Reed was also an alumnus of Morton Blackwell's Leadership Institute, and in the future he would become a guest speaker.[64]

In 1989 Reed wrote an influential memorandum supporting the notion of millions of untapped fundamentalist voters, arguing that they simply lacked organization. He set about proselytizing. Within three years, the

Christian Coalition's budget soared to $8.5 million, and its following rose to a quarter of a million dues-paying members in a thousand chapters across the country.[65] It is not known when Reed joined the Council for National Policy, but its directory listed him as a member as of 1998.[66]

In 1992 the fundamentalist networks encountered some new obstacles. That January the Internal Revenue Service revoked the CNP's tax-exempt status as an "educational" institution, pointing out that it had failed to publish a journal or hold public lectures. The 501(c)(3) designation allowed donors to write off their contributions, and saved the organization on everything from payroll taxes to postage. The CNP fought the IRS decision and eventually won, though it had to pledge to produce a quarterly journal to educate the public. (As of April 2019, no such journal appeared to exist. CNP and CNP Action did launch websites with two online periodicals, *Policy Counsel*—mostly recorded speeches to and by members—and the monthly newsletter *Heard Around the Hill*.[67])

In 1996 the bipartisan Federal Election Commission filed a lawsuit against the Christian Coalition, charging the organization—whose membership had grown to 1.7 million—with acting illegally to advance Republican candidates, including CNP members Senator Jesse Helms and Oliver North.[68] As a 501(c)(4) organization, the Christian Coalition was required to be nonpartisan, but the FEC found that over the 1990, 1992, and 1994 elections it had used voter guides, mailings, and telephone banks to campaign for conservative Republicans. The contributions that paid for these efforts should have been reported as campaign contributions.[69]

The FEC cited the "Reclaim America" packets mailed out in the 1994 campaign. These included a cover letter from Pat Robertson and a "scorecard" that promised to "give America's Christian voters the facts they will need to distinguish between good and misguided Congressmen." The FEC further claimed that the Christian Coalition distributed 750,000 voter guides and made 29,800 calls on behalf of Jesse Helms' Senate campaign in North Carolina in 1990.

The *New York Times* reported, "That same year, the suit said, the coalition coordinated with the National Republican Senatorial Committee to produce and distribute 5 million to 10 million voter guides to help Republican Senate candidates in seven states." The coalition also worked in "coordination, cooperation and/or consultation" with the 1992 Bush campaign. Its activities included spending funds to identify and transport voters to the polls, and to produce and distribute 28 million voter guides. Oliver North's unsuccessful 1994 bid for the Senate benefited from 1.7 million voter guides.[70]

The issue of barring religious organizations from politicking was a bipartisan thicket, however. The Christian Coalition's voter guides tended to avoid mentioning candidates by name, but their criteria exclusively favored conservative Republican candidates. But Democrats who wanted to enforce the Johnson Amendment faced the history of African American and other churches that had worked to their advantage. It could be—and was—argued that various environmental, civil rights, and labor unions produced voter guides that raised similar concerns. As a result, both the AFL-CIO and the American Civil Liberties Union supported the Christian Coalition's case. In 1999 a U.S. district judge dismissed most of the charges, with two exceptions: those that concerned mailing a flier in support of Newt Gingrich, and sharing a political list with Oliver North's campaign.[71]

The 1999 judgment widened the avenues for targeted advocacy by various tax-exempt organizations, but there were important differences among them. The environmental and civil rights groups that favored the Democrats worked discretely, focusing on their narrow issues and constituencies. They were also eager to reach across the aisle to helpful Republicans, as in the case of environmentalists' work with President George H. W. Bush and Senator John McCain on cap-and-trade legislation. They trained their own activists and managed their own messaging.

Furthermore, groups with similar agendas, such as the Environmental Defense Fund and the Natural Resources Defense Council, competed with each other for funding and attention. These organizations relied heavily on the traditional news media to make their case, and media coverage could also generate criticism and debate.

The CNP partners, in contrast, operated within a closed system. Their ensemble of single-issue organizations harmonized like a well-tuned choir. The CNP leadership set the agenda, the donors channeled the funding, the operatives coordinated the messaging, and the media partners broadcast it unquestioningly. Every element of the operation worked toward getting out specific votes in support of hand-picked candidates. They were relentless in helping their friends and punishing their enemies. There was little interest in engaging Democrats in constructive debate or reaching across the aisle. Theirs was a Manichean vision of good versus evil. They were the elect, chosen by God to set the nation on His path. Democrats were demonized. It was a battle for the hearts and minds of Middle America on an epic scale.

Some members of the coalition were more strategically minded than others. In 1993 Ralph Reed produced a paper called "Casting a Wider Net," expressing his doubts that the issues of abortion and homosexuality would be enough to build a winning coalition.[72] A recent poll had showed that only 12 percent of the voters and 22 percent of evangelicals considered abortion to be a key issue. Reed was particularly interested in broadening the movement's appeal to conservative Catholics.[73]

The situation called for new tactics. If the electorate wasn't sufficiently worried about their issues, the issues would need to be refined, reframed, and sold to their voters. For this, the movement turned to its professionals.

FIRST, THE REPUBLICAN Party required attention. The party ranks still included moderates such as Pennsylvania senator Arlen Specter and New Jersey governor Christine Todd Whitman, both of whom had taken pro-choice positions.[74] The hardliners objected. In 1995 James Dobson threatened to bolt both the CNP and the Republican Party on the grounds of insubordination on both fronts. He arrived in Washington with a small entourage, including Ralph Reed and Betsy DeVos, to lecture Republican presidential hopeful Phil Gramm. They sternly informed Gramm that he needed to run on a "morality" platform, but Gramm balked at the idea. The following year, candidate Bob Dole proved equally uncooperative on the question of appointing antichoice judges to the Supreme Court. Dole committed a further offense by suggesting he would make a place in his cabinet for Colin Powell, a moderate Republican with a pro-choice stance. Dobson and company made it clear that they would rather see the Republicans lose than win with a maverick, and punished Dole by withdrawing their support.[75] In November Dole went down in defeat to Bill Clinton's bid for a second term.

One factor was the evangelical turnout, which dropped 6 percent from 1992 to 1996.[76]

In February 1998, Dobson returned to the CNP fold with an appearance at its Phoenix meeting. Following an introduction by Elsa Prince Broekhuizen, matriarch of the Prince-DeVos dynasty, he delivered a diatribe blasting the Republicans for abandoning God's law.[77] "Does the Republican Party want our votes—no strings attached—to court us every two years, then to say, 'Don't call me. I'll call you?'" he demanded. "If I go, I'll take as many people with me as possible."[78] His audience understood that Dobson's weekly radio audience numbered twenty-eight million—when the combined audience for all three network news broadcasts had dropped to thirty-two million viewers.[79]

The following month Dobson delivered his ultimatum to twenty-five House Republicans in the Capitol basement, threatening to pull his support from the party unless it backed his agenda.[80] He detailed his demands in a letter to Rep. Tom Coburn of Oklahoma. The list included defunding Planned Parenthood, eliminating "so-called safe-sex and condom distribution programs," and cutting off support for the National Endowment for the Arts. It added supporting school choice and "a ban on partial-birth abortion, the defense of traditional marriage, and opposition to any legislation that would add 'sexual orientation' to any civil rights law, educational program, or any congressional appropriation."[81] The CNP would adhere to this menu with astonishing consistency over the next two decades.

The bullying tactics worked. "Keeping Dobson and other Christian-right leaders happy has become the central preoccupation of Republican lawmakers," CNN reported. "In the House, the legislative agenda is crammed with 'pro-family' votes aimed at Dobson's constituency."[82] In May the Republican House leadership invited Dobson and a group of CNP activists to brief them at a "values summit" at the Library of Congress. The meeting resulted in a Values Action Team that gave right-wing Republicans access to the Family Research Council's vast mailing lists and media outlets for their lobbying efforts.[83] It also gave the FRC and the CNP a new hold on Republican congressmen.

The Values Action Team met every week while Congress was in session. After leaving the House in 2000, Coburn joined the board of directors of the Family Research Council.[84] In 2004 he won a bid for the Senate, where he served as a leading voice for climate denial and gun rights, and against same-sex marriage.

Despite its newfound clout on Capitol Hill, the coalition was losing momentum among voters. Its members saw the 2000 presidential primaries as a wake-up call. They favored George W. Bush, self-identified as "born again," though his "compassionate conservative" slogan left them cold. They shunned his strongest challenger, Senator John McCain. The stubborn Arizonan was a cradle Episcopalian who attended a Baptist church, but refused immersion and the label "born-again," even when it would have benefited him politically. Furthermore, McCain was willing to work with Republican moderates and even Democrats when it suited him.

In 1999 Bush delivered a closed-door address to the CNP, promoting his candidacy. Word leaked out and the press demanded the remarks in the name of transparency, but Bush and the CNP stonewalled.[85]

When the November elections came around, Gore won the popular vote by half a million, thanks to support on the coasts and the Rust Belt states of Pennsylvania, Michigan, and Wisconsin. But Bush won the electoral college by a hair—after the Supreme Court halted the recount in Florida.

Sixty-eight percent of the white evangelicals voted for Bush over Al Gore, but Bush advisor Karl Rove—another Leadership Institute graduate—told *Christianity Today* that although evangelicals accounted for a third of Bush's votes, four million of them had failed to turn out.[86] Neither the pulpits nor the pews were fully engaged, and the close race boded ill for the future.

Over the previous two decades, the CNP had made impressive gains. Its leadership had built a constellation of organizations and convinced Congress and the news media to treat them as independent grassroots representatives. They had recruited a network of donors who could shop for their favorite causes at the CNP meetings three times a year. Their Leadership Institute populated Capitol Hill, the Beltway, and the statehouses with its graduates, ready to network for the cause. They had enlisted a broadcast empire of hundreds of radio stations, many of them in areas that were off the radar for national media, providing an uncritical amplifier for their message. But people had to vote; without them, the movement was stalled.

What was to be done? It fell to CNP cofounder Paul Weyrich to decide. In 2001 he oversaw the creation of a manifesto drafted by his protégé Eric Heubeck at the Free Congress Foundation. The essay was called "The Integration of Theory and Practice: A Program for the New Traditionalist Movement."[87]

It began on a somber note: "The conservative movement is defensive, defeatist, depressed, and apologetic." Unfortunately for the movement, conservative values ran counter to the prevailing popular culture—in fact, "conservatives themselves often no longer understand or support a truly culturally conservative vision of America."

Bertolt Brecht had once ironically suggested the same approach in a vastly different context: if the people didn't support the movement, the answer was "to dissolve the people and elect another."[88]

The "Program" amounted to a virtual declaration of war on American culture and governance—shocking in its ruthlessness and antidemocratic spirit.

> Our movement will be entirely destructive, and entirely constructive. We will not try to reform the existing institutions. We only intend to weaken them, and eventually destroy them. We will endeavor to knock our opponents off-balance and unsettle them at every opportunity . . .
>
> We will use guerrilla tactics to undermine the legitimacy of the dominant regime. We will take advantage of every available opportunity to spread the idea that there is something fundamentally wrong with the existing state of affairs . . .
>
> Most of all, it will contribute to a vague sense of uneasiness and dissatisfaction with existing society. We need this if we hope to start picking people off and bringing them over to our side. *We need to break down before we can build up*. We must first clear away the flotsam of a decayed culture.

The new movement advocated "intimidating people and institutions" such as Hollywood celebrities and university administrators: "We must be feared, so they will think twice opening their mouths. They must understand that there is some sort of cost in taking a 'controversial' stand."

The movement would stoke the flames of alienation: "It is a basic fact that an us-versus-them, insider-versus-outsider mentality is a very strong motivation in human life." The movement would transform the political culture by laying siege to the popular culture through dedicated organizations. These new associations would watch movies together and "feel part of the group as we watch it." They would engage in charitable activities, partly to create a positive public image and "partly to create an alternative to government solutions." The groups "should provide everything that a person could want in terms of social interaction," other than the office and the church, although some churches would be affiliates. It would include sports leagues to recruit people who were otherwise uninterested.

The essay echoed authoritarian philosophies, emphasizing groupthink to the detriment of independent inquiry and open debate. "The movement should imitate the communist distinction between party members and fellow travelers," it continued. "There is no medium more conducive to propagandistic purposes than the moving image, and our movement must learn to make use of this medium." Effective television and movie propaganda would require creative talent and considerable capital, "but these hurdles *must* be overcome sooner or later."

Over 2002 and 2003 Weyrich and the Arlington Group considered their next moves in coordination with other right-wing organizations; when it published a list of its members a few years later, more than half of them belonged to the CNP.[89]

The evidence suggested that they were losing ground on abortion and gay rights, but there were promising signs that they could make same-sex marriage their next hot-button issue. The cause was making headlines. In 2001 the Gay and Lesbian Advocates and Defenders (GLAAD) had filed a lawsuit on behalf of same-sex couples, and the following year the Massachusetts Court ruled in their favor. The temperature rose further in 2004, when Massachusetts governor John Kerry won the Democratic nomination for president. Kerry, a Catholic, had reservations about same-sex marriage but upheld the law.[90] His office made him a prime target.

The CNP's enthusiasm for George W. Bush had grown since the last election. The *New York Times* reported that shortly before the Republican National Convention, Bush had greeted the CNP at the Plaza Hotel in New York in an event described as a "pep rally."[91]

The Arlington Group promoted ballot measures banning same-sex marriage in eleven states, and Republicans were especially keen to ride on their coattails.[92] The front line shifted to the battleground state of Ohio. There, the Focus on the Family and the Family Research Council coordinated an extensive campaign with the support of a Cincinnati activist and Arlington Group member named Phil Burress and his organization, Citizens for Community Values.

CNP partners helped on the national level as well. The Salem Radio Network aired hundreds of advertisements across the country from a new group called Americans of Faith, chaired by Salem's Edward Atsinger III, encouraging fundamentalists to register to vote.[93] Tony Perkins, the boyish new president of the Family Research Council, began to organize pastors to enter the political arena. James Dobson personally campaigned for five Republican Senate candidates, including Tom Coburn in Oklahoma.

Bush won Ohio, a critical swing state, by less than 120,000 votes, boosted by white evangelical votes in rural areas.[94] He won the electoral college by thirty-six votes; Ohio was responsible for twenty of them. Nationally, 3.5 million more evangelicals cast their votes in 2004 than in the previous election, raising their turnout rate by 9 percent.[95] Equally electrifying, the Republicans swept the Senate with a net gain of four seats. The coalition was making progress.

New rules were emerging in Washington. Morton Blackwell had spelled them out in a 1998 letter to an unnamed, recently elected friend:

> Your constituency is the voters, especially the coalition which elected you. You can't count on the news media to communicate your message to your constituency. You must develop ways to communicate with your coalition which avoid the filters of the media. Focus on your base. Write to them. Meet with them. Honor them. Show yourself to be proud of them. Support their activities. Show up at their events. Help other politicians and activists who share their priorities.

"Liberals in the media failed to defeat you," he added. "Now they will use carrots and sticks to tempt and to intimidate you. They will define any betrayal of your coalition as a sign of 'growth.' Don't fall for that nonsense."[96]

Your constituency is the coalition. Avoid the filter of the media. It was a winning formula. The CNP could turn to the NRA for a prototype for face-to-face social networking that would be emulated by other organizations. In the future the NRA would pioneer new technologies to link Blackwell's trainees and leverage their political activism. The NRA had come a long way from the gentlemen's shooting club cofounded by Mr. Conant in 1871, and it was in good company.

CHAPTER 7

IDEOLOGY 101: THE CNP'S CAMPUS PARTNERS

The Council for National Policy's demographics problem continued. The bedrock of its support, the older white Protestant population, was aging. Younger, more racially diverse voters skewed liberal, especially on social issues, and the causes that mobilized fundamentalist voters didn't play as well with the new generations.[1] Young women who had come of age with abortion rights weren't ready to surrender them—especially to a movement that maintained that life began with conception. Millennials had grown up around openly gay friends and relatives, and the sky hadn't fallen—even when they enlisted, married, or had children.

But these experiences never touched the CNP crowd. Its founders had been born old. In the 1960s, as his contemporaries were protesting the Vietnam War in sandals and blue jeans, young Paul Weyrich welcomed it in a suit and tie.[2] Nevertheless, Weyrich understood the pressures of time. In the introduction to the 2001 manifesto, his protégé Eric Heubeck wrote, "We must, as Mr. Weyrich has suggested, develop a network of parallel cultural institutions existing side-by-side with the dominant leftist cultural institutions." The roadmap specified: "There will be three main stages in the unfolding of this movement. The first stage will be devoted to the development of a highly motivated elite able to coordinate future activities. The second stage will be devoted to the development of institutions designed to make an impact on the wider elite and a relatively small minority of the masses. The third stage will involve changing the overall character of American popular culture."[3]

The first stage—developing "a highly motivated elite"—had already been advanced by the Council for National Policy. The second stage, the development of institutions, was well underway through the groups clustered under the CNP umbrella. The third stage, changing American popular culture, had been set in motion through the fundamentalist broadcast media, but there was a long way to go.

The manifesto specified that none of these efforts would bear fruit if they didn't address a vital demographic: "We will accomplish the goal of retaking our country only when large numbers of young people are educated outside of the indoctrinating environment of many public and private schools, universities, and of course, the popular culture. At this point in their lives, many of their ideas are still in the formative stage, the more so the younger they are . . . College students must be a key audience for our movement, since they are free of excessive time commitments and they find themselves in an environment that (theoretically) encourages activism and exposure to new ideas."

The movement, it argued, needed to establish "alternative fraternities" as well as study groups and book clubs that could "build each other up in every possible way: in terms of public speaking skills, debating skills, physical skills, intellect, manners, aesthetic sense."[4]

But the CNP's most visible efforts were focused not on fraternities and book clubs but on cultivating entire colleges. It started in Hillsdale, Michigan, 130 miles southeast of the DeVos redoubt to the west.

At first glance, Hillsdale College appears to boast little more than some middling sports teams and larger-than-life statues of Ronald Reagan and Margaret Thatcher gazing over a path called Liberty Walk. But what Hillsdale has in spades is money. As of 2017, the tiny Michigan college had an enrollment of some fourteen hundred students, but an outsize endowment of $574 million—much of it courtesy of CNP members and their donor networks.[5] On a per capita basis this amounts to over $380,000 per student, outstripping many colleges, including Columbia, Brown, and Vanderbilt.[6]

Hillsdale was founded in 1844 by Baptist abolitionists. Its formal relationship with the radical right began with college president George C. Roche III, an early member of the CNP. In 1971 Roche founded a quasi-alumni journal called *Imprimis,* offered free of charge to Hillsdale graduates. It evolved into a platform for CNP members, such as the Family Research Council's former director Gary Bauer and Judge Roy Moore of Alabama.[7] Roche began to distribute *Imprimis* to a vastly expanded audience—still free of charge.

One of Hillsdale's star recruits was Erik Prince, scion of the Prince-DeVos dynasty, who found his way to the class of 1992.[8] He had previously served as one of the first interns at the Family Research Council (which his family supported with large infusions of cash).[9] Family influence also helped him to a low-level internship at the Bush White House and a coveted spot at the U.S. Naval Academy. He lasted three semesters at Annapolis before he departed, going to Hillsdale to complete his studies.[10]

Like many other institutions with ties to the CNP, Hillsdale has been racked by scandal. Roche fell from grace in 1999, when he was accused of carrying on a nineteen-year-long affair with his daughter-in-law, the editor of *Imprimis*. She killed herself on campus with a handgun she took from his gun cabinet.[11] Roche denied the allegation, but he was obliged to resign and went into seclusion until his death in 2006.

Roche was succeeded by political scientist Larry Arnn, a native of Pocahontas, Arkansas, and the son of a Phillips Petroleum employee.[12] Arnn also joined the CNP. Eager to expand the college's footprint, he built on his predecessor's initiatives to transform Hillsdale into a CNP platform. The college developed a distinctive curriculum based on an originalist interpretation of the Constitution, parallel to fundamentalists' literal reading of the Bible. Hillsdale worked in close partnership with the Federalist Society, whose leadership also joined the CNP, and argued that "the job of the judiciary is to say what the law is, not what it should be." This position suggested that the Federalists and their hand-picked jurists should be in charge of defining "what the law is."[13]

In their view, America had been corrupted by liberal lawyers and judges who sought to adapt the law to modern society, legalizing practices such as same-sex marriage and abortion. Constitutional originalists danced on the ledge of contradiction. The Founding Fathers had crafted a document that condoned slavery and denied voting rights to women. For much of the nineteenth century, the Constitution allowed states to deny the right to vote to slaves, free blacks and Native Americans, as well as to white males without property.[14] Originalists allowed that history had moved on in some areas, but they tended to cherry-pick the principles that suited them.

Even as George Roche disappeared from view, his journal lived on. In 2010 *Salon* described *Imprimis* as "the most influential conservative publication you've never heard of." By 2018 it claimed a circulation of 3.9 million, "read by as many people as the *New York Times* and the *Wall Street Journal*." It still arrived free of charge and often unrequested. The publication made a special effort to blanket the legal profession. American attorneys found it unbidden in their mailbox, uncertain as to who paid for it and for what purpose. Many of its articles consisted of verbatim speeches by conservative visitors to the Hillsdale campus, closely tracking the prevailing winds at the CNP, and a reader would be hard pressed to find a voice that strayed from CNP orthodoxy. *Imprimis* was used to recruit participants for the Hillsdale National Leadership Seminars, held two to three times a year in different parts of the country. Hillsdale claimed that more than thirty thousand people have attended the program since it was founded in 1982.[15]

Besides CNP members such as Bauer, Moore, and Arnn, *Imprimis* published many friends of the organization, offering a preview of the policies they would enact in the future. In 2008 John Bolton, future national security advisor, explained why the United States should disregard the United Nations' human rights policies.[16] In 2016 Scott Pruitt, months away from his appointment to the Environmental Protection Agency, explained why the Supreme Court should dismantle environmental protections.[17]

Hillsdale's mission statement declares, "As a non-sectarian Christian institution, Hillsdale College maintains 'by precept and example' the immemorial teachings and practices of the Christian faith." It derides the "dehumanizing, discriminatory trend of so-called 'social justice' and 'multicultural diversity.'"[18] The college's finances depend on conservative donors. Following a series of disputes with federal and state authorities over affirmative action requirements, Hillsdale decided to relieve itself of such obligations by refusing federal funding. Contributions from major donors, led by the DeVos family, allowed the college to offer extensive financial aid to its largely homogenous student body.[19]

But Hillsdale still stood apart from the fundamentalist colleges associated with the Council for National Policy, which maintained affiliations with specific religious leaders or denominations. The CNP designated Hillsdale to serve as its "constitutionalist" bulwark and groomed it to feed the coalition's operations on Capitol Hill and in partner media.

In 2010 Hillsdale created an important resource in Washington. The Allan P. Kirby Jr. Center for Constitutional Studies and Citizenship occupies three identical red brick town houses with crenellated towers on Massachusetts Avenue, a short walk from Union Station. Across the street looms the Heritage Foundation, eight stories of somber gray stone.

The Kirby Center serves as a (tax-exempt) home for Hillsdale's Washington program, which overlaps neatly with CNP programs and partners. It has been fully integrated with the Hillsdale curriculum, and provides both a pipeline for student aides for conservative congressmen and a social center to attract like-minded young people to the movement. The center's James Madison Fellows Program brings high-level congressional staff to annual retreats and networking luncheons.

The tiny college has served as a feeder for higher positions as well. Soon after Donald Trump took office, the *Hillsdale Collegian* ran an article called "Hillsdale Alumni Take Over Trump's Administration." The lengthy list of appointments included chief of staff for Betsy DeVos's Department of Education, associate counsel for President Trump, and speechwriters for Trump and Vice President Mike Pence.[20]

Hillsdale's CNP connections have brought rich economic rewards beyond the DeVos and Prince families and their foundations. The families have also contributed through their participation in the Donors Trust and the National Christian Foundation. Other leading donors included the Castle Rock Foundation, the family philanthropy of CNP founding father Joseph Coors, which has contributed over $5 million in multiple grants over the years. In 2002 the Foster Friess family foundation donated a handsome $100,000.[21]

In 2007 Morton Blackwell's Leadership Institute contributed $1,000 to Hillsdale. This may have been more of a fee than a donation, explained by the Leadership Institute and the Kirby Center's joint training activities. In 2012 the Leadership Institute held its Capitol Hill Staff Training School, intended to help aspiring activists, aides and interns "develop your networking strategy" and learn the basics of email campaigns and budgets, at the Kirby Center.[22] The Kirby Center also hosted the Leadership Institute's "Intro to Fundraising Workshop" to teach "the psychology of major gifts" and "one-on-one solicitation."[23] One hand washes the other: the Leadership Institute has trained Kirby Center interns, and the Kirby Center has provided the Leadership Institute with staff.

One of the Kirby Center's major assets is the Boyle Radio Studio on the top floor, which enjoys a close relationship with Salem Media. The studio was launched in 2015, at the same time as WRFH ("Radio Free Hillsdale"), a new station on the Michigan campus. At the inauguration the Kirby Center's director announced, "That station and these studios are part of a new and unique Hillsdale program to train students in broadcast journalism."[24] The "journalism training" in question differed from standard journalism curricula; one Hillsdale student intern reported, "We visited the National Rifle Association's headquarters to learn how to cover gun-related issues and topics."[25] Hillsdale and the Kirby Center were set to groom future generations of fundamentalist and right-wing talk show hosts as well as traditional journalists.

Another inauguration speaker was Vince Benedetto, owner of a Pennsylvania radio network and the donor who launched the Washington and on-campus stations. Benedetto was an evangelist for the medium, whose influence was often overlooked. He cited a recent Nielsen survey that found that over 91 percent of Americans over the age of twelve listened to the radio each week—nearly 90 percent of every demographic age group.[26] "It's now surpassed television as the largest mass reach medium," Benedetto said.[27]

Salem Media was prominently featured at the event. The keynote speaker was Salem's syndicated talk show host Hugh Hewitt, who claims an audience of two million listeners every week in more than 120 cities. Hewitt hosts weekly broadcasts from the Kirby Center, which he describes as "the

Hillsdale College lantern of reason, the lighthouse of sweet argument and persuasion in the shadow of the Capitol."[28]

The CNP's partner media platforms were as networked as its organizations. Hillsdale College enjoyed a cozy relationship with the *Daily Caller*, founded in 2010 by Tucker Carlson and CNP member Neil Patel, and seeded with $3 million from former CNP president Foster Friess. Described as the radical right's answer to the *Huffington Post*, the *Daily Caller* claims more than twenty million unique readers a month on its home page, and millions more on its partner sites and social media. (As of 2019 its Facebook page has more than five million followers.) The *Daily Caller* creates and distributes its content through the Daily Caller News Foundation, or DCNF—another tax-exempt 501(c)(3) organization. The foundation shares content with over 250 publishers, and its website states that its content "is available without charge to any eligible news publisher that can provide a large audience."[29]

Hillsdale president Larry Arnn has been the subject of admiring coverage in the *Daily Caller*, disseminated by "eligible" news publishers ranging from the *New Boston Post* to *American National Militia*.[30] In February 2019 the Hillsdale College National Leadership Seminar in Orange County featured Arnn and the Daily Caller News Foundation's editor-in-chief as two of the five speakers.[31] The *Daily Caller* also hosts Hillsdale interns, some supported by a two-year paid reporting fellowship.[32] In December 2017 the *Daily Caller* hailed Arnn (as well as CNP elders Ed Meese and Richard Viguerie) as "Conservative Leaders Who Impacted American Culture."[33]

Hillsdale College acquired another powerful tool for persuasion through its free online courses, with its ideology on full display. A course on the Supreme Court argued that "judicial decisions have done much to advance a Progressive agenda that poses a fundamental threat to liberty." Constitution 201 chronicled the "rise of bureaucratic despotism" through FDR's New Deal and LBJ's Great Society programs.[34] In 2015 Hillsdale announced that its enrollment for online courses had surpassed a million; the college claims that eight hundred thousand people have taken its Constitution 101 course, to help so "America can begin to turn around and restore lost liberty."[35]

Hillsdale has amplified its reach across social media. *Imprimis,* for example, has garnered almost 50,000 followers on Twitter and more than 660,000 on Facebook.[36]

Hillsdale wasn't the CNP's only foothold in academia. Other partners arrived by way of the revolt against the federal government's integration requirements. Jerry Falwell's Liberty University illustrates both the deep roots of these relationships and the benefits they can yield. Falwell was one of Paul Weyrich's earliest fundamentalist allies, serving on the founding board of governors of the CNP.

Falwell was an eager entrepreneur. In 1971 he founded a small Baptist college in Virginia as a subsidiary of his multimillion-dollar televangelism business. But his revenues stumbled in the 1980s with the fallout from the Jim Bakker and Jimmy Swaggart sex scandals, and his college suffered too. Rebranded as Liberty University in 1985, the school made a partial recovery, but it still labored under heavy debt. Liberty started to explore the economic potential of an online curriculum, propelled by the vision of Falwell's son, Jerry Jr., a bearded version of his father.[37]

There were limits to that vision. One was a series of scandals involving a number of for-profit schools with online curricula, which were issuing worthless diplomas while skimming vast amounts of federal scholarship funds. (Liberty is officially "non-profit.") In 1992 Congress responded by passing the 50 percent rule, requiring colleges to hold at least half of their courses on a physical campus to qualify for federal support. But in 2006 the Republican Congress quietly passed legislation removing those consumer protections, stealthily inserting eight lines into a vast budget bill. This benefited a massive number of commercial educational institutions, including many fundamentalist colleges.

Liberty University's fortune was made; it quickly expanded to become the second-largest online college in the United States. As of 2015, its on-campus student body numbered around 15,500, while its online enrollment approached 95,000. The school, like many similar institutions, makes a special effort to recruit military veterans, who have access to additional government funding. By 2016 the university was pulling in more than $1 billion a year, most of it courtesy of U.S. taxpayers, and clearing a net income of $215 million; Falwell Jr.'s salary was set at almost $1 million a year. The university has dismissed faculty concerns and student complaints about the quality of online instruction.[38]

Like Hillsdale College, Liberty University maintained close ties to the CNP. As of 2014, the dean of its school of public policy and the associate dean of its law school were members. Many other CNP members were graduates. Tony Perkins, president of the Family Research Council and then vice president of the CNP, graduated in 1992 and received an honorary doctorate in theology in 2006.[39] CNP member Penny Nance, president of Concerned Women for America, serves on Liberty's board of trustees.

Liberty's Jesse Helms School of Government, founded in 2004, furnishes another pipeline of staff for conservative congressmen.[40] The university has also worked closely with Morton Blackwell's Leadership Institute, cosponsoring and hosting the Grassroots Campaign School to train students in strategic campaign planning, alliance building, and get-out-the-vote programs.[41]

Liberty University's quarrels with federal government didn't end with segregation. The school continues to ban transgender students, and its honor code states that "sexual relations outside of a biblically ordained marriage between a natural-born man and a natural-born woman are not permissible at Liberty University."[42] Obama-era federal guidelines banned sex discrimination on college campuses under Title IX, but Liberty University claims a religious exemption.[43]

The Council for National Policy has rich hunting grounds in America's evangelical colleges, which number over a hundred. The CNP roster includes Everett Piper, president of Oklahoma Wesleyan until his retirement in 2019. Although the former college rebranded itself as a "university," this tiny school enrolls only six hundred students on its main campus, with an additional online enrollment. The school has a dismal four-year graduation rate of 23 percent.[44] Its name is confusing to traditional Methodists, who also name institutions after founder John Wesley; Oklahoma Wesleyan was established by the Wesleyan Church, a nineteenth-century splinter group from the Methodists.

The United Methodist Church, with nearly seven million members in the United States, is affiliated with almost 120 U.S. colleges and universities and historically linked to many more, including Duke, Emory, Syracuse, the University of Southern California, Southern Methodist University, and Wesleyan University in Connecticut. The tiny Wesleyan Church, on the other hand, has approximately 141,000 members in the United States and five affiliated colleges scattered across North America. Oklahoma Wesleyan, like its fellows, long struggled in obscurity—until the 2002 arrival of Dr. Piper, who, as it happens, is a native of Hillsdale, Michigan. Piper is mediagenic, with a strong chin, crisp white hair, and a trim build. He grew up in a blue-collar family just down the road from the school George Roche was transforming into a CNP stronghold.

Piper joined the CNP at some point after he assumed the presidency of Oklahoma Wesleyan. There he developed an institutional relationship with Tony Perkins and the Family Research Council. Piper is a regular guest on *Washington Watch*, Perkins's syndicated radio show, and often fills in as host for the program. In 2016 Oklahoma Wesleyan announced "a new partnership" with the Family Research Council "to advance faith, family, and freedom in public policy and the culture from a Christian worldview."[45] Piper is another *Daily Caller* favorite, sometimes appearing with Supreme Court justice Clarence Thomas's wife, Ginni, a *Daily Caller* correspondent (and CNP attendee).[46] In one story, Piper recommended five books for college students—all put out by Regnery Publishing, a conservative house founded by CNP member Alfred Regnery and acquired by Salem Communications in 2014.[47] Piper also appeared on the National Rifle Association's NRATV and the Christian Broadcasting Network.[48]

The college board's description of Oklahoma Wesleyan's academic program stresses its commitment to the OKWU Pillars: "primacy of Jesus Christ, priority of Scripture, pursuit of Truth, and practice of Wisdom."[49] Like Liberty University, Oklahoma Wesleyan's Christian worldview requires it to claim exemption from regulations governing sex discrimination, refusing to accommodate transgender students.[50] In 2018 Piper came to national attention with an editorial in the *Washington Times*, stating that "in this brave new world of hyphens and acronyms, we paint ourselves into a corner of 'tolerance' where we must affirm the proclivities of anyone who 'identifies' as ISIS just as much as we do all who identify as

LGBTQ. After all, in both cases it could be easily argued 'that's just who they are.'"[51]

Through the CNP's energetic networking of media, money, and institutions, messages from minor-league schools like Hillsdale and Oklahoma Wesleyan could reach a national audience. A college president like Everett Piper could forgo the rigors of scholarship in favor of talk radio and blog posts on *BullyPulpit*.[52]

By 2014, the Council for National Policy counted a dozen college and university administrators among its 350 members, all of them at the level of president, vice president, or dean at their institutions. Most of their schools maintained a modicum of respectability, even if they generally fell short of academic excellence.

But the odor of corruption never disappeared. One striking case involved CNP member Oren Paris III. Paris's father, Oren Paris II, founded Ecclesia College to train missionaries as an appendage of his fundamentalist country music empire. The younger Paris, a tall man with the hearty build and receding blond hairline of an aging quarterback, inherited the presidency from his father. The college, organized as a "church," was located in a suburb of Fayetteville, Arkansas, about thirty miles from the Oklahoma border.[53] It offers a limited curriculum—heavy on Bible studies—with 232 students and a 14 percent graduation rate.[54] (Arkansans joked that Ecclesia's commencement speeches better be long if there were only a dozen people graduating.)

Like his academic counterparts in the CNP, Paris had an entrepreneurial streak, but he lacked their skills. In 2013 he struck up a deal with a young Arkansas Republican state senator named Jon Woods. Paris asked Woods to procure state development funds for the college, reinforcing his case with a text message stating, "Good selling point to conservative legislators is that [the college] . . . produces graduates that are conservative voters. All state and secular colleges produce vast majority of liberal voters."[55] Woods steered hundreds of thousands of dollars in state funds to Ecclesia College over several years in return for a series of kickbacks. In 2017 Paris and Woods were indicted along with several coconspirators. In September 2018 Paris was sentenced to three years in federal prison, and Woods to more than eighteen.[56]

The CNP's major donors understood that reaching a broader student population would require them to go beyond individual colleges. In 2012 an enthusiastic eighteen-year-old named Charlie Kirk approached Foster Friess at the Republican National Convention, pitching his idea for a new organization. Turning Point USA proposed to update the messages and the networking capacity of CNP partners to energize a new generation of conservative college students. Friess agreed to bankroll the new group and joined its advisory council (along with Ginni Thomas).[57] The Richard and Helen DeVos Foundation is reported to have made a contribution in 2015, and Betsy DeVos spoke alongside Kirk at a Turning Point USA summit in 2018.[58]

Kirk had a natural grasp of Paul Weyrich's guerrilla tactics, updated for the digital age. Turning Point USA set out to use conservative media and social media platforms to advance its cause, with Kirk as public spokesman and student activists as ground troops. The organization uses memes posted by shadowy groups such as ConservativeMemes.com ("Registration Private" via "Domains by Proxy, LLC"). One example was as a photo with a caption reading "NRA HERO: THE HERO WHO SHOT THE TEXAS CHURCH SHOOTER WAS A CERTIFIED NRA INSTRUCTOR ARMED WITH AN AR-15."[59] The *New York Times* reported that the "pre-made, sharable graphics on sites like ConservativeMemes.com" match many posts on Being Patriotic, a Facebook page managed by Russian interests.[60] (A further connection arose in a 2019 report requested by the Senate Intelligence Committee, which found that Russian agents routinely shared content created by Turning Point USA.[61]) Kirk's organization stands out as unusually combative in an already contentious field, exploiting the troubled boundary between free speech and hate speech on campus.

The organization's goals included mobilizing college students for the movement, and challenging the trends of political correctness on campus. These efforts would undermine the authority of professors and administrators and disrupt the knowledge industry from a new direction, challenging American institutions that play a leading role in independent research and the advancement of science and social policy.

Kirk grew up in suburban Chicago and started his organization as soon as he graduated from high school. (His higher education consisted of some general education classes at a community college following his rejection from West Point.[62]) Kirk was a highly effective fund-raiser and self-promoter. By 2018 Turning Point USA claimed a budget of around $8 million, fed by a network of conservative donors (most of them undisclosed), as well as ongoing contributions from Foster Friess.[63] By 2019 the TPUSA website listed chapters on more than a thousand high school and college campuses in all fifty states and the District of Columbia, as well as "5000+ activism events" and "500k face-to-face conversations."[64]

TPUSA maintains open ties to organizations run by members of the CNP. The NRA has cosponsored TPUSA events. TPUSA works hand in hand with Morton Blackwell's Leadership Institute, listing it as one of its three partner organizations.[65] The Leadership Institute plays an essential role in TPUSA's "Professor Watchlist," a site that publishes photos and denunciations of professors. The accused's offenses range from joking about Republicans to documenting gender bias in economics textbooks. (*Politico* recorded 226 "watchlisted" professors at 156 schools in 2018.[66])

The site encouraged students to inform on their professors through the Leadership Institute's Campus Reform project.[67] Campus Reform works alongside TPUSA to equip and train conservative student activists across the country, through twelve regional field coordinators.[68] Its "Balance in Media" grants fund conservative student publications whose staff members have been trained at the Leadership Institute.[69]

Another Turning Point USA initiative, the Campus Victory Project, consists of a plan to "commandeer the top office of Student Body President at each of the most recognizable and influential American Universities." In 2017 the *New Yorker*'s Jane Mayer published the content of a brochure from the project, which outlined the stages of its campaign. "Once in control of student governments," Mayer wrote, "Turning Point expects its allied campus leaders to follow a set political agenda. Among its planks are the defunding of progressive organizations on campus, the implementation of 'free speech' policies eliminating barriers to hate speech, and the blocking of all campus 'boycott, divestment and sanctions' movements. Turning Point's agenda also calls for the student leaders it empowers to use student resources to host speakers and forums promoting 'American Exceptionalism and Free Market ideals on campus.'"[70]

There is evidence that Turning Point USA, like other groups linked to the CNP, vastly exaggerates its effectiveness. In 2018 *Politico* reporter Joseph Guinto found that TPUSA claimed to have helped fifty conservative students win elections for student body president, but when he called the student leaders in question, some of them disavowed the connection and others condemned TPUSA. Guinto noted that although the TPUSA staff had grown to 130, some of its four hundred registered chapters were dormant.[71]

Turning Point USA's greatest utility may have been in its optics. Charlie Kirk has been a highly visible symbol of the coalition's inroads with Weyrich's longed-for student demographic. Donald Trump has tweeted his praises and granted Kirk numerous photo opportunities and an exclusive television interview at the White House.[72] Kirk receives ample coverage on Fox News and Breitbart, and he publishes frequent editorials on the *Daily Caller*.[73] It is not known whether Charlie Kirk is a member of the CNP, but the CNP's Policy Council includes him as a featured speaker, and CNP Action prominently displays his endorsement on its website.[74]

TPUSA implements the coalition's drive to enlist minorities as well as youth, but these efforts can backfire. In 2017 Kirk hired the controversial African American commentator Candace Owens, another Trump favorite, and promoted her to director of communications. The following year Owens told a British audience, "If Hitler just wanted to make Germany great and have things run well, okay, fine." She blamed "leftist journalists" for the resulting controversy.[75] A few months later Juan Pablo Andrade, an advisor for a Trump surrogate organization, attended a Turning Point USA conference in West Palm Beach. Andrade released a Snapchat video from his hotel room (booked on the TPUSA tab) declaring, "The only thing the Nazis didn't get right is they didn't keep fucking going!" He too blamed the "leftist media" for the ensuing storm.[76] Owens and Andrade recanted their statements. TPUSA's 2018 summit featured a partnership with a new group called Young Jewish Conservatives, cofounded by Rabbi Ben Packer, a follower of the late ultranationalist rabbi Meir Kahane.[77] In April 2019 the Young Jewish Conservatives hosted a Leadership Institute training session on lobbying in Hoboken, New Jersey.[78]

Turning Point USA chapters have racked up a series of petty gaffes, usually when their attempts to deride their opponents go wrong. In 2018 the Kent State chapter staged an event for Free Speech Week designed to disparage the idea of "safe spaces" on campus. A male student posed on campus dressed in diapers, awkwardly sucking a pacifier and distributing bubbles. He promptly became an object of ridicule; memes and counter-memes went viral in a matter of hours.[79] "Free speech" is a major theme of the initiative, often used to challenge administrators' attempts to limit hate speech on campus. The Leadership Institute provides TPUSA chapters with giant "free speech" beach balls, which students are invited to inscribe. At the University of California San Diego, a student popped it with a pocket knife.[80] At the University of Delaware students drew a penis on the ball, which prompted the campus police to remove it.[81]

There is concern about the organization's involvement in electoral campaigns. Designated as another 501(c)(3) "charity," Turning Point USA is required to be nonpartisan, but students told Jane Mayer that TPUSA staff asked them to engage in campaign activities on behalf of Ted Cruz and Marco Rubio in the 2016 presidential primaries.[82] According to *Politico*, Kirk told a 2015 audience that TPUSA "members and those people associated with our organization were able to knock on over 58,000 doors and make over 107,000 phone calls" in the 2014 gubernatorial campaign of Illinois Republican Bruce Rauner—a major TPUSA donor.[83] It's unlikely that the IRS, given the incoherent policy governing the political activities of "nonpartisan" nonprofits, will address the question anytime soon.

Another CNP youth affiliate is Students for Life of America. This antiabortion organization was founded by student volunteers in 1977 and relaunched in 2006. President Kristan Hawkins is a member of the CNP. Students for Life claims more than eleven hundred chapters in all fifty states, with a budget of over $6 million and a staff of forty, including nineteen regional coordinators.[84] Its Facebook page peddles T-shirts reading "Equally Human, Born and Preborn" and promotes Hawkins's lecture "Lies Feminists Tell." Students for Life starts recruiting students as early as in middle school for antiabortion activism and continues through high school and college, with additional chapters in medical and law schools.[85] It holds dozens of training workshops and summits across the country every year, together with the Susan B. Anthony List, the Family Research Council, and the Alliance Defending Freedom, all run by prominent CNP members.[86] A page on its website states that Students for Life "frequently partners" with these groups.[87] The Students for Life's Planned Parenthood Project accuses the organization of supplying "faulty birth control" and "deceptive counseling" in order to carry out abortions for profit, and lobbies to defund it.[88]

Students for Life encourages followers to create their own "Cemetery of the Innocents" as a school activity, offering detailed instructions for assembling it on school grounds: "Your Regional Coordinator may be able to provide your group with little pink crosses from SFLA," the group advises. "One idea is to use paint stirring sticks and wire them together. You can get these for free at local paint stores." There's a cafeteria option for high schools: "You can also stick your crosses into large sheets of Styrofoam and display them during lunch periods!"[89]

The Council for National Policy cultivates upcoming members through the William F. Buckley Jr. Council, a group of sixty. (This may have been its response to the Council on Foreign Relations' term membership for promising candidates under thirty-five.) The CNP's youth council is heavy on senior members' offspring; one founding member of the Buckley council was Paul Pressler IV, the son of the Houston judge and founding member of the CNP.[90] Another member is the daughter of CNP member Charmaine Yoest, the antiabortion activist who directed public affairs at the Department of Health and Human Services from 2017 to 2018. Other spots are occupied by staff of the leadership and their organizations. Judge Pressler's personal assistant is a member, and so is the assistant to Jenny Beth Martin, head of the Tea Party Patriots. The youth council has also included the executive director and director of field operations of Students for Life.

The William F. Buckley Jr. Council has experienced its own whiffs of scandal. Reality television star Josh Duggar (*19 Kids and Counting*) was listed as a member in 2014, when he was serving as executive director of the homophobic Family Research Council Action, the FRC's lobbying arm. In 2015 Duggar was caught up in a series of scandals. Duggar confessed to various transgressions, including pornography addiction and adultery. "The last few years, while publicly stating I was fighting against immorality in our country I was hiding my own personal failings."[91] He resigned from the Family Research Council; Tony Perkins responded, "We are praying for the family."[92]

Perkins had his hands full. For years conservative Republicans had been grooming a young Ohioan named Wesley Goodman, who worked under CNP member Paul Teller on the House Republican Study Committee. Goodman had built his political career lobbying against LGBT rights, as a relentless foe of same-sex marriage. In 2015 the thirty-one-year-old Goodman had been elected to the Ohio state legislature with the benefit of funds raised by the CNP from various members, including Paul Pressler, Richard Viguerie, Morton Blackwell, and Ed Meese.[93] Goodman was also the director of the CNP's Conservative Action Project, created to oppose the Affordable Care Act and other Obama initiatives.

But earlier that year Goodman, another rising star on the CNP youth council, was accused of molesting the eighteen-year-old stepson of a CNP member in his hotel room at the annual meeting of the CNP at the Washington Ritz-Carlton. The stepfather complained to Tony Perkins.[94] Perkins sent Goodman a private letter saying he could no longer support his bid for office, but chose to remain silent as Goodman pursued his winning campaign. Eight weeks later he suspended Goodman from the CNP.[95] Perkins managed to keep the CNP incident under wraps for over two years, until it finally broke in the *Washington Post* in November 2017. Rod Dreher, a columnist for the *American Conservative*, fumed, "*This is how it works!* Play the game, and you'll get ahead. If you won't play the game, then at least keep your mouth shut about the players . . . Tony Perkins of the Council for National Policy showed how to do it."[96]

A few days after the story broke, Caleb Hull, an investigative journalist for the conservative *Independent Journal Review*, reported that he had also been approached by Goodman, and cited testimonies by an additional thirty men and boys who had been stalked by Goodman, some after he had spoken at a 2017 Turning Point USA conference.[97] Goodman had reached some of them online through Craigslist, Snapchat, and Facebook Messenger, often with promises of mentorship and political connections. Goodman resigned from public office following the revelations and went into a career in public relations.

The Council for National Policy took these speed bumps with aplomb, wrangling college presidents with feeble academic credentials, media moguls with no commitment to journalism, and self-righteous crusaders who committed criminal abuses. The CNP's uncompromising vision required a surprising amount of compromise.

CHAPTER 8

KOCH, DEVOS, SOROS: DONORS, POLITICS, AND PASTORS

Leading figures of the Council for National Policy compromised their partnerships as well. At first glance, Charles and David Koch were unlikely allies for the fundamentalist right. Religion has played little part in their rhetoric; they preach the free market gospel. Fundamentalists should have been dismayed at the way the Kochs extended their free-wheeling notions to the private sphere. David Koch advocated civil liberties that the fundamentalists bitterly opposed, including same-sex marriage and abortion rights.[1] Outlining his philosophy in a 2014 interview, he explained, "I'm basically a libertarian. And I'm a conservative on economic matters and I'm a social liberal." Koch didn't care whether the candidates he backed agreed with him. "That's their problem," he told Barbara Walters in an interview. "I'm really focused intensely on economic and fiscal issues, because if those go bad the country as a whole suffers terribly."[2]

But the Kochs and the core of the CNP also shared common ground. The Koch and DeVos families had both suffered irksome run-ins with the law. The DeVos company Amway was investigated by the United States and other governments for various forms of fraud, while the Kochs' companies tangled with the federal government on both environmental and financial grounds.[3] In 1974 a Koch oil company, along with two other oil companies, was cited for violating federal price controls, and the following year federal regulators found another Koch company guilty of overcharging for propane gas.[4]

A month after the first offense, the *New York Times* covered Charles Koch's Dallas speech about his new approach to promoting Koch family values: "The development of a well-financed cadre of sound proponents of the free enterprise philosophy is the most critical need facing us today," he said.[5] By 1977 the Kochs had begun to establish their "well-financed cadre" with a handsomely endowed think tank called the Cato Institute.[6] Their initiative would expand into a complex web of donors, front organizations, and shadowy alliances that defy a full accounting.

Charles Koch saw the Nixon-era price controls as evidence of "the bankruptcy of the Republican alternative to Democratic interventionism."[7] His brother David decided to take things a step farther, with an attempt to disrupt the bipartisan status quo. In 1980 he ran as the Libertarian Party's candidate for vice president, on a platform that can only be described as bizarre. It called for the elimination of all restrictions on immigration and the abolition of the Immigration and Naturalization Service, the repeal of all gun laws, opposition to all taxation, the abolition of the FBI and the CIA, and the repeal of Social Security.[8] It added that no one, no matter how psychotic, should be involuntarily committed to an institution for care. The platform also called for the legalization of homosexuality, prostitution, abortion, and all forms of drug use.

David Koch campaigned enthusiastically in twenty-seven states, traveling to most of them on his own dime. But his platform was too radical and the entrenched parties too powerful for him to get traction. Koch's ticket garnered a humiliating 1 percent of the national vote. Brother David had basked in the limelight, but brother Charles was unimpressed, given the amount of David's own money he had invested to float the campaign.[9]

The two brothers reluctantly turned back to the GOP. Like Richard Viguerie and Morton Blackwell, they were dismayed by centrist Republicans. Nixon had founded the Environmental Protection Agency, and moderate Republicans were willing to reach across the aisle to collaborate and compromise with Democrats on taxes and entitlement programs. But Reagan's "Southern strategy" showed new potential to widen the country's political divide, and Texas was a key component. It was no coincidence that Reagan's alliance with the South was launched in Dallas.

There was a regional affinity with the Kochs. Charles and his younger brother David were Wichita born and bred, but their father, Fred Koch, hailed from the tiny town of Quanah, Texas, eight miles from the Oklahoma border. Fred was born in 1900, at the dawn of the automobile era.[10] In 1901, when Fred was a babe in arms, prospectors struck oil at the Spindletop salt dome in Beaumont, Texas, a small town near the Gulf of Mexico, some thirty miles from the Louisiana state line. According to the American Oil & Gas Historical Society, "The Spindletop oilfield . . . would produce more oil in a day than the rest of the world's oil fields combined," launching the modern oil and gas industry.[11]

Fred Koch grew up along with the industry. He launched his career with a degree in engineering from MIT—a rare achievement for a kid from a Texas cow town—and returned home to witness a feverish army of wildcatters blasting the prairie. The lucky few struck oil.

Joining forces with an MIT classmate from Wichita, Fred Koch parlayed his education into a network of refineries and pipelines to monetize their strikes. Over the 1930s Koch expanded his operations to build refineries in the Soviet Union and Nazi Germany.[12] In 1940—just in time for the war—he founded the company that would become Koch Industries. This grew into an industrial behemoth with subsidiaries in chemicals, minerals, and finance, as well as petroleum. By 2019 it had grown into the second-largest privately held company in the United States (after the Cargill agricultural conglomerate), with over $120 billion in revenues and over a hundred thousand employees in sixty countries.[13]

Fred Koch and his wife Mary had four sons. Frederick, the oldest, devoted his life to the arts as a connoisseur of paintings, rare books, and historic properties. David and Bill were fraternal twins. Bill's passion was for sailing; his team won the America's Cup in 1992. He pursued the energy business but quarreled with David and their youngest brother Charles. David and Charles bought out their brothers in 1983, leading to a lengthy and acrimonious lawsuit. Frederick and Bill retained fabulous fortunes, but they were dwarfed next to their brothers'.[14]

Charles and David were left with a total of 84 percent of Koch Industries, and a net worth of over $50 billion each. The company operated refineries in the frozen reaches of Minnesota and the Gulf of Mexico. Their pipelines snaked four thousand miles across the continent, through Oklahoma, Texas, and Louisiana—which happened to be the buckle on the Bible Belt.

Charles Koch was indisputably the richest man in Wichita, the largest city in Kansas, with a population approaching four hundred thousand, some fifty miles north of the Oklahoma border. In the days of the Wild West, Wichita represented the southern edge of civilization. Young Bat Masterson herded cattle a few miles up the road, while Wyatt Earp kept the peace. In Edna Ferber's 1929 novel *Cimarron*, her heroes, displaced from the Confederate South, start out in genteel Wichita before they set off for the Oklahoma land rush.

In modern Wichita, Koch Industries employs over thirty-five hundred people, and the brand is affixed to everything from the Koch sports arena to the Koch Orangutan and Chimpanzee Habitat at the zoo.[15] But much of Charles Koch's philanthropy, distributed through countless outlets, has gone toward promoting his vision of free market absolutism and a government that disregards all forms of public welfare, limiting its purview to keeping the peace.

Koch's son Chase has joked about his upbringing, first as a six-year-old, listening to Milton Friedman read aloud at story time, and later as a teen dispatched by his father to a family feedlot where he—literally—shoveled shit. "About five miles away, you can smell it," he recalled.[16] In the family tradition, young Koch was rewarded with a corporate position and a mansion in Wichita, while the residents of western Kansas were left with the stench.

Charles may have been the richest man in Wichita, but his brother David became the richest man in New York City, a far more competitive position.[17] David shared his brother's libertarian philosophy, but he aspired to a different place in society. After some years as a confirmed bachelor, he married a beautiful young fashion assistant from Conway, Arkansas, more than twenty years his junior. The *New York Times* magazine published a chatty article wondering how far Julia Koch would ascend as a "fin de siècle society wife." The couple made a good start with their patronage of the Metropolitan Museum, but, socialites cautioned, Julia Koch "must find one or two more causes, besides the Met, to which she needs to give serious amounts of David's money and her time."[18]

The causes multiplied, and the Koch name blossomed across the city. As a trustee to the Metropolitan Museum, Koch donated $65 million to construct the David H. Koch Plaza on Fifth Avenue. As a ballet patron, he gave Lincoln Center $100 million toward the renovation of the renamed David H. Koch Theater. His $1.1 billion bought him the David H. Koch Center for ambulatory care at New York–Presbyterian Hospital. He took a long-term interest in public television, joining the boards of the influential stations WGBH in Boston and WNET in New York (though he resigned from the WNET board in 2013, after the station aired a documentary that portrayed him in an unflattering light).[19] Despite these efforts, the couple's social profile seemed to lower over time. One factor was David Koch's ongoing battle against prostate cancer. But his reputation was also affected by the mounting criticism of Koch Industries' record of pollution and influence peddling, detailed in another major documentary and Jane Mayer's prizewinning reporting.

New York society had turned a skeptical eye on new money for generations, but in Charles Koch's western fiefdom, the Koch fortune was old money. The fiefdom extended for miles. Just as New York's tri-state area subsumes Connecticut and New Jersey suburbs, the four south-central states function as a cultural and economic unit. "Kansmatexiana" is a virtual petrostate, made up of four of the nation's top dozen oil-producing states. Its politics are marked by a deep-seated resistance to federal authority, shaded by a pervasive sense of loss.

As an antebellum sugar producer, Louisiana was the richest state in the Union, and its francophone past included waves of French refugees from the Haitian revolution bent on re-creating their plantocracy on U.S. soil. After the defeat of the Confederacy, they were dispossessed once again. With the dismantling of the slave economy, carried out under federal authority, Louisiana would plummet from the wealthiest state in the Union to one of the poorest.

Texas had an equally rebellious history, first as an independent republic and then as a member of the Confederacy. It would become the leading oil producer in the country, responsible for 40 percent of the national output, Houston overtaking Tulsa as the oil capital of the world.[20] Texans felt a long-standing rivalry with New York, a resentment shared throughout the West. They produced tangible goods: oil, beef, cotton, wheat. New York City money men traded numbers in the air. When commodity prices plummeted, it was easy (and sometimes justifiable) to blame Wall Street. So it was deeply satisfying when, in 2006, Texas's gross domestic product surpassed New York's, coming second only to California; soon its population did the same. Texas's growth rate, fueled by the oil boom, outstripped New York's in the 2010s.[21]

The independent spirit was reflected in the Texas economy; it is one of seven states with no state or local income tax. In oil-dependent states such as Texas and Oklahoma, state budgets rise and fall with revenues from oil and gas severance taxes. (These are state taxes applied to resources "severed" from the ground.) State legislators walked a fine line: lower the taxes and lose budgets for roads and schools, or raise them and lose campaign contributions. Votes were at stake as well; roughly a fourth of the jobs in Oklahoma are connected to the energy sector.

The same game took place in Washington, with different stakes. Oil and gas campaign contributions come in fifth among U.S. industries, and Koch Industries leads the sector.[22] Unlike the top four industries, the energy sector political contributions are utterly lop-sided; the vast majority go to Republicans, and a major share of those go to legislators from oil-producing states.

The oil and gas industry's principal antagonists are the Environmental Protection Agency and its supporters in the Democratic Party. Here too there was resonance with the nineteenth century, when northern abolitionists' campaigns led to war and the federal government's dismantling of the plantation economy. There were more echoes in the late twentieth century, when the South's lucrative tobacco industry was decimated by lawsuits and public health campaigns leading to government smoking restrictions. In the minds of the oil barons, the environmentalists and their Washington allies were threatening to dethrone their petrostate just as it reached its apex.

Whatever their divergence over abortion and same-sex marriage, the Kochs and the CNP leadership shared a profound faith in petroleum. Morton Blackwell and CNP president Tony Perkins both arrived in Washington by way of Baton Rouge, and Louisiana was a key state for the oil industry. There is no indication that the Koch brothers joined the Council for National Policy, but their organizations funded a number of groups run by CNP members over two decades, and leaders of the Kochs' key organizations are members of the CNP.

The web of relationships between the Kochs and the CNP can be traced back to at least 1995, when there is a record of a Charles G. Koch Charitable Foundation contribution to Morton Blackwell's Leadership Institute.[23] The Kochs and the Council for National Policy needed each other. The Koch brothers had proved themselves to be master corporate strategists, but David's 1980 campaign demonstrated they hadn't a clue how to appeal to the electorate. The Council for National Policy leadership was well on the way to creating a network of "grassroots" organizations and the strategists to manage them, but they needed timely infusions of cash.

The Koch brothers and their subordinates thought along the same organizational lines as Paul Weyrich and Morton Blackwell, with higher social aspirations. In the winter of 1996 a member of the Kochs' inner circle, Richard Fink, published a paper in *Philanthropy* that echoed the CNP approach. "From Ideas to Action: The Role of Universities, Think Tanks, and Activist Groups" called for a three-stage model of social change—a political assembly line in which universities would generate "intellectual raw materials," think tanks would process them into "useable form," and "citizen activist" groups would "press for the implementation."[24] The process was not unlike oil production: academic wells of ideas, think tank refineries, and pipelines to propel them into the mass culture.

The Kochs had already laid the foundations. In 1974 the brothers launched their think tank, the Charles Koch Foundation, later renamed the Cato Institute. In 1980 they founded an academic base, the Mercatus Center, to promote their brand of radical free enterprise. It was later moved to George Mason, a public university in the Washington suburbs that became the Kochs' academic flagship. "Grassroots operations" were the most problematic. The Kochs launched Citizens for a Sound Economy in 1984, but it failed to thrive.

Koch Industries operations continued to provoke outrage and lawsuits. In 1996 a Koch butane pipeline exploded in the hamlet of Lively, Texas. Two teenagers who had set out in a truck to get help and warn their neighbors were burned alive. Exposure to dangerous substances was a way of life for the people who lived near Koch facilities. The federal government sued Koch Industries for more than three hundred oil spills from Koch pipelines in 1995 and 1997. Fresh water supplies in six states were affected; the Department of Justice reported that most of the spills took place in Texas, Oklahoma, and Kansas. The lawsuits sought amounts ranging from $71 million to $214 million in penalties. But when the Bush administration took office in 2001, the suit was settled for $35 million. This sum, greatly reduced, still represented the largest civil fine for violating an environmental law ever imposed until then.[25]

The Kochs fared even better with a second lawsuit over the same period. As the Center for Public Integrity explained,

> In late 2000—as the Clinton Administration was preparing to leave office—Koch was hit with a 97-count indictment for covering up the discharge of more than 15 times the legal limit of benzene, a carcinogen, from a refinery in Corpus Christi, Texas. The company faced penalties of more than $350 million. Four Koch employees were also charged individually and faced up to 35 years in prison.
>
> Three months after the Bush administration took office—and just before the lawsuit went to trial—the Justice Department abruptly settled the case. Koch agreed to pay $20 million and plead guilty to a single count of concealment of information. In return, the Justice Department dropped all criminal charges against Koch and the four employees.[26]

The Kochs had gotten off lightly, but looking to the future, they stepped up their political activity. They focused most of their efforts in the realm of donor activity, often described as philanthropy, informed by their talent for corporate strategy. Like their father, Charles and David Koch were MIT graduates. Every major undertaking showed the careful assembly of the interlocking parts: the political equivalent of wells, refineries, pipelines.

The brothers funded their political machine from multiple pockets, described by Jane Mayer in her essential book on the Koch empire, *Dark Money*. Between 1998 and 2008 the Charles G. Koch Charitable Foundation donated over $48 million, mostly to groups supporting his agenda. Another $28 million came from the Claude R. Lambe Charitable Foundation, named after a Wichita real estate developer and early investor in Fred Koch's business. Lambe left his fortune in the care of Charles Koch; the foundation board was comprised entirely of Charles Koch, his family members, and his employees. (It was dissolved in 2013.)

Over the same decade, Koch Industries disbursed over $50 million in lobbying activities, and the Koch PAC donated $8 million to political campaigns.[27] The sums added up to a vast fortune—but that didn't tell the whole story. The Koch brothers spent millions more in personal contributions, and the privately held Koch Industries conglomerate was exempt from the reporting requirements of publicly held companies.

The dark money didn't stop with the Kochs; they were keen to leverage their influence with other donors. Like the founders of the CNP, they looked to their rivals for inspiration. Many philanthropic foundations had taken a liberal bent, even when their founders, such as Henry Ford, were reactionary; the liberal Council on Foundations helped its member groups reinforce each others' projects, contributing to initiatives ranging from the civil rights movement to the green revolution. The Koch brothers set out to create a parallel universe of philanthropy. Through various dark money trusts and donor networks, their millions would serve as a magnet for like-minded plutocrats.

The Kochs coordinated their efforts through the Philanthropy Roundtable, founded in 1987, a conservative version of the Council on Foundations. A young woman named Whitney Ball, the director of development at the Koch's Cato Foundation, left to work for the roundtable, which received massive support from various Koch outlets, as well as CNP donors such as the Dick and Betsy DeVos Family Foundation.[28]

In 1999 the Kochs helped to launch a new consortium called the Donors Trust, with Whitney Ball in charge. Donors who committed $1 million or more per year could join the affiliated Donors Capital Fund.[29] These groups functioned as tax-exempt "donor-advised funds," obscuring the relationship between donor and beneficiary. Donors knew their contributions went to a list of approved causes, and they received a tax write-off in return.

The result was a merry-go-round of reciprocal funding. The Koch network and CNP donors—especially the DeVos family—grew ever closer, despite their religious differences. The DeVoses joined the Kochs' Seminar Network, and Charles Koch attended CNP meetings. In January 1999 he received the Richard DeVos Free Enterprise Award at the Council for National Policy's biannual meeting in Naples, Florida.[30]

The Koch brothers and the CNP took the 2000 elections as a warning signal, after George W. Bush lost the popular vote to Al Gore and squeaked into the presidency by a single vote in the Electoral College. The contest was stained by serious voting irregularities in Florida and elsewhere. (A study by the Carnegie Corporation found that as many as four to six million votes "were lost" in the election.[31]) It was a narrow escape for the Kochs. Former Texas governor George W. Bush was a longtime friend to the oil industry, but Al Gore was a committed environmentalist who promised to lead the nation in tackling climate change and pollution. But the plutocrats were also concerned by the course of the new administration. Once in office President George W. Bush began to behave more like a traditional Republican than a libertarian, taking an interventionist position in the Middle East and proposing expanded Medicare benefits.[32]

The Kochs regrouped. In 2003, with the 2004 elections in sight, they launched their donor summit. The initial event was a modest affair, consisting of some fifteen friends of Charles who sat through lectures on libertarian philosophy. Not surprisingly, even fewer participants returned for the next round; Charles Koch admitted that his target audience lacked motivation so long as Republicans were in office.[33] That would change. In time, the summits would expand to hundreds of donors—including the CNP's DeVos and Friess families—meeting on a biannual basis to renew their contributions to the Kochs' Seminar Network.[34] A $100,000 commitment was required to get in the door. The Seminar Network, even less transparent than the Donors Trust, would channel millions of dollars toward reshaping the U.S. government on behalf of the one percent.

The Koch-funded Citizens for a Sound Economy, founded in 1984, was harder to manage. Many observers described it as "astroturf": an artificial grassroots organization, driven by funding from the top, designed to resemble a popular initiative.[35] In 2003 Dick Armey became head of Citizens for a Sound Economy. Armey was an outspoken former congressman from Texas, a Republican majority leader, and a member of the CNP. Although he was resolutely antiabortion, Armey, the bearer of a PhD in economics from the University of Oklahoma, focused more on lowering taxes than promoting fundamentalist concerns. Over the 1990s he had encouraged a sputtering movement that became the Tea Party, whose scattered local activists agreed on vague notions of lowering taxes but little else.

In 2003 Armey fell out with David Koch, and Citizens for a Sound Economy split into two organizations. Both maintained their 501(c)(4) status as nonpartisan "social welfare" organizations that were allowed to conduct political activity so long as it was not their primary function. They were also allowed to fund other 501(c)(4) groups.[36] Armey's faction was dubbed FreedomWorks, and continued to receive major funding from the Donors Trust as well as from the Richard and Helen DeVos Foundation.[37]

The second group, Americans for Prosperity, was chaired by David Koch and became the hub of Koch-sponsored political activity. The Koch brothers still found financial strategy more intuitive than politics. As investigative reporter Lee Fang pointed out, the Kochs "struggled with ways to engineer public support for their extremely unpopular ideas, such as slashing the size of state government, thus laying off teachers and firemen, and reducing services."[38]

It was a unique challenge: to engineer the mechanisms of American democracy and media to convince voters to support candidates who would compromise the safety of their water, soil, and air, and limit their families' access to health care and public education. It would require all the strengths of American corporate culture, including strategy, messaging, and marketing. But the Kochs, increasingly impatient with the traditional Republican Party, were ready to make an end run.

Over time, Americans for Prosperity developed into an organization to rival the traditional GOP. In their ground-breaking 2018 paper, Columbia professors Alexander Hertel-Fernandez and Jason Sclar and Harvard sociologist Theda Skocpol described it as "a new political-party-like federation . . . to synchronize lobbying and grassroots mobilization for elections and policy battles in dozens of states as well as in Washington, DC."[39]

The CNP connection was bred in the bone: the director of Americans for Prosperity, Tim Phillips, attended Jerry Falwell's Liberty University before completing his studies at Virginia Tech. In 1997, at the age of thirty-three, he cofounded a consulting firm called Century Strategies with Ralph Reed, a leading figure in the CNP.[40] Phillips and Reed handled financial operations for the corrupt lobbyist Jack Abramoff, also a CNP member at the time. Phillips himself joined the CNP sometime before 2014.

The Koch organization made a strategic decision to focus on state-level activity, with Americans for Prosperity as their lever. "A nation-spanning organization," wrote Skocpol and her colleagues, "AFP is by far the most important political organization in the overall network supported by the Koch seminars . . . By 2007, before Barack Obama even declared his candidacy for the presidency, AFP had installed paid directors and usually additional paid operatives in fifteen states spread across all U.S. regions and encompassing close to half the U.S. population."[41] By 2019, Americans for Prosperity would expand across thirty-five states and claim an army of 3.2 million activists.[42]

The reciprocal funding accelerated. Over its first two decades, the Koch-founded Donors Trust disbursed over $218 million. Its number-one beneficiary was the Koch-funded "grassroots organization" Americans for Prosperity. The top fifty beneficiaries included the Koch-funded FreedomWorks Foundation (the "charity" arm of FreedomWorks), the Mercatus Center, and the Cato Institute.[43] The DeVoses were surely pleased to see that organizations headed by fellow CNP members also benefited, including the Federalist Society (ranked no. 4), the State Policy Network (no. 23), and the NRA, through the NRA Freedom Action Foundation (no. 42).[44] The DeVoses reciprocated. Between 2007 and 2011, the DeVos family foundation gave $800,000 to the Kochs' FreedomWorks Foundation.[45]

The Koch-CNP cross-funding brought other benefits. Morton Blackwell's Leadership Institute received funding from the Donors Trust, the Donors Capital Fund, and the Charles G. Koch Charitable Foundation.[46] Tim Phillips served as volunteer faculty for the Leadership Institute, and the Leadership Institute provided training and seminars for Americans for Prosperity interns.[47]

The idea of the consortium was popular among donors. CNP donors not only supported the Koch-backed consortium but were also active in the National Christian Foundation, a donor network comprised of affluent evangelicals. Launched in the 1980s by a fundamentalist network known as "The Family," the National Christian Foundation became a major, if obscure, force in U.S. philanthropy. Its meetings, held in luxury resorts, were known as "the Gathering"; adult attendees were charged $2,200 for admission and required to commit upward of $200,000 a year.

The National Christian Foundation hosted a broad array of donors and many traditional charities, overlapping with the Council for National Policy. Its key donors included CNP members from the DeVos, Prince, Friess, Coors, and Templeton families; its major beneficiaries included many groups run by CNP members, including the Family Research Council, Focus on the Family, and other anti-LGBT organizations—as well as a host of Koch-backed organizations.[48] By 2017 the National Christian Foundation had grown to be the eighth-largest charity in the United States, raising $1.5 billion a year.[49]

But the conservative donor networks faced a challenge from the left. One rival—who would become a bête noire for the CNP—was Hungarian-born financier George Soros. Soros began his philanthropic career in 1979, and eventually he assigned more than $32 billion of his fortune to his philanthropic network, the Open Society Foundations (leaving him with over $8 billion).[50] Unlike the Kochs, Soros launched his philanthropy with an international emphasis, and only added U.S. domestic projects after the end of the Cold War.

In 2005 Soros and his son Jonathan provided seed funding for a liberal donor consortium called the Democracy Alliance, in partnership with an Ohio insurance executive named Peter Lewis.[51] (Lewis was small fry compared to Soros, with a fortune of a mere $1.3 billion at the time of his death in 2005.[52])

The Democracy Alliance bore some structural similarities to the Koch seminars and the National Christian Foundation. The *Washington Free Beacon* published a story about the alliance, based on documents left behind from a meeting. It reported that the group met several times a year, maintained a veil of secrecy regarding donors and grants, favored luxurious venues, and demanded a steep price for admission: $30,000 in annual dues and pledges of at least $200,000 a year.[53] The Democracy Alliance's approach allowed it, like the Koch seminars, to focus on long-term policy issues instead of the short-term electoral agendas of most political action committees (PACs). Both provided seed money to new organizations that promised to advance their values.

There were also significant differences. Three-quarters of the Democracy Alliance partners were coastal, concentrated in three areas: the Boston–New York–Washington corridor, the Bay Area, and Los Angeles. In contrast, almost two-thirds of the Koch Seminar participants lived in the South and the Midwest.[54] In electoral terms, this meant that the Democratic donors' focused on zones that weighed heavily in the popular vote, while the Koch seminar donors were more likely to inhabit critical swing states that tilted the Electoral College, and sparsely populated states with disproportionate influence in the Senate. Both networks featured a preponderance of donors from the fields of finance, insurance, and real estate. But the Koch seminars were weighted toward the extractive industries and manufacturing, while the Democrats skewed toward the information industries, the legal profession, and entertainment.[55]

In the short term, the demographics of the Democracy Alliance were to their advantage. In the fall of 2005 the alliance, with its depth in the information industry and Silicon Valley, seized the initiative to fund new approaches to digital campaign technology. Over the next three years the Democrats established a clear lead in digital technology, making a major contribution to Obama's victory.

But these same qualities contributed to a disadvantage. The Koch seminars' corporate culture produced a structured approach, with a clear sense of command and control and a defined hierarchy. Combined with the Council for National Policy and its affiliates, the network resembled a vertically and horizontally integrated corporation. A closely held circle of strategists and CEOs determined the policy, supported by a cohort of investors, executed by obedient franchises. Network donors contributed to a fund, and the management directed it to bankroll a chosen few network organizations.

As a result, the Koch network could, as the Skocpol study states, "nimbly form and revise overall strategies, while [the Democracy Alliance's] rules have promoted scattering of resources and undercut possibilities for advancing any coherent strategy."[56] The Democracy Alliance expected its beneficiaries to collaborate, but the approach often resembled the tech start-up culture, with all of its exuberance, creativity, and chaos. Scores of organizations were invited to the meetings to make their pitches. Donors offered winning contestants the equivalent of venture capital, and they were placed in competition with each other to scrabble for a longer-term commitment. Many went broke along the way.

The Skocpol study noted that logically, Democrats should have enjoyed a competitive advantage, given that wealthy liberals are more prevalent in the United States than wealthy conservatives. Nonetheless, their network proved less effective. The Koch seminars "have fueled a tightly integrated political machine" that moved national and state-level Republicans toward the ultra-free-market right. The Democracy Alliance, on the other hand, achieved "more limited results by channeling resources to large numbers of mostly nationally focused and professionally managed liberal advocacy and constituency groups."[57] These differences would have a dramatic impact on the battle royal to come.

Fueled by massive investments into their networked organizations, the Council for National Policy members made many political inroads, particularly through activities of the Family Research Council. The year 2003 marked a new chapter for the organization, as founder James Dobson took up the cause of fellow CNP member and Alabama judge Roy Moore. Moore was fighting to retain a massive monument to the Ten Commandments at the Alabama Supreme Court after it had been ruled unconstitutional by a federal court.[58]

After Dobson brought in Tony Perkins as FRC director, Perkins launched a new FRC "ministry" called Watchmen on the Wall, after Isaiah 62:6: "On your walls, O Jerusalem, I have set watchmen." This organization served to recruit and network fundamentalist pastors in critical electoral districts. In their home states, members were treated to periodic "pastor appreciation breakfasts." The FRC took the opportunity to distribute complimentary organizing materials, including a manual for organizing their own "Culture Impact Team" and "IRS-compliant voter guides produced by FRC."[59]

Many pastors continued to be uncomfortable with preaching politics from the pulpit, and the Family Research Council offered them a menu of arguments and workarounds. One video, narrated by Tony Perkins, listed religious figures who challenged authority, including Moses, Elijah, and John the Baptist, demanding, "Were these men of God throughout history being too political?" FRC voter guides scrupulously avoided endorsing candidates in a literal fashion; they simply rated candidates according to their criteria, which led to an inescapable conclusion in favor of Republicans. Pastors were encouraged to join the P3 Pastor Program ("Praying for the nation, Preaching the whole counsel of God, and Partnering with others"). Members could access the FRC's "church-friendly Bulletin Insert" to print and distribute to the congregations on Sunday, tucked into the order of worship. The FRC also produced compelling antiabortion videos to show in the church. They even offered a menu of ready-made sermons, including PowerPoint presentations written by Perkins and his partners for download and delivery from the pulpit.[60]

The Family Research Council sponsored regional briefings with names like "Keep God in Texas."[61] In 2003 Watchmen on the Wall hosted its first national conference, which became an annual event. Pastors and their wives enjoyed a heavily subsidized three-day junket in Washington at the swanky Hyatt Regency on Capitol Hill.[62] There they received FRC policy briefings, training sessions, and a "Spiritual Heritage Tour" of the U.S. Capitol.[63] Then they were dispatched to Capitol Hill to carry the FRC message to their congressmen, whose office addresses were helpfully listed in the conference program. The materials also included painstaking guidelines for the legal boundaries for church politicking, and tips for setting up a "Culture Impact Team" in the home church. The orientation materials included a budget—suggesting that pastors should contribute 1 percent of their church's undesignated receipts to the Family Research Council.[64]

The shadow network operated at full force. Watchmen on the Wall was heavily promoted on the CNP radio partner networks, which in turn recruited their followers for training at the Leadership Institute. The pastors' training sessions instructed them in methods not only for getting their congregants to the polls but also for extending their influence to family and friends and recruiting their followers to run for political office. Any churchgoer who was misguided enough to support a Democrat was pounded with messaging on the twin virtues of "sanctity of life" (antiabortion) and "sanctity of marriage" (anti-same-sex marriage). The FRC website added a downloadable "Election Prayer Guide" asking worshippers to "pray that America's Christians will all register to vote" and cast their votes based on candidates' "biblical values," in order to elect "godly men and women as leaders who fear the Lord and honor Him."[65]

The FRC's first iVoterGuide was drafted in 2004 by two Southern Baptist pastors, Kenyn Cureton and Richard Land, a CNP member.[66] The guides routinely awarded high marks to conservative pro-gun, anti-tax Republicans for defending "biblical values," at the expense of Democratic candidates. Soon after the guides were launched, Richard Land, head of the Ethics and Religious Liberty Commission of the Southern Baptist Convention at the time, described the promotional strategy in a question-and-answer session: "We currently have an 18-wheeler, which used to be used to sell merchandise from the Charlie Daniels Band—after all, we are based in Nashville—and it is now the iVoteValues.com Express. It's part of a yearlong campaign to heighten awareness of people in the Southern Baptist and evangelical community, that they ought to be registered to vote, to help them get registered to vote, to help them get informed on the issues, and then to encourage them to vote their values, their beliefs and their convictions."[67]

The guides didn't tell Baptists who to vote for, Land said—they were just "printing up platform comparisons": "We will be printing a significant number this year, and we're encouraging folks to order them from iVoteValues.com [linked to the Family Research Council] or Faithand-Family.com [a Southern Baptist Convention site]."

The iVoter guides defined the issues, and their wording influenced the reactions. At the top of their list they placed appointing conservative [or "originalist"] judges and banning same-sex marriage. Environmental issues were not worthy of mention.[68]

Voter guides are standard issue for all sorts of political parties and activists, of course, and it's standard practice for the wording of the "questions" and candidate ratings to nudge the reader in the desired direction. But by making pastors and churches their vehicles of distribution, the iVoter guides gave their recommendations the imprimatur of spiritual leaders—perhaps even an air of divine authority.

In 2006 the Family Research Council appointed iVoter coauthor Kenyn Cureton as its vice president for church ministries, a post that included oversight of Watchmen on the Wall. Under his leadership, the website's listing of its national pastors network grew from a base of 1,800 pastors to 75,000.[69] Many were located in critical swing states, including Wisconsin (with 891 members), Michigan (1,778), Pennsylvania (2,464), and Florida (7,372).[70] In a tight race, a cohort of pastors who influenced as few as fifty votes apiece could swing an election.

In 2006 Tony Perkins created an annual rally and networking event in Washington, D.C. The Values Voter Summit was hosted by FRC Action, the Family Research Council's lobbying arm, and cosponsored by a long list of groups run by CNP members: the American Family Association Action, Alliance Defending Freedom, Oklahoma Wesleyan University, Liberty University, the Susan B. Anthony List, and many more.[71]

The summit offered the movement's middle tier of supporters—many of whom had never heard of the Council for National Policy—a chance to see CNP stars in person. Tony Perkins was the host. Oliver North was a regular, as were media figures such as Todd Starnes.[72] The Values Voter Summit grew to more than three thousand attendees from across the country, some of whom paid over $600 for the full three-day package (not including travel and lodging). This included training workshops in political campaign techniques by staff from Morton Blackwell's Leadership Institute and briefings from movement pollster George Barna.[73] The summits wound up with a black-tie "Faith, Family and Freedom Gala," with a 1950s-style stage band rocking gospel tunes and standards to a danceable beat. A few non-Baptists even danced. No alcohol was served.[74]

Perkins promoted the summit on his *Washington Watch* broadcasts on the Bott and American Family Radio networks. CNP member Richard Bott himself sometimes attended, and Bott Radio sponsored the meeting's "radio row." This was an improvised studio in the exhibition hall, where speakers could follow up with an interview and fans could snap pictures of them as they spoke. The exhibition hall featured booths and tables from a broad range of organizations: Liberty University recruited students, fundamentalist movie companies promoted feature films, and the NRA handed out bumper stickers.

The Values Voter podium became a required stop for Republican politicians seeking the FRC's blessing and presidential hopefuls auditioning for the fundamentalist voting bloc. The Values Voter Summit became a media event for mainstream news outlets as well, a rare opportunity to view the shadow network in the spotlight.

Other American Christians agonized over the conflicts generated by the gaps between the world's political realities and the ideals of their faith. What was a Christian position on the torture practiced by the U.S. government in the post-9/11 period in pursuit of combating terrorism? How could the biblical commandment "Thou shalt not kill" be reconciled with capital punishment and the epidemic of gun violence? What would a humane refugee policy look like in a world beset by millions of suffering refugees?

These matters were absent from the prayer menu for Watchmen on the Wall and the program for the Values Voter Summit. Children's welfare was only mentioned from conception until birth. The Family Research Council held that fundamentalist Christians "*are* victims of religious discrimination . . . From the Senate chamber to a corner bakery, Christians with natural or biblical views of marriage and sexuality have a bullseye on their backs."[75] Their sense of victimization left little compassion for anyone else.

CHAPTER 9

THE OBAMA CHALLENGE

The Council for National Policy was still racing against time. As of the early 2000s, evangelical Christians remained the largest religious group in the United States, with about a quarter of the population, but their numbers were starting to drop. The Southern Baptists, the largest Protestant denomination in the country, peaked in 2006 at sixteen million members, then went into a precipitous decline.[1] At the same time, the percentage of atheists and unaffiliated Americans rose sharply; it was only a matter of time before the "unchurched" overtook the Southern Baptists.[2]

The fundamentalists held on to several major advantages. First, older white Protestants were likely to vote. The generational difference was stark: between 2000 and 2016, over 66 percent of eligible voters over forty-five turned out to vote, while eighteen-to-twenty-nine-year-olds averaged around 45 percent.[3] In an era of razor-thin margins, getting additional white evangelical voters to the polls was a make-or-break strategy.

Second, they still held sway in the Senate, which allotted disproportionate representation to sparsely populated states, many of which were fundamentalist bastions. The Senate controlled the all-important federal judiciary appointments. CNP and Koch network donors had invested millions in state and local campaigns to take over the statehouses, where the decisions on redistricting and gerrymandering were made, but these and many other issues were ultimately settled—or not—in the courts. National policy was made in Washington, but the devilish details were often left to the state and local levels.

For the Council for National Policy, court battles were another way to promote its agenda. Once again it took inspiration from the left, specifically the American Civil Liberties Union (ACLU), which had martialed armies of pro bono attorneys to argue its cases since its founding in 1920.

In 1993 the CNP's James Dobson and a group of fundamentalist leaders launched a rival organization that came to be known as the Alliance Defending Freedom. The ADF was created to fight for the "religious liberty" of fundamentalists, starting with the right to skirt the tax code. Its founding director was CNP member Alan Sears, coauthor of the 2003 book *The Homosexual Agenda: Exposing the Principal Threat to Religious Freedom Today.* CNP members on the board of directors include vice chairman Tom Minnery, president emeritus of Dobson's Family Policy Alliance, and Marjorie Dannenfelser, a former staffer on the Hill who became head of the Susan B. Anthony List. ADF's general counsel, Michael Farris, is a CNP member as well.[4]

Sears, a former official in the Reagan Justice Department, made a priority of rolling back civil rights for the LGBT population, one case at a time. His organization also worked to expand the presence of fundamentalist values in the public square, and pushed back against women's rights to contraception under the Affordable Care Act.[5]

The ADF grew into a legal powerhouse. As of 2015 it had a staff of over forty lawyers and a $50 million budget.[6] Its army of 3,300 "Allied Attorneys" argue cases on a local level, contributing over a million pro bono hours of service.[7] The ADF claims to have litigated cases in over sixty countries.[8]

The ADF's Blackstone Legal Fellowship has recruited over 2,100 law students from more than 225 law schools in 21 countries. The Blackstone fellowship included a nine-week summer immersion program—complete with daily worship services—as well as internship and job placement, building the ranks for future litigation.[9] The alliance funded hundreds of lawsuits nationwide and "played various roles in 54 U.S. Supreme Court decisions . . . including representing parties directly, assisting in amicus efforts, and providing financial assistance."[10]

The organization's stated goal was to "restore religious freedom," but some faiths were favored over others. In 2014 the Blackstone Fellowship website stated that the movement "seeks to recover the robust Christendomic theology of the 3rd, 4th and 5th centuries" which is "catholic, universal orthodoxy and is desperately crucial for cultural renewal."[11] "Christendomic" appeared to refer to the period when Roman emperor Constantine imposed Christianity as a state religion throughout the Roman Empire as a vehicle for expanding his imperial cult.

Alliance Defending Freedom contributors have included the Koch brothers' Donors Trust, but the largest contributions have come from the DeVos and Prince families and the National Christian Foundation, which granted it nearly $14 million in 2014 alone.[12] CNP member Foster Friess is among the major donors to the NCF.[13]

Like many of the CNP affiliates, the Alliance Defending Freedom has experienced embarrassing setbacks. One of its central claims was that children of same-sex couples were "more likely to experience emotional and developmental problems than those with opposite sex parents," citing the research of Texas sociology professor Mark Regnerus.[14] In 2013 Regnerus filed an amicus brief in federal court in a case opposing same-sex marriage in California.[15]

But an expert analysis published in the journal *Social Science Research* found Regnerus's methodology highly deficient, full of bogus data. One of his survey respondents, for example, reported he was seven feet eight inches tall and weighed eighty-eight pounds. Less than a quarter of the few cases of same-sex parenting cited in his study could be confirmed, and these produced no evidence of emotional or developmental disadvantages to their children.[16]

The same could not be said of ADF attorneys. In November 2012, charges were filed against Lisa Biron, a pro bono attorney for the Alliance Defending Freedom who had defended the Destiny Christian Church of Concord, New Hampshire in a tax case.[17] Biron was found guilty of forcing her fourteen-year-old daughter to take part in a threesome with a man she solicited on Craigslist—the ad read "two girls, 18 and 33, looking to party"—and making an iPhone video of her daughter in the act.[18] She was sentenced to forty years in prison for what the judge called an "egregious" crime causing "incalculable" harm to her daughter.[19]

The Alliance Defending Freedom created the ADF Young Lawyers Academy and the Blackstone Legal Fellowship to steep young lawyers in their values and train them in their tactics. The organization has received over $45 million from the National Christian Foundation, as well as grants from the Richard and Helen DeVos Foundation and the Koch brothers' Donors Trust and Donors Capital Fund.[20] Alliance Defending Freedom has provided pro bono representation for Turning Point USA and Students for Life, and describes the Family Research Council, Students for Life, and other groups run by CNP members as "allied organizations."[21]

The Council for National Policy put a strong emphasis on the courts. Presidents are limited to two terms, congressmen come and go, but judges are forever—or more precisely, federal judges can serve for life.[22] Most Americans' experience with the judiciary is limited to traffic or family courts that deal with day-to-day issues. But these courts are subordinate to three federal levels of the judiciary. District court judges are appointed to ninety-four district courts and supervise civil and criminal trials. Judges for the Courts of Appeals, or circuit judges, serve on twelve regional circuit courts, plus a court of appeals in Washington, D.C. They review appeals from district court cases and decisions from federal agencies. The Supreme Court is the ultimate arbiter of the law.

District court judges, circuit judges, and Supreme Court judges are all nominated by the president and confirmed by the Senate, though few appointments receive national attention below the Supreme Court.[23] But together, the three courts have the power to transform American society. Elected officials are chosen in the glare of publicity, holding their personal histories, public records, and political positions up for examination. Supreme Court nominees can face similar scrutiny, but historically the appointment of district and circuit court judges has been less contentious, more a matter of jurisprudence than politics.[24]

One reason for this was the set of arcane practices in Congress—hardly visible to the public—that served to mediate regional differences and keep American society on an even keel. The Senate confirmation process for federal judges was a prime example. The Constitution requires Supreme Court justices to be confirmed with the "advice and consent" of the Senate, which is also required by the statutes regulating the district courts and courts of appeal. The Senate has also maintained procedures for the confirmation of judges, such as "blue slips": a time-honored tradition by which the Senate Judiciary Committee chairman only proceeded with hearings for nominees who received both home state senators' support, as expressed by a piece of blue paper.

Another element was the rating system of the Standing Committee on the Federal Judiciary, an independent arm of the American Bar Association. Under this practice, the White House submitted names to the committee in advance of their official nomination, so that their integrity, professional competence, and judicial temperament could be reviewed. Philosophy, political affiliation, and ideology were not part of the assessment.[25] They were graded at three levels: "highly qualified," "qualified," and "not qualified." The names of poorly rated individuals were often withdrawn before their nomination.

The premise was that while elected officials may not like all nominees equally, they could agree on common standards of professionalism and impartiality.[26] The ABA review began in 1953 at the request of Republican president Dwight Eisenhower, and every president from Eisenhower to Barack Obama participated in the process except George W. Bush. Conservatives claimed that the ABA ratings had a liberal bias, but the ratings did not adhere to party loyalty: for example, none of George H. W. Bush's nominees received the ABA's lowest rating, while four of Bill Clinton's did.[27]

The various elements of the confirmation process reflected the belief that extreme rulings can cause social disruption when they radically alter the status quo. Many members of the Council for National Policy argued that such disruption had occurred when a liberal Supreme Court ruled on school desegregation, abortion, and same-sex marriage. The CNP started out as an organization of preachers, politicos, and moneymen, but over time it developed three legal organizations, each of which spun networks in its own right. These were the Alliance Defending Freedom (ADF), led by CNP member Alan Sears; the Federalist Society, headed by CNP members Eugene B.

Meyer and Leonard Leo; and the American Center for Law and Justice (ACLJ), run by Jay Sekulow, a member of the CNP board of governors.

The Alliance Defending Freedom represented legal boots on the ground. Its website included a form for local pastor and activists to apply for free legal aid for related causes. The Federalist Society, by contrast, was effectively the officers' corps, founded in 1982 at a symposium at Yale Law School organized by a group of Yale, Harvard, and University of Chicago law students who supported an originalist interpretation of the Constitution. One of the speakers was University of Chicago law professor and future Supreme Court justice Antonin Scalia, who became a mentor to the Chicago chapter.

The Federalist Society quickly grew to a membership of seventy thousand, with more than two hundred law school chapters and professional chapters in ninety cities. Its conservative views made its members a minority on many campuses, but it won respect through both the prestige of its members and the quality of its programs, which encouraged wide-ranging debate. The society was more secular than other CNP affiliates, but it was equally single-minded. Its piece of the CNP portfolio was judiciary nominations.

Meyer, the Federalist Society's president, was the son of a Communist Party organizer who defected and became a founding coeditor of the conservative *National Review*. But much of the lobbying effort was carried out by the society's executive vice president, Leo.

The election of George W. Bush gave the Federalist Society cause to celebrate. Bush's two Supreme Court nominees, John Roberts and Samuel Alito, were members of the Federalist Society. According to an Alliance for Justice review, so were almost half of the appeals court judges Bush appointed. Federalist Society member Brett Kavanaugh served as associate White House counsel until 2003, when Bush nominated him for the Washington, D.C., Circuit Court of Appeals—a traditional stepping stone to the Supreme Court.[28]

Leonard Leo was one of the "four horsemen" of the Bush administration who advised the president on court appointments; the others were Sekulow, White House counsel C. Boyden Gray, and former CNP president (and former attorney general) Ed Meese. In 2005 they formed a working group that came to be known as the Judicial Crisis Network. This organization was led by Carrie Severino, a former clerk for Clarence Thomas, who had been a member of the Federalist Society since the 1980s. Severino was a frequent guest on Perkins's *Washington Watch*. Her husband, Roger Severino, was the director of the DeVos Center for Religion and Society at the Heritage Foundation. In 2017 Trump appointed him to oversee the office that addresses abortion access and LGBT rights at the Department of Health and Human Services.[29]

Federalist Society donors included the DeVos family, the National Christian Foundation, and an array of Koch foundations and consortia.[30] Harvard law professor Noah Feldman called the Federalist Society a "remarkably open and transparent" organization whose members form relationships through intellectual exchange: "The informal hierarchy that results informs judicial appointments, as it was always intended to do."[31] On the other hand, one retired judge described the Federalists as "good people, smart people, who are put off by people going too far to the left—but they can also identify people a tyrant wants."[32]

THE CNP'S MOST visible legal advocate was attorney Jay Sekulow, who appears to have been a member since the 1990s. Sekulow was born to a New York Reform Jewish family and moved to Atlanta in his youth. An indifferent student, Sekulow graduated from a tiny Atlanta Baptist college and its even tinier law school, where he converted to Messianic Judaism under the influence of Jews for Jesus.[33] After a stint as an attorney with the IRS, he founded a firm that challenged tax regulations governing religious and conservative organizations, based on his inside knowledge. He soon came to the attention of the CNP's Pat Robertson.

In 1990 Robertson recruited Sekulow to run his new organization, the American Center for Law and Justice, based at Robertson's Regent University in Virginia. According to *Time* magazine, the ACLJ was another "conservative answer to the [ACLU]," whose acronym it echoed. Sekulow became the movement's legal bulldog, serving as lead counsel on a number of high-profile cases that advanced its causes, including antiabortion activism and school prayer.[34] In 1997 Sekulow established the European

Centre for Law and Justice, based in France, and the next year he opened the Slavic Centre for Law and Justice in Moscow.

Sekulow's enterprises served him well. In 2017 the *Guardian* obtained tax documents revealing that Sekulow and his family had reaped more than $60 million since 2000 from the ACLJ and an affiliated charity, Christian Advocates Serving Evangelism. Much of the money was extracted as donations from retirees on fixed incomes, susceptible to a finely tuned telemarketer script: "We wanted to make sure you were aware of the efforts to undermine our traditional Christian values" effected by Barack Obama, and so on.[35] The bounty bought Sekulow a private jet, extensive properties, and his own law firm operating for the benefit of the fundamentalists.

He also became a CNP media star. His radio show *Jay Sekulow Live!* has been carried by more than 1,050 stations, including Salem Communications and the Bott network. Sekulow is telegenic, with expensive suits, a perpetual tan, and an authoritative baritone. He appears as a frequent guest on Robertson's Christian Broadcasting Network, and his weekly program is carried on the fundamentalist Trinity Broadcasting Network, Daystar, and Sky Angel.[36] Fox News and the three networks made him a regular commentator.

Sekulow is adept at self-promotion—so adept that a George Barna poll of Christian conservatives named his American Center for Law and Justice the "most effective organization in leading positive cultural change in the U.S. during 2016."[37]

The National Rifle Association might seem an unlikely arbiter of federal judicial appointments, but it has played a surprisingly large role in the process. This became part of its remit in 2009, with President Obama's first Supreme Court nomination. Judge Sonia Sotomayor enjoyed wide bipartisan support, but according to the *New York Times*' legal expert Linda Greenhouse, then Republican Senate minority leader Mitch McConnell took strong objection to her nomination. McConnell, a graduate of Morton Blackwell's Leadership Institute, turned to the National Rifle Association, run by CNP member Wayne LaPierre. He requested that the group publicly oppose Sotomayor and "score" the vote to activate its members. "The NRA had never scored a vote on a judicial nomination," wrote Greenhouse. "Judge Sotomayor had no record on gun issues. But the organization obliged Senator McConnell and announced that it would score the Sotomayor vote.

Republicans melted away. Only seven voted for confirmation. The scenario was repeated the following year for the nomination of Elena Kagan, who had no track record on gun cases because she had never been a judge."[38]

The NRA took similar actions against other nominees, with mounting success. In 2016 the NRA pulled out all the stops to derail the confirmation of Obama nominee Merrick Garland to the seat left vacant by Scalia's death, issuing an "instant and evidence-free denunciation," Greenhouse wrote. The NRA mobilized its supporters to lobby Congress against Garland, listing the congressional switchboard number on NRATV spots.[39] On March 20, 2016, Mitch McConnell broadcast the NRA's influence on Fox News, stating he "can't imagine" a Republican majority in the Senate wanting to confirm a nominee opposed by the National Rifle Association.[40]

Greenhouse concluded, "If the affirmative act of passing legislation is out of reach, it seems to me that there is one thing an aroused and disgusted public ought to focus on: reclaiming the judicial confirmation process from the National Rifle Association."

Instead, the opposite occurred. McConnell and the Republican senators declined to hold proceedings of any kind on Garland's nomination, for the first time in over a century. The nomination was stalled, and the seat on the Supreme Court was held in escrow for the next administration.

CNP MEMBERS WERE also making important inroads into the realm of information. Traditional newspaper advertising peaked, then started to plummet in the early 2000s.[41] Newspapers closed, and tens of thousands of journalists were thrown out of work, depriving local communities of statehouse reporting and the services of national wire services. Media watchdogs worried over the influence of Fox News and the Sinclair Broadcast Group, but they paid less attention to the burgeoning fundamentalist broadcasting outlets that sprang up to fill the vacuum.

According to Adam Piore in *Mother Jones*, in 2005 Frank Wright, president of the National Religious Broadcasters, reported that one hundred million Americans tuned in to Christian stations at least once a month, up 43 percent from 2000. This was four times the weekly audience of National

Public Radio at the time. According to Wright, the trailblazer was Salem, the CNP's most powerful media affiliate.[42] It was a close relationship: Salem founder and former CNP president Stuart Epperson Sr. was a longtime board member of the National Religious Broadcasters, where his son Stuart Junior would join him.[43] (Frank Wright would become Salem's president and chief operating officer in 2013.[44])

Salem Communications was growing rapidly. In 2004 it acquired sixteen news and talk stations, doubling its number of secular stations at the expense of the local independent and public stations they acquired. In 2005 author Sarah Posner reported, "Salem is the seventh largest owner of radio stations in the country." If it were combined with American Family Radio, she added, it would be placed fourth.[45] Salem's programming was now available to a third of the U.S. population, and its online publications had an audience of three million.[46] Its news division website described it as "the only Christian-focused news organization with fully-equipped broadcast facilities at the U.S. House, Senate, and White House manned by full-time correspondents," with news "specifically created for Christian-formatted radio stations."[47] This meant "news" based on "biblical values"—not fact-based, multisourced professional practice. Salem also provided an unabashed platform for fellow members of the CNP, such as Kenneth Blackwell, former Ohio secretary of state, and lawyer Jay Sekulow.

But the CNP's leading radio personality was James Dobson. By the mid-2000s his broadcasts were carried on over two thousand U.S. radio stations, reaching six to ten million weekly listeners. Dobson reached additional audiences through his frequent appearances on the Trinity and Christian Broadcasting networks and his specially produced videos, which were projected in church services.[48]

New digital platforms appeared. In 2004 Southern Baptist leader and CNP member Richard Land—coauthor of the iVoter guides—launched the *Christian Post*, an online evangelical news service. The *Christian Post* published diverging opinions regarding Republican politicians, but adhered to strict CNP orthodoxy regarding abortion and same-sex marriage. It amassed a monthly audience of ten million viewers.[49] The *Daily Caller*, launched by CNP member Neil Patel and Fox News host Tucker Carlson and bankrolled by the CNP's Foster Friess, would be added to the stable in 2010.

The 2004 elections presented a new challenge for the CNP coalition. John Kerry came out of the Democratic convention with a lead over George W. Bush in the polls. That August the *New York Times* had a rare opportunity to cover the Council for National Policy's meeting at New York's Plaza Hotel in advance of the Republican National Convention. The *Times* described the event as "a pep rally" for George Bush.[50] In the weeks that followed, CNP partners went all out on Bush's behalf. Salem Communications ran hundreds of radio ads on behalf of a fundamentalist voter registration drive called "Americans of Faith," cochaired by Atsinger.[51]

In November 2003 the Massachusetts Supreme Judicial Court made its ruling legalizing same-sex marriage. The fundamentalists drew a line in the sand and made this issue their driving concern for 2004—although polls showed that voters placed it dead last among fifteen issues in the campaign, far behind the economy, terrorism, and jobs.[52]

The national indifference to the perils of same-sex marriage suggested that a state-level approach might be more successful, starting in the swing states with a strong fundamentalist presence. Gary Bauer, a member of the CNP's board of governors, served as a national spokesman for the initiative.[53] Ballot initiatives to ban same-sex marriage were launched in thirteen states. Ohio was ground zero; its proposal for a state constitutional amendment, known as Issue One, was one of the most extreme measures, proposing to restrict "governmental bodies in Ohio from using your tax dollars to give official status, recognition and benefits to homosexual and other deviant relationships that seek to imitate marriage."

Issue One threatened domestic partnerships and civil unions as well as same-sex marriage. Critics charged that it could also penalize people who received health benefits through domestic partners, single mothers seeking maternity leave, and unmarried couples who owned joint property.[54] To rural Ohioans sitting in fundamentalist pews, the initiative played as a local issue—to counter an external attack on tradition and the "sanctity of marriage." It was actually a brilliant electoral maneuver, rooted in a national strategy and designed by the kingpins of the CNP.

Campaign strategists saw Ohio as crucial. The Massachusetts ruling sanctioning same-sex marriage presented a wild card, a case of the judiciary getting out in front of national public opinion: a UCLA study showed that when the decision was made, no single state had more than 50 percent support for same-sex marriage. Thirteen states had passed measures banning it, and thirty states would adopt similar prohibitions. But support for same-sex marriage was growing rapidly, and polls indicated that it had won majority acceptance in thirty-six states by the time the Supreme Court ruled the bans unconstitutional in 2015.[55]

Democrat John Kerry, a Catholic, disapproved of same-sex marriage at the time, but he chose to campaign on other issues.[56] But James Dobson detected an opportunity in Kerry's Massachusetts origins, and the campaign tied Kerry to his state's court ruling.

As author Dan Gilgoff explains, Dobson's Focus on the Family created a blueprint for the state ballot initiatives. "All but two of the thirteen campaigns were led by Focus on the Family's state-level Family Policy Councils . . . Nowhere would amending the state constitution prove more consequential than in Ohio."[57] The Ohio campaign was orchestrated by a recovered pornography addict named Phil Burress, who headed a group called Citizens for Community Values, an Ohio state affiliate of the Family Research Council, Focus on the Family, and the Alliance Defending Freedom.[58]

Getting Issue One on the ballot was a complicated process. For advice on the signature drive, Burress turned to Kenneth Blackwell, the Ohio secretary of state and a member of the CNP's executive committee. Blackwell pointed him toward the state's network of evangelical churches, and Burress expanded his church contact list by 70 percent, to seventeen thousand churches.[59] His roster of volunteers grew to six thousand. Burress used mailing lists from groups run by CNP members Gary Bauer and Don Wildmon. But, Gilgoff reports,

> It was the Family Research Council . . . that provided the most crucial aid. On top of mailing letters to thirty thousand Ohio supporters, FRC gave two million dollars to Citizens for Community Values, helping to underwrite Burress's contract with a professional signature-gathering firm . . . It was FRC's biggest investment in any state in 2004, and it was undertaken with an eye toward winning Ohio for Bush. "Politically speaking, I knew it was a swing state, and an important state in the election," said Family Research

> Council president Tony Perkins in an interview after the election. "It's all about turnout, and we wanted to encourage our people to turn out and vote because the results would be more votes for pro-family, pro-marriage, pro-life candidates."[60]

Same-sex marriage became a signature issue for Perkins and other CNP activists. Indiana congressman Mike Pence joined Perkins for a photo op on Capitol Hill following a failed 2004 vote on the ban in the House.[61] Once again, the framing of the issue was critical: liberals argued for same-sex marriage as "marriage equality"; Perkins and Pence opposed it by calling for "marriage protection" in defense of the "sanctity of marriage."

Burress's efforts in Ohio delivered the bonus of registering nearly 55,000 new voters. He paid a firm to call every home in the state to identify 850,000 supporters, then call each of them the day before the election, encouraging them to vote. His organization placed nearly three million inserts into church bulletins the Sunday before the election.[62] Burress told the Baptist Press news service that he had seen preliminary polling data that indicated that if the issue was on the ballot, it could boost the Bush vote by 3 to 5 percent.[63]

Burress's efforts were leveraged by Kenneth Blackwell, who oversaw the state electoral process at the same time he chaired the state Bush-Cheney campaign committee. His polling places were rife with irregularities. The Brennan Center at the NYU School of Law published a report after Blackwell was named to the Presidential Advisory Commission on Election Integrity in 2017. It found that in 2004, "Blackwell issued a series of decisions that both restricted access to voting . . . and invited criticism for the appearance and substance of partisanship."[64] His measures included disqualifying some voter registrations based on the weight of the paper stock they were printed on.[65]

Kerry's campaign was further derailed by the Swift Boat campaign, a fraudulent attack on his war record launched by CNP member Jerome Corsi.[66] (Corsi and Kenneth Blackwell coauthored a book two years later.[67])

Bush won Ohio by 118,457 votes—with 50.8 percent of the vote.[68] As Gilgoff noted, "switching fewer than sixty thousand votes [in Ohio] would have given the national election to John Kerry."[69]

The 2004 elections revealed both the strengths and the weaknesses of the CNP's focus on the evangelical vote. James Dobson personally campaigned for five Republican senators and drafted letters of support for many more. The Republicans took the Senate, with a net gain of four of James Dobson's candidates. CNP member Ralph Reed undertook the organization of evangelical activists on a national basis, collecting thousands of fundamentalist church directories across the country and submitting them to the Bush-Cheney campaign (over the objections of many pastors). Their listings were fed into phone banks and registration drives.[70] The campaign sent the names of unregistered evangelicals back to their local volunteers, who would contact them and encourage them to register. A Bush campaign director estimated that this campaign yielded new voters "in the range of millions."[71]

Then there was the question of money. As mentioned, in the six years leading up to the 2004 elections, Salem Communications and its executives contributed $423,000 to federal candidates, 96 percent of it to Republicans, making it the sixth-largest donor in the industry.[72] Other CNP partners and 501(c) "action" organizations followed suit—to say nothing of the donor networks.

According to Gilgoff, "Evangelicals had constituted the same portion of the electorate as in 2000, about 25 percent, but had turned out in higher numbers than in any presidential election for which statistics are available. White evangelicals supplied two of every five Bush votes . . . media created a new demographic category to describe them—values voters.[73]

But it was also clear that as the evangelical population aged and declined, public opinion on their hot-button issues was turning against them. The handwriting was on the wall.

The 2006 midterms emphasized that point. The Republicans were battered by Bush's war in Iraq, which had been propelled by claims of weapons of mass destruction that never materialized. A series of scandals led to the resignation of four Republican congressmen, including House Speaker Tom DeLay. Three more tainted Republican representatives lost their bids for reelection. Democrats gained control of both houses of Congress and won a majority of the governorships.[74]

The CNP and its partners geared up for a fight in 2008. The National Rifle Association, led by CNP member Wayne LaPierre, was set to spend

$40 million, $15 million of it opposing Obama.[75] Tony Perkins's Watchmen on the Wall were energized. In Oklahoma, Southern Baptist pastor and CNP member Paul Blair took action through his organization, Reclaiming Oklahoma for Christ. Blair, a former lineman for Oklahoma State and the Chicago Bears, hosted a "Rally for Sally" Kern, a state legislator who made headlines declaring that homosexuality "is the biggest threat our nation has, even more so than terrorism or Islam."[76]

CNP members invested heavily in Proposition 8, California's campaign to ban same-sex marriage. These included John Templeton Jr. ($900,000), the American Family Association ($500,000), and CNP dowager Elsa Prince Broekhuizen, mother of Betsy DeVos and Erik Prince ($450,000).[77]

The money didn't dispel some looming problems. The Council for National Policy had an uneasy relationship with maverick Republican John McCain, who refused the endorsements of CNP televangelists Pat Robertson and Jerry Falwell, calling them "agents of intolerance" who exerted an "evil influence" over the Republican Party.[78] But the influence remained. According to journalist Max Blumenthal, the members of the CNP were the "hidden hand" behind McCain's choice of running mate, having withheld their support—and their fundamentalist base—until he accepted their candidate, fundamentalist Sarah Palin, over his first choice of moderate Joe Lieberman, a decision he later regretted.[79]

If the results of the 2006 elections were a setback to the coalition, 2008 was a nightmare. Barack Obama won the election by a large margin, sweeping the swing states of Florida, North Carolina, and Indiana.[80] The tides were in his favor: Pew Research Center found that 53 percent of the electorate identified as Democrats or leaned Democratic, compared to 36 percent Republican. The wedge was widened by the growing populations of minority voters who supported the Democrats, bolstered by support from educated white female voters.[81] The Democrats gained seats in the Senate and the House, securing control of both chambers. They also held thirty-two governorships (in twenty-nine states plus three territories) and both houses of the legislatures in twenty-seven states.

Barack Obama received most of the credit. A young multiracial community organizer—the face of new America—he appealed to traditional Democrats and inspired special passion among African Americans and youth. For years the strategists of the radical right had counted on older, less-educated white Protestants turning out to vote. Now Obama's campaign showed that, given the right encouragement, young people and minorities could be coaxed to the polls too.

Obama's liberal record on social issues alarmed the fundamentalists, and he represented an additional threat to the Koch brothers and their counterparts in the extractive industries. His platform included a pledge to reenergize U.S. environmental policies and tackle the challenges of climate change, especially greenhouse gases.[82] Controls aimed to protect clean air and water would add to their overhead, and cleaning up their toxic waste would add to their costs. Adding to their anxiety was the wild volatility of the oil market. In June 2008 oil was selling for over $160 a barrel. Six months later, the global financial crisis had knocked it down to just over $50.[83] These developments threatened not just the petroleum industry but also the state governments that depended on its tax revenues and, by extension, the entire regional economy.

Obama's victory challenged the fundamentalists' electoral strategy, and they were obliged to assess their weaknesses. Once again, they had to regroup.

It was the end of an era, further marked by Paul Weyrich's passing. In 1996 he'd taken a fall on black ice, broke his spine, and was confined to a wheelchair.[84] Weyrich, once blond and rosy-cheeked, grew gaunt and grim; life and loss turned the puckish cherub to a vengeful prophet.

But he was still in the action. In 1983 Weyrich had founded a weekly, by-invitation-only lunch near Capitol Hill. The lunches served as interim meetings for CNP activists to discuss their efforts to lobby for their causes and to purge moderate congressional Republicans, with the lobbying arms of the Family Research Council and the American Family Association as important sponsors.[85] The grand old man of the CNP spent his twilight years traveling to Moscow, building new alliances between his conservative constituency and the ruling class of the New Russia.[86]

The month after the 2008 election, Weyrich died at the age of sixty-six.[87] His lunches were taken over by the Leadership Institute's Morton Blackwell and Colin Hanna, both members of the CNP's board of governors. They convened the sessions in an evangelical coffee shop called Ebenezers, a convenient five-minute walk from the Heritage Foundation and Hillsdale College's Kirby Center. According to investigative reporter Lee Fang, "During the first two years of the Obama administration, Representative Mike Pence, then the third most powerful Republican in the House, promised to attend every single meeting of the lunch to update the members about the activity in the GOP caucus, legislative fights, and what to expect that week."[88]

The political crisis had a silver lining for the coalition: wealthy conservatives were complacent no more. Every sector of the coalition responded in character, according to its strengths. Money poured into the Kochs' Seminar Network, more than quadrupling its income from 2008 to 2012.[89] The budget for Americans for Prosperity leapt from $2 million in 2004 to $15.2 million in 2008, and again to $40 million in 2012.[90] The money came in handy: with the loss of Congress in 2006 and the White House in 2008, a lot of Republican staffers needed jobs, and the Koch network could provide them.

The Council for National Policy turned to organizing. Two days after the election, L. Brent Bozell III, head of the Media Research Center and a member of the CNP's board of governors, rallied a band of conservatives to his country house in the Shenandoah Valley to plan a counterattack. The CNP members included Morton Blackwell, Tony Perkins, Richard Viguerie, Grover Norquist, and Leonard Leo of the Federalist Society, as well as pollster Kellyanne Conway.[91]

Perhaps, they decided, the CNP had been too secretive. Soon after the 2008 debacle, the CNP's Ed Meese and Conway founded a spin-off called the Conservative Action Project to mobilize CNP members and provide a public platform to oppose Obama policies. Meese was its first president, and other leading members included the CNP's Tony Perkins and Gary Bauer. The Conservative Action Project didn't trumpet its connections to the CNP, but they weren't hard to find; its email address included @cfnpaction.org, and the CNP's URL was cfnp.org. The project prepared to fire off memos attacking policy initiatives from the Obama administration. The Family Research Council expanded the reach of the Weyrich lunches by adding a Wednesday-morning Conservative Action Project breakfast in its Washington office.[92]

The rout also brought new life to the Tea Party. It had formerly consisted of sputtering, semicoherent eruptions of local protests, encouraged by CNP member Dick Armey and nurtured with modest grants from the Koch brothers. Now the movement took off, supposedly sparked by a February 2009 rant by CNBC reporter Rick Santelli against Obama's mortgage bailout plan.[93] March 2009 marked the emergence of a new spin-off called the Tea Party Patriots, initially organized by Dick Armey's FreedomWorks and headed by Jenny Beth Martin, a columnist for the conservative *Washington Times* and future member of the CNP executive committee.[94] "Before long," investigative reporter Lee Fang wrote in his book *The Machine*, "Americans for Prosperity, the group David Koch serves as chairman, became the premier Tea Party organization, hosting the largest rallies, employing the greatest number of organizers, and generating lots of media buzz. The ability of the Koch brothers to quickly build a national anti-Obama movement came as the result of thirty years of infrastructure building."[95]

The reinvigorated Tea Party lowered the standards of American political discourse. Protests erupted across the country over the spring of 2009, unleashing a cult of invective and incivility. When Democrats returned to their home districts for the summer recess to promote the Obama health care plan, Tea Partiers invaded their town halls and shouted down the legislators, bringing the proceedings to a halt. Their disruptions led to fistfights, arrests, and even hospitalizations.[96] The protests were largely organized through Facebook and Twitter and amplified by Fox News and other right-wing outlets.

In September 2010, BBC correspondent Katie Connolly reported that the Tea Party was "decentralised—not so much an organisation as a network of small groups with a loose affiliation to similar fiscal principles." She noted that the protesters tended to be "overwhelmingly white and older than 45, and more likely to be male." They had little use for Republicans who reached across the aisle. "What use is a Republican to us, if all they do is vote with Democrats?" Tea Party activist Christina Botteri told Connolly.[97]

The Council for National Policy noted the Tea Party's wildfire growth, but feared it lacked fundamentalist principles. But the movement was brought into the CNP orbit, thanks to the extraordinary efforts of three CNP members who had been working together for years: Ralph Reed, Tim Phillips, and Grover Norquist. Reed and Norquist were longtime friends who both got their start with the College Republican National Committee. Reed and Phillips had cofounded the consulting firm Century Strategies in 1997.

Mother Jones reported that in March 2010, Norquist, president of Americans for Tax Reform, vouched for the Tea Party movement at the CNP's meeting. The following September, the CNP's Ralph Reed organized a gathering to introduce a new voter registration drive, including a panel with CNP executive director Bob Reccord and Jenny Beth Martin from the Tea Party Patriots.

Tarnished by his connection to the Abramoff scandals in 2006, Reed had reinvented himself with a new organization called the Faith & Freedom Coalition. This group could harness his organizational skills to the muscle of the fundamentalist movement and the energy of the Tea Party.[98] Reed told reporter Sarah Posner that there was "synergy" between his new group and the Family Research Council's Voters Values groups, and featured FRC's Tony Perkins and Ken Blackwell as speakers on the program. He added that FFC "brings something to the table" in the form of get-out-the-vote techniques and new proprietary software called Voter Trak.[99]

"In 2010 and 2012," Reed declared, "FFC will register an estimated one million new faith-based voters and make tens of millions of voter contacts in what may be the largest conservative get-out-the-vote effort in modern political history."[100] Voter Trak introduced many of the characteristics that would be advanced by CNP partner organizations in the future.

It was all in the family. The Tea Party Patriots had begun to receive major support from the Kochs' Americans for Prosperity, headed by Tim Phillips, Reed's old business partner and fellow CNP member. That same September Phillips introduced the Kochs' digital strategy at the Seminar Network.

In October 2010 the Tea Party Patriots leaders attended a CNP meeting in Orange County and delivered a shopping list in the form of a memo. (It was leaked by Mark Williams, a Tea Party Express chairman who had recently been purged for a racist blog post.[101])

The Tea Party Patriots wanted CNP money—in large quantities. Lee Fang recorded the list:

> To fund the Tea Party Patriots' "traditional" get-out-the-vote walk and phone lists, they asked for $150,000, as well as $250,000 for "GPS-enabled smart-phone walk lists and technology," $125,000 for help setting up house parties, and finally $250,000 for "collateral material" . . . For efforts after the election, the memo demanded $110,000 for help protesting possible legislation during the lame-duck session of Congress, $175,000 for a summit to entertain newly elected Tea Party politicians, $300,000 for "Younger Generation Outreach," at least $500,000 for a renewed advertising budget, $200,000 for help organizing tax-day Tea Parties in 2011, and a litany of other high-priced requests.[102]

The Tea Party Patriots also wanted money for polling to test which of their efforts were most effective. They suggested they'd need a cool $100 million over the next forty years to achieve their goals.

It's not clear whether CNP members bankrolled the shopping list in 2010.[103] But the visible connections between the CNP and the Tea Party organizations multiplied. Lee Fang reported, "The Weyrich Lunch and its affiliated meetings and groups provided a nexus for right-wing front groups organizing the Tea Parties to collaborate with other conservative group and corporate fronts."[104] Reed's new Faith & Freedom Coalition expanded rapidly. Its Washington summit became an annual affair and it retained Richard Viguerie's American Target Advertising to promote its efforts.[105]

On election night in 2010, CNP elder statesmen Richard Viguerie and Morton Blackwell hosted a victory party for 350 "conservatives" and Tea Party activists at Blackwell's Leadership Institute in Arlington, Virginia, billed as a "one-stop conservative central." It doubled as a CNP celebration. Although the CNP wasn't mentioned on the press release, nine of the ten "conservative leaders" listed as available for interviews were CNP members as of 2014, including Tony Perkins, Kellyanne Conway, the Koch brothers' Tim Phillips, and Tea Party Patriots president Jenny Beth Martin.[106]

Richard Viguerie was delighted. From the beginning, the godfather of the CNP had argued that his movement had created a "two-legged stool" through combining national defense conservatives and economic conservatives. It might be able to win some elections, but it didn't constitute a stable coalition. Reagan added the third leg with the social conservatives who formed the core of the Council for National Policy. "In 2009 a fourth leg was added to the Reagan coalition," Viguerie wrote, "the limited-government constitutional conservatives of the Tea Party."[107]

The Tea Party joined the funding merry-go-round. In 2012 the Koch brothers' FreedomWorks poured $800,000 into the coffers of the Tea Party Patriots and the Tea Party Express. That same year the Richard and Helen DeVos Foundation donated $50,000 to the FreedomWorks Foundation and $2 million to Donors Trust.[108] Jenny Beth Martin reaped the benefits of their largesse. When she came to the Tea Party movement in 2009, she was facing bankruptcy and had taken to cleaning houses to make ends meet. Three years later she was set to earn over $450,000 through her Tea Party salary and consulting fees.[109]

The Tea Party funding was part of the growing collaboration between the Koch and CNP donor networks. In 2011 the Richard and Helen DeVos Foundation made a massive $3 million grant to the Americans for Prosperity Foundation—the largest grant to the Koch group recorded for the year.[110]

Charles Koch returned the favor. Between 2010 and 2012, he donated a total of $100,000 to the Council for National Policy through the Claude R. Lambe Charitable Foundation (which closed in 2013).[111]

In 2005 a major new player appeared on the scene. The Mercer Family Foundation, founded by hedge fund mogul Robert Mercer and his daughter Rebekah, gave the CNP $50,000 a year between 2009 and 2012. The foundation also gave seven-figure grants to Brent Bozell's Media Research Center.[112]

The Council for National Policy's fundamentalist members went back to their roots. In 1979 preacher James Robison had convened a secret meeting in Dallas to organize opposition to Jimmy Carter—leading to the alliance with Ronald Reagan.[113] In November 2009, Robison hosted an introduction to Ralph Reed's Faith & Freedom Coalition.

On September 8 and 9 of 2010, Robison convened a group that could help put Reed's plan into action, this time to defeat Barack Obama. The *Ethics Daily* reported that about forty fundamentalist leaders gathered near the Dallas airport to seek a "new Ronald Reagan." The Council for National Policy was well represented at the meeting; the CNP members included Paige Patterson, cofounder of the Southern Baptists' Conservative Resurgence; Southern Baptist leader Richard Land; Washington pastor Harry Jackson; and the Family Research Council's Tony Perkins. The CNP's executive director, Bob Reccord, was present, as well as Bob McEwen, who would hold that position in the future.

They were joined by megachurch pastors who could influence legions of potential voters. One was Craig Groeschel, who had founded Life. Church in an Oklahoma garage in 1996. It expanded to a network of thirty-two churches and claimed a combined weekly attendance of about one hundred thousand, connected by satellite to share Groeschel's sermons and tech-savvy fund-raising operations.[114] Another attendee was Tom Mullins, founding pastor of Christ Fellowship, a multisite church based in Palm Beach, Florida, with nearly thirty thousand members. Johnnie Moore represented Jerry Falwell's Liberty University. Moore was well on his way to becoming the movement's leading marketing and public relations expert.[115]

The meeting prepared the fundamentalists' firepower for future presidential elections. Robison listed his criteria for candidates: pro-life, pro-Israel, against same-sex marriage, for smaller government and reducing government spending, for a strong defense to fight "Radical Islam," for the free market, and against "excessive, foolish taxation."[116]

Robison's group would serve as the core of a fundamentalist "brain trust" for the GOP in the period to come. The pastors favored coreligionists such as Mike Huckabee and Texas governor Rick Perry, but they were prepared to support any Republican candidate who met their criteria and supported their agenda.[117] After all, Ronald Reagan was a worldly, divorced former Democrat who drank Orange Blossom Specials and puffed away in cigarette ads. ("I'm sending Chesterfields to all my friends. That's the merriest Christmas any smoker can have."[118]) There was clearly room for sinners.

* * *

AS THE FUNDAMENTALISTS planned their assault, the demolition of the traditional news industry continued apace—especially between the coasts. The revenues for the Associated Press peaked in 2008, and plummeted 65 percent the following year.[119] The AP constituted a critical circulatory system for American journalism. The cooperative was traditionally financed by member newspapers, broadcasters, and other news outlets, whose members contributed funds to support reporting, including breaking news, investigative journalism, and foreign correspondence beyond the means of their individual resources. The local members gave the AP an ear to the ground in their locales. As communities lost their local papers, the AP lost their revenues as well as their local reporting.[120]

As a result, national news tilted further toward urban coastal areas, in both coverage and audience. Conservative broadcasters, including Fox News, Sinclair stations, and fundamentalist radio and television outlets, took advantage of the trend, claiming a growing share of the local audiences.[121] Flyover country became ever less visible to the coastal elites, ever more influenced by conservative outlets, and ever more resentful of elite news organizations.

The loss of local newspapers had deeper consequences. Just as hometown journalists were disappearing from city hall, statehouse reporters were disappearing from state capitols. These were the professionals who were supposed to assess state governance, reveal corrupt practices, and explain how tax dollars were being spent. "By 2009," *Governing* magazine reported, "nearly one in four full-time newspaper reporter positions in the country's statehouses had been eliminated," and their numbers continued to drop.[122]

The Koch brothers had a plan for this too. In 2009 the Kochs' Donors Trust and Donors Capital Fund provided startup funding for the Franklin Center for Government and Public Integrity—its name oddly reminiscent of the prestigious investigative journalism organization the Center for Public Integrity.[123]

The Franklin Center formed a network of information services based in the State Policy Network think tanks. The State Policy Network's president, Tracie Sharp, was a member of the CNP as of 2014. These outlets placed personnel in statehouses to issue reports in support of the coalition's platform. The Conservative Transparency database reports that between 2009 and 2014 the Franklin Center received over $34 million in grants to funnel to its statehouse partners, 95 percent of it from the Kochs' Donors Trust.[124] By the end of its second year, it had established bureaus in forty-one out of fifty states, and its Watchdog.org websites operated in over twenty states.[125]

The Franklin Center's website stated its activist goals: "We change the prevailing narrative, and lay the foundation for long-term change."[126] In 2012 the *Daily Signal* (whose cofounder Tucker Carlson was on the Franklin Center board) reported the launch of the Franklin Center's new Breitbart Awards (cosponsored with the Heritage Foundation), presented at its "Future of Journalism Summit." As the Franklin Center vice president explained, "Breitbart set an example of what any individual can do, and showed people that you don't need to go to journalism school or be a professional to make a big impact."[127]

A 2013 study from the Pew Research Center found that within the expanding universe of nonprofit news sites, "The most consistently ideological content appeared in the two formally organized families of sites—the American Independent News Network sites, which had a liberal tone to their coverage, and the Watchdog.org operations, whose content carried a conservative tone."[128]

Franklin Center funding declined sharply after 2015, and a number of its outlets closed.[129] But a decade after its founding, it was still active. As of 2019, its online platform, Center Square, listed twelve "state pages," many of them—including Wisconsin, Michigan, Pennsylvania, Ohio, and Florida—in critical swing states.

The Franklin Center maintains state-level "projects," such as Oklahoma's CapitolBeatOK. CapitolBeatOK offered enthusiastic coverage of Oklahoma state attorney general Scott Pruitt's ongoing lawsuits against the Environmental Protection Agency. These included his campaign against the EPA's attempt to enforce the Clean Air Act by limiting emissions of sulfur dioxide, a toxic substance that contributes to asthma, acute bronchitis, and emphysema, especially among children and the elderly. According to CapitolBeatOK, the EPA was merely applying "an aesthetic visibility standard," citing frustrated "advocates of energy independence." One of them, as it happened, was the director of the Koch brothers' Americans for Prosperity–Oklahoma.[130]

The decimation of traditional news outlets in Middle America left a vacuum that CNP- and Koch-funded outlets were eager to fill. But this was only half the story. The other half lay in the manipulation of massive data collections and their deployment on digital platforms. The CNP, along with the Koch brothers, would have a hand in that too.

CHAPTER 10

DATA WARS

The Koch brothers and their fundamentalist partners had launched impressive campaigns, expanding their use of traditional tools, including phone banks, bus tours, and direct mail. But a digital revolution loomed on the horizon, approaching at dizzying speed.

By 2002 the Democrats and the Republicans had launched the opening salvos of a digital arms race. The initial weapon consisted of information to predict and influence voter behavior. The Democratic National Committee called their database Demzilla; the Republican National Committee called theirs the Voter Vault.[1]

The dangers were obvious from the start. "Think about the possibilities for abuse, for manipulation," warned Beth Givens, director of the Privacy Rights Clearinghouse, in 2003. "Democracy suffers when you tailor your message twelve different ways depending on who you want to reach out to. The data that can be purchased is mind-boggling."[2]

Both parties set out to segment and target voters. The RNC's Voter Vault (later renamed the GOP Data Center) collected data on everything from fishing licenses to property records.[3] Demzilla took a similar approach, but Brian Reich, a former Democratic operative, wrote an article on the Personal Democracy Forum website complaining that Demzilla didn't provide useful information to grassroots organizers and canvassers, or allow them to feed updated and corrected data into the system, while the Democratic National Committee often lacked access to data gathered on a state level.[4]

But the digital revolution waited for no one. Facebook debuted in 2004, Twitter in 2006, iPhones the following year. These innovations further upended the American way of life, including the business of politics.

Veteran Democratic operative Harold Ickes decided to address his party's deficit. In 2006 Ickes, the ginger-haired son of a legendary New Deal cabinet member, raised more than $11 million in venture capital, including backing from the Democracy Alliance, $1 million of which was from George Soros. Ickes used the money to launch a for-profit startup called Catalist, briefly named the Data Warehouse.[5] (It was said that Democrats found it easier to recruit young technologists than the Republicans.[6]) Equipped with a crack team, Catalist built the largest and most advanced political database to date.[7] It pioneered the use of data for micro-targeting political campaigns, compiling information about voters to inform phone banks and craft messages to appeal to individual voters. The project mined voter registration files and business databases to identify likely Democratic voters, then sold the information to Democratic campaigns and partner organizations. Ickes and his investors stood to make money from the enterprise, though they cautioned that they didn't expect to turn a profit until 2010.[8]

However, they had an additional reason for making the company private. The Federal Election Commission had fined at least two other organizations for conducting campaign activities without registering as political action committees, or PACs.[9] Catalist's private status meant it was not required to reveal its investors or the amount of their investments—an example of the Democrats' version of dark money.[10]

Catalist's 2008 customer base included some ninety organizations that traditionally supported Democrats. The NAACP, founded in 1909, was one of the oldest. NARAL Pro-Choice America, dating from 1969, lobbied at a state level for abortion rights, and Emily's List, founded in 1985, raised money for pro-choice female Democratic candidates. Environmentalists were represented by the Sierra Club (1892) and Clean Water Action (1972).

MoveOn.org was one of the few relative newcomers, founded in 1998 in response to the attempt to impeach Bill Clinton. MoveOn was also noteworthy for its roots in the tech community.[11]

Catalist sold its data to Democratic candidates, but it operated outside the control of the DNC. This led the Democratic National Committee to commission a company called Voter Activation Network to create its own internal database platform, VoteBuilder, in 2006.[12] (VAN merged with NGP Software to become NGP VAN in 2011.[13])

Critics feared that Catalist's external operation would compete with the DNC's, offering candidates and organizers a way to circumvent cumbersome party machinery. Rather than uniting the party, Catalist's approach could foster costly competition. Ickes was a longtime Clinton ally, but Catalist sold data to the competing Barack Obama campaign as well.[14] Once Obama won the primaries, Catalist clients used its data to orient phone bank callers and door-to-door canvassers, drawing from information on some 230 million Americans and tailoring messages to speak to their personal issues. Labor unions provided much of the manpower to translate data into votes with phone banks and canvassing.[15]

VAN and Catalist software could be integrated, and the two organizations made their products available for purchase to any candidate or cause that had the support of a progressive or Democratic organization, whether state-level party, union, or political action committee.[16] Catalist offered the additional benefit of allowing canvassers to feed contact history back into the database.

The Republicans were falling behind, as symbolized by their candidate. In July 2008 the *London Telegraph* ran a profile titled "John McCain 'Technology Illiterate' Doesn't Email or Use Internet," quoting him as saying that "he prefers to conduct his communications by phone." The Republican candidate reported that he relied on his aides to pull up the few websites he scanned. "I don't expect to be a great communicator," he stated.[17]

Barack Obama, on the other hand, was a modern communicator from the start. His campaign seized the new tools of social media and deployed them with panache. "Like a lot of Web innovators, the Obama campaign did not invent anything completely new," observed David Carr in the *New*

York Times. "Instead, by bolting together social networking applications under the banner of a movement, they created an unforeseen force to raise money, organize locally, fight smear campaigns and get out the vote that helped them topple the Clinton machine and then John McCain and the Republicans."[18]

After the Democrats swept the 2008 elections, the *Atlantic* published a report called "How Democrats Won the Data War in 2008," identifying Catalist as a major factor. "Registered voters contacted by Catalist member groups turned out at a rate of 74.6%; the voters who weren't turned out in proportions roughly equivalent to the national average—about 60.4%." The new votes were especially critical in four battleground states: Ohio, Florida, Indiana, and North Carolina.[19]

Obama's victory contributed to the Democrats' sense of euphoria: surely their growing demographic advantage, plus their ingenious grasp of technology, would guarantee their hold into the future. But the very nature of their victory suggested future obstacles. Obama shortchanged the DNC and state party organizations, playing to the media and entertainment cultures on the coasts. His powerful campaign organization promoted the candidate himself rather than the Democratic Party.[20]

In 2009 the Koch brothers launched their response. It began with a funding mechanism: a secretive new entity called the TC4 Trust. The following year TC4 funneled $2.5 million in seed money to the Themis Trust, a new Koch-controlled voter database.[21] Named after a Greek deity who imposed divine law on human affairs, the Themis Trust was even murkier than the Kochs' previous dark money outlets. It operated in strict secrecy; the Koch brothers did not appear on its regulatory filing, and reporters' inquiries went unanswered.[22] Its single trustee was Paul W. Brooks, who appeared on the roster of the Council for National Policy as chairman of the Institute for Faith, Work and Economics. (Paul W. Brooks was also the name of a former vice president for Koch Industries.) The chief operating officer was Benjamin Pratt, another Koch Industries veteran.[23]

The Themis database would network the Koch organizations and CNP partner organizations, outgunning both the Democrats' Catalist and the Republican National Committee's Voter Vault. Its registration as a nonprofit

501(c)(4) allowed Themis to serve advocacy groups but not political candidates. Themis contracted the services of a voter data-mining company called i360.[24]

The annals of digital media are littered with projects that failed not because of flawed technology but from the lack of a user base to implement it. The Council for National Policy brought ready-made "communities" to the table, preassembled into a network of organizations and informed by its broadcasting empire. The target audiences were heavily concentrated in sparsely populated states between the coasts. This demographic presented a disadvantage for winning the popular vote in national elections, but a strong advantage in the Senate, where Wyoming's population of under six hundred thousand enjoyed the same representation as California's forty million.

There was more untapped potential in the Electoral College. For years, conventional wisdom held that the arithmetic of the Electoral College favored the Democrats. In 2014 Matt Mayer, a conservative Republican strategist, challenged this notion. His analysis of the elections leading up to 2012 showed that the Democrats "almost always win" eighteen key states plus the District of Columbia. Mayer's key states included Michigan, Wisconsin, and Pennsylvania, which were increasingly contested. The Republicans, Mayer argued, could be confident of winning twenty states between the coasts, plus Alaska. The key to tipping the balance in the Republicans' favor lay in winning northern industrial states, and Mayer believed they lay within reach.[25]

This strategy came to be known as the "Northern Path," and the question was whether the Democrats might be foolish enough to take these states for granted.

The Kochs and the CNP coalition turned to their strengths: the ability to develop a long-term strategy; a massive funding base; and enduring associations such as the NRA and churches. The business moguls understood how to build an integrated corporate structure; their marketing experts knew how to create a new consumer base from existing social relationships. The challenge was to connect the real-world communities to the digital platforms.

Some technologists thought these questions could be answered by their machines, but others turned to an influential 1973 treatise by Stanford sociology professor Mark Granovetter. "The Strength of Weak Ties" described how human connections functioned at different tiers. "Strong ties" involved close relations, such as family, friends, and colleagues, but "weak ties" to acquaintances and members of larger associations could also be influential in networking and decision-making.[26] Placed in a political context, the theory suggested that people may be more likely to respond to digital prompts to act—or vote—in concert when they are combined with sustained interactions with members of their social circles.

While the Democrats emphasized "pushing" their messages out to the public through advanced use of social media, the Koch brothers and the CNP partners concentrated on addressing existing networks and communities in a double-edged campaign. The first item of business, aimed squarely at the electoral college targets of Wisconsin and Michigan, was eroding the Democratic trade unions, state by state.

The CNP had advanced their cause with the election of Scott Walker, son of a Baptist minister, as governor of Wisconsin in 2010.[27] Walker turned Wisconsin into a flashpoint by proposing legislation that would cripple public sector unions by limiting collective bargaining. Democrats responded by demanding his recall.[28] Walker raised $30.5 million for his campaign, two-thirds of it from out-of-state donors. The CNP's Richard DeVos gave a quarter of a million to his campaign.

The CNP's Foster Friess gave Walker over $100,000 to fight off the recall attempt.[29] Other Walker donors included the Wisconsin Family Council (an affiliate of James Dobson's Focus on the Family) and the American Federation for Children, chaired by Betsy DeVos.[30] The Koch brothers' Americans for Prosperity contributed to television ads.[31]

When he was running for office in 2007, Barack Obama had declared, "Understand this: If American workers are being denied their right to organize while I'm in the White House, I'll put on a comfortable pair of walking shoes and I'll walk on that picket line with you as President of the United States."[32] Instead, Wisconsin Democrats, fighting for the life of their party, were stunned when Obama declined to show up, despite the frequent trips he had made to the state on his own behalf in 2009 and 2010.

Political scientist Peter Dreier wrote, "Had Obama gone to Wisconsin and campaigned for Democrats, or even made a few public statements endorsing the Democrats seeking to unseat six of Walker's right-wing

Senate allies, the liberal Democrats might have turned a narrow defeat into a spectacular unprecedented victory."[33] Instead, Walker won the recall election and crushed the union. Wisconsin slid from blue to purple. Crippling the public employees' unions translated into a blow for the Democrats as well as their union allies.

As the Democrats' allies struggled, many of their opponents were thriving. Some, including fundamentalist churches and the NRA, had deep and ample roots. Others were new organizations, such as the Tea Party Patriots: spawned, bankrolled, and networked for the occasion. The coalition leveraged these organizations by constructing a complex digital operation that linked data to apps to voters. While the Democrats were bedazzled by Obama's charisma and shiny new technologies, the coalition fell back on a deep knowledge of its target audience and its user behavior, combining it with polling and messaging in targeted districts.

Their digital strategy was fully integrated into their own dedicated media sphere of broadcast and online platforms—an option that wasn't available to the Democrats. The radical right could stream its messaging through CBN, TBN, Salem Communications, Bott Radio, American Family Radio, and hundreds of other outlets. The liberal response was feeble: liberal Air America, an internet radio service launched in 2004, lasted only a few years before it went bankrupt and was dissolved in 2010.[34] Although Air America and left-leaning news outlets such as MSNBC often concurred with Democratic positions, there was little to suggest that they carried unidirectional messaging, networked through other data platforms and apps. (Indeed, given the divisive nature of the Democratic Party, such unified messaging hardly exists.)

The new digital strategy was unveiled by the Koch brothers at a Seminar Network gathering in Aspen in September 2010. The agenda was leaked to the press. Tim Phillips, head of the Kochs' Americans for Prosperity and a member of the CNP's board of governors, was a presenter. Other CNP members in attendance included Bill Walton (chairman of Rappahannock Ventures, LLC, and CNP vice president as of 2014), Foster Friess (former CNP president) and his son Steven, and Richard DeVos (former CNP president) and his wife Helen. Other big money people included two longtime Koch allies, Oklahoma oil moguls Larry Nichols and Harold Hamm.

A Koch spokesman introduced Themis Trust in a session called "Mobilizing Citizens for November."[35]

The new political machine was still missing some gears—specifically, to connect the data to the ground troops. Over 2010 and 2011 another new organization emerged to fill the gap. United in Purpose was funded by two Silicon Valley venture capitalists, Reid Rutherford and Ken Eldred, and registered with the IRS as a tax-exempt "non-partisan organization that actively supports Christian involvement in the civic arena."[36] Nonetheless, the group's March 2016 website stated that "United in Purpose is a 501c4 whose mission is to unite and equip like-minded conservative organizations to increase their reach, impact, and influence through the latest technology, research and marketing strategies for the purpose of bringing about a culture change in America based on Judeo-Christian principles."[37] The "non-partisan" organization was actively extending its influence to the Republican platform, and condemning any Democratic candidate who had a different perspective. (The organizers may have been responding to America Votes, a "coordination hub" organized by Democratic supporters in 2004, seeking to network unions, interest groups, and political media firms in a get-out-the-vote effort.[38])

United in Purpose hired Bill Dallas, a CNP member as of 2014, as CEO. Dallas, a California real estate entrepreneur who had served two years in San Quentin for grand theft embezzlement in the early 1990s, reported that he "found a deep relationship with God when I got in prison."[39] Dallas was fined $1.5 million; upon his release he started paying it down, parlaying his celebrity into a new business called the Church Communication Network, "a satellite and Internet communications company which served over 8,000 churches across North America" (now defunct).[40]

Church communications provided the perfect groundwork for United in Purpose. Dallas was marketing to the religious equivalent of America's sprawling shopping malls. As evangelical churches expanded into megachurches across the country, they outfitted their sanctuaries with giant video screens to project the preacher and song lyrics to the audience. Churches were replacing their choirs with praise teams and stage bands, complete with electric guitars, trap sets, and in the case of First Baptist Dallas, a full forty-piece orchestra.[41]

Entrepreneurial pastors, such as Craig Groeschel of Life.Church, took advantage of opportunities to merge church, money, and media. In 2010 *Ethics Daily* had reported that Groeschel had joined CNP members Tony Perkins, Richard Land, and Harry Jackson in a group of fundamentalist pastors in Dallas to discuss how to replace Obama with a fundamentalist-friendly president.[42] From his home pulpit in Edmond, Oklahoma, Groeschel simulcast his sermons to his affiliates and their hundred thousand weekly attendees. Church members were encouraged to download a tithing app on their phones and purchase church videos and publications on its website. The Prosperity Gospel promised a tangible reward.

At one Life.Church service, I joined the congregants watching a presentation about "Chris and Jessica," who "had a hard time tithing." But after Jessica took a screen capture of her first tithe and posted it, "Good things happened to Chris and Jessica. God put his blessings on them."[43]

Megachurch families were encouraged to visit the boutiques outside the sanctuary. At one megachurch I saw the "store" where boys could claim toy machine guns and girls could get Barbie dolls as a reward for learning their Bible verses. In-church kiosks offered one-stop shopping for the families' entire information needs, from books to magazines to videos, often leaving their homes untouched by professional news media.[44]

Bill Dallas's Church Communication Network operations offered satellite training and online materials, and taught churches how to build networks. It was interwoven with the CNP from the start. CNP stalwart James Dobson appeared in their promotional videos as one of the group's "experts in their ministry fields." Fundamentalist pollster George Barna was listed on its roster of sponsored speakers.[45] In 2010 Dallas added a book to the mix called *Lessons from San Quentin*, coauthored with Barna and promoted on the fundamentalist media circuit, including Pat Robertson's Christian Broadcasting Network.[46] In 2014 Bill Dallas addressed the Family Research Council's pastors organization, Watchmen on the Wall, citing George Barna on ways to get out the fundamentalist vote.[47] Bill Dallas was fully networked into the Council for National Policy.

Under Dallas's direction, United in Purpose linked sophisticated data-mining operations to a consortium of partner organizations, many of them run by members of the CNP.[48] It sent a mailing to the participants of a Rick

Perry prayer rally in Texas, signed by CNP member Don Wildmon of the American Family Association.[49] The group planned to dispatch a hundred thousand canvassers, called "champions," to recruit unregistered evangelical voters and secure their votes.[50] Other critical partners included the Family Research Council, the Tea Party Express, and Concerned Women for America, and Ralph Reed's new Faith & Freedom Coalition, all headed by CNP members. Barna was a key strategist.[51]

United in Purpose called its project "Champion the Vote." This was an attempt to engage five million unregistered conservative evangelical voters for 2012. For his polling, Dallas turned to Barna, who was placed in charge of a United in Purpose division called the American Faith and Culture Institute. His expertise on SAGE Cons—the demographic he had described as "spiritually active governmentally engaged conservatives"—would make him the ideal person to help target the voters who would become the movement's secret weapon.

"There are some 20 to 25 million adult SAGE Cons across the country. Two-thirds of them live in the South and Midwest," Barna wrote. "The demographic profile of SAGE Cons differs significantly from that of the rest of America's adults. These Christian conservatives have a median age around 60 and are primarily white."[52]

Barna noted that his SAGECons were anything but representative of the U.S. population. "Almost nine out of ten of them attend a Protestant church. Nearly nine out of ten are married but relatively few (23%) have a child under the age of 18 living in their home. One out of every five of them has served in the military—again, about double the national average . . . The driving force behind their faith is that nine out of ten of them (90%) have developed a biblical worldview. That compares to just 1% of the rest of U.S. adult population."[53]

This voting bloc, neglected by urban elites, was concentrated in areas that could play an outsize role in the Senate and the Electoral College. But Barna knew exactly where to look, and he made it clear that traditional news coverage was irrelevant to the political proposition:

> At this point you may be shaking your head and wondering how it was possible that you never heard about SAGE Cons during the

> election cycle even though they are a larger voting block than blacks, Hispanics, gays, college students, or any of the other small but interesting segments that the liberal media love to highlight. One reason is that the mainstream media were locked in their own polling about evangelicals.
>
> . . . A second reason for many people's ignorance of the group was that the movers and shakers in the SAGE Con world were not hiding, but they were happy to avoid wasting their time in meaningless conflicts with the mainstream media. Their task was to directly educate, motivate and activate their own constituency, and the mainstream media was not likely to aid them in that quest.
>
> The goal was not to gain exposure in the mainstream media; it was to elect conservatives to public office so that biblical principles were more likely to be reflected in public policy. Finally, the public remained blissfully unaware of SAGE Cons because the primary research uncovering the segment was performed outside the information networks that the media are comfortable using.[54]

More gears were starting to mesh. United in Purpose accessed church directories provided by pastors from Watchmen on the Wall, the Family Research Council "ministry." The Family Research Council recruited canvassers in churches to cultivate the new voting bloc.

The Koch brothers' Americans for Prosperity launched new astroturf operations of their own, targeting the 2012 election, determined to build a bigger, smarter, and better financed digital operation than anything the Democrats could produce. The Kochs announced the next phase at their June 2011 meeting at the Ritz-Carlton in Vail, Colorado.

This time, despite extensive security operations to guarantee secrecy, a recording of the proceedings was leaked to *Mother Jones* magazine. Charles Koch told his audience that the Obama administration presented a unique challenge. "We have Saddam Hussein, this is the Mother of All Wars we've got in the next 18 months. For the life and death of this country."[55] He read out the names on the "million-dollar club" of donors, among them CNP members the (Richard and Helen) DeVoses, the Friesses, and the Templetons.[56] (Friess was on the board of advisors for the $3 billion John Templeton

KMMJ was one of the first radio stations in Nebraska, founded by the Old Trusty incubator company. U.S. news outlets began as hyper-local institutions with strong engagement with the community, informed by national news services that kept the nation "on the same page."
AMERICANRADIOHISTORY.COM

OK 7
Oil Wells on State Capitol Grounds
Oklahoma City, Oklahoma
16534

Oil wells dominated the grounds of the Oklahoma state capitol for decades, just as the oil and gas industry have dominated the state's political economy.

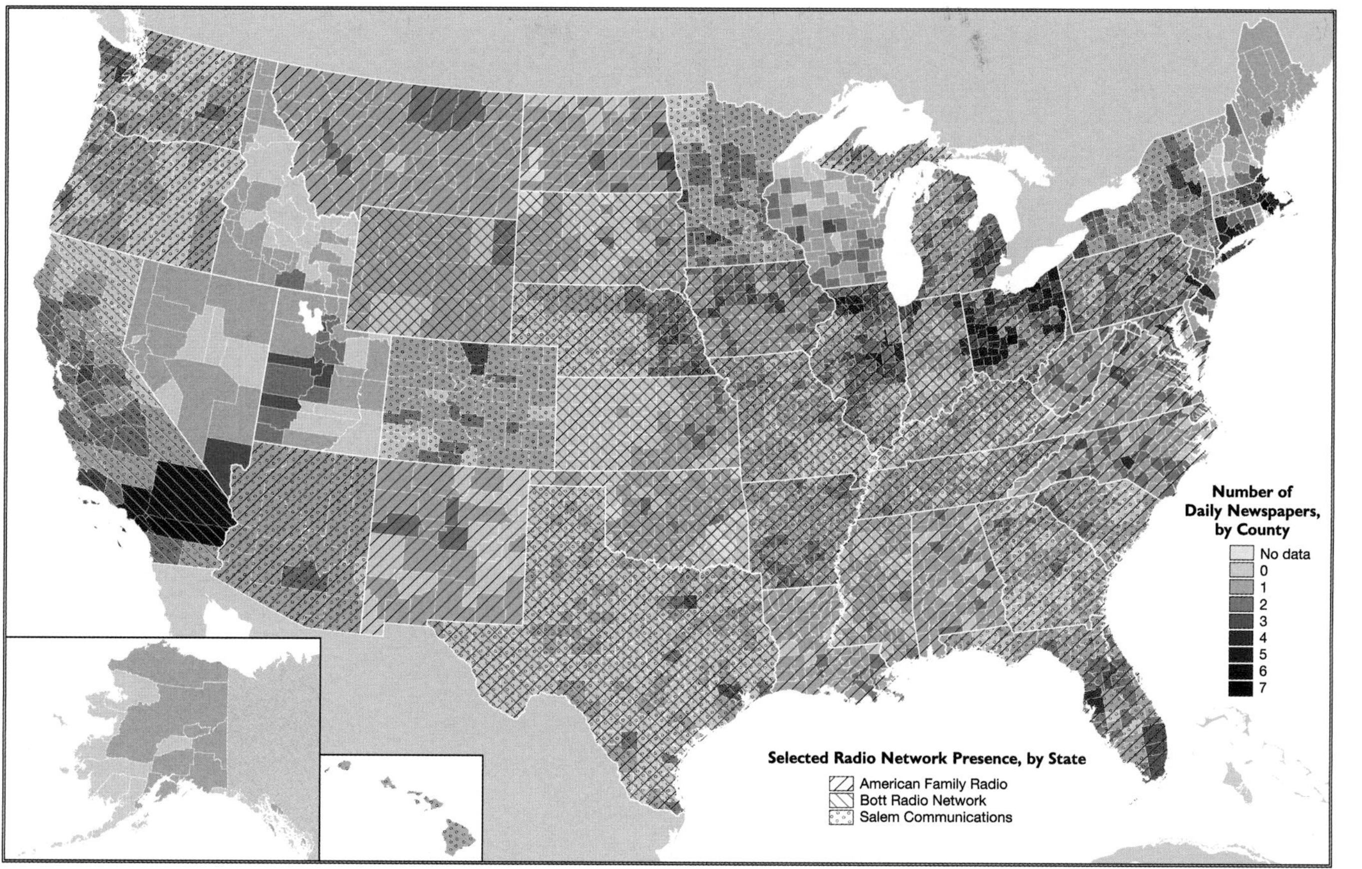

As local newspapers disappear, fundamentalist and conservative talk radio networks rush to fill the vacuum. Darker areas indicate the areas with the greatest number of local newspapers; paler areas are those with fewer or none. The lines and dots indicate states with stations owned by Salem Communications, Bott Radio Network, and American Family Radio—all run by members of the CNP. MAP BY GARY ANTONETTI

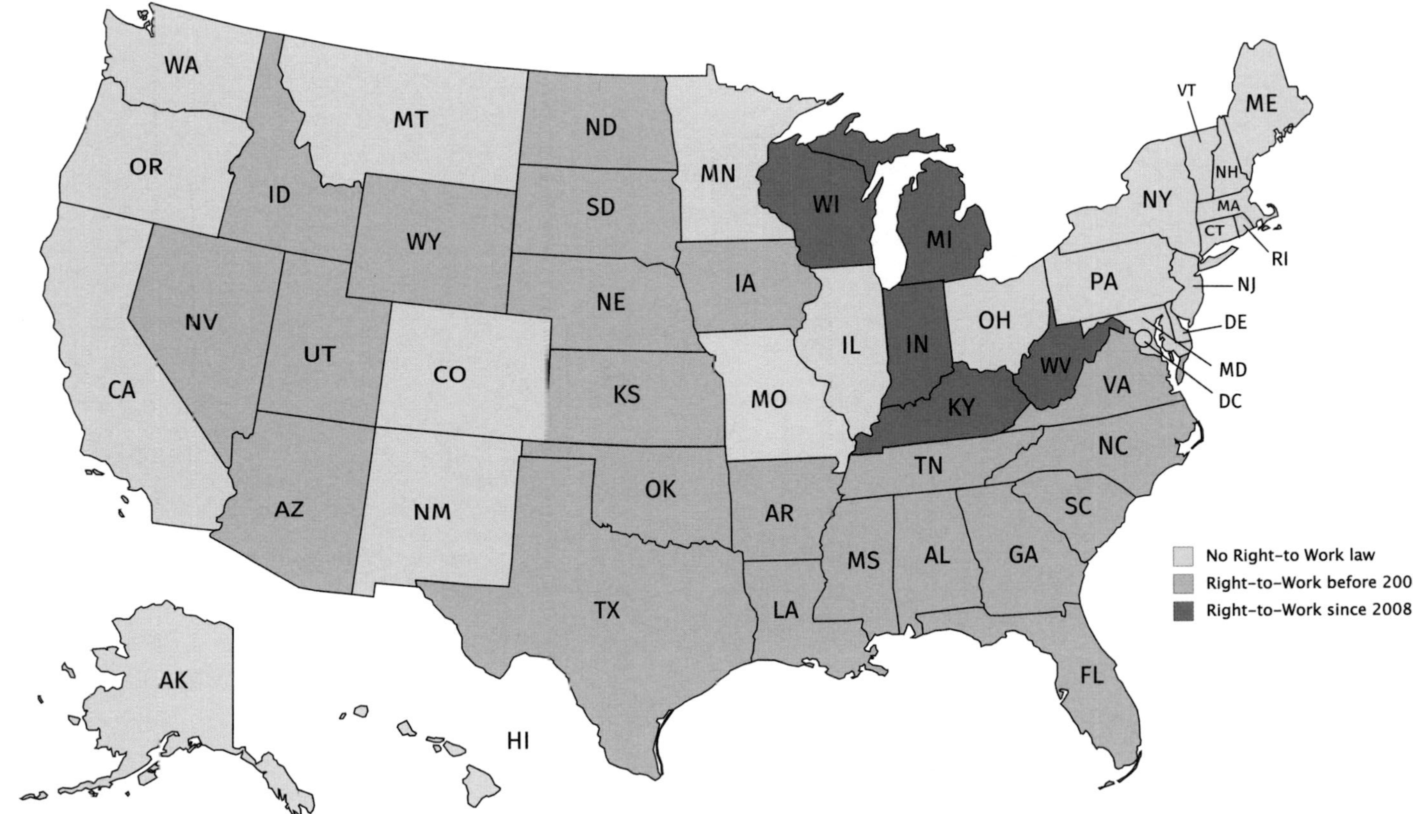

The Kochs made their billions in the oil and gas industry. The Koch brothers and the DeVos family poured millions of dollars into campaigns to pass right-to-work legislation, which has crippled labor unions and the Democratic candidates they supported, especially in crucial swing states such as Michigan and Wisconsin. Hillary Clinton won the popular vote by 3 million in 2016, but Donald Trump won the Electoral College by fewer than 80,000 votes in Wisconsin, Michigan, and Pennsylvania (states Obama won in 2008 and 2012). "RIGHT TO WORK STATES TIMELINE," NATIONAL RIGHT TO WORK COMMITTEE. CREATED WITH MAPCHARTS BY ELEANOR ZAFFT.

Okahoma-born Tony Perkins, president of the Family Research Council and the Council for National Policy, broadcasts *Washington Watch* on several radio networks promoting the fundamentalist agenda and recruiting supporters for the Leadership Academy and the Values Voter Summit.

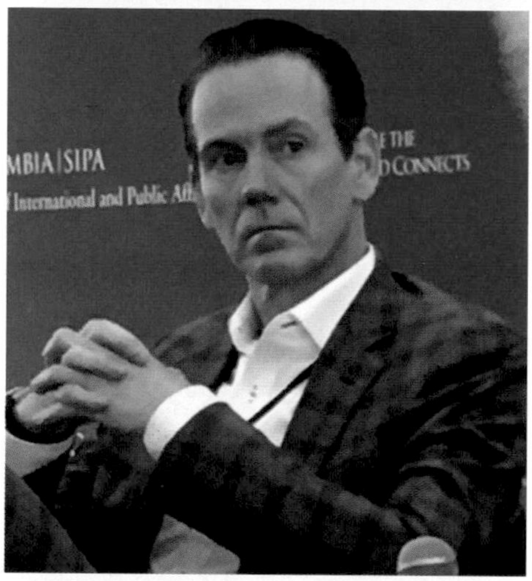

Oklahoman Chris Wilson of WPA Intelligence oversaw the innovations in apps and data deployed in the 2016 Ted Cruz campaign, in concert with the Koch-financed i360 data platform, Cambridge Analytica, and the uCampaign apps. Once Cruz lost the primaries, the Trump campaign inherited Cruz's app template.

George Barna served as a leading pollster for the fundamentalists for decades, and ran a division of United in Purpose get-out-the-vote campaign. In 2016 Barna identified 17 million unengaged evangelical voters who offered a path to Republican victory.

ALL PHOTOS BY THE AUTHOR UNLESS OTHERWISE CREDITED

FROM TOP TO BOTTOM:
Robert Jeffress, pastor of First Baptist Dallas, is a leading voice on Donald Trump's Evangelical Advisory Counsel. Jeffress called Islam and Mormonism heresies "from the pit of hell" and claimed "you can't be saved being a Jew." The U.S. Department of Defense carries his program *Pathway to Victory* on the American Forces Network.

Carter Conlon is pastor at the Times Square megachurch in Manhattan, the former Mark Hellinger Theatre. Conlon has been a featured speaker at the Family Research Council's national "ministry" for pastors, Watchmen on the Wall. According to Tony Perkins's introduction, Conlon's New York church stands "at the gates of hell."

Event

Sunday, November 04 2018

02:30 PM

Las Vegas Sunday GOTV Knock 11/4 - NRA-ILA Frontlines

Thank you, patriot, for joining us to ensure pro-gun voters make their voices heard at the polls! There is no more important work you can do this day to advance the cause of freedom than making sure our supporters realize the magnitude of this election, and we need them to turn out!

Please bring a fully charged smartphone, or if you own a tablet with a data plan, please bring that for the convenience of the larger screen. You can be extra prepared by downloading our door-knocking app, i360 Walk. W...

NRA-ILA Las Vegas Office

Event

Friday, August 31 2018

05:00 PM

Cedar Gap Baptist Church Outdoor Gala'18 - NRA-ILA Frontlines

Looking for a fun Friday night event for the whole family? Come out to Cedar Gap Baptist Church's Outdoor Gala'18 to enjoy a catfish dinner, take part in multiple outdoor attractions that include specials activities for kids, and meet your Missouri NRA-ILA team to pick up some free NRA gear and find out how you can get involved to protect your Second Amendment Rights!

The event will be hosted on Friday, August 31, 2018, from 5PM-9PM, at the Cedar Gap Baptist Church in Seymour, Missouri.

Ad...

Cedar Gap Baptist Church

The uCampaign app template has been used by various organizations in their get-out-the-vote efforts. In the 2018 screenshot on the left, the NRA-ILA app encourages Nevadans to bring their smartphones to connect to the Koch-funded i360 data platform when they canvas. In the screenshot on the right, a Southern Baptist church hosts an NRA pre-election event in Missouri.

i360 DATA DICTIONARY | CONSUMER DATA

INTEREST IN GOLF BHAV_GOLF	Indicates someone in the household is interested in golf. *Information gathered via survey, subscription or reported information.*
FREQUENT HEADACHES BHAV_HEADACHES	Indicates someone in the household has frequent headaches. *Information gathered via survey response.*
HEARING DIFFICULTY BHAV_HEARINGDIF	Indicates someone in the household has loss of hearing. *Information gathered via survey response.*
ANGINA/HEART DISEASE BHAV_HEARTDISEASE	Indicates someone in the household has angina related to heart disease. *Information gathered via survey response.*
HEAVY INTERNET USER MODEL BHAV_HEAVYINET_SCORE	A regression technique is used to predict the heaviest users of the internet, using the internet more than once a day in a typical month. The raw score is recoded into a decile value. VALUES: 1 - 10 : 1= most likely to use , 10= least likely to use
PURCHASER OF HIGH-TICKET MERCHANDISE BHAV_HITICKET	Indicates someone in the household has purchased a "high ticket" product via mail, including artifacts and antiques (average price of $100). *Information gathered via survey response.*

The Koch-funded i360 data platform gave select users a state-of-the-art guide to individual voters, based on voter registration information, consumer data, and social media activities, combining political and commercial data. Information such as cholesterol count could be surprisingly indicative of voting patterns. The technologies, networked into the activist organizations, outstripped the Democrats' capabilities.

Joined the Council for National Policy, leaders in the conservative movement, who w/ @POTUS are renewing the conservative vision in our time

1:48 PM - 19 May 2017

Vice President Mike Pence is a CNP favorite. He is a graduate of the Leadership Institute, run by Morton Blackwell, a leading figure in the CNP. Pence and Tony Perkins have been friends for more than twenty years. In May 2017, Pence tweeted this celebration of the CNP. Whether he merely "joined" the event or also joined the organization remains ambiguous.

2016 Voter Breakdown

Eligible; Unregistered
7.3%

Clinton
28.5%

Registered; Didn't Vote
33.5%

Other
3.4%

Trump
27.3%

Note: the value for Registered Voters used in these calculations does not include data for North Dakota (which does not require registration) and American Samoa (which did not fill out the EAVS).

The path to victory in recent elections has lain in mobilizing targeted blocs of Americans who are eligible to vote but failed to do so. The battle isn't over: Didn't Vote won the 2016 election, with over 40 percent of the eligible electorate (registered and unregistered). "2016 NOVEMBER GENERAL ELECTION TURNOUT RATES," UNITED STATES ELECTIONS PROJECT; "2016 ELECTION ADMINISTRATION AND VOTING SURVEY," US ELECTION ASSISTANCE COMMISSION; "PRESIDENTIAL ELECTION RESULTS," *THE NEW YORK TIMES*, AUGUST 9, 2017; "ELECTION RESULTS FOR THE U.S. PRESIDENT, THE U.S. SENATE AND THE U.S. HOUSE OF REPRESENTATIVES," FEDERAL ELECTIONS COMMISSION / CREATED WITH GOOGLE SHEETS BY ELEANOR ZAFFT / CREATIVE COMMONS WITH ATTRIBUTION

AND BY THE
WORD OF THEIR
TESTIMONY,
AND
THEY DID
NOT LOVE
THEIR
LIVES TO
THE DEATH.
REVELATION 12:11
SHE HAS
DONE
WHAT
SHE
COULD...
MARK 14:8
Paige Patterson
Dorothy Kelley Pat

ALL SCRIPTURE
IS INSPIRED
BY GOD...
- 2 TIMOTHY 3:16 -
PREACH
THE WORD...
- 2 TIMOTHY 4:2
Nancy Avery Pressler
Judge Paul Press

Paige Patterson and Paul Pressler III led the Conservative Resurgence in the Southern Baptist Convention, and went on to become leading members of the Council for National Policy. Patterson commissioned stained glass windows to honor the movement at the Southwestern Baptist Theological Seminary in Fort Worth, where he was president. The windows were removed in 2019 following a series of scandals.

Foundation, which funded many educational and scientific institutions as well as Koch projects.[57])

Charles Koch warned his audience, "The media's ninety-plus percent against us . . . It isn't just your money we need. We need your energy. We need you bringing in new partners, new people. We can't do it alone. This group can't do it alone. We have to multiply ourselves."[58] The Council for National Policy stood ready to help.

In 2011 the Kochs founded a new funding clearinghouse called Freedom Partners to replace the TC4 Trust, and staffed it with Koch Industries personnel. Freedom Partners was described as a "chamber of commerce"—specifically, "nonprofit, nonpartisan 501(c)6 chamber of commerce that promotes the benefits of free markets and a free society." It was a highly unusual representative of its category from the start. Freedom Partners, a "trade association," didn't represent any trade. It existed almost entirely as a grant-making organization, disbursing nearly $236 million over 2012. According to the Center for Responsive Politics, "Much of that money went to limited liability companies that are wholly owned by better-known nonprofits—what the IRS refers to a 'disregarded entities.'"[59]

Freedom Partners' initial 2012 tax filing acknowledged that its grants were "subject to express prohibitions or protections against the use of grant funds for electioneering purposes," and affirmed that the group did not engage in any "direct or indirect political campaign activities."[60] However, five of its ten beneficiaries spent nearly $70 million on behalf of Republican candidates in 2012, mostly in television advertising.[61]

Freedom Partners' tax status allowed it to hide its donors but required it to disclose its grants and their recipients. It recruited some two hundred members, each of whom paid at least $100,000 to participate.[62] The annual winter meetings were held in luxurious resorts in Indian Wells, California, near a home and golf course owned by Charles Koch.[63] Republican presidential hopefuls added it to their list of "beauty contests."[64] The organization created a subsidiary called Freedom Partner Shared Services, a full-service recruitment, employment, and training agency to staff employees for the extended network.[65]

The Koch empire was invisibly populating the colorless downtown of Arlington, Virginia. At the outset of the Civil War, Arlington was a northern outpost of the Confederacy; the Union seized it early in the conflict, making it a southern outpost of the North.[66] Now the Kochs made it the base of their national operations.

The Koch walk began with an entire floor of a nondescript modern office building off the main courthouse square. Good luck finding it. There was no sign on the outside and no listing on the building directory; most of the staff entered through the Gold's Gym on the ground floor or from the parking garage. The lobby guard said not even he has access to the seventh floor; that's the floor that housed Americans for Prosperity and the Grassroots Leadership Academy. The Freedom Partners Shared Services employment bureau occupied another floor in the building—with the same address as the Kochs' millennial "grassroots organization," Generation Opportunity.[67] Freedom Partners was three blocks away on Wilson Boulevard; the suite was also unmarked, unlisted, and inaccessible. The headquarters of Kochs' data platform i360 were only steps away in a building on Clarendon Avenue, made of glass and steel, yet equally opaque.

Freedom Partners and the Themis Trust worked in concert. Their activities were harder to track than other Koch dark money operations, but the *Washington Post* and the Center for Responsive Politics succeeded in documenting at least $407 million the two groups raised in advance of the 2012 elections, along with a number of the recipients.[68] Americans for Prosperity received $44 million.

Other CNP partners were also on the short list; one was EvangChr4 Trust (at over $5 million), whose sole trustee—once again—was CNP member Paul W. Brooks.[69] This organization passed $1.2 million along to CitizenLink, a lobbying arm of James Dobson's Focus on the Family—which in turn spent over $2.5 million on advertising for Republican candidates in 2012.[70]

Another CNP beneficiary was Concerned Women for America, which received $8 million from the Koch machine. (The CWA is an outlier among women's organizations. It opposed the Violence Against Women Act in 2012 on the grounds that it "creates new protections for homosexuals."[71]) Concerned Women of America was one of about a dozen CNP partners in the United in Purpose get-out-the-vote campaign. These groups could provide United in Purpose with foot soldiers to test and implement the digital platforms in development.

Foot soldiers had to be trained. Morton Blackwell's Leadership Institute became the nerve center for instruction in digital political technology. It had received funding from the Donors Trust and Donors Capital Fund for years, but after Obama's victory the two consortia stepped up their contributions. In 2012 grants arrived from the Charles G. Koch Foundation and the Claude R. Lambe Charitable Foundation as well.[72] The Leadership Institute has had its own five-story building on North Highland Street in Arlington since 1996, a fifteen-minute stroll from the Kochs' Americans for Prosperity. (The Council for National Policy had formerly occupied the adjoining building, but moved into the District of Columbia.)

In February 2012 United in Purpose, rich in manpower and flush with cash, launched a massive door-to-door get-out-the-vote campaign, drawing on its new data to reach five million of George Barna's targets: unregistered white fundamentalist conservatives.

National Public Radio reporter Barbara Bradley Hagerty followed some of the volunteers, or "champions." United in Purpose had obtained data on 180 million Americans and assigned points for characteristics ranging from homeschooling to an affinity for NASCAR. "If your score totaled over 600 points," UiP's Bill Dallas told Hagerty, "then we realized you were very serious about your faith. Then we run that person against the voter registration database . . . If they were not registered, that became one of the key people we were going to target to go after."

Hagerty traveled to several locales to observe the canvassing. A Florida canvasser told her that the Family Research Council had recruited him at his church. Reviewing the track record, Hagerty found that the data was flawed in Florida, South Carolina, and Iowa, sending canvassers on wild goose chases, but highly effective in Ohio. She concluded, "United in Purposes' experiment shows the promise and peril of having a bottomless well of data to draw upon: Accessing it is one thing—using it effectively is another thing entirely."[73]

The 2012 election, pitting Obama against Mormon Mitt Romney, sowed dissension among the Southern Baptists. Their animosity toward Mormons went back for generations, and resurfaced in 2010 with a diatribe on the Trinity Broadcasting Network by Southern Baptist pastor Robert Jeffress, who had harsh words for other faiths: "Islam is wrong, it is a heresy from the pit of Hell," he said. "Mormonism is wrong, it is a heresy from the pit of Hell. Judaism, you can't be saved being a Jew."[74]

Jeffress, the slight, white-haired pastor of the First Baptist Dallas megachurch and an influential ally of Tony Perkins, poured salt on the wound at the 2011 Values Voter Summit. There he informed reporters that Mormonism was "a cult" and that Romney was "not a Christian."[75] Romney's campaign was further undermined by other members of the coalition. The CNP's Richard Viguerie complained that Romney was an "establishment Republican" who slighted true conservative values to run a "content-free" campaign.[76]

Romney had serious competition in the eyes of the Council for National Policy. One contender was Mike Pence, a congressman from Indiana. Pence was a CNP favorite, a Leadership Institute alumnus who considered James Dobson "a friend and a mentor to me."[77] The 2010 Values Voter Summit greeted Pence with cries of "Pence for President!" In the summit straw poll, Pence narrowly triumphed over Southern Baptist pastor Mike Huckabee, with Mitt Romney running a distant third.[78]

The results were nonbinding, but Tony Perkins said they were "descriptive of the type of candidate values voters would be looking for."[79] Pence was encouraged enough to explore a presidential run, but the CNP's Ralph Reed advised him to run for governor of Indiana first. In 2012 Pence ran for governor and squeaked to victory in a three-way race. Reed commented, "If you're Mike Pence, and you believe what he believes, you know God had a plan."[80]

Reed was a man who kept his options open. At the second Faith & Freedom Coalition conference in 2011, he had hosted a familiar roster of fundamentalist favorites, including Michele Bachman of Minnesota and the FRC's Tony Perkins. But he also invited someone the *New York Times* called "a famous almost-candidate"—Donald Trump.[81]

AS THE 2012 elections approached, the Obama campaign went into overdrive, especially in the area of digital operations. Obama's team built on his

2008 success with Project Narwhal, which integrated information regarding a voter's social media, contributions, and volunteer efforts into a database.[82] The Obama campaign took the smartphone revolution into account. In July it issued an iPhone app, Obama for America, that allowed canvassers to sign up and retrieve data as they went door to door, then enter updates into Obama's central database.[83]

The Romney campaign, playing catch-up, developed an app too—but it was mostly limited to photo sharing.[84] Romney's team also attempted to digitize the campaign, but it did not go well. Their answer to Project Narwhal was Project Orca—which one of its own web developers described as "an unmitigated disaster."[85]

When November rolled around, Obama defeated Romney by five million votes in the popular election. Not surprisingly, he swept the urban coastal areas. Less predictably, he won a total of twenty-six states, including the Rust Belt states of Ohio, Wisconsin, Michigan, and Pennsylvania, as well as Iowa and Florida.[86] Obama's digital campaign, described in the *Washington Post* as "bleeding-edge tech," was given much of the credit.[87]

But even as the Democrats celebrated Obama's victory, Republicans saw a silver lining. Obama's triumph didn't tell the whole story. In 2008 he had beaten McCain by 9.5 million votes, but in 2012 his advantage fell to less than 5 million. There was erosion in the South. Obama had won North Carolina's fifteen electoral college votes in 2008 and lost them in 2012. Nationally, Democratic candidates for the House of Representatives won 1.4 million more votes than Republicans, but thanks to gerrymandering and other factors, that vote translated into a thirty-three-seat gain by the Republicans in the House.[88] This gave them the House majority, as well as thirty-three state governorships, handing them control of the congressional budget process and greater influence on state-level policy.[89] The election offered further evidence of the Democrats' lack of long-term strategy and their focus on national elections and urban coastal areas, at the expense of "flyover" districts.

There was more good news for the Republicans in the Rust Belt. The November elections brought the DeVos family a long-awaited victory in its battle to defeat the right to collective bargaining in the Michigan state constitution, overcoming opposition from the United Auto Workers and the public employees' union.[90] This was critically important, as evidenced by the National Bureau of Economic Research finding that "right-to-work laws reduce Democratic Presidential vote shares by 3.5 percentage points," through reducing campaign contributions from organized labor and limiting outreach to potential Democratic voters.[91] Michigan's sixteen electoral votes moved out of the safe Democratic column, and other states would follow. CNP member Grover Norquist wrote that if right-to-work laws were passed in a dozen more states, "the modern Democratic Party will cease to be a competitive power in American politics."[92]

Republican technologists went back to the drawing board. The conservative *Washington Examiner* reported, "The Republicans concluded that President Obama's technologically advanced digital operation—including how his re-election campaign culled, analyzed and utilized voter data and demographic statistics to motivate turnout—was significantly responsible for GOP presidential nominee Mitt Romney's defeat. Data Trust has been charged with bridging that divide."[93] The Republicans' Data Trust was instructed to create an information hub available to all approved GOP candidates, local parties and organizations.

United in Purpose's parallel efforts had failed to win the presidency, but there was untapped potential. George Barna reported that thirty-eight million born-again Christians didn't vote in the election, twenty-six million of whom were registered to vote but stayed home.[94] (Up to a quarter of the Republicans, he noted, said they could not vote for a Mormon.[95]) Activating them would be a priority.

The Koch brothers postponed the meeting of their Seminar Network from January to April 2013 as they conducted a postmortem on the lost election.[96] Then they refocused their efforts, handing out over $41 million in grants to a small group of organizations. The following year they gave 80 percent of their funding to eight Koch organizations, mostly through Freedom Partners, concentrating their influence.[97] One short-term goal was to derail Obama's health care initiative. They gave a $5 million grant to Generation Opportunity, one of the "nonpartisan" partners of Americans for Prosperity. One objective was to dissuade millennials from signing up for health insurance under the Affordable Care Act.[98] Eliminating young, healthy members from the pool would drive up the costs for everyone else and undermine the program.

But the data contest remained a priority. The Center for Media and Democracy's PR Watch recorded that the Kochs' Freedom Partners 2013 tax return reported another $5.8 million investment in Themis Trust, the parent organization for the i360 data platform.[99]

At the same time, the CNP members conducted an ongoing assault on moderate Republicans. The CNP had already shown some muscle on this front. In 2009 it launched a campaign against upstate New York Republican Dede Scozzafava, a candidate in a special election for the House. Scozzafava drew the fundamentalists' ire with her moderate stand on labor unions and her support for abortion rights and same-sex marriage. The antiabortion Susan B. Anthony List, run by Marjorie Dannenfelser, dispatched staff members to her district to campaign against her.[100] CNP member Dick Armey endorsed her Conservative Party rival, and his Tea Party partners followed suit. Running a distant third, Scozzafava withdrew from the race. The National Organization for Marriage, directed by CNP member Brian Brown, turned the candidate's name into a synonym for blacklist: "If you try to elect pro-gay-marriage Republicans, we will Dede Scozzafava them."[101]

Lee Fang wrote, "While many forces—especially the influence of talk radio and Fox News—affected the outcome of [the 2010] Republican primaries, the Weyrich Lunch–drawn line in the sand against moderate Republicans reverberated in campaigns across the country."[102] Just as the Conservative Resurgence had reshaped the Southern Baptist Convention and the Cincinnati Revolt transformed the NRA, the CNP was determined to purge the GOP.

In April 2013, Tony Perkins told his followers to withhold contributions to the Republican Party and other Republican organizations until they "grow a backbone." Instead, they should "give directly to candidates who reflect [their] values and organizations [they] can trust—like FRC Action."[103] Later that year the Republican National Committee hired the FRC's senior director, Michael Mears, to the position of director of strategic partnerships.[104]

Tony Perkins was relentless. That fall he announced at the Values Voter Summit that House Speaker John Boehner "was really in trouble" because he didn't give the ultraconservative membership of the House an adequate hearing. Freshman senator Ted Cruz, Perkins proclaimed, "has become the de facto leader of the Republican Party."[105]

The coup against the traditional Republican Party gathered momentum, coalescing around Boehner's leadership. The fuse was lit by CNP member Paul Teller, executive director of the conservative Republican Study Committee. Teller took exception to Boehner's attempts to work out a historic budget deal with the Obama administration. In the words of Matt Bai of the *New York Times*, "The speaker occupied what may have been the toughest spot in Washington—trying to control a nihilistic rebellion in his own caucus."[106]

In December 2013 Teller was fired for leaking confidential committee information and sending emails to undermine some Republican lawmakers "in an alliance with conservative advocacy groups."[107] The CNP's Conservative Action Project fired back a letter protesting his dismissal, signed by CNP executive director Bob Reccord, former CNP president Ed Meese, and over a dozen other CNP members, as well as the heads of Koch organizations and other conservatives.[108] A month later Teller was hired as chief of staff by Texas senator Ted Cruz, the "de facto leader" of the party; John Boehner resigned from Congress in October 2015.[109]

Ted Cruz counted on the support of the fundamentalists. They were less interested in his Princeton and Harvard Law School degrees than in his father's embrace of Seven Mountains Dominionism, the theology that preaches that fundamentalists should take control of the "seven mountains" of society: family, religion, education, media, entertainment, business, and government.[110]

Cruz faced an ongoing likability problem, as well as competition from Mike Huckabee, an ordained Southern Baptist minister, but he possessed a keen intellect, an iron will, and a formidable work ethic. In September 2014 Cruz and Huckabee headlined a ninety-minute webcast from a church in North Carolina, *Star Spangled Sunday*, sponsored by a number of CNP partner organizations, including Concerned Women for America. The event promoted a new video from United in Purpose called "1,2,3 Vote," offering new online tools to show pastors which members of their congregation were registered to vote, and how to recruit the rest.[111]

Cruz actively courted Watchmen on the Wall, which had reportedly grown to thirty-eight thousand fundamentalist pastors nationwide.[112] Cruz's father, Rafael, attended their annual gathering in Washington, where hundreds of pastors paid $199 for a three-day affair.[113] (The Family Research Council subsidized their junket for an additional $800 per person, amounting to a half-million-dollar investment.) The conference served as a prime distribution point for FRC's Voter Impact Toolkit and its get-out-the-fundamentalist-vote instructions.[114]

Ted Cruz campaigned hard. He was the only presidential candidate to address the Watchmen on the Wall in May 2014, at the side of pastors-cum-CNP members E. W. Jackson and Harry Jackson, and CNP president Tony Perkins. In June 2014 Cruz addressed the CNP, where an attendee reported that "Cruz blew everyone else out of the water."[115] Cruz worked the Values Voter Summit as well. He triumphed in its 2013 straw poll with 42 percent of the vote, in a contest with five major contenders.[116] In 2014 Cruz's first-place showing was whittled down to 25 percent, with a strong challenge from Ben Carson, but Cruz regained his ground in 2015, winning 35 percent of the vote in a field of eight. Donald Trump reaped a paltry 5 percent.[117] Tony Perkins, now president of the Council for National Policy, endorsed Ted Cruz for president in January 2016 in the final week of the Iowa campaign.[118] The CNP machinery fell into place.

It was an ideal match on many levels. The ground troops were ready to canvas and the digital platforms were ready to process their findings—they just needed a candidate. Unbeknownst to most, Ted Cruz happened to be one of the leading digital innovators in American politics. His background told part of the story; his mother was a computer programmer, and his father, a Cuban exile, had been a pro-Castro mathematician before he became a fire-breathing Dominionist preacher.[119] Cruz put together a formidable political machine, based on his own innovative brand of digital campaigning.

One of his key advisors was the lanky Oklahoman Chris Wilson, founding director of WPA Opinion Research, which changed its name to WPA Intelligence, or WPAi, in 2017. Wilson had long-standing ties to the CNP. In 1998, as vice president of the market research firm Fabrizio,

McLaughlin & Associates, Wilson was listed as a speaker for the CNP meeting at Tysons Corner, Virginia.[120] Wilson parlayed his background in corporate marketing into a lucrative business in political strategy, and scored wins for several Tea Party–backed candidates.[121] But his biggest client was Cruz, whose campaigns paid out millions of dollars to his firm, starting in 2011.[122] Together, Cruz and Wilson set about assembling Koch-based funding, CNP organizing, and digital technology.

As of mid-2015, Wilson was working full-time for Cruz as his director of research, analytics, and digital strategy, overseeing a team of more than forty data scientists and developers in preparation for the Iowa primaries.[123] That summer he added the political consulting outfit Cambridge Analytica to his roster, at the behest of New York hedge-fund millionaire Robert Mercer and his daughter Rebekah, who were major investors in the British firm and converts to the CNP fold.[124] Again, one hand washed the other; the Mercers donated $11 million to a Cruz super PAC.[125]

Skeptics have taken the management of Cambridge Analytica to task for inflating the company's importance, but it played a significant role in a larger effort to expand Cruz's digital operations. The company was experimenting with psychological profiling, surveying over 150,000 households and scoring them on a version of the Myers-Briggs personality test. The *Washington Post* reported that the Cruz campaign modified the Cambridge template to create an "enhanced voter file" with "as many as fifty thousand data points gathered from voting records, popular websites, and consumer information such as magazine subscriptions, car ownership, and preferences for food and clothing."[126]

Politico's Mike Allen and Kenneth P. Vogel reported that the Koch brothers' i360 data analyzed a potential voter's television habits to target advertising more effectively. The Koch operation leveraged i360 data with "in-house expertise in polling, message-testing, fact-checking, advertising, media-buying, dial groups and donor maintenance," *Politico* noted. "Add mastery of election law, a corporate-minded aggressiveness and years of patient experimentation—plus seemingly limitless cash—and the Koch operation actually exceeds the RNC's data operation in many important respects."[127] By 2014 the Koch brothers had spent $50 million developing i360.[128]

More gears began to turn. One emerged from the gloom of a 2012 Romney "victory party." Thomas Peters was a fresh-faced twenty-six-year-old Catholic blogger. Peters didn't have a problem with Mormons, but he hated losing. As the returns came in, he watched his friends pull out their smartphones to relay the news and realized that mobile technology was everywhere, but the GOP hadn't developed a single app that advanced their cause.

The Republicans, he wrote, needed to learn from "President Obama's superb digital operation and grassroots mobilization [which] combined to defeat Republicans for a second time in a row. I became convinced that night the only way to defeat Democrats was to learn from their tech advances, and then leapfrog them. The biggest obstacle was bridging the gap between digital and field. It took over two years to read up and plan, but eventually I found backing and a (really, really good) developer, and we got to work."[129]

Peters was the founder of the ultraconservative American Papist, described on his LinkedIn page as "one of the most popular Catholic blogs in the world." He served as an advisor for Catholic Vote, one of United in Purpose's "parachurch" member organizations, which brought antiabortion Catholics into the fundamentalists' political fold.[130]

Peters looked for ways to incorporate the attraction of video games into political apps: "I wasted a lot of my youth on computer games, so I understood that 'gamification'—awarding badges, points, and social recognition—drives activity."[131] He embarked on a quest to outdo the Democrats' mobile apps. Peters's big idea was connecting mobile-based gamification to the coalition's grassroots organizations. In July 2013 he launched a small startup called Political Social Media LLC, with the operating name uCampaign.

That month Peters had a devastating swimming accident that left him partially paralyzed; with time, he regained some use of his arms.[132] Over the course of his recovery, he advanced his project to develop cell phone apps for conservative Republicans. He shopped his prototype to various campaigns, and Chris Wilson from the Cruz team said yes. Peters received $150,000 in seed funding from Sean Fieler, a close associate of Robert Mercer and, like Mercer, a strong Cruz supporter.[133]

Peters represented the company, but the app was developed by its chief technological officer, Vladyslav Seryakov. Seryakov—Peters' "really, really good developer"—was a mystery man described by a British parliamentary report as "an Eastern Ukranian military veteran who trained in computer programming at two elite Soviet universities."[134] His professional profile showed that he earned a degree in computer science from the Military University in Kharkov, Ukraine, between 1987 and 1990, when Ukraine was still part of the Soviet Union.[135] According to white-hat hacker Chris Vickery, the framework for Cruz's version of the app was written in English and translated only into Russian and Ukrainian.[136]

The team developing the Cruz Crew app worked with AggregateIQ, a small Canadian data firm that also served Cambridge Analytica. The smartphone app harvested information from Facebook Login, a tool that facilitated registrations on multiple platforms, and shared its data with AggregateIQ, which could distribute it to other networked organizations.[137]

Seryakov brought Soviet expertise to the app development, but Thomas Peters brought a feel for the target audience's user behavior. "We began with the supposition that effective digital grassroots activism should be mobile, social, and sticky (=easy to use, hard to discard)," Peters wrote. "(It's a given that it will be driven by, and produce, data.)"[138] Peters sold the idea to the Cruz campaign. "Chris Wilson, director of Cruz's polling and analytics department, and mastermind of the Cruz big data push, saw the potential in the early product," Peters noted.[139] The campaign launched the Cruz Crew app in May 2015.[140]

The design showed a keen understanding of the strong and weak social ties that can lead voters to the polls. When the user downloaded the app, it requested access to the phone's entire directory of contacts. "That allows it to match those contacts to Cruz's voter universes and prompt *existing* supporters to reach out personally to identified potential supporters," Peters wrote.[141] As of February 2016, the app matched over three hundred thousand potential supporters with active supporters. This data was supplemented with users' political surveys about themselves and their acquaintances, and data culled from their activities on the phone—especially their preferred calls to action.[142]

The app's gamification element awarded points to certain practical actions, such as checking in, sharing contacts, and making phone calls. These points added up to badges, ranging from "Bald Eagle" for a novice to

"U.S. Constitution" for an enthusiast. The app built in additional rewards for high achievers, including bumper stickers, T-shirts, and tickets to opening-night screenings of *Star Wars*.[143]

The RNC had been investing massive resources in its attempt to catch up with the Democrats, but the Koch operation made the biggest advances in integrating data from the field in real time. The Kochs played favorites, selling i360 data to Ted Cruz, Jeb Bush, Marco Rubio, and Wisconsin governor Scott Walker, but spurning others.[144] In July 2015 the Republican National Committee's Data Trust and the Koch brothers' i360 struck a bargain to share data.[145]

The 2016 primaries would serve as a laboratory for the new array of digital tools. Over the run-up to the elections, the Koch and CNP organizations and the digital projects meshed in new ways. The National Rifle Association sat at the center of these operations, fueled by nearly $5 million from the Kochs' Freedom Partners in 2014.

Much of the NRA's political activity was conducted by two of its affiliates: its lobbying arm, the Institute for Legislative Action (NRA-ILA), and its political action committee, the Political Victory Fund (NRA-PVF). The NRA billed itself as "America's longest-standing civil rights organization," but the Second Amendment was the only "right" that it considered. Following the Cincinnati rebellion of the 1970s, the NRA and its many subsidiaries were unabashedly political, despite the NRA's qualification as a "nonpartisan," tax-exempt 501(c)(4) organization that "operated exclusively to promote social welfare."

The NRA's Political Victory Fund rated candidates for office according to their positions on gun control. The ratings, which overwhelmingly favored Republicans, were complemented with "action" measures. The organization's website recruited "dedicated, educated volunteers like you to assist with phone banks, literature drops, precinct walks, voter registration, Election Day activities, and other campaign volunteer activities."[146] The NRA's 2016 campaign contributions favored Republican congressional candidates at a ratio of almost sixty to one ($5.9 million to $106,000).[147]

The NRA presented itself as a public organization; it was required by the IRS to be "engaged in promoting in some way the common good and general welfare of the people of the community." But its inner workings were obscure, and there were no hard numbers for its membership. Dave Gilson of *Mother Jones*, exploring its record, found that the NRA reported "more than 5 million members" in 2016, but its magazine distribution, included with paid membership, put the number closer to four million. (The NRA has interpreted a Pew survey to suggest that some fourteen million respondents claimed they were NRA members, implying that they identified with the organization without paying dues.[148])

The money was murky as well. Five million members paying the $35 in dues required at the time would have resulted in $175 million. But the NRA and its five affiliates reported nearly $434 million in 2016 revenues, plus approximately $42 million carried over from the previous year.[149] This steep rise in income was fueled by the organization's political donors, whom it was not required to reveal.

New money was pouring in. In 2013 *Mother Jones* reported that "an organization allied with the donor network of billionaire brothers Charles and David Koch gave between $2 million and $3 million to the NRA's election efforts, according to two Republican fund-raisers familiar with the gun group's campaign work."[150] The Kochs' Freedom Partners Chamber of Commerce 2014 tax return recorded a $4.9 million donation to the NRA's Institute for Legislative Action, which ran many of its campaign activities.[151]

A few years earlier the NRA Freedom Action Foundation had launched a project called Trigger the Vote, a "national non-partisan voter registration effort to ensure gun owners across the country are registered to vote."[152] It could build on the NRA's vast secret database of gun owners, assembled from state and local lists of gun permits (permits that the NRA opposed), as well as purchased lists from gun shows and magazines. A former NRA lobbyist told BuzzFeed's Steve Friess that the NRA was tracking "tens of millions" of gun owners, most of them without their knowledge.[153]

There were plenty of untapped Republican voters who didn't attend fundamentalist churches or hold strong opinions about same-sex marriage. Trigger the Vote offered an avenue to reach them. This was apparent to hedge fund millionaire Robert Mercer, a CNP member and a lifetime member of the NRA.[154] In 2016 the *Guardian* reported, "Cambridge Analytica, a voter data firm in which Mercer is a key investor, has worked with the Herald Group, a DC-based consulting firm, to implement the NRA's 'Trigger the Vote' drive to register new voters and get them to the polls. i360, a big voter data firm that is closely tied to the Koch donor network, has also been involved in the Trigger the Vote campaign."[155] An unnamed donor from the Koch network reported that LaPierre had attended Koch meetings, "affording him a chance to pitch and schmooze with big network donors such as investor Foster Friess."[156] But these encounters were redundant. Friess and LaPierre went on hunting trips together—and both were active members of the CNP.

On December 30, 2015, the NRA Political Victory Fund made its initial payment to the i360 data platform—a disbursement of $414.84 to i360 for "phone calls." This was the first of eight disbursements, totaling nearly $1,700 in less than a month.[157] There would be many more to come.

The Susan B. Anthony List's Women Speak Out PAC paid i360 nine larger sums, totaling nearly $15,000, from October 2015 through November 2016, for "data subscriptions," "digital revenue share," and "software management." The Susan B. Anthony List was another uCampaign app client.[158] But Cruz for President was the big spender, investing nearly $315,000 in i360 services in eleven payments over 2016.[159]

It was another illustration of the network in action. Hundreds of millions of dollars flowed from the networked donors to the partner organizations. A state-of-the-art "database of over 250 million 18+ adults, including the 190 million who registered to vote" and an innovative app stood ready to reach them. Armies of lawyers supported platoons of strategists. Grassroots organizers appeared on multiple fronts, including NRA volunteers, Tea Party activists, and tens of thousands of fundamentalist pastors. Salem, Bott, and American Family radio stations carried the movement's messaging in unison, and the Christian Broadcasting Network and Trinity Broadcasting Network appealed to millions of viewers.[160] Social media were generated from a great distance and went viral in a heartbeat. Lists of nominees for federal judgeship were drawn up by the Federalist Society.

Once again, the impact of these forces would be magnified by their location, in states with disproportionate weight in the Electoral College and the Senate—populations that were all but invisible to many on the coasts.

The Iowa caucuses were scheduled for February 1, 2016. The Cruz Crew's online community expanded as the date approached. The app functioned like a closed Facebook feed, in which Cruz supporters interacted exclusively with other Cruz supporters and with the candidate himself, without encountering differing opinions.

Three days before the Iowa caucuses, the app went into overdrive. Cruz Crew app users were prompted to send out over 230,000 invitations, share get-out-the-vote messages on Facebook and Twitter, and check in at their caucus locations on Google Maps. Nearly 3,800 Iowans received targeted messages from friends who had downloaded the app, saying "I hope you will Caucus for Ted Cruz on Monday. Here's how: https://www.tedcruz.org/caucusforcruz/."[161] Peters wrote, "In the final 24 hours the app served over 850,000 requests to the 11,000 supporters who were online, pulling 2GB of data through the system."[162]

Donald Trump had taken the lead in a number of polls, but on February 1, Ted Cruz took Iowa—by a mere 6,239 votes.[163] The Cruz Crew app wasn't his only advantage. The Family Research Council had an app too, and it promoted Tony Perkins's guests "like Senator Ted Cruz."[164] As of 2019, the FRC's Watchmen on the Wall had over a thousand pastors in Iowa alone. The *Washington Post* reported that evangelicals made up about two-thirds of the Iowa Republican caucus-goers, and "Cruz won them convincingly."[165]

The runner-up in Iowa was Donald Trump, who found himself at a disadvantage. *Politico* reported that in the summer of 2015 Trump had appealed to the Koch brothers to allow him to purchase i360 data, and been turned down. He also asked to speak at the Kochs' summer gathering alongside other Republican candidates, but was spurned again. Although Trump was friendly with David Koch, the brothers disapproved of his immigration and trade policies.[166] The Kochs announced that their network was primed to spend $889 million on the 2016 elections, and Trump was not on their list. The Cruz campaign, on the other hand, purchased some $315,000 worth of data from i360 in 2015, more than any other campaign.[167]

Trump faced additional obstacles with the fundamentalists. In September 2015 he appeared at the Values Voter Summit, introduced by CNP member David Bossie, president of Citizens United. Trump addressed the crowd clutching his Bible. His only problem at the debates, he declared, was that "people were not sure I'm a nice person. And I am! I am! I am! I'm a giving person. I believe in God, I believe in the Bible, I'm a Christian, I've got a lot of reasons. I love people."[168] But Russell Moore, head of the Ethics and Religious Liberty Commission of the Southern Baptist Convention, published a retort in the *New York Times*. "To back Mr. Trump," he stated, evangelicals and social conservatives "must repudiate everything they believe."[169]

In February 2016, Southern Baptist leader Richard Land—the CNP member who had helped launch the FRC's iVoter guides for church leaders—went even further. He published an editorial in the *Christian Post*, the largest online fundamentalist publication, headlined "Donald Trump Is a Scam. Evangelical Voters Should Back Away." The editor's note stated, "The *Christian Post* has not taken a position on a political candidate before today. We are making an exception because Trump is exceptionally bad and claims to speak for and represent the interests of evangelicals."[170]

Nonetheless, Trump took off after Iowa, winning primary after primary, and other candidates fell by the wayside. On May 3, 2016, Ted Cruz exploded to reporters, "I'm going to tell you what I really think of Donald Trump. This man is a pathological liar . . . Whatever he does, he accuses everyone else of doing. The man cannot tell the truth, but he combines it with being a narcissist, a narcissist at a level that I don't think this country's ever seen . . . The man is utterly amoral."[171]

Ted Cruz, the last man standing, dropped out of the race.

Some observers of the campaign's data game rushed to judgment. Issie Lapowsky wrote in *Wired* that the result "suggests that data—the kind Cruz fastidiously gathered—might not matter all that much to a presidential campaign . . . Cruz is proof that you can have all the fancy trappings, but if people don't love the candidate it doesn't matter."[172]

But maybe this was the wrong lesson to draw. Perhaps Cruz's Iowa upset was a proof of concept, not final product—demonstrating that in certain districts, digital strategy combined with fundamentalist ground troops and dark money could overcome a candidate's deficits. What would happen if the coalition applied its formulae on behalf of a candidate with the advantage of a manic charisma that played into America's ripest fears and fantasies?

The trick, it seemed, came down to identifying the vulnerable districts and determining which ones would count in the electoral math to come. But first, the coalition needed to overcome many fundamentalists' distaste for the Republican candidate-in-waiting. Luckily, the CNP had a political wizard for the job.

CHAPTER 11

THE ART OF THE DEAL: NEW YORK, JUNE 21, 2016

The candidate was the problem. Ted Cruz had won the hearts, minds, and purses of the CNP and the Koch network, but as of May 4, 2016, Donald Trump had undeniably won the primaries. Now the shadow network faced a distressing choice: either accept a victory by their nemesis Hillary Clinton, who was running a healthy lead in the national polls—or embrace Donald Trump, the man Ted Cruz had just labeled "utterly amoral" and a "pathological liar," and the CNP's Richard Land had denounced as "exceptionally bad."[1]

A group of female conservatives, including CNP members Marjorie Dannenfelser and Penny Nance, had sent an "anyone but Trump" letter to Iowa voters, stating, "As women, we are disgusted by Mr. Trump's treatment of individuals, women in particular."[2] As far as the movement's key issues were concerned, Trump's loose-cannon rhetoric had been all over the place; he was on record saying he didn't care to challenge same-sex marriage, and he was wobbly on abortion.[3] His religious credentials were spotty, to put it mildly.[4] For a coalition that depended on getting out the fundamentalist vote, these were poor optics indeed.

For George Barna, the taste of victory was turning to ashes. For the past three decades his polls had informed the political campaigns of Christian fundamentalists and the funding strategies of right-wing donor networks. Now, in the spring of 2016, those years of work appeared to be paying off—until they threatened to evaporate.

Barna combined analysis with evangelical zeal. With his neatly trimmed hair and horn-rimmed glasses, he looked like an aging Harry Potter. Besides his polling, Barna produced a stream of books and presented his research in seminars for the faithful. At the Family Research Council's Values Voter Summit, Barna briefed rooms full of dedicated fundamentalists with chapter and verse on election tactics, including turnout projections, generic ballots, and favorability ratings to apply toward their campaigns.[5]

Barna claimed that his efforts were all the more successful for taking place, quite intentionally, off the national radar. He boasted that he followed every heartbeat of the "opposition media—the major networks, CNN, MSNBC, the *New York Times* and the *Washington Post*," but what he called "the other side" had little notion of the coalition's project.[6]

Barna had every notion of the challenge ahead. The Republicans had held control of both houses of Congress since 2014, with the biggest House majority since World War II.[7] This allowed them not just to stymie the Obama's judiciary appointments in the Senate but also to derail his budgets from the House. The odds were excellent for holding on to the Senate in 2016, thanks to a favorable map for the Republicans. This also would be the case in 2018, and somewhat less so in 2020.[8] The polls favored Hillary Clinton to win the popular vote and the Republicans to hold the Senate.[9] A Democratic presidency and a Republican Senate would once again stall governance on many fronts, but it could well result in more seats for moderate judges.

But if the Republicans won the presidency and retained the Senate, they would hold the power to reshape the American judiciary. That's when the real change would unfold. They would have the ability to roll back abortion rights, gay marriage, and gun laws; they could revoke environmental regulations, abolish entire federal agencies, and assail IRS restrictions on churches' right to operate as tax-free political platforms. Decisions on gerrymandering and redistricting would set the scales for many elections to come. Their aspirations would no longer be limited by the system of checks and balances designed by the founders of the Republic to guard against extremism.

It was not looking promising. The Republican primaries had been crowded and messy, with sixteen contenders and a rogue. The members of the CNP looked with favor on Ben Carson (a Seventh-Day Adventist) and Mike Huckabee (a Southern Baptist pastor), but they divided their active support between Ted Cruz (a Southern Baptist) and Marco Rubio (a Catholic who converted to Southern Baptist and back again).[10] The DeVos family in Michigan had donated millions to super PACs for Cruz and Rubio, and the Koch brothers had placed both men on their short list.

But Trump broke through, riding on his uncanny charisma, the caché of celebrity, and a powerful backlash against political business-as-usual. All the same, Trump the candidate was at a decided disadvantage. He had run a seat-of-the-pants operation, lacking donors, infrastructure, and a ground game, while his Democratic opponent possessed all three.[11] Hillary Clinton's well-oiled campaign held its comfortable lead through the primary season, and the national news media constantly assured her that the presidency was hers to lose.[12]

The *New York Times Magazine* described the challenge. "Trump, after accumulating enough delegates to win the nomination with almost no visible operation or recognizable strategy, has only nominally scaled his campaign beyond where it was a few months ago. There is barely any fund-raising or field apparatus to speak of, and Trump has outsourced a great deal of the nitty-gritty of an enormous general-election campaign to the overtasked R.N.C."

In May, soon after Ted Cruz acknowledged defeat, *Time* magazine's Elizabeth Dias reported that Tony Perkins, Ben Carson, and Bill Dallas had begun organizing a closed-door meeting for Trump and fundamentalist leaders.[13] It was a hard sell. The evangelical media had stewed over Trump's January 2016 appearance at Jerry Falwell's Liberty University. Speaking at a quasi-religious convocation following some hymns, Trump proceeded to shock young fundamentalist ears by saying "damn" and "hell" in his speech—finable offenses on the Liberty campus.[14] He further startled his audience by referring to Second Corinthians as "Two Corinthians, 3:17, that's the whole ballgame"—a blunder he blamed on CNP president Tony Perkins, who had written out his briefing notes.[15] Perkins accepted the blame, responding, "It shows he's not familiar with the Bible. Donald Trump's a very interesting guy."[16] Like Ralph Reed, Perkins was keeping his options open.

The fundamentalists measured a man's worth by his church attendance, marital fidelity, and knowledge of the Bible, and Trump came up short on every count. He claimed to be a Presbyterian, but didn't attend regular services (unlike Hillary Clinton, who was a devout Methodist).[17] Trump's speech was laden with vulgarities and devoid of religious sentiment. He shocked pastors by declaring he was above the need to ask God for forgiveness, and told a radio host that his favorite Bible verse was "an eye for an eye"—an Old Testament concept repudiated by Jesus, who said "turn the other cheek."[18]

Major donors distrusted Trump's business practices and grasp of economic principles. In early March Betsy DeVos told the *Washington Examiner* why her family supported Marco Rubio: "I don't think Donald Trump represents the Republican Party . . . I think more and more people are going to realize that they really don't trust him."[19] A month later, as Trump pulled further ahead, ABC News asked Charles Koch if he might prefer Clinton to the Republican candidate. "It's possible," he answered.[20] The Koch network was actively exploring an alternative to Trump.

In past elections, evangelicals who didn't care for the candidates had stayed home by the millions. This time, without their backing, Trump would go down at best as a historical footnote, and at worst, as an embarrassment that could cripple the GOP for years to come.

George Barna couldn't watch that happen, and neither, in the end, could the donors. The Republican Party was the coalition's only path to power, and whatever Trump's failings, its leadership held Hillary Clinton to be the greater evil. Her pro-choice stance was anathema to the fundamentalists, along with her support for same-sex marriage and gun control. Her commitment to social programs and environmental protections offended their free market absolutist donors.

But the Republican Party was in disarray. The national convention was only a few weeks away, and there were stirrings of a Dump Trump rebellion. In June CNN reported that "Donald Trump faces an extraordinary money deficit unheard of in modern presidential politics."[21] Clinton's campaign had $42 million in the bank as of May 31, while Trump's campaign had $1.3 million.[22] Trump claimed that contributions were pouring in to the Republican National Committee, but this was not so. The RNC had only $20 million in cash at the end of May—a third of what it held in May 2012.[23]

By the start of the summer, Barna wrote, his polls showed "a huge number of conservative Christian votes either unavailable or up for grabs. Some 15% planned to vote for an independent or third-party candidate. About 7% were still trying to decide what to do. Another 5% said they would vote, but not for a presidential candidate."[24]

The machine was assembled and ready to roll: the CNP grassroots organizations, the Leadership Institute alumni, the fundamentalist and NRA get-out-the-vote drives, and the Koch brothers' i360 data platform. There were also the uCampaign apps, acquiring data and contacts from different grassroots canvassers and organizations. But many of these elements had been assembled for the benefit of Ted Cruz, and Cruz was in a sulk. Furthermore, according to George Barna, Jerry Falwell Jr. and Robert Jeffress were the only early Trump supporters among the pastors.[25] That would have to change before the convention.

It fell to Ralph Reed to test the waters. Reed had been cultivating Trump for years. On May 20, *Time* magazine's Elizabeth Dias noted that Ralph Reed had been neutral in the primaries, but had decided that "he will personally support Trump and do everything he can in his personal capacity to help Trump's campaign in general." She added that Reed promised to bring a lot to the table: he was planning the largest "voter education program of his career," with 200 million voter contacts, "directed at 32.1 million faith-based voters primarily in battleground states like Iowa, Florida, North Carolina, Virginia, Colorado and Ohio," including 25 million pieces of mail and an average of 7 digital messaging impressions per voter.[26]

But there was work to be done. Cruz's bitter words over his primary defeat were still fresh, and Dias noted that key members of the coalition still doubted Trump's sincerity. But the Faith & Freedom Coalition, which now claimed a million members, was a core partner in the United in Purpose coalition, and Reed and Perkins joined forces to present the candidate in a new light.

Reed scheduled Trump's dress rehearsal for June 10, 2016, at a Faith & Freedom Coalition conference in Washington, D.C. In his opening remarks Reed gave a "shout-out" to Concerned Women for America president Penny Nance, and announced a lifetime achievement award for its founder, Beverly LaHaye.[27] He introduced "a man who has become a good friend"—Donald Trump. Trump in turn praised Jerry Falwell Jr. and Robert Jeffress, "who we all know and love." Trump singled out three CNP members in the audience for his appreciation: fundamentalist broadcaster Richard Lee, California pastor Jim Garlow and Father Frank Pavone, director of Priests for Life.[28]

Then Trump moved on to his list of goals, which, he said, he had put together "just the other night, for this meeting." His mastery of the fundamentalist rhetoric was word-perfect, beginning with "We want to uphold the sanctity and dignity of life," the code for an anti-abortion plank, followed by his support for "marriage and family" and "religious freedom." Trump added that he had "put a list together of highly, highly respected judges, and you will see, and I think you've seen it. . . . these judges are all pro-life."

In the meantime, George Barna and his associates at United in Purpose went to work. They decided to reach out to two hundred fundamentalist leaders who were still undecided and invite them to "hear from the two major-party candidates. They'd start with Donald Trump."[29] (Hillary Clinton's campaign never responded to the invitation, Barna wrote. She would spend June 21, 2016, giving a speech in Columbus, Ohio.[30])

They called it "A Conversation about America's Future with Donald Trump and Ben Carson." It was organized by United in Purpose, headed by CNP member Bill Dallas, and the parent organization for Barna's American Culture and Faith Institute. Another official host was My Faith Votes, a new online get-out-the-vote project aimed at "25 million Christians who are registered to vote [who] won't vote unless we motivate and equip them to vote!"[31] The "non-partisan educational" organization had received a huge influx of cash over the previous year from undisclosed donors; its contributions and grants ballooned from $154,000 in 2015 to over $7.5 million in 2016.[32]

Fox News personality Todd Starnes—himself a member of the Council for National Policy—published a preview on May 23, headlined

"Mega-Christian Leaders Having Private Meeting with Donald Trump."[33] Tony Perkins was "one of the key conservative leaders spearheading the gathering," which was "convened by a who's who among evangelicals." At least five of the nine leaders named were members of the CNP, and a sixth was CNP executive director Bob McEwen. "Specifically," Starnes reported, "the leaders want to hear detailed plans on potential Supreme Court nominees and the vetting process."[34]

They decided to hold the meeting in the ballroom of the New York Marriott Marquis, a massive glass-and-steel structure on Forty-Sixth Street and Seventh Avenue in Times Square. To Barna's surprise, legions of fundamentalist leaders answered the call—some one thousand in all.[35] They came from all over the country, reflecting the movement's Southern Baptist roots but including Pentecostal and Nazarene charismatics.[36]

The invitees passed through a Secret Service screening and made their way to the Broadway Ballroom, a twenty-nine-thousand-square-foot cavern with a sprawling red carpet.[37] The event was carefully curated, beginning with inspirational speeches from movement all-stars, including pollster George Barna and CNP members Ralph Reed and Ken Blackwell, the former Ohio official who had overseen the disputed 2004 elections.

The warm-up act for the afternoon was Ben Carson. Shortly after he ended his primary campaign, Carson accepted the position of honorary national chairman of My Faith Votes. Now he softened up his audience for Trump, asking them to view him in a new light, however unflattering. "This is like a chess match, and God is the great grand master," he told the packed ballroom. "Sometimes he uses a pawn."[38] (If Trump minded Carson calling him a pawn, he didn't say so in public.)

Carson passed the microphone to Franklin Graham, heir to Billy Graham's evangelical empire, which claimed $600 million in annual revenues.[39] Graham offered Trump more backhanded support. Was Trump a sinner? Well, Graham reminded his audience, the God of the Old Testament worked through lots of sinners: Abraham lied, Moses disobeyed God. David committed adultery and had a man killed.[40]

The organizers of the event had agreed that Trump should not be allowed to give a speech; that was too dangerous. Only the day before, the GOP had obliged him to fire his brash young campaign manager, Corey Lewandowski, for his tendency to "let Trump be Trump."[41] This occasion called for exquisite control.

National Public Radio reported that before Trump was allowed to appear, he attended a small meeting with members of the steering committee for the event. These included CNP president Tony Perkins and CNP members James Dobson, Gary Bauer, and the Reverend E. W. Jackson.[42] At the end of the day he emerged with a list of his new "evangelical advisory council," including many of those present.

The candidate had already addressed one of the group's primary concerns by sending them a list of a dozen judges he would consider nominating. In March Trump had met with CNP member Leonard Leo from the Federalist Society and assembled an initial list.[43] In an April 2 *Washington Post* interview, he named the sources of the candidates: "I'm getting names. The Federalist people. Some very good people. The Heritage Foundation."[44]

For the plenary session's master of ceremonies, the organizers tapped Mike Huckabee. He hosted a chat session with Trump, his former rival, leading into a question-and-answer period with a panel of handpicked leaders. The proceedings were recorded in a blog post by Dr. Billye Brim, founder of the A Glorious Church Fellowship of Collinsville, Oklahoma, and the Billye Brim Bible Institute: "Trump entered confidently and smiling from stage left. The audience was warm in its welcoming reception. He spoke to us for a while. In this he pointed out something that stayed with me the whole day and until now, this election is about the Supreme Court. The next president will appoint 2, 3, 4, or possibly 5 life term Justices . . . He said all his judges would be vetted by the Federalist Society."[45]

The Marriott audience was familiar with all of the panelists, in part thanks to their regular appearances on Tony Perkins's daily radio program *Washington Watch*. George Barna, Ken Blackwell, Ralph Reed, Ben Carson, Mike Huckabee, Mike Pence: Perkins had hosted them all on his show, and they all stayed on message.

The members of Mike Huckabee's panel—which also included the CNP's James Dobson and Kelly Shackelford—reported they had received fifty thousand questions from their constituencies. They whittled them down to twenty, of which Trump answered a handful. Trump handled the situation confidently, touching on all their priorities. He promised to nullify the Johnson Amendment, the IRS regulation that restricted tax-exempt institutions—including churches—from engaging in electoral politics. He pleased the audience with his responses on abortion, terrorism, and immigration issues.[46]

"He stayed with us past the allotted time," Billye Brim marveled. "Governor Huckabee kept pointing out that it was past the time we had agreed for. Mr. Trump said, 'There is no place more important for me to be than here.'"

At the end of the session, Huckabee stood at Trump's side and declared victory. "There's one thousand people representing millions of people across America who understand that this election is really not a hard lift. We have Hillary Clinton, and we have you. You want to make America great again. You bring disruptive leadership to this country that will challenge the institutions that have virtually ruined the America that many of us know, grew up in, appreciate, and want to hand to our kids and grandkids."[47]

This day would go down in history, Huckabee said. "God willing, you will look back in your first year as president of the United States and you will say that this event at the Marriott Marquis in New York was one of the seminal events—if not the seminal event and turning point in taking you to the presidency."[48] The audience gave a standing ovation to the man they had condemned only weeks earlier.

Immediately after the event, Tony Perkins led a press conference with eight fundamentalist leaders, largely attended by religious media outlets. They praised Trump's appearance—but none of them would commit to endorsing him. In an article headlined "Trump Struggles to Close the Deal with Evangelicals," the conservative *National Review* rated the event a failure. "Many of these individuals were present Tuesday due to their leadership roles in large, grassroots-oriented organizations; strikingly, none of them are yet willing to extend Trump an endorsement that could mobilize their constituents on his behalf."[49]

CNP member Michael Farris, longtime head of the Alliance Defending Freedom, was particularly unmoved. "I think he is without a moral core," he said coming out of the meeting.[50]

National news organizations showed limited interest in the event, and local television stations paid more attention to the anti-Trump demonstrations outside.[51] Two reporters who made it into the ballroom were Sarah McCammon from NPR and Todd Starnes from Fox News (formerly of the *Baptist Press*, where he was fired for "factual and contextual errors."[52]) Starnes was an insider, but even he missed the larger significance of the event, tweeting that it was "basically a campaign rally."[53]

The Council for National Policy took pride in the event. In July its lobbying arm, CNP Action, published an account in its online newsletter, *Heard around the Hill*:

> On June 21 in New York City, United in Purpose and My Faith Votes with Global Fund Group, FCCI, CNP Member Charles Herbster, Vision America Action, AFA Action and Family Research Council presented "A Conversation About America's Future" with Donald Trump and Ben Carson. The meeting was a chance for attendees to get to know Trump, his position on important issues and vision for America's future. It also helped him to better appreciate matters of importance to the faith community. The following CNP Members helped to convene the meeting: Art Ally, Gary Bauer, Ken Blackwell, Dick Bott, Rich Bott, Brian Burch, Ken Cuccinelli, Marjorie Dannenfelser, James Dobson, Jim Garlow, Kristan Hawkins, E.W. Jackson, Harry Jackson, J. Keet Lewis, Penny Nance, Tony Perkins, Ralph Reed, Lila Rose, Kelly Shackelford, Rick Scarborough, Richard Viguerie and Tim Wildmon.[54]

The wheels were turning. After Trump emerged from the gathering, his campaign announced the formation of his Evangelical Advisory Board.[55] The idea wasn't new; in 2009 Barack Obama had established the President's Advisory Council on Faith-Based and Neighborhood Partnerships, made up of Catholic, Protestant, Jewish, and Muslim leaders, plus some community organizers.[56]

But Trump's new council was something else again. Most of its twenty-six members had participated in the Marriott Marquis event. At least ten were Southern Baptist clergy, and others were affiliated with Southern Baptist institutions. At least three were Pentecostal pastors, while others led urban megachurches. There were no Catholics, Jews, or representatives of the other faiths that together make up the majority of the U.S. religious population. There weren't even any Methodists, Episcopalians, or Presbyterians, Trump's putative denomination.

But the list did include Texas Baptist James Robison, who had led the 1980 rally that brought Ronald Reagan into the fold, as well as CNP members James Dobson, Ralph Reed, Richard Land, and Harry Jackson.[57]

Robert Jones, the CEO of the Public Religion Research Institute, noted an even more salient feature. "If you look at his evangelical advisory council, it's people with media connections, more than broad church-based connections," he told *Politico*. "That's a weird slice of the evangelical world."[58] These included stars from the fundamentalist broadcasting networks, whose programming reached hundreds of millions in the U.S. and abroad.

One of the "media connections" on the Evangelical Advisory Board was Sealy Yates, a savvy attorney and "Christian literary agent" from Orange County. Yates had founded the country's biggest fundamentalist literary agency, representing CNP member Jim DeMint, Ben Carson, and various other authors.[59] He was also the founder and chairman of My Faith Votes.[60]

"Trump's bounce from the New York event was almost immediate," Barna noted with satisfaction. "Some of those who attended the meeting made a personal shift from 'undecided' to becoming secret Trump voters, but did not discuss that change publicly (this seemed most common among the pastors who attended the event)." Barna added that "while pastors had little role in the recalibration process, Christian nonprofits and Christian media (especially radio) started building some momentum for Trump."[61] These "Christian nonprofits" included the Family Research Council, the Alliance Defending Freedom, and other CNP affiliates, while the CNP member-owned Salem, Bott, and American Family radio networks captured a large segment of the "Christian" radio market.

Now came the question of Trump's running mate. Trump's team had reviewed several dozen candidates. Trump himself favored Chris Christie, an old acquaintance who had joined the Trump campaign as soon as he abandoned his own.[62] But Christie was a cradle Catholic, and the fundamentalists had someone else in mind.[63] "None would do as much to shore up Trump's standing in the conservative Christian world as Mike Pence," Barna wrote.[64] Two out of three members of Barna's fundamentalist voting bloc reported that they had more confidence in Trump's ticket with the addition of Pence.[65] It wasn't just the problem of adding the scandal-soiled Christie to an already troubled ticket. Tony Perkins and Morton Blackwell embraced Mike Pence as one of their own, and he had risen to congressional office on a tide of their support.

Trump and Pence had differed on a number of policy matters. Pence had promoted homophobic policies for decades, while Trump had been known to voice support for gay rights.[66] As governor, Pence had attacked Planned Parenthood and rolled back abortion rights, while Trump had publicly praised Planned Parenthood and supported abortion rights until 2011.[67]

In early July CBS News reported that Trump had offered the vice presidential slot to Christie, but Trump's campaign chairman, Paul Manafort, took matters in hand.[68] One day when the candidate was scheduled to fly out of Indianapolis, Manafort invented a story that his plane had mechanical problems, requiring him to stay the night. The next morning a breakfast was arranged for Trump and the Pence family. Pence forcefully made his case. The next day Trump rescinded his offer to Christie and extended it to Pence, who accepted in a heartbeat.[69]

Election Day was less than four months away. The coalition went to work. The hidden machinery that had advanced the candidacy of Ted Cruz now pivoted to Trump, giving him the donor base, ground game and campaign technology he lacked—strategically concentrated in critical districts of swing states. George Barna's polling monitored the target population and adjusted the campaign's regional messaging based on the results. They found that the three hot-button issues were abortion, the Supreme Court, and immigration.[70]

The pastors from the Marriott Marquis went back to their congregations and told them it was their Christian duty to go to the polls and to cast their vote based on "biblical values."

The Evangelical Advisory Board wasn't the fundamentalists' only payoff. The Republican National Convention was approaching in August, and the party needed a platform. In July the *CNP Action* newsletter published a notice:

> On July 18, delegates to the Republican National Convention adopted the official 2016 Platform, which declares the Party's

> principles and policies. The Republican Party is energized to lead a turnaround from the failed policies of Barack Obama and Hillary Clinton, and this platform provides a thorough look at how we will restore prosperity and security to our country. It is said to be the most conservative platform by any political party in American history. Please use this platform for your continued efforts to advance the Conservative Movement.
>
> CNP President Tony Perkins was instrumental in the development of the platform. Among the Platform Committee Members were CNP Members Len Munsil and Timothy Houseal.

The RNC's platform staff included "Mike Mears, Director of Strategic Partnerships." The burly, bearded Mears had worked his way up from spokesman for Concerned Women for America to senior director for Family Research Council Action. In 2013 the Republican National Committee hired him as director of strategic partnerships, where he was charged with "keeping the lines of communication open between the RNC and our friends in the conservative movement."[71]

"Creating and presenting the platform," Barna commented, "is where the policy wonks reap their 15 minutes of fame (and that's about how much time the television networks covering the conventions devoted to the platform discussion, despite the ultimate significance of the document.)"[72]

But those journalists who did a deep dive into the fifty-eight-page document found surprises. Vox Media's Matt Yglesias wrote, "The platform also includes a *lot* of more or less wacky notions that highlight the continued influence of talk radio—rather than, say, the US Chamber of Commerce—over the practical day-to-day concerns of most Republican Party activists."[73]

"An amendment offered by the Family Research Council's Tony Perkins," *Time* magazine noted,

> in the subcommittee on healthcare, education, and crime offered support for the controversial practice of "conversion therapy" for children who identify as LGBT.
>
> "We support the right of parents to determine the proper treatment or therapy of their minor children," the amendment said.

> Perkins originally drafted a more explicit embrace of the practice, but amended the text after consultations with top RNC officials. Perkins' amendment, which passed the subcommittee and subsequently the full committee, also calls for legislation to require parental consent for minor women to cross state lines for the purpose of obtaining an abortion.[74]

Conversion therapy, through which practitioners attempt to "cure" homosexuality through treatments that can amount to torture, has been widely condemned in the medical community, including the American Medical Association, and banned in sixteen states, the District of Columbia, and a number of other countries.

Conversion therapy wasn't the only controversial element of the new GOP platform. It also came out strongly against abortion and Planned Parenthood. It urged the reversal of same-sex marriage, supported the right of businesses to deny service "to individuals for activities that go against their religious views" (a code for allowing discrimination against LGBT individuals), and called for the repeal of the Affordable Care Act. It opposed environmental and food safety regulations and called for the development of all "marketable" forms of energy, including coal, oil, and natural gas.

The RNC platform committee listed CNP members Len Munsil and Timothy Houseal among the state committee members, but it was Tony Perkins, one of two Louisiana representatives, who captured the spotlight.[75] The *New York Times* reported, "It was the lack of much interference by Mr. Trump or his aides that seemed to set the tone for the platform's direction. That allowed conservative activists like Tony Perkins, the president of the Family Research Council, to exert greater influence. Mr. Perkins's hand could be seen in dozens of amendments on issues like gun control, religious expression and bathroom use."[76] This point was echoed by George Barna: "One striking element of the 2016 Republican platform debate was the lack of intervention by the Trump campaign."

The *Times* was puzzled by the reactionary approach to homosexual and transgender rights: "While public and legal opinion has moved steadily in one direction, the official declaration of Republican Party principles appears to be heading sharply in the opposite direction." Tony Perkins, the hidden hand of the Republican Party, was hiding in plain sight. But the record showed that party platforms mattered: their congressional representatives had a habit of voting them into law.

At the Republican National Convention in Cleveland, Ted Cruz pointedly withheld his endorsement for Donald Trump, earning a round of boos.[77] But when Tony Perkins took the podium, he announced, "I will be voting for Donald Trump in November, and I will urge my fellow Americans to do the same."

"From his judicial nominees, to his running mate, to the party platform and the policies it promotes," Perkins said, Donald Trump was committed to "upholding and protecting the first freedom, and therefore our ability to appeal to and unite under God"[78] By Tony Perkins's scorecard, Donald Trump had covered all the bases.

Now Perkins and his associates delivered their combined forces to Trump's campaign. George Barna estimated that the fundamentalist leaders in the Marriott ballroom "cumulatively held direct influence over 60 million voters."[79] This included the bloc Jerry Falwell Jr. signaled in his remarks at the meeting: "In the last presidential election, there were 25 million Christians who were registered but who didn't bother to show up at the polls. We are the single most influential voting bloc."[80] Getting them to the polls was the task at hand.

The fundamentalists' network of organizations and linked media, constructed over decades, would be an area of particular strength. By comparison, the Democrats and the traditional news media swam in a pond of divisive debate. Hillary Clinton had to contend with scathing criticism from Bernie Sanders and ongoing investigations in the *New York Times*—even if it ultimately endorsed her.[81] But the Republicans fell into line as soon as Trump's nomination was confirmed, and the CNP media complex responded to a central command. Once it embraced a candidate, the criticism ceased. Winning the crucial uncommitted votes wasn't a question of reflecting national public opinion; the majority of Americans rejected the fundamentalists' social platform. Polls showed that most Americans continued to believe that abortion should be legal in all or most cases.[82] Over 60 percent of the population supported same-sex marriage, and over 90 percent supported expanded background checks for firearms.[83] These percentages increased among the younger citizens who represented the country's future.

But it wasn't about majority rule. "God never waits until He has a majority on His side," George Barna declared, "to move forward in power and to claim a decisive victory."[84]

The fundamentalists reconciled Trump's character with their goals by defining him as not a man of God but an instrument of God. Barna's operational term for him was "God's wrecking ball."[85] He wanted Trump aimed squarely at the federal government and certain citizens its officials were elected to serve. His task was to destroy.

CHAPTER 12

"THE MIRACLE"

The Trump campaign benefited from the fundamentalists' get-out-the-vote ad campaign, but Hillary Clinton's campaign bought television ads too. In fact, it outspent Trump's campaign by almost two to one; the campaign finance watchdog Open Secrets reported that Clinton spent $768 million compared to Trump's $398 million.[1] If television ad buys determined outcomes, 2016 would have been no contest. Instead, the campaign was like Dunkirk: your sense of how it was going depended on whether you were in the air, on the ground, or in a submarine.

The CNP project ran silent and deep. The digital innovations were moving ahead at full speed, with the strategic focus and financial might of a corporate enterprise. Perhaps Ted Cruz's computer-programmer mother deserved the credit for her inspiration; or his strategist Chris Wilson, for electoral map reading; or young Thomas Peters, for his addiction to gamification. Regardless, it was clear that Trump didn't create the package; he inherited it. The irony was that the package had been developed to defeat him.

In December 2015, the *Washington Post* had reported that Ted Cruz's novel smartphone app included a number of features that were new to campaign technology. Its geofencing capacity could be activated to allow the campaign to locate supporters and allow them to find each other. Cruz's "enhanced voter file" contained as many as fifty thousand data points from voting records, online activity, and consumer sources. Cambridge Analytica embedded staffers and behavioral psychologists in the campaign to interpret the results and craft the messages accordingly. Cruz's team experimented on members of the National Rifle Association, testing messaging and psychological approaches at an annual meeting. A subject tagged as a "neurotic" could be approached with a pitch that emphasized the menace of home invaders and the benefit of a bedside firearm. A subject whose data reflected traditional values might be wooed with heart-warming messages of hunting as treasured family time.[2]

Chris Wilson, Cruz's director of data and analytics, told the *Washington Post* that "he didn't know what the campaign would do with the personal information it gathered after the election. 'We will take great care,' he said, 'knowing that our supporters provided this data to us for a limited purpose.'"[3] History would prove otherwise.

In December 2015 data security expert Chris Vickery found a massive database leak containing the personal information of 191 million American registered voters, including names, contact information, and voting records.[4] Shortly afterward, Vickery found a second online breach concerning another approximately eighteen million individuals. This data included far more personal information: cell phone numbers, religious views, "Bible lifestyle," and whether their hobbies included hunting or NASCAR racing. Vickery found evidence that the database was created by a company called Pioneer Solutions, headed by former convict Bill Dallas. Dallas was also the CEO of United in Purpose, the organization that cosponsored Trump's Marriot Marquis summit with My Faith Votes. "The data is made available to church pastors who want to know what percentage of their congregations is registered to vote," the Center for Investigative Reporting found. "Pastors can even search for individual members of their congregations . . . With the help of the data, campaign foot soldiers arrive at the door of such Americans, or call or email them, to urge them to register and show up at the polls."[5]

There had been plenty of efforts to mobilize religious groups for political purpose, but this initiative represented a new level of sophistication. George

Barna, employed by a division of United in Purpose, wrote that "United in Purpose proved to be an effective convener and bridge-builder among conservative faith-driven non-profits . . . The virtual company had proven its organizational and strategic abilities in the 2014 mid-term election effectively providing infrastructure, technology, and research at no cost to dozens of partnering non-profits."[6]

In 2016, Barna wrote, United in Purpose adopted a "more aggressive approach." It recruited some seventy-five "faith-oriented non-profit organizations, along with a few thousand conservative churches in the nation, who strategically cultivated support for a variety of pro-life, pro-family, limited government candidates in swing states across the nation."[7]

Barna listed thirty-five cooperating conservative Christian nonprofits. At least a third of them were headed by members of the CNP, including the Family Research Council, Focus on the Family, the National Religious Broadcasters, and Concerned Women for America. Another six were state-level affiliates of Focus on the Family. Media partners included Blue Diamond Media, headed by Mike Huckabee, and Catholic Vote, which published Thomas Peters's blog.

The organizations narrowed their issues down to five: abortion, same-sex marriage, Supreme Court appointments, limited government, and "religious liberty." Other issues were discussed, Barna noted, but "these ministries kept their focus on what mattered: saving the United States from further moral and spiritual cannibalization by the radical Left, represented by Mrs. Clinton."[8]

Their target was a pool of "38 million born-again Christians who had not voted in the prior two presidential elections, 26 million of whom were already registered to vote." The partners shared videos, digital voter registration software, and voter guides, as well as research from United in Purpose suggesting persuasive language and messaging. The media campaign began with the organizations' messages to their followers. "Between social media postings, emails, and website listings that included articles, videos, and blogs, the partner organizations initiated just shy of one billion unique digital contacts with targeted voters."[9]

The CNP's partner media were full participants. Barna reported that his fundamentalist conservative target audience "essentially gave up on the mainstream channels—ABC, CBS, NBC, CNN, and their various offshoots—in favor of smaller cable channels, a variety of independent online sources, and some handpicked radio analysts." The "independence" of the online sources was relative. Barna's "most trusted and influential news sources" included CNP president Tony Perkins and Tim Wildmon, CNP member, head of the American Family Association, and host on its two hundred radio stations.[10] These outlets pursued a relentless campaign to erode trust in professional news organizations, which their followers liked to call the "lamestream media." Barna noted that by Election Day, 99 percent of his fundamentalist conservatives believed that the media's reporting of the election was unfair and biased.

The movement broadcasts enhanced the networking. In the months leading up to the election, Tony Perkins's *Washington Watch* hosted CNP members who headed other partner organizations: Penny Nance from Concerned Women for America, Tim Wildmon from the American Family Association, Thomas Fitton from Judicial Watch. On August 22, 2016, Todd Starnes hosted Perkins's program "from the Fox News bunker in New York City."[11] Tony Perkins, in turn, was repeatedly featured on the Christian Broadcasting Network.

Other CNP partners pursued their own initiatives. NRA CEO Wayne LaPierre named Dana Loesch, a raven-haired Tea Party veteran from Missouri, as his special advisor on women's policy in June 2016, the same month she published *Flyover Nation: You Can't Run a Country You've Never Been To*. Loesch became an important NRA spokeswoman on the circuit, and brought *The Dana Show*, a popular syndicated daily radio program, to the mix. In 2014 she had been named Missouri's number-one radio personality.[12]

The fundamentalist media campaigns were leveraged with radio, online content, and live appearances. On Tuesday, October 25, for example, the American Family Association's Urban Family Talk network posted a video of CNP member E. W. Jackson, who was completing a "non-partisan five state tour to turn out the Christian vote in Ohio, Pennsylvania, Virginia, North Carolina and Florida"—all battleground states. Jackson declared, "Today's Democrat party does not represent the values of any Christian—black, white, Hispanic, or any other ethnicity." The site added, "Devout Christians—Catholic, Protestant, black, white, Latino, and others—will be persecuted under a Clinton presidency."[13]

At the Values Voter Summit in September, Tony Perkins announced that he was embarking on his own twenty-two-state "Your Values, Your Vote, Your Future" bus tour to speak with "Christians wrestling with the Trump candidacy." The fundamentalist outlet *Charisma News* reported that "the Values Bus Tour will focus on turning out the Christian vote in key battleground states," noting that less than 350,000 votes in four states won the election for Obama in 2012.[14]

Perkins's broadcasts reiterated that he would not endorse any specific candidate, but on November 2 he called in from the battleground state of North Carolina, reporting how disturbed people were at the "latest revelation of corruption from the Clinton administration." His colleague added, "You just have to throw the bums out sometimes."[15]

"FRC used Perkins' daily radio program along with an extensive and highly-targeted digital marketing campaign to educate and motivate its constituency," Barna reported. "If there was a medium available, FRC used it: phone calls, videos, door-to-door canvassing, voter guides, radio advertising, radio interviews, digital voter registration, and so on."[16] All in all, the FRC made millions of contacts, he noted, and the American Family Association made millions more—in addition to the other CNP affiliates.

The National Religious Broadcasters, headed by CNP member and Southern Baptist pastor Jerry Johnson, also played a role. Its "Christians Vote" campaign was broadcast on more than a thousand member stations across the country, reminding listeners that voting was a Christian obligation. Barna estimated the NRB's audience at sixty million per week.[17] (By comparison, National Public Radio had some nine hundred member stations as of 2016, when its weekly listenership reached an all-time high of thirty-seven million.[18])

The crusade was taken to church sanctuaries. The partner organizations delivered sermon notes to thousands of churches "to encourage and assist pastors in communicating about the election with congregants."[19] Perkins's bus tour—cosponsored by Concerned Women for America—made whistle stops at fundamentalist colleges as well as churches.[20]

Barna believed that his movement had learned a vital lesson that the Democrats had apparently missed: the most effective way to reach a voter was through a printed—not online—guide, delivered by hand, preferably by a member of the community.[21] WallBuilders, a United in Purpose affiliate run by Texas Christian nationalist David Barton, distributed more than six million printed voter guides in twelve swing states. Barna reported they had partnered with a total of 112,000 churches—a third of all the churches in the country.[22]

The results of get-out-the-vote efforts began to appear. In August 2016, the Democratic firm Catalist scrutinized the primary results from ten battleground states through June to seek the reasons for the record-breaking vote in the Republican primaries. They found that 1.4 million new voters had been registered since 2012. The share of white voters had risen 16 percent, while the share of black voters fell 12 percent.[23]

Rather than trying to sell congregations on Donald Trump's virtues, the fundamentalist campaign preached the evils of his opposition. In January 2015 Trump had effectively recanted his previous pro-choice position by signing a petition condemning abortion and same-sex marriage. The petition was proffered by CNP member Paul Blair, pastor of the Fairview Baptist Church in Edmond, Oklahoma.[24] Blair, a regular on fundamentalist radio networks owned by CNP hierarchy, had endorsed Ted Cruz. Blair attended the Marriott Marquis meeting with Donald Trump, stating on his departure, "I was not a Trump supporter, but I wasn't anti-Trump either . . . We know Hillary Clinton will be a disaster."

Like many of the participating pastors, Blair deployed his church in the political causes of the CNP. At Fairview Baptist, a modest, warehouse-like building north of Oklahoma City, his pulpit was flanked by giant screens that displayed hymn lyrics, Bible verses, and Technicolor images of souls writhing in hell. After one fire-and-brimstone sermon, he urged his flock to join an antiabortion march on behalf of "the 40 million babies murdered in the Holocaust of abortion."[25]

Organizations headed by CNP members developed videos to stir opposition to abortion, which dovetailed with the campaign. One gruesome example used animated drawings of fetuses and procedures, accompanied by a narration emphasizing the woman's pain and the possibilities of complications and death.[26] The videos were produced by Live Action, run by Lila Rose. The Susan B. Anthony List, headed by Marjorie Dannenfelser, broadcast its antiabortion, anti–Hillary Clinton videos in advance of the elections.[27]

Abortion became a centerpiece of the Republican campaign, far eclipsing policies that affected the health and welfare of those children already born. The messaging focused on misleading—and often outright false—arguments abouts highly dramatic but rare scenarios, devised by message framers such as the Leadership Institute's Robert Arnakis long before. The videos, messaging, and church bulletin inserts all carried gruesome depictions of "partial-birth abortion" and tied it to Hillary Clinton's alleged support of "unlimited abortion on demand." The Susan B. Anthony List advertisement stated: "Hillary Clinton supports late-term abortions."[28]

There were various problems with this argument. According to the Guttmacher Institute, only 1.3 percent of abortions take place at or over twenty-one weeks from conception. The procedure the fundamentalists labeled "partial birth abortion"—dilation and extraction—is extremely rare, and often involves instances where the life of the mother is at stake.[29] Such cases could involve uterine tumors, membrane rupture, or infections leading to blood loss, stroke, or sepsis. Other cases involve severe abnormalities in which the fetus has no hope of viability outside the womb.

This issue illustrates the disequilibrium of the debate: one can imagine a pro-choice campaign that dramatizes and "visceralizes" the agonizing plight of expectant parents who must choose between the health of the mother and the life of the child. Such cases raise existential questions, but they held no place in the fundamentalist campaign rhetoric. Instead, voters were besieged by an alternate drama: women bearing a healthy child to term and capriciously deciding to terminate it "on demand," with the support of callous medical staff. No one seemed able to show that this had actually happened.

Hillary Clinton's record was clear and consistent. She opposed late-term abortion except where the health or life of the mother was at stake.[30] But over the course of the campaign, Republican candidates and their networked media pounded away on a false representation of her position. Ted Cruz laid out the fiction in a September 2016 appearance at the Texas Tribune Festival: "The views of Hillary Clinton on abortion are radical and extreme. She supports unlimited abortion on demand, up until the moment of birth, including partial birth abortion, with taxpayer funding."[31]

Marco Rubio had made a similar charge the previous February, asking, "Why doesn't the media ask Hillary Clinton why she believes that all abortions should be legal, even on the due date of the unborn child?"[32] Donald Trump repeated the notion in the final presidential debate, using the visceral language deployed by the long fundamentalist campaign: "You can take a baby and rip the baby out of the womb of the mother just prior to the birth of the baby."[33]

The image took hold in the popular imagination. I was sitting in an Oklahoma living room with a group of sixtyish matrons, chatting about the election, when of one them burst out, "I just don't understand how Hillary Clinton could want to kill those full-term babies!"

ON AUGUST 26, 2016, the Trump campaign introduced America First, its first mobile app, on the Apple App Store and Google Play. It was a product of Thomas Peters's uCampaign, or Political Social Media LLC, the company that created the Cruz Crew app. In fact, it used the same template and sported many of the same features, including gamification "action points," an events schedule, and a news feed. The National Rifle Association had launched its version of the uCampaign app at its national meeting the previous July.[34]

Another version of the uCampaign app had been acquired by the Vote Leave campaign in the United Kingdom; the June referendum on Brexit would serve as its debut.[35] The vote was predicted to be an uphill battle for the Brexiteers. The polls indicated that British public opinion, especially in urban areas and among younger and educated segments of the population, favored remaining in the European Union. The population that favored leaving tended to live in rural areas and "old industrial areas," where high unemployment bred fears of immigrant competition for jobs. The Brexiteers' challenge was to enlist the unengaged Leave voters and suppress the Remain voters by convincing them to skip the referendum—not a million miles from the November challenge in the United States.[36]

The main goal of his British app, Peters reported, "was to make it easy for Vote Leave activists to inform their friends and family that they were supporting Leave, so that as many individuals as possible would know they were not alone in supporting the 'unpopular' side of the vote." The Vote Leave app included the Cruz Crew gamification features, awarding points and badges based on ranks in the British army. The result, Peters reported, was "a self-contained social network for activists of Vote Leave to connect, mingle and take action." At the climax of the campaign, the app prompted users to access their entire mobile address book and send everyone on it a "personal" scripted message telling them why they should vote Leave. The approach, Peters said, achieved a 99 percent delivery and read rate.[37]

The Brexit vote took place on June 23, 2016 (two days after the Marriott Marquis meeting in New York). It was a stunning upset, at 51.9 percent Leave to 48.1 percent Remain. A University of Warwick study showed that the highest numbers of Leave votes were cast in regions that experienced "deprivation in terms of education, income and employment."[38]

Two years after the Brexit vote, the British Electoral Commission determined that the Vote Leave campaign violated British law in its payments to AggregateIQ and Cambridge Analytica.[39] Vote Leave's advertisements claimed that millions of Turkish migrants were on the verge of flooding the UK, and falsely claiming that leaving the EU would free 350 million pounds to invest in the National Health Service.[40] TechCrunch reported, "In general, dog whistle racism appears to have been Vote Leave's preferred 'persuasion' tactic of microtargeted ad choice."[41] The Brexit vote unleashed ongoing chaos in the British political system and economy, and ongoing damage to the European Union.

The Trump app tweaked the features of the Vote Leave app and built on its success. Peters repeated the process of mining the users' phone directories. The personal invite code allowed them to track invitations. "This encouraged the app to grow virally," Peters wrote on his blog; "they could invite friends not just via email and text, but through their phone's share-to-other apps function." Peters intentionally kept the app simple, which favored older demographics; the app users were concentrated among people in their forties and fifties, which dovetailed with Barna's target population.[42]

Within five minutes of the user granting permission, the app downloaded his contact list from his phone and sent a pre-scripted message tailored to the recipients. Peters described his approach in an interview with Karen Jagoda from the e-Voter Institute:

> We do tie in with Facebook and Twitter, so people can share pre-populated messages there. But when we started out at the very

> ground level—why are we getting people to download an app as opposed to just visiting a website? One of the big reasons is that only a smart phone app has access to your phone address book contacts. These are the people you actually know, this is your mom, this your brother, this is your co-workers, this is your friend that you know from high school that you actually still text with. And so the big thing that we focus on is getting people to send and share messages to those people.

Peters added,

> When we bring in some big data it can become very powerful. So for instance with the Trump campaign when we built their official app, we could match people's phone address books to the voter data file. So even if you were living in upstate New York, we could find out, if you chose to opt in, that you knew people in Florida who were potentially swing voters, and here was a message we thought you should send them. We sent hundreds of thousands of those types of messages. It's one of the most effective things that we do for campaigns.[43]

Wired magazine dismissed the uCampaign app as a "minimum viable product." By comparison, Hillary Clinton's campaign retained a DreamWorks Animation team to create an interactive app that allowed supporters to visit her campaign headquarters to water the plants and pet the office dog—"immersive, cartoon-like, and colorful, as if the cast of South Park could walk through the door at any moment." The lead developer speculated that the more people petted the dog or watered the plant, the more likely they were to return.[44]

Peters had an answer. "What we focus on is the messenger . . . When my brother sends me a text message explaining that this is the reason why he's going to vote for your candidate, that's the message I have to pay attention to, because I actually have to care about what my brother thinks."[45]

In a speech to the American Association of Political Consultants, Peters listed his accomplishments: The uCampaign app was downloaded by some

150,000 Trump supporters who carried out 1.2 million actions and delivered over three million contacts.[46] In the final seven weeks of the campaign, the app sent 300,000 person-to-person get-out-the-vote messages, targeting persuadable voters in swing states. Supporters were rewarded with badges ranging from "Apprentice" to "Big League."[47]

Peters launched partner apps over the same period. One was for the Koch brothers' Americans for Prosperity, run by CNP member Tim Phillips. Another supported the reelection campaign for Wisconsin senator Ron Johnson. Canvassers for Johnson's Democratic opponent called or knocked on doors of 299,000 voters; the Kochs' Americans for Prosperity, guided by the new app, contacted three million. Another app served the Republican National Committee's Lead Right 2016 campaign, which granted Republicans up and down the ticket access to the platform. The National Rifle Association's NRA-ILA app helped to organize its millions of supporters for campaign activities.

Peters reported that his networked apps "generated hundreds of thousands of additional actions . . . Because of the shared nature of our platform, all the apps we run benefit from the improvements and breakthroughs we make for one app."[48]

The Kochs' i360 data platform continued to advance the Republican ticket. In 2014, i360 had tested its new products in the real-world laboratory of the Kochs' Americans for Prosperity campaign to defeat Democratic senator Mark Udall of Colorado, informed by extensive polling. According to *Politico*, "About 60,000 voters were broken into six 'treatment groups.' One group got a knock on the door, plus a volunteer phone call and a mail piece. Another got door plus mail. Another got door only, and so forth. Within those groups, the message varied."[49] Michael Palmer, a founder of i360, stated that i360's strength arose from its steady stream of money and its independence from the political calendar. Its innovations included "mobile canvassing apps or data management interfaces, so our clients can actually access that data, report against it, manipulate it, and put it to use."[50]

Americans for Prosperity deployed another "secret weapon" called the Grassroots Leadership Academy, a free six-week training program in Colorado, launched in 2014, that trained activists in election technology and other campaign techniques.[51] Offering free workshops, such as "community mobilizer certification," across the country, the academy complemented Morton Blackwell's Leadership Institute in Arlington, reaching beyond Blackwell's base.

The financial nerve center for these operations was the Kochs' Freedom Partners, headed by Marc Short, a close advisor to Mike Pence. Short had worked for Pence in the Senate, run Freedom Partners from 2011 to 2016, and then rejoined Pence's team, where he was considered Pence's ambassador.[52]

On Arlington's "Koch walk," Freedom Partners Shared Services, sharing a suite with Americans for Prosperity, functioned as an employment agency for the entire network, in partnership with the Leadership Institute. Freedom Partners vice president Kevin Gentry was formerly vice president of the Leadership Institute, and Freedom Partners Shared Services recruited staff from Morton Blackwell's shop.[53] Veteran GOP operatives viewed Mike Pence as a key player in the enterprise. They told Politico that they didn't believe the Koch operations had the power to create a presidential candidate, but "their weapons could make a decisive difference for someone who was already running a viable campaign for the nomination—someone like Pence, whose record could make him a bridge between the GOP's evangelical and establishment wings."[54] By selecting Pence, Trump could ride on his coattails.

The fundamentalists weren't the only ones who needed to be wooed to the Trump camp; the Koch brothers had needed some convincing too. In July 2016 Charles Koch convened his donor summit, including influential Republican figures such as Wisconsin governor Scott Walker, Colorado senator Corey Gardner, and Kansas representative Mike Pompeo, a close fundamentalist ally of Tony Perkins. At that point Koch told the attendees that his network didn't plan to support either Clinton or Trump. This offended some of Koch's traditional allies, but it kept the door open if Clinton won, and also allowed Trump to accuse her of being a patsy of billionaires without a rebound.

But Koch also told his donors that the network planned to spend a record $750 million in the election cycle—and it so happened that the money was going to be spent to the benefit of Republicans. It was reasonable to expect Trump to share the spoils, directly or indirectly.

The *Washington Post* reported that $250 million of the Koch network funds would go toward "the policy and political campaigns" of their own "grassroots" organizations—including Americans for Prosperity, Concerned Veterans for America, the Libre Initiative (to court Hispanic voters), and Generation Opportunity, aimed at millennials who could be deployed as field troops in the campaign to come.[55] The Koch network's money, media, and digital operations benefited Republicans up and down the ticket, from voter registration drives to the last-minute push. Everyone agreed that the key was to identify unengaged conservative voters and get them to the polls. The fundamentalists argued abortion; the NRA argued guns; Americans for Prosperity argued taxes; and they all used uCampaign apps. At least some could access and feed information into the Kochs' i360 database.

George Barna offered a trenchant assessment of the candidates: "Both Hillary Clinton and Jeb Bush were mediocre campaigners, policy wonks who didn't enjoy retail politics, approached the office as a birthright."[56] Trump, on the other hand, "was more interesting: he was a whack job perhaps, risky for sure, but more life-like, less robotic and scheming, more of a real person than Hillary the Elitist."[57] Trump's uncanny (and sometimes perverse) charisma would set the gears in motion, and the Democratic Party's campaign shortcomings would help.

The debilities of the Obama-Clinton era—overreliance on data, a weakened DNC, and neglected state-level politics—were catalogued in the book *Shattered: Inside Hillary Clinton's Doomed Campaign*, by Jonathan Allen and Amie Parnes. These qualities played into the hands of the CNP and Koch operations, which had been networking their data with their ground operations for years. They disciplined the Republican Party to a high degree of unity by rewarding the compliant and purging the recalcitrant, and devoted serious resources to state-level politics. These efforts paid off. In the years since Obama became president in 2009, the Democrats had lost 919 of the country's 7,382 positions in state legislatures.[58]

It wasn't just an issue of data analysis, it was a question of sourcing the data. According to *Shattered*, Clinton's young digital strategist, Robby Mook, played a major role in the plan. Polling and canvassing were expensive. Clinton was eager to save money, and Mook commissioned cheap analytics surveys, dispensing with more costly operations.[59]

Both Clinton and Trump understood that the electoral college would depend on a handful of battlefield states, including Pennsylvania, Florida, and North Carolina. But the Clinton campaign took Michigan and Wisconsin for granted, discounting the electoral impact of the DeVos family's successful campaign to crush Michigan's unions and the Koch brothers' parallel victory over unions in Wisconsin.[60] Barack Obama passed up opportunities to support unions in Wisconsin when they came under fire, and Hillary Clinton never traveled there for her campaign. Wisconsin state party organizers complained that the campaign didn't even send them campaign literature to hand out.[61]

The Clinton campaign took a lot for granted—including the Latino vote. Hispanics traditionally voted for Democrats, but they had moved steadily into the evangelical fold, where they served as prime targets for CNP partner organizations and the Koch brothers' Libre Initiative.[62]

As George Barna and i360 were crunching the responses from the ground troops and churning them into messaging, the Clinton campaign made a strategic decision not to emphasize the votes of undecideds.[63] But both Clinton and Trump were unusually unpopular candidates (for very different reasons). The undecideds held back, distorting the results of the surveys and the conclusions of the strategists. In the language of computer programmers, it was "GIGO—garbage in, garbage out"; or in the vernacular, bad input data that resulted in flawed conclusions. The Clinton campaign was asking the wrong questions in the wrong places.

But to be fair, bad data was coming from many directions. If Clinton and her team were overconfident for most of the campaign, they were echoing the leading news media. Over the years many national media organizations had also cut back on expensive polling operations, and as local and state news organizations declined and disappeared, their polling went with them. This made it even harder to take the pulse of regional populations, especially when little effort was made to do so. The coastal media tended to emphasize national polls, which showed Clinton leading by a healthy margin. The day before the election, the *New York Times* election blog *The Upshot* gave Clinton an 85 percent chance of winning. The night of the election, millions watched the *New York Times'* "election meter" swing from an overwhelming prediction for a Clinton win to the Trump victory over a few hours.

And indeed Clinton won the popular vote by some three million (compared to Obama's five million in 2012). She lost the electoral college by a total of less than 80,000 votes in three states (Michigan, Pennsylvania, and Wisconsin), and by less than 1 percent in each case.

In the postmortem, every expert had an explanation. The political analysis site FiveThirtyEight's Harry Enten showed how Clinton's loss could be attributed to registered voters who stayed home—especially nonwhites, Hispanics, and those under forty-five. "Simply put, Trump got more of his voters to turn out than Clinton did. That's quite a turnaround from the pre-election conventional wisdom that the Clinton campaign had the better turnout machine." Furthermore, Trump benefited from an increased turnout among white voters without college degrees. Enten added, "It's pretty remarkable that a group of voters that is shrinking as a percentage of the population made up a larger share of the electorate in 2016 than in 2012."[64]

Olga Khazan of the *Atlantic* detected the role of the fundamentalist campaign. "Seven in 10 voters on Tuesday said the next president's appointment of a new Supreme Court justice was an important factor—presumably because this judge could have a decisive vote in cases involving abortion and other social issues," she wrote.[65] She quoted a tweet by Tony Perkins: "It isn't that folks like him more than previous candidates. They were mobilized by what's at stake & the clear contrast w/Hillary on life."[66] Khazan added that Richard Land "believes evangelicals were motivated to vote in unprecedented numbers because of Hillary Clinton's record on abortion." Both men had pulled levers behind the scenes, in their roles at the Council for National Policy.

Many factors determined the outcome of the election, and the margin was so close that any one of them could have swung it in another direction. The U.S. Census noted a peculiar phenomenon in its election data: "When analyzed alongside race and Hispanic origin, in 2016 a large portion of the additional reported voters (2.8 million) were non-Hispanic whites who were also 65 years of age and older."[67]

Did the CNP and Koch operations make the difference? Given the sheer quantity of money, media, and manpower—much of it clever, most of it legal, some of it perhaps not—it's easy to see how they could have swung eighty thousand votes.

Word traveled among the fundamentalists. In March 2017, a video was posted online recording Canadian pastor Craig Buroker's explanation how it all worked, from a layman's perspective:

> I met this week for an hour and a half with the head of Canada Family Action Coalition . . . He had a chance to be with somebody this past week, who was very very well known in American circles, in government circles and also business circles and he's a very successful Christian. And he asked them a question, he said I need to know one thing, how did they get Donald Trump in as President when there was so much against him . . . There was an extremely wealthy Christian businessman, funded what they call a big data campaign in the eleven swing states. So this businessman connected with a guy who had the system, and what they did was they contacted 20,000 pastors in the eleven swing states . . .
>
> They targeted with this big data campaign, 20,000, they asked 20,000 pastors, got their data bases and what they did was, they sent information to people, for 15 million people, to find out do you know who you are voting for . . . They targeted from emails to text to phone calls to actually sending them a letter. They targeted right down to people who weren't decided who they were voting for yet. So once they sent the information out and the person said yeah, I'm voting for so and so, they were taken off the list because they knew who they were voting for. And they just targeted down to the people who didn't know. And at the end of the day when they found this certain number of people with this data campaign, they sent them the information on here's what Hillary Clinton and the Democratic Party stand for, here's what Donald Trump and his platform stands for. And when the Christians saw side by side what the values were, past voting records and the moral issues, it was . . . very clear.

Ralph Reed took his victory lap with a press conference at the National Press Club the day after the election. "Conservative Christians," he stated, had made up 33 percent of the electorate, and 79 percent of them had voted for Trump. (Exit polls showed an even higher count of 80-81 percent.[68])

"Donald Trump made the most full-throated, aggressive and unapologetic appeals to the evangelical voters that we have arguably seen in a general election environment, since Ronald Reagan spoke to the Religious Roundtable in 1980 . . ." Reed and his staff laid out the millions of interactions their coalition had delivered for the Trump campaign, and listed the policies they expected to be enacted in return. It was transactional politics in its purest form.

George Barna had a more mystical explanation, proclaiming, "The outcome was a miracle—an inexplicable, unanticipated, extraordinary event of human history attributable to God's intervention."[69] Inexplicable indeed—until the fundamentalists and the Koch machine were factored in.

DONALD TRUMP KNEW how to show his gratitude. The benefits to the Council for National Policy and the Koch network were tangible and immediate. Trump turned to his Evangelical Advisory Board for nominations for positions in his administration.

"They are inquiring on a regular basis if we have any other people, 'give them to us,'" Richard Land stated. "I've never had that level of solicitation from an administration before." Johnnie Moore, the Southern Baptist media strategist on the evangelical board, was exultant. "This White House, the front door is open to evangelicals," he told the *New York Times*, estimating that he had visited at least twenty times in the previous year. "Not a day goes by when there aren't a dozen evangelical leaders in the White House for something."[70]

The week after the election, Trump subjected his old friend Chris Christie to a second humiliation by dismissing him as head of his transition team and replacing him with Mike Pence. In the past, Pence had worked closely with Marc Short, until recently head of the Kochs' Freedom Partners and soon to be Trump's director of legislative affairs.[71] The new administration took shape accordingly.

The qualifications of Trump's appointees caused some puzzlement. CNP member Kellyanne Conway, a pollster, became counselor to the president. CNP royalty Betsy DeVos, a sworn enemy of public schools, was named secretary of education. Her credentials were so scanty that her confirmation resulted in a tie. For the first time in U.S. history on a cabinet position, the vice president—Mike Pence—had to cast the deciding vote. CNP member Charmaine Yoest, a former vice president of the Family Research Council, was placed in charge of public affairs at the Department of Health and Human Services.

Trump tapped CNP member Jay Sekulow to run his defense team in the Russia investigation,[72] and placed CNP vice president Bill Walton in charge of his "landing team" for the Treasury; Walton doubled as a donor in the Kochs' Seminar Network. Proposed as head of the IRS, Walton advocated eliminating corporate income tax.[73] The all-stars from the Marriott Marquis began to make frequent front-page appearances at the White House. Their influence was most obvious on Trump's Evangelical Advisory Council, and that influence only grew. In September 2017 the council was refreshed with new members, including Tony Perkins and Gary Bauer, member of the CNP board of governors and Perkins's predecessor at the Family Research Council.[74] In all, Trump appointed no fewer than eight of the speakers and panelists from the Marriott gathering to the council.

On April 28, 2017, Trump became the first sitting president to address the National Rifle Association in Atlanta. "You came through for me, and I am going to come through for you," he told them. "You have a true friend and champion in the White House."[75] On October 13, 2017, Trump became the first sitting president to address Tony Perkins's Values Voter Summit, proclaiming "We are stopping cold attacks on Judeo-Christian values." Trump was followed by CNP member and campaign manager Kellyanne Conway, introduced as "the woman who saved the world" by helping to elect Trump.[76]

A *New York Times* article marveled at the fundamentalists' influence:

> Mr. Trump and members of his administration have spent their first six months in office cultivating and strengthening ties to the movement's key groups and players with a level of attention and care that stands out for a White House that often struggles with the most elementary tasks of politics and governing.
>
> Their outreach extends to groups across the ideological spectrum—small government, tax-averse Tea Party followers; gun

> owners; abortion opponents; evangelical Christians and other culturally traditional voters. And it reflects the importance that Mr. Trump and his aides have placed on the movement politics of the right, which they recognize as the one base of support they cannot afford to alienate since conservatives, according to Gallup, are 36 percent of the electorate.[77]

CNP member Paul Teller, who had been fired from the Republican Study Committee and hired as Ted Cruz's "agitator in chief," was named special assistant to the president for legislative affairs. After the election he gave a talk to the CNP's junior division, the William F. Buckley Jr. Council, outlining his plans. The priorities were to repeal Obamacare and various executive orders on the environment, he said: "We're setting up a big Supreme Court fight." There was "more filling of administration jobs—some of the top folks," he told the young activists. "Also just filling in the staff positions, getting frankly guys like you, [CNP] folks upstairs, good conservative leaders into good places where they can have influence so that folks are surrounded by implementers who are themselves conservatives. You hear this a lot: Personnel is policy."

Teller predicted that in the new year the new administration would "dive right into a debt limit fight," and that "the Supreme Court fight will probably kick into full high gear." He was eager to tackle government agencies. "If you're talking about draining the swamp, the best way to do it is, a lot of government employees leave—attrition—don't rehire them. Make it easier to fire them. Go after the State Department folks too. Everybody always talks about the civil service domestically—no one ever seems to go after the foreign service. Let's go after the foreign service." Teller viewed the knowledge and experience of the diplomatic corps as an impediment to Trump's foreign policy. "Because nobody in the Trump administration wants to come in and feel like their hands are tied because there are like a thousand bureaucrats beneath them telling them what to do, and they've been there before, and blah blah blah."[78]

The Council for National Policy celebrated Trump's first two weeks in office with a scorecard in their monthly newsletter. Trump was moving on their agenda with dizzying speed. On January 20 he signed an executive order aimed at rolling back Obamacare. On the twenty-third he signed a memorandum to prevent U.S. funds going to international health charities that counsel abortions. On the twenty-fourth he signed an executive order to restart the Keystone XL oil pipeline, and the following day he signed an order to deny federal grant money to sanctuary cities.

But the bonus occurred on January 31. The previous year the Republican Senate had successfully stalled Obama's nomination of Merrick Garland to the Supreme Court. Now Trump nominated Neil Gorsuch to the seat.[79]

The next day, an 11:30 meeting appeared on the president's calendar. The White House labeled the transcript "Remarks by President Trump in meeting with SCOTUS Groups."[80] The "Supreme Court of the U.S." groups consisted of the leaders of eleven organizations. At least seven of the eleven were members of the Council for National Policy, including elder statesman Morton Blackwell. "I appreciate all of the help in deciding who to pick for the United States Supreme Court," Trump told them. "Leonard [Leo, CNP member from the Federalist Society], you were fantastic. All of you were. And Jim DeMint [CNP member from the Heritage Foundation]."

He invited the people around the table to introduce themselves, starting with CNP member Wayne LaPierre from the NRA. "Wayne, I would say they know you. Perhaps they know you better than they know me." There was laughter. LaPierre was followed by CNP member Penny Nance, from Concerned Women for America, who was followed by CNP member Charmaine Yoest, soon be appointed to the Department of Health and Human Services. The CNP's economic lobby was represented by Grover Norquist, and its legal front by Leo. Finally, there was the grand old man of the movement, CNP cofounder Morton Blackwell of the Leadership Institute.[81]

Over his first year in office, two of Trump's councils of economic advisers would be disbanded. His cabinet would become a revolving door, and White House staff would arrive and depart as frequently as the Washington metro. Federal agencies were purged of dissenters, and thousands of positions were cut—but the Evangelical Advisory Board prospered.

The benefits extended into 2017. In July a group of Council for National Policy leadership were invited to the Oval Office for a prayer session with the president during a day-long "listening session" at the White House. Tony Perkins was there, along with members Ralph Reed, Gary Bauer, Jim

Garlow, Richard Land, and some additional friends from the Evangelical Advisory Board.[82]

Perkins was anticipating a big announcement. He had been working with Mike Pence for months, maybe years, to ban transgender people from the military—although neither the Pentagon nor the courts could find a reason to do so.[83] Trump announced the ban by Twitter on July 26, blindsiding the Pentagon.

Fundamentalist media partners benefited as well. On July 25, 2017, Trump granted Salem Communications, co-owned by former CNP president Stuart Epperson, an exclusive "Day at the White House," with a series of interviews with top officials. Over 2017, Trump gave more interviews to Pat Robertson's Christian Broadcasting Network (often conducted by the CNP's Jay Sekulow) than to CNN, ABC, or CBS.[84]

As of 2017, the Republicans held all the cards. They controlled the White House, both houses of Congress, and thirty-three of the state legislatures. Furthermore, their ranks were filled with fresh blood: the average age of the Democratic House leadership was seventy-two, and the Republicans' was forty-eight.[85]

Trump moved quickly to fulfill his promise to reshape the judiciary. He had inherited 103 circuit and district court vacancies, compared to Obama's 54, thanks in large part to the Republican Senate's delaying tactics on Obama nominations. Now, with the Republican Senate behind him and the Federal Society nominations in hand, Trump prepared to fill the vacancies in record time.[86]

Toward the end of 2017, the Kochs took their own victory lap in the form of a Seminar Network paper called "Advancing Principled Public Policy." The new administration had overturned the Bureau of Land Management's Stream Protection Rule, rescinded the fracking ban on federal and Indian lands, and initiated the withdrawal of the U.S. from the Paris climate agreement. Justice Neil Gorsuch was confirmed to the Supreme Court. The Koch network's "grassroots" organizations mobilized twenty thousand people to contact their senators in his support. In the end, three targeted Democrats—Joe Donnelly, Heidi Heitkamp, and Joe Manchin—all voted for Gorsuch in fear of losing their seats. (Donnelly and Heitkamp would lose them anyway.)

It was ultimately about money, in the form of the Republican tax bill. An internal document from Americans for Prosperity, published by Lee Fang and the Intercept, showed the scope of their efforts. To build support for the bill, the Koch network organized more than a hundred rallies in thirty-six states, contacted over 1.8 million activists, knocked on over thirty-three thousand doors, and spent millions on digital and broadcast advertising.[87] On December 22, 2017, Trump signed the bill into law, giving massive tax cuts to the wealthy and to corporations and paving the way for a record federal deficit. It was another major step toward restructuring the American economy. A third of the corporate tax cuts benefited the top 1 percent of the population; 70 percent went to the top fifth.[88] The Center for American Progress Action Fund estimated that Betsy DeVos saved some $10 million in taxes the first year alone.[89] Americans for Tax Fairness estimated that the Koch brothers would benefit by saving between $840 and $1.4 billion in income taxes a year.[90] DeVos and other cabinet members began a litany of regret in their congressional testimonies, regarding the "difficult decisions" they had to make. It appeared that there wasn't enough money in the federal budget for after-school programs, heat subsidies for low-income families, and operations to clean up toxic waste dumps.[91]

The Republicans set their sights on slashing Social Security, Medicare, and Medicaid—entitlements many Americans had paid into all of their adult lives—betting that American middle-class voters would trade them off for a few crumbs by way of tax refunds. As *Forbes* magazine pointed out, "The higher deficits caused by the tax cuts of 2017 will fuel the chronic attack to cut the programs."[92] The social and economic damage would follow for years, perhaps generations, to come.

As the Kochs' fundamentalist friends might say, "God helps those who help themselves."

CHAPTER 13

MIDTERMS

On May 3, 2017, Donald Trump and Mike Pence hosted a dinner in the Blue Room of the White House for what they called "faith leaders," and what *Time* magazine called a "campaign advisory board." It was old home week for CNP fundamentalists. The guests included CNP members James Dobson, Richard Land, and Ralph Reed; member Steve Bannon attended as a White House official. Billy Graham's son Franklin was there, and so was their fundamentalist wingman, Robert Jeffress of the First Baptist Church of Dallas—according to Vox, "an unofficial leader of Trump's de facto evangelical advisory council." Jeffress had made headlines in the past, stating, "Not only do religions like Mormonism, Islam, Judaism, Hinduism—not only do they lead people away from the true God, they lead people to an eternity of separation from God in hell."[1] Nonetheless, the American Forces Network, operated by the U.S. Department of Defense, carried Jeffress's radio show *Pathway to Victory* in its programming for military personnel.

Jeffress and his colleagues were in the mood to celebrate. Earlier that day Trump had signed an executive order creating the White House's Faith Leadership initiative, designed to give faith-based groups a stronger voice in the government and to advise the administration on policies affecting their programs.[2] The first name on their judiciary list, Neil Gorsuch, had just been confirmed. Pence introduced the president as "a man of faith" who showed "courage, conviction and compassion."[3] Fundamentalists who had denounced Trump only a year earlier gave him a standing ovation.[4]

On May 19, 2017, Pence tweeted, "Joined the Council for National Policy, leaders in the conservative movement, who w/@POTUS are renewing the conservative vision in our time."[5] It was accompanied by a photo of him at a CNP podium, flanked by its vision statement: "A united conservative movement to assure, by 2020, policy leadership and governance that restores religious and economic freedom, a strong national defense, and Judeo-Christian values under the Constitution."

The CNP's plans for a 2020 takeover were—remarkably—on schedule. The leadership was well pleased by the way Donald Trump and the Republican Congress had been keeping their promises over the course of 2017. The judicial appointments and confirmations, drawn from the list presented to him before the June 2016 summit, were rolling along briskly, in the circuit and appeals courts as well as the Supreme Court.

In December Trump invited a group of fundamentalists, led by CNP member Ralph Reed, to the White House to discuss his plan to move the U.S. embassy to Jerusalem. There they discussed the executive order he had signed to repeal the Johnson Amendment. (Only Congress held the power to repeal it, however, and Congress demurred.[6])

The Republican Congress was going to extraordinary lengths as well. In December, Republican senator Patrick Toomey introduced a provision to the Senate tax bill to exempt colleges with certain endowments that didn't accept federal funding from a 1.4 percent tax on endowment investment income. Democrats and reporters could only identify one college in the country that qualified for the exemption: Hillsdale College. After the Democrats expressed their outrage, the language was stripped from the bill.[7] Six months later, Mike Pence gave the commencement address to Hillsdale's 367 graduates. "I don't use the word 'mentor' loosely," he told them, "but the President of Hillsdale College has been a mentor to me."[8]

The CNP president continued to cultivate the evangelical vote in return for favors. On May 14 Tony Perkins—the man who had declared that "Islam is not a religion . . . it is a comprehensive system which is incompatible with the Constitution"—was named to the U.S. Commission on International Religious Freedom.[9]

The following week Perkins convened the pastors from the Family Research Council's "ministry," Watchmen on the Wall, for its annual gathering in Washington.

Not everyone was a pastor; the gathering included representatives of state-level Focus on the Family groups and other related organizations. The annual three-day "National Briefing Programs" typically included Family Research Council briefings and training sessions. Then the pastors would be dispatched to Capitol Hill to lobby their congressmen, whose offices were helpfully listed in the program.[10] Over the weekend attendees would hear a series of speakers, many of them Family Research Council staff members, with Tony Perkins himself delivering introductions.

The Family Research Council was rallying the troops for the midterms a year and a half in advance, offering a combination of prayer meetings, pep rallies, and coaching sessions for preaching its gospel from the pulpit. One 2017 session was billed as "An Interactive Workshop: a panel of pastors discuss what you can do starting tomorrow."[11] Panelist Scott Craig was a Republican member of the South Dakota House of Representatives at the time, and pastor of the Landmark Community Church in Rapid City. Craig urged his listeners to overcome their fear of the IRS and the media when they took their message to the pulpit.

His point was echoed by another panelist, Dr. Gary French, pastor of Life ReNewed Ministries in Buckner, Kentucky (population four thousand). French reported that his involvement in the movement had brought him unexpected political influence:

> We've reached into Kentucky and I'm telling you, though it might seem like it's small, we helped elect a God-fearing Christian governor. We helped last year elect, for the first time in, I don't know how many decades, both a conservative Republican Senate and House of Representatives. I had a representative from the governor text me this morning for a meeting.
>
> I'm telling you, once you take that stand and just start doing these things, and organizing these events, people will come to you. We have presidential candidates come to our ministry seeking endorsements, because we were willing to take a stand. I've had my

> automobile keyed, I've had homosexual activists call me, and I'm telling you, God stands with me, and I stand with Him.[12]

The chair of the panel, Pastor J. C. Church, closed the session by intoning, "When we preach an uncompromised message, we will partner with the kingdom-thinking people that God has given the DNA to build a network that can capture the future in your cities and your nation."[13]

Tony Perkins closed the gathering by presenting the Watchmen Award to James Robison, who had done so much to spread his lifelong homophobic crusade across the nation and into the public sphere. Robison's speech bookended his 1980 rally in Dallas. Now, almost four decades later, he recounted the advice he gave in 2016 to Republican fundamentalist candidates: "When this campaign started a year ago, we had seventeen candidates. I was very close friends to at least ten of them. I got to be close to most all of them, I prayed with all of them. I don't care whether it was Ben Carson or Mike Huckabee—he used to work for me, I bought Mike his first suit." Ted Cruz, he said, "grew up listening to me preach, and Rafael his dad was in my inner circle, he helped me when Reagan was elected."[14]

Back in March 2016, Robison said, he met with Tony Perkins and conservative groups in Orlando to discuss the Republican primaries. It was becoming obvious that Robison's favorite, Ben Carson, wasn't going to make it. Carson told Robison that he had decided to endorse Trump—with a condition: "'The only way I'll endorse him is if he agrees to spend extensive time with you alone, and it has to start with a private meeting of at least an hour. And then it must continue . . . He's agreed.' The meeting happened in April . . . For one and half hours [Trump] told all the pastor leaders in his council, and I was privileged to bring in all the major denominational leaders, from the Assemblies of God, Southern Baptists, the various major groups . . . along with a few Pentecostal friends."[15]

The movement had come full circle. Robison had brought Reagan to Dallas, and now he delivered the fundamentalist war council to Trump. This was a man who made history, yet few Americans outside fundamentalist circles had ever heard of him.

The digital tools for engagement were advancing briskly, linking fundamentalists, antiabortion activists, and the NRA through a single app template, thanks to Thomas Peters' uCampaign, Chris Wilson's WPAi, the Canadian firm Aggregate IQ, and Cambridge Analytica, sponsored by CNP members Robert Mercer and Steve Bannon. The beneficiaries included the Brexit campaign, the Cruz campaign, and the Trump campaign.[16]

In September 2016 Peters and uCampaign followed with the Lead Right app for the Republican National Committee to advance its get out the vote campaign. Peters's stated goal was to "leapfrog the Democrats." "There isn't any mobile app," he told CNET, "offering as much data and offering as many ways for activists to engage as we are."

The following year uCampaign released another way for activists to engage. On December 22, 2017, anticipating the midterms, it launched the RumbleUp text-based app, which drew on several texting apps developed by Democrats. One Democratic strategist characterized it as "laggard technology," left in the dust by early adopters. "When it comes to campaign technology," RumbleUp's marketing materials admitted that, "Democrats invent, Republicans perfect."[17] The process of perfection involved connecting the information gleaned from the app to the network of digital platforms and organizations that could utilize it. Thomas Peters told the American Association of Political Consultants that the goal for 2018 was to "win everyone's attention with peer-to-peer text messages—even if they haven't opted in." RumbleUp, he reported, was slated to send 75 million texts in 2018.[18]

The Family Research Council joined the uCampaign family of apps in 2018. In May 2018 Todd Starnes told a Watchmen on the Wall audience that they could download the new Stand Firm app and use it to text their questions to the panel.[19] The app's privacy policy specified, "We may, with your permission, collect third party contact information (including, without limitation, names, telephone numbers, emails and social media handles, if available) from your mobile address book." These would be made available to the uCampaign client (in this case, the Family Research Council). The pastors' cell phone directories offered a rich opportunity to weave them and their congregations ever more tightly into the network.

The Watchmen's 2018 gathering showed how far fundamentalist politics had come. Its attendees enjoyed a special tour of Washington's new Museum of the Bible, created as a showcase and a gathering place for the movement. It had opened six months earlier a few blocks from the Capitol, in the former Terminal Refrigerating and Warehousing Company. Most of the museum's half-billion-dollar budget came from the fundamentalist Green family of Oklahoma City, owners of the Hobby Lobby craft stores. Hobby Lobby had made headlines with a landmark Supreme Court ruling that allowed it to deny some forms of contraception to employees covered under its health insurance plan, on the grounds of religious belief.

More recently, the company agreed to pay $3 million in federal fines for smuggling thousands of Iraqi artifacts into the country for display in the museum, shipped to Oklahoma City in boxes labeled as tiles. Thousands of items from the approximately forty-thousand-piece collection were forfeited.[20] Experts charged that other items in the collection were fakes, and they were subsequently removed.[21]

The Green family members were major donors to the National Christian Foundation, where they joined the DeVoses and the Friesses in funding such CNP regulars as the Family Research Council, Focus on the Family, and the Alliance Defending Freedom.[22] The Richard and Helen DeVos Family Foundation is also prominently featured on the Museum of the Bible's donor wall.[23]

The visiting Watchmen gravitated toward a sound-and-light show that allowed them to relive Moses' journey from burning bush to the Promised Land. They visited a Holy Land village re-created in mud and wattle, populated by reenactors in dun robes who demonstrated olive presses and other period devices. They found refreshment in the Milk + Honey café.

The program included two Republican congressmen (and no Democrats). One was Mark Meadows of North Carolina, who had helped lead the conservative revolt against House Speaker John Boehner in 2015, and who opposed the Affordable Care Act and any form of gun control.[24] Another was Mike Johnson, a youthful congressman from Louisiana and former legal counsel for the Family Research Council and the Alliance Defending Freedom. Johnson demonstrated the effectiveness of the Family

Research Council political pipeline. "Tony Perkins is like a big brother to me," Johnson told the pastors. "I literally began carrying his bags when he was a junior legislator in Louisiana, and the Lord's brought us all a long way."[25] In 2005 the Family Research Council honored Johnson's work for the Alliance Defending Freedom to block same-sex marriage in Louisiana.[26]

It would be a mistake to assume that the program was limited to pastors from flyover country. A place of honor was given to Carter Conlon, senior pastor of the Times Square Church, the megachurch at 237 West Fifty-First Street in the heart of Manhattan. As the Mark Hellinger Theater, it had hosted the 1955 debut of *My Fair Lady*.[27] Now Conlon and his praise team packed in shifts of up to fifteen hundred people at a time, who worshipped beneath a ceiling decorated with half-nude rococo nymphs and cherubs, landmarked relics of the theater's past life.

In his introduction, Tony Perkins wryly suggested that Conlon's Times Square Church stood at "the gates of hell," and Conlon echoed the message:

> While we slept, as a nation, while we failed to take the stance that we ought to in many cases, an enemy came in to the borders of this nation by night and surrounded the city . . . As a snake he slithered into the wombs of the nation and began to murder the children. The devil always goes after the children . . . Not content with that, he slithered into our grade schools and began to gender-confuse our children and lie to them about many things. Then he went into our high schools and told our high school children you cannot pray, you cannot do this, you cannot speak about God . . . He went into our colleges and began to radicalize our young people in the nation . . . Not content with that he went into the homes and began to divide and destroy the homes. Not content with that he began to redefine family and marriage in the nation.[28]

The 2018 conference included a personal appearance by Vice President Pence. The audience of over five hundred pastors, spouses, and church leaders received him with standing ovations and shouts of "USA! USA!" He responded, "This President, his Vice President, his administration couldn't be more grateful for Tony Perkins' unwavering leadership in Washington, D.C."[29] Pence recounted the various measures Trump had taken on the attendees' behalf, starting with the nominations of a record number of conservative judges.[30]

The Watchmen on the Wall activities didn't end with the conference. Katherine Stewart, who has covered the fundamentalist movement extensively, wrote in the *New York Times* that its briefings for pastors were "concentrated in contested states like North Carolina, Ohio and Missouri."[31]

The September 2018 Values Voter Summit was focused on the midterm elections. Tony Perkins convened the meeting at its usual venue, Washington's venerable Omni Shoreham Hotel, a massive brown brick structure that has hosted inaugural balls for every president since FDR, including Bill Clinton's celebrated saxophone performance.

The summit brought together some two thousand supporters and forty networked organizations, ranging from the NRA to the American Society for Tradition, Family and Property of Hanover, Pennsylvania. The event had been heavily advertised on fundamentalist radio networks across the country, offering listeners a chance to hear the rock stars of their movement and to tour an exhibition hall for stickers, leaflets, and swag. Freckled young scouts from Trail Life USA, the fundamentalist alternative to the Boy Scouts, guided participants through the maze of hallways to the meeting rooms. They came from all over the country: burly men in leisure suits and polo shirts, contrasting with the crisply tailored suits of their Washington chiefs; midwestern dowagers in pastels and pearls; stylish young interns in sheaths and spike heels; and a scattering of tagalong teens.

The movement's clout was demonstrated by the number of the nation's leaders who took a break from running the country to appear. The crowd warmly welcomed secretary of housing and urban development Ben Carson, who strode the stage with far more confidence and mastery than he'd shown during the primaries. The new secretary of state, Mike Pompeo, gave an address, and so did Senate majority leader Mitch McConnell. Vice President Mike Pence engaged in cheerful banter, pointing an imaginary trigger finger at people who spoke up from the audience. Donald Trump had spoken at the summit the previous year (the first time a sitting president had done so), but this time he sent his regrets.

The plenary sessions were billed as the main events, but the smaller workshops positioned the attendees for the midterms ahead. The name of the Council for National Policy wasn't used, but its leadership was much in evidence. Tony Perkins was master of ceremonies; other participating members included Gary Bauer, Ralph Reed, Tim Wildmon, and Richard Bott. Oliver North, the new president of the NRA, responded to recent school shootings with the news that the NRA was ready to send teams to do school "recons" to arm them against future assaults.

The summit opened with the United in Purpose breakfast, "The 2018 Crystal Ball: How Conservatives Can Gain Ground and Prevent a Wave Election." George Barna and CNP veteran Ralph Reed, the two speakers, focused on recent polls and the upcoming midterms. Barna reported that there had been a drop in engagement among the SAGE Cons, his sector of socially conservative older voters, which would hurt the Republicans. There had also been a major voter registration drive that brought in 1.75 million new Democrats. "The media is our biggest opponent," he stated. SAGE Cons were looking for a new media universe. "We can point them towards FRC, AFA, and CBN. Social media and blogs have impact, but research shows that radio has the biggest reach of any media."

As always, they had their eyes on the prize. The House race was tilted against them, but they stressed the Senate contest, which would leave them with the all-important judiciary appointments. The key Senate races, Barna noted, would take place in Arizona, Nevada, Tennessee, Texas, and Missouri—where the networked apps were already doing their job.

Ralph Reed emphasized that door-to-door canvassing was the critical factor: every engaged volunteer reaped an average of seven votes. The goal was over forty visits or calls a day per volunteer, in nineteen target states. It was all the more important because their research had shown that Trump underperformed with women and young voters, and considerably more voters described themselves as Democrats than Republicans. Then again, as Barna never tired of saying, it wasn't about winning a majority. It was about tipping the target districts in the battleground states. A look at the electoral map in most of these states showed bright blue dots in cities, surrounded by a sea of suburban, small town, and rural red. Strategy was all.

At the Leadership Institute workshop, staff coached attendees on how to approach nonconservatives, stressing storytelling and "situational awareness." They should anchor their points with a "handprint"—a gesture or a touch. "If you disagree with someone, put your hand on their shoulder and say, 'I'm praying for you.'"

They received instructions for their lobbying sessions on Capitol Hill, included in the summit schedule: "Don't burn bridges, smile. We need to be winsome. Take a page of talking points with you and send a hand-written thank-you letter." ("Winsome" is a popular term among fundamentalists, describing a display of "childlike charm.")[32]

The presenters were particularly focused on the Brett Kavanaugh confirmation process, and gleeful at the way the opposition had botched its lobbying effort: chanting, shouting, and blocking hallways in the attempt to persuade Susan Collins and other undecided senators. "Planned direct actions on the other side have been ineffective with our members and pushed them back into our arms—their direct actions are helpful to us." They were confident of their coming victory, and aware of its lasting importance: "Brett Kavanaugh will be Ruth Bader Ginsburg's age in 2050."

The presenters announced that the Leadership Institute had scheduled training programs in thirty states, starting with Georgia. Their question was, "How do we get evangelicals out of the pews and into the polling places?"

The audience heard, many times over, about the rapid pace of Trump's court appointments. By February 2010 the Senate would confirm a record number of Trump's nominees for the circuit courts, subject to lifetime appointments.[33] "If we can hold on for two years," Mitch McConnell told them, "we're going to transform the federal judiciary."[34]

The Values Voter Summit was also a cultural showcase for figures the movement and its media had elevated to celebrity. Jack Phillips, a soft-spoken baker from Colorado, won fame through the Masterpiece Cakeshop decision by the Supreme Court. Phillips didn't believe in same-sex marriage and declined to make a wedding cake for a gay couple; he added that he also refused other requests, such as "adult" cakes or cakes that denigrated anyone, including LGBT individuals. In a halting voice, he explained that he had welcomed the gay couple to his store, and he was willing to sell other products to the couple. Then he recounted how his business had been ruined by the controversy despite the decision in his favor.

Dr. Lance Wallnau's speech was more emphatic. A leading proponent of Seven Mountains Dominionism, he drew a dizzying maze of diagrams on the board and informed his audience that their duty was to "go into the den of Goliath" and set up "bands of believers within the halls of influence." Copies of Wallnau's new book, *God's Chaos Candidate: Donald J. Trump and the American Unraveling*, were available in the exhibition hall. Mammon was represented as well. A firm called Inspire Investing gave a presentation describing how their company organized investor protests against corporate funding for objectionable causes. So far, they reported proudly, they had convinced Chevron to stop contributing to Planned Parenthood, and Costco to stop supporting "divisive issues," starting with gay pride parades. Inspire Investing was the fifth-fastest-growing investment firm in the nation, they said, which earned them prominent coverage in the *New York Times*.[35]

But the conversation kept coming back to the challenge of the midterms. The political strategy sessions reported that evangelicals were ambivalent about Trump: they didn't like the man, his values, or his behavior, but they responded to the idea that he had kept his promises. The session leaders reported that they had been testing their messages. They found that immigration, for example, worked best when it was framed as a matter of law and freedom, not racism versus compassion. Other key issues were taxes, economic growth, crime and violence, and national defense. Their best mechanism was to deflect the voters away from the traditional news media and point them toward media generated by the Family Research Council, American Family Media, and the Christian Broadcasting Network.

The speakers alerted the audience to a dozen close Senate races—within two points, they said—where turnout was key. They reported that the voting rate in the 2014 midterms had been 36.4 percent, the lowest since 1942. But they called for a selective turnout. "Don't get everyone in your church to vote," Barna warned, echoing Paul Weyrich's dictum decades earlier. "Some will vote against you." It was also a question of where they voted. "The polls didn't call 2016 wrong," Barna reminded them. "The lesson is, look at what media isn't showing you—it showed generic national polls, not states."

The battleground states were what counted. The strategists highlighted fifteen: the key Senate races in Arizona, Florida, Indiana, Missouri, Montana, North Dakota, Nevada, and Tennessee, and the competitive races in Michigan, Minnesota, Ohio, Pennsylvania, Texas, Wisconsin, and West Virginia.

In the summit's exhibition hall, the Leadership Institute offered copies of its guide *Door-to-Door Campaigning: Everything I Know about Politics I Learned Going Door-to-Door*, with sections devoted to data management and "Talking with Liberal Voters." The Family Research Council provided a fat binder for pastors, including instructions to help their congregations in "Voting Your Values," complete with voter registration materials, voter guides, and tips for proselytizing. Liberty University handed out recruiting materials and branded lip balm. The iPray app offered pink plastic bracelets. You could purchase a copy of a book by Ben Carson, MD, titled *You Have a Brain*. There were lapel pins, Twix bars, and souvenir pens galore.

But the real prize swag came in the form of a shiny disc of base metal, offered on behalf of Lance Wallnau. Wallnau's "Cyrus-Trump Proclamation" compared "God's Chaos Candidate" to the pagan king of Persia, who issued the edict for the rebuilding of the Temple in Jerusalem.

Many fundamentalists believed that moving the U.S. Embassy to Jerusalem was a fulfillment of a biblical prophecy that would lead to the Rapture. In the End Times—which could come at any minute—believers would rise into the air to encounter Jesus, leaving nonbelievers (including Jews) among the "remnants" who faced an eternity in hell. In 2015 Mike Pompeo had delivered a speech at the Summit Church God and Country Rally in Kansas, denouncing the Supreme Court ruling on same-sex marriage and stressing the importance of evangelical Christians in public office. The future secretary of state solemnly declared, "We will continue to fight these battles. It is a never-ending struggle until . . . the Rapture."[36]

The Values Voter Summit closed with a gala honoring Elsa Prince Broekhuizen. A petite woman with a fluffy white pompadour, she gazed placidly at the masses. But she embodied power: an elite Gold Circle member of the Council for National Policy, mother to Betsy DeVos and Erik Prince, confidante to James Dobson, and major donor to the Family Research Council, Focus on the Family, and the Alliance Defending Freedom.

Inspired, the two thousand faithful left for home, determined that nobody was going to take flyover country for granted. They left the Omni bearing Voter Impact DVDs to organize church voter registration on Voter Impact Sunday. They passed Tony Perkins's Values Bus, which would be making a tour to churches and county fairs in a dozen states across the country, with special attention to Montana, North Dakota, Wisconsin, Tennessee, and Missouri—Senate battleground states.[37] The Kansas City stop was billed as a rally with Mike Pence at the Hy-Vee Arena, where the vice president would support Josh Hawley's campaign against incumbent Claire McCaskill.[38] Its October 11 Yorba Linda stop in Orange County was billed as a Salem Radio Life Broadcast & Candidate Forum. The bus supported a rally for Marsha Blackburn in Tennessee and joined a Total Christian Television rally in Akron, Ohio.[39]

WPAi, the consultancy run by Ted Cruz's advisor Chris Wilson, was going national too. Its website proclaimed that it "provided analytics and polling for key races at the state and federal level around the country," including the Ted Cruz–Beto O'Rourke contest in Texas and the Kevin Cramer–Heidi Heitkamp race in North Dakota.[40]

The networked apps entered the fray well before the November elections. The National Rifle Association's Institute for Legislative Action's app was particularly active. The NRA-ILA app offered extensive training sessions and campaign events focusing on battleground states. In July the app announced a Nevada session that included training in the use of the Koch brothers' i360 data platform.

Such events were scheduled in all of the battleground states. The coordination was exquisite: members downloaded the apps, the apps fed the i360 database, and i360 informed the canvassers. Morton Blackwell's Leadership Institute and the NRA worked hand-in-glove. Glen Caroline, the director of the NRA-ILA Grassroots Programs and Campaign Field Operations Division, had taught at the Leadership Institute. He oversaw the NRA's "campaign field operations, voter registration drives, and Get Out the Vote campaigns at the national, state, and local levels," while also supervising over two hundred of the Leadership Institute's "FrontLines Activist Leaders (FALs) nationwide."[41]

The NRA app offered a stream of events leading up to the midterms. An August 10 meetup in St. Louis served "to recruit new volunteers to help support pro-gun candidates this election cycle." On August 29 the Wisconsin NRA-ILA team presented "an important FREE Grassroots Activism Workshop" to "provide you with all the tools you need to defend our rights and help elect pro-gun candidates in Green Bay" at the Cabela's sporting goods shop. On August 31, the NRA partnered with the Cedar Gap Baptist Church in Seymour, Missouri, for a catfish dinner.[42]

It's impossible to list all of the 2018 campaign activities carried out by groups connected to the Council for National Policy, or to recount all of the ways they complemented the Koch operations. But the available examples are suggestive of the influence the CNP exerted in key races.

In January 2018, the Koch donor network gathered in Indian Wells, California, to commit $400 million to the 2018 midterm election cycle.[43] Much of the meeting focused on a new bid to privatize public education and to break the teachers' unions. CNP member Tim Phillips, the president of the Kochs' Americans for Prosperity, reported that his organization had created an impressive field operation in thirty-six states to promote its cause. "We have more grass-roots members in Wisconsin than the Wisconsin teachers' union has members. That's how you change a state!" he said.[44] Phillips's presentation was accompanied by AFP's chief executive, Emily Seidel. She reported that the network was "analyzing" fourteen Senate races and was fully supporting four Republicans racing against Democratic incumbents: Joe Donnelly in Indiana, Tammy Baldwin in Wisconsin, Claire McCaskill in Missouri, and Bill Nelson in Florida. "The list will continue to grow," Seidel said.[45] The effort would begin with a massive direct mail campaign and turn to mass mobilization in the fall. Americans for Prosperity was hiring en masse, and its website promised that its paid "grassroots army" would be supplied with "the best equipment, technology and teammates." (Unlike the populations it was set on dispossessing, AFP's "army" enjoyed full medical, education, and retirement benefits, plus paid vacation.[46])

On June 19 the *New York Times*'s Hiroko Tabuchi described how the Kochs' ground troops and the Koch network's technology converged in a story on AFP's campaign to defeat public transit initiatives. There was widespread support for a transit plan in Nashville, the *Times* reported, but then the AFP's Tennessee division came into the picture. It made almost forty-two thousand phone calls and knocked on more than six thousand doors, arguing that public transit violated liberties, and the measure was soundly defeated. The national campaigns also utilized phone banks, advertising campaigns, public forums, reports, and editorials in local media.

"Central to the work of Americans for Prosperity," the *Times* stated, "is i360, the Kochs' data operation, which profiles Americans based on their voter registration information, consumer data and social media activities. The canvassers divided the neighborhoods into 'walkbooks' or clusters of several dozen homes, and broke into teams of two."[47] The canvassers were equipped with iPads running i360 software. AFP funneled the money for the Nashville campaign through a local organization that was not required to name its donors.

Leading into the midterms, the Koch grassroots army rolled out its social media campaign in full force, inviting supporters to training programs to implement its apps and feed its data platform.

In Ocala, Florida, the Kochs' Libre Initiative invited Hispanics to free English classes at the Open Door Church. In Lincoln, Nebraska, the Kochs offered a free lunch to high school students who joined their training program. These programs were replicated across the country, recruiting local and national staff and volunteers for their campaigns.

There were additional efforts by CNP partner organizations. One was the Susan B. Anthony List. The antiabortion organization's website reported that it raised $28 million to send out 1,105 pro-life canvassers in ten states. These visited more than 2.7 million low-turnout pro-life voters at their homes and reached over 350,000 voters with live get-out-the-vote calls.[48] They concentrated their forces on the Senate races that had been highlighted by analysts at the Values Voter Summit, including Indiana, Missouri, Florida, North Dakota, and Tennessee. The Susan B. Anthony List's PAC, Women Speak Out, had made nine disbursements to the Koch-funded i360 data platform from 2015 to 2016, and four more in the 2017 to 2018 cycle, this time for "operating expense," "video production," and "digital ads." The Susan B. Anthony List wrangled its supporters on its own uCampaign app, Life Impact, launched on October 2, 2017. Its gamification features offered "prizes like pro-life sunglasses" and "precious feet pins" depicting feet at ten weeks.

The National Rifle Association's NRA-ILA app had developed innovative features over the previous two years. One was the use of geofencing: local gun shops and shooting ranges joined as partners, and the app facilitated meetups there among local supporters, reinforcing their activism through social interaction.

The NRA Political Victory Fund app organized volunteers for phone banks and canvassing. ("Please bring a smart phone or tablet along with a comfortable pair of shoes.")

In sparsely populated or heavily fundamentalist states, the combined forces of the CNP groups and the Koch network could make an outsize impact. Over the week of November 3, the NRA app promoted campaign events in Arizona, Indiana, Missouri, Montana, Nevada, Washington State, and Wisconsin.

The NRA was testing the boundaries. An investigation by *Mother Jones* revealed that the NRA appeared "to have illegally coordinated its political advertising with Republican candidates in at least three recent high-profile US Senate races," in "apparent violation of laws designed to prevent independent groups from synchronizing their efforts with political campaigns." In Claire McCaskill's Missouri Senate race, for example, the NRA "flooded local TV stations with ads supportive of Hawley in the month before the election."[49]

But synchronization was the name of the game, and i360 was the key. Its Federal Election Commission filing listed 884 clients from 2017 to 2018, including the NRA, the Susan B. Anthony List PAC, and Americans for Prosperity, as well as the Republican Parties of Wisconsin and Virginia, the National Republican Senatorial Committee, and myriad Republican candidates at every level.[50] Its capacity for data collection was extraordinary. Besides the usual voter files, i360 tracked voters' marital status, interest in diet and weight loss and cholesterol levels, preference for internet ads or outdoor ads, hearing difficulty, home equity, and household monthly expendable income, in addition to a category labeled "Bible."[51] When the various canvassers bearing their smartphones and iPads knocked on the door, their devices gave them an excellent idea of who would answer, and offered a tailored script.

Despite the Republican efforts, the Democrats had a window of opportunity. Public disapproval of Trump was building, and there was talk of a "blue wave" that could take both houses of Congress and bring the Trump Revolution to a halt. But there were many shortfalls on the campaign front. Democratic volunteers in Texas, New York, and California told the same story. Many of them used a mobile canvassing app called MiniVAN, which offered and collected data on registered voters and their voting history. But the data was limited to address, phone number (if you were lucky), party registration, and when they last voted. A New York Democratic organizer reported that his workers had to input their information on paper forms, which had to be passed along to be digitally recorded. Some presidential campaigns lent volunteers burner phones, but congressional races asked volunteers to use their own phones. Lower-level candidates couldn't afford the VAN services. Other companies were entering the digital space—including Voter Circle, Tuesday Company, Team, and Hootsuite—but they hadn't gained traction, and there was little coordination, either among the digital platforms or the state Democratic parties. In Texas, Beto O'Rourke's campaign was trying a new app called Polis. But it was competing with Ted Cruz's mature digital and field operations, run by Chris Wilson and WPAi in coordination with uCampaign and Cambridge Analytica.

The fundamentalists rallied their own grassroots army on multiple media platforms. On Sunday, November 4—two days before the election—Tony Perkins cohosted a preelection television marathon called *The Event*, carried on cable television and a Facebook feed. *The Event* was sponsored by the Truth & Liberty Coalition, and included CNP members Tony Perkins, E. W. Jackson, and Kristan Hawkins among its six featured guests. The program's website included resources from the Family Resource Council, including the iVoter Guide and materials for church Culture Impact Teams. There were also links to a Whitehouse.gov page titled "Trump's

Accomplishments" and another to a site selling a DVD called *Politics: Easy as P.I.E.* by CNP executive director Bob McEwen.[52] The cosponsors included an array of CNP partner organizations, among them the Family Research Council, the American Family Association, Alliance Defending Freedom, and Students for Life of America. United in Purpose and My Faith Votes were additional sponsors, as were various Baptist and other churches.

I streamed *The Event* from my perch for the midterm elections in Dallas. A few days earlier I had attended a Cruz rally in Fort Worth, standing next to supporters who called Democrats "demons" and described O'Rourke as "the son of Satan."

Early on election night the mood at the Ted Cruz victory party in Dallas was confident. Beto O'Rourke had generated some buzz, but the crowd anticipated a Cruz victory. We lined up for our repast of beef brisket ladled into a Fritos bag, topped with sour cream, and washed down with root beer. When the votes were finally counted, Cruz won easily, but the pundits who predicted a "blue wave" faced a contradictory landscape. Voter turnout leaped, especially among sectors that benefited the Democrats—eighteen- to twenty-year-olds, urban voters, and minorities. The Democrats won the House but suffered a setback in the Senate.[53]

At the Values Voter Summit, the experts had warned their listeners that the Democrats would need to win twenty-three seats to flip the House. They won forty. This reflected a marked increase in the national voting population that supported Democratic candidates and policies—but of course, the national majority was not the only question. On a practical level, it meant that the Trump administration would face an obstructionist House that would object, delay, and confront the White House on everything from budgets to investigations.

But in the Senate, the Republicans expanded their majority of fifty-one seats to fifty-three, versus the Democrats' forty-five and two independents. Democrat Claire McCaskill went down in defeat in Missouri, as did Heidi Heitkamp in North Dakota. Republican Rick Scott won a razor-thin victory over Bill Nelson in Florida. Chris Wilson claimed some credit, reporting: "For the fifth consecutive cycle, WPAi clients outperformed the partisan average in both their primary and general election contests by double digits."[54] The Senate victory gave the coalition another two years to push its federal judicial appointments, with the potential to benefit from rulings on redistricting, voting restrictions, and other factors to tip the balance.

But time could be running out. The CNP coalition was starting to wobble.

CHAPTER 14

"DEMOCRACY IN AMERICA"

The Founding Fathers created a marvelously complex structure, a system of political bulwarks that allowed one strut to compensate for the weakening of another. Their system of checks and balances placed the legislative, administrative, and judicial branches as counterweights. The federal, state, and local governments balanced local values against national interests. The framers of the Constitution enshrined the rights of a free press as a watchdog on corruption and government malfeasance. But they may not have anticipated a prolonged assault on every institution at once.

At the end of 2018 a group of young Family Research Council staff members touted their achievements at the state and national level with a Facebook Live video.[1] Matt Carpenter, deputy director of state and local affairs for the FRC, listed bills passed in the statehouses to support their causes, some of which drew on the support of partner organizations. "On the pro-life side," Carpenter said, "we were able to help our state policy council in Kentucky get a dismemberment ban across the finish line." In California, he reported, the FRC mobilized thousands of emails and phone calls to prevent the state from requiring universities to carry chemical abortion pills. Some victories represented the thin edge of a wedge. The FRC's legislative assistant celebrated the introduction of "unborn child language" into the tax code for education accounts, in the form of "any homo sapien at any stage of development."

Host Matthew Mangiaracina, FRC's manager of digital strategy, exclaimed, "I can't even keep track of all the wins, there's so much winning going on!"

Over the first two years of the Trump administration, movement activists concentrated on their missions to roll back women's access to abortion and civil rights for the LGBT community. In 2019 the Alabama legislature passed a law banning abortion altogether, except in cases where a woman's life is in danger or the fetus has a fatal abnormality, making no exceptions for rape or incest.[2] Other states have passed the so-called heartbeat law, prohibiting abortion after the fetus has a detectable heartbeat. This occurs around the sixth week of pregnancy, which is before many women learn they are pregnant.

There was little nuance in the antiabortion movement. The Susan B. Anthony List, seven hundred thousand strong, maintains that "life begins at conception."[3] In fact, the movement argues that life can even begin before conception: it is adamantly opposed to the morning-after pill, which pauses ovulation and prevents the release of an egg.[4] The Family Research Council's answer to it was: "Plan B No Substitute for Plan A: Abstinence!"[5]

The movement based its antiabortion propaganda on a falsehood: that Democrats support, in the words of Ted Cruz, "unlimited abortion on demand up until the moment of birth."[6] True to Robert Arnakis and the Leadership Institute playbook, its language and imagery became ever more distressing, beginning with campaigns to end "partial birth" and "birth day" abortions, and proceeding to the "Born-Alive Abortion Survivors Protection Act."[7]

Fearing an erosion of abortion rights under the Supreme Court, New York and Virginia passed laws giving women and their doctors increased latitude for their decisions, allowing them to address rare cases of nonviable pregnancies, severe untreatable abnormalities, and other dire contingencies. (One example is anencephaly, in which a fetus forms without a brain or entire skull.) Donald Trump exploited the issues by falsely claiming that these laws gave doctors and mothers the power to "execute" a newborn baby.

The Family Research Council and its affiliates declared war on Planned Parenthood, seeking to close down its health and contraception services for low-income women, as well as its abortion clinics. It has waged its battles by accosting patients with pictures of mangled fetuses, dispatching middle-school American Heritage Girls to protests, and harassing clinics' landlords and their children.[8] In 2019 the movement renewed its efforts on the cultural front, with the release of the feature film *Unplanned*. The film was an attack on Planned Parenthood, depicting its clinics as a craven venture bankrolled by "George Soros, Bill Gates and Warren Buffett."[9] One character states that Planned Parenthood's "business model" is simple: "Fast-food outlets break even on their hamburgers. The French fries and soda are the low-cost, high-margin items. Abortion is our fries and soda."[10]

The film's heroine, based on an actual Planned Parenthood employee, defects after she is told to double her "quota" of abortions. This is done by strong-arming tearful teenagers into getting abortions they don't want, and by inflicting unsuspecting patients with life-threatening hemorrhages (through what are statistically safe and routine procedures). But statistics were of no interest; *Unplanned* was melodrama, and it worked. It opened on more than eleven hundred screens across the country and recouped its $6 million budget in the first week.

The film offered an organizing platform for the movement. CNP member Lila Rose, founder of the antiabortion group Live Action, had a cameo role as a television reporter, which was put to use in the publicity campaign. The Susan B. Anthony List promoted the movie on its Facebook page, Tony Perkins devoted a column to it, and Mike Pence, Ted Cruz, and Donald Trump Jr. tweeted its praises.[11]

I watched *Unplanned* among a sparse audience at a theater in Times Square. I had a special interest in the film: it was shot in my hometown, and extras for the climactic antiabortion rally included students from my high school. I learned that the casting call emails had made no mention of abortion, Planned Parenthood, or the name of the film. Instead, they invited locals to appear in "an exterior scene" in a film called *Redeemed*, which was "based on a true story of a woman's journey and God's redeeming love and forgiveness."[12]

The movement's second crusade was to erode the rights of the LGBT population. It has already achieved some successes. Tony Perkins took credit for the push on banning transgender people from the military, which Trump announced in 2017.[13] That year, Texas lawmakers introduced thirteen anti-LGBTQ "religious freedom" bills, including a ban on adoption from taxpayer-funded adoption agencies by same-sex couples.[14] In May 2019 the Trump administration announced a new regulation in the name of "religious freedom," allowing health care providers to deny services on religious or moral grounds. Opponents fear it could lead to withholding health care from women and LGBT patients.[15]

Many CNP partners, starting with the Family Research Council and Focus on the Family, have been tireless advocates of conversion therapy. The Family Research Council defends what it calls "sexual orientation change efforts" as "effective and beneficial," and looks to the Supreme Court to reverse the bans in the future.[16] The same organizations have resolutely opposed same-sex marriage; the Family Research Council filed an amicus brief, which they claimed "debunks" the idea that homosexuals have the "fundamental right to marry."[17]

Laws govern behavior, but they also shape public opinion. In many states the passage of same-sex marriage laws has led to greater public support for it, and diminished homophobia.[18] But by the same token, as Dr. Dhruv Khullar pointed out in the *New York Times*, antigay laws can have the effect of poisoning public opinion toward the LGBT population, at the risk of increased discrimination and violence.[19]

There would be profound social consequences in carrying this crusade to its conclusion. As of June 2017, there were over half a million same-sex marriages in the United States, concentrated on but not exclusive to the East and West Coasts. Couples have been filing joint returns, bearing and adopting children, and serving as valued members of their communities for years. A large and growing majority of Americans support both same-sex marriage (67 percent) and the right to abortion "in all or most cases" (58 percent).[20] Historically, once political and civil rights are enshrined in law, there are few successful examples of revoking them—and those have ended badly.

There are broader issues at stake. The United States is a large and complex society, navigating a turbulent period of history. Its leaders face urgent decisions concerning climate change, public health and education, and international conflict. How can the country countenance the reduction of its entire future to a litmus test on abortion and same-sex marriage—debated under false premises?

Yet similar principles affect the U.S. judiciary as well. As of May 5, 2019, Donald Trump's 102nd judicial nominee was confirmed; his nominations comprise thirty-seven appeals court judges, sixty-three district judges, and two Supreme Court justices. Congressional Republicans expedited the process. In April 2019 the Republican-controlled Senate altered its rules to accelerate confirmation by limiting debate to two hours, and suspended the power of the "blue slip" to allow home-state senators to essentially veto nominees. (Republicans noted that it was Democrat Harry Reid who, as then Senate majority leader, invoked the "nuclear option" to confirm Obama nominations in 2013.[21])

The circuit courts can exert a major influence on national policy. Trump has encouraged the overwhelmingly conservative Fifth Circuit Court, corresponding to Louisiana, Mississippi, and Texas, to do away with the entire Affordable Care Act.[22] Trump appointments achieved a Republican-appointed majority in the Third Circuit Court, covering New Jersey, Delaware, the U.S. Virgin Islands, and parts of Pennsylvania, and they are well on the way to flipping the influential Ninth Circuit Court, based in San Francisco.[23] This court has attracted Trump's ire by challenging the administration's Muslim travel ban and other controversial measures.[24]

The new judges are distinguished by their ideology and their youth. In March 2019, for example, the Senate confirmed thirty-seven-year-old Allison Jones Rushing to the Fourth Circuit, with jurisdiction over Maryland and districts in the Carolinas, Virginia, and West Virginia. Rushing served as a legal intern for the Alliance Defending Freedom, and has publicly opposed the Supreme Court decision on behalf of same-sex marriage.[25] As of March 2019, Trump was responsible for a fifth of the seats in the appeals courts, guided by the Federalist Society, the Heritage Foundation, and the NRA. There were more than three dozen appeals and circuit court nominees in waiting.

The ideological litmus tests for court appointments grew starker. The American Bar Association, which instituted its ratings system at the request of President Dwight Eisenhower, gave more "not qualified" ratings to Trump nominees than to the previous four presidents combined.[26]

Some ideology tests were blatant, such as the appointments for the Board of Veterans Appeals, which adjudicated veterans' issues under the aegis of the Veterans Administration. The appointments had always been nonpartisan, and the White House confirmation routine. But in 2018, for the first time, the White House required a slate of eight nominees to disclose their party affiliation and other political details. The candidates, already heavily vetted serving judges, were winnowed according to party: the three Democrats and an independent were rejected, the three Republicans and an independent who voted Republican approved.[27] It was an unprecedented move.

But the Supreme Court represented the highest stakes. By blocking Obama's nomination of Merrick Garland, the Republican Senate left one seat open for Trump to fill. The retirement of Anthony Kennedy left another. Trump's appointees, Neil Gorsuch and Brett Kavanaugh, have not always agreed. But on June 27, 2019, they joined the court's other conservatives in a 5-4 ruling that federal courts lacked the power to hear challenges to partisan gerrymandering, a practice that has increasingly stacked the deck on behalf of Republicans in a number of states. This decision would impact local, state, and national elections for years to come.

The electoral process faces other risks as well. The infrastructure of American democracy, like the country's roads and bridges, is aging. The Constitution, however revered, was hammered out as a compromise among men defending very specific economic and political interests, over two centuries ago. The Electoral College undermined the principle of "one man, one vote," and rewarded Donald Trump's narrow victories in Pennsylvania and Wisconsin over Hillary Clinton's much wider margins in New York and California.[28] The creation of the powerful institution of the Senate has resulted in a citizen in Wyoming exercising around sixty-seven times the voting power of a Californian.[29] The nation has bumped along with these anomalies, but their liabilities are increasingly called into question.

The 2018 electoral map showed other aspects of the great divide. Once again, the Democrats won the coasts and the cities, while Republicans dominated the South and the Plains states. But the rift was even obvious in individual states. One example was Missouri, where Democrat Claire McCaskill's victories in St. Louis, Kansas City, and the college town of Columbia marked three blue dots in a sea of red.

The crisis in the news media compounded the problems. The impact of Sinclair stations was extensively reported, but there has been equal concern over the partisan nature of Fox News. According to the *New York Times*, "the symbiosis between Fox News stars and the Trump administration means the network will not treat Democrats fairly." (Fox News's Washington headquarters are located in the Hall of the States building on North Capitol Street, the same office complex that houses the CNP's.) The channel's influence was growing. In April 2019, Fox News finished first among cable news channels with a prime-time audience of nearly 2.4 million viewers. That's still well under 1 percent of the U.S. population—but the same month, CNN's prime-time audience plummeted 26 percent, to 767,000.[30] Televisions are permanently set to Fox News in bars, airport lounges, and waiting rooms through many stretches of the South and the Midwest.

Fox's influence is multiplied across its many platforms. CNP member Todd Starnes is a good example. The FoxNation streaming service carries his program *Starnes Country*. In 2018 Fox News Radio announced that it was expanding *The Todd Starnes Show* to a full three-hour program every weekday. Starnes's Facebook page—with a quarter of a million followers—states that "his daily commentaries are heard on more than 500 [radio] stations."

The media organizations run by CNP members are less celebrated than Fox News, but they have their own impact, especially in the states where they are concentrated. Consider, for example, the case of Missouri, where Claire McCaskill lost a tightly contested race against Josh Hawley in 2018. The Bott Radio Network owns forty-eight stations in the state of Missouri alone. The CNP is well represented in its schedule, which carries Tony Perkins's *Washington Watch*, James Dobson's *Family Talk*, and Gary Bauer's *End of Day Report*.[31] National Public Radio, by comparison, had thirteen stations.[32] Both of the state's leading dailies endorsed McCaskill, but the *Kansas City Star* and the *St. Louis Post-Dispatch*'s combined circulation represented around 6 percent of the state's more than six million citizens.[33]

The combination of partisan media and ground troops can be powerful indeed. McCaskill faced attacks from a battery of organizations run by CNP members. The Family Research Council excoriated her for supporting abortion rights and gun control.[34] The FRC's Watchmen on the Wall, boasting 1,927 Missouri pastors in its network, distributed iVoter guides in their churches labeling her as "very liberal" and linking to a Project Veritas video tying her to Planned Parenthood.[35] (Project Veritas was launched in 2010 as a project to discredit news media and liberal organizations through sting operations. Its founder, James O'Keefe, had received training and modest financial support from Morton Blackwell's Leadership Institute.[36])

The NRA ran a campaign called "Defend Freedom. Defeat Claire McCaskill," giving her an F in its ratings. Its app announced that its Missouri team was going door-to-door "to build support for Missouri's Pro–Second Amendment candidates."[37]

The Susan B. Anthony List went all out. Its press release announced that it had sent a "field team of 117 canvassers to visit more than 310,000 Missouri voters ahead of Election Day to elect pro-life Josh Hawley and defeat incumbent Senator Claire McCaskill. Additionally, it held eight in-state media events, reached 448,144 voters through persuasive voter contact mail and digital ads, made 90,399 live voter calls, and raised $34,392 in bundled contributions for Hawley's campaign."[38]

The Koch brothers' Americans for Prosperity–Missouri assailed McCaskill with a $1.8 million multimedia campaign, including television, cable, and digital ads.[39] The national Americans for Prosperity organization ran five ads against McCaskill on Facebook in Missouri between August 31 and September 16 alone, informed by its powerful data collection.[40]

The Democrats' response to this situation has been colored by troubles of their own. The party faces a generational divide between the traditional "white men" who have run the party in the past, and a newly energized generation that reflects the growing diversity of the nation. But both camps have been slow to grasp the realities of the new electoral map, a fact exemplified by Hillary Clinton's failure to show up in Wisconsin, a major stop on what Nate Silver calls the "Northern Path" to electoral victory. The Democratic Party has taken its traditional constituencies for granted and missed the ground shifting beneath its feet. With their party's headlong rush to diversity, Democratic activists tended to underestimate the role of the Electoral College in the swing states, but without the Rust Belt it was hard to make the math compute.

In the words of *Atlantic* senior editor Ronald Brownstein, the trigger for Trump's victory was "a mass uprising by the GOP's 'coalition of restoration'... the older and blue-collar whites, evangelical Christians and non-urban voters who in polls have consistently expressed both the most economic pessimism and cultural unease about a changing America."[41] This demographic sounded surprisingly similar to George Barna's SAGE Cons.

The Democrats' Rust Belt problem has often been ascribed to the loss of industrial jobs in the region, a major factor.[42] But one should not overlook the impact of the massive targeted get-out-the-vote efforts conducted by CNP and Koch partners, combined with a multiplatformed media, advertising, and canvassing campaigns informed by state-of-the-art data and a keen understanding of their audiences.

The playing field was far from level—the military would call it asymmetrical warfare. The Democratic Party fostered a culture of infighting and debate, pitting candidates and constituents against each other and amplifying infractions and gaffes. These were aired in the traditional news media, which turned a critical eye on every candidate from every party. This played into the hands of the new Republicans, who imposed a high degree of discipline on their organizations, of which every component—including dedicated media operations—executed its appointed tasks.

One question that arises is the legality of certain actions of the CNP and Koch organizations, in view of the requirements of their tax-exempt, nonpartisan status. But it would be a mistake to focus exclusively on this question. These groups operated within a framework that was constructed under both Democratic and Republican administrations. Both parties bear responsibility for an American political system that has been increasingly corrupted by skewed campaign finance laws, undermining participatory democracy and surrendering power to wealthy individuals and corporate interests. The laws governing the political activities of nonprofits are soft and unenforced, benefiting special interests on both sides. The complex legal questions of campaign finance and data gathering are far from settled. But it should not be denied that the CNP and the Koch operations owe a large measure of their success to smarter strategies, stronger coalitions, and that abiding but often forgotten principle, "Know your audience." Their approach was honed and informed by the likes of Weyrich and Barna: "God doesn't need a majority." Neither does the U.S. electoral system as it is currently constituted.

As the CNP members pursued their social policies, the Koch network advanced its economic plan. On December 22, 2017, President Trump signed the most radical revision of the U.S. tax code in thirty years, without a single Democratic vote. The Koch brothers, DeVoses, and their counterparts benefited—but at the cost of a massive national deficit. The Committee for a Responsible Federal Budget projected that the shortfall for the fiscal year would approach $900 billion, about a quarter of which was the result of the new tax bill.[43]

Nonetheless, in March 2019, the Trump administration released its 2020 budget request, with large increases for defense and border security and cuts in social programs and federal agencies. Medicare, Medicaid, and student loans were all on the chopping block. The budget aimed for a 15 percent cut for the Department of Agriculture, including drastic reduction of its programs for food stamps and conservation. The Department of Education was slated for a 12 percent cut. At Health and Human Services, the National Institutes of Health would lose about 12 percent of its budget, and the Centers for Disease Control around 10 percent. The State Department and the U.S. Agency for International Development would lose almost a quarter of their budget, and the Environmental Protection Agency nearly a third.[44] "God's wrecking ball" was on a tear, battering the institutions of the U.S. government.

Trump continued to turn to his CNP supporters to implement key policies. In June 2019 he appointed CNP member Ken Cuccinelli to head U.S. Citizenship and Immigration Services. In a December 2018 op ed in the *Washington Times*, Cuccinelli had suggested, "The president could continue adding troops to the border and turn border security entirely over to the military."[45]

Trump's fundamentalist supporters girded themselves for the battle ahead. On June 16, 2019, the *Washington Times* published an account of Ralph Reed's plans for 2020, "to register 1 million evangelical voters, knock on 3 million doors, and put literature in more than 117,000 churches in key states, with the hopes of contacting roughly 30 million people." Reed reported, "It's going to be roughly three times the level of what we did in 2016.[46]

The strategists of the CNP had long been cultivating right-wing Catholics such as Frank Pavone, seeking to expand their remit from evangelicals, or the "born again," to conservative Christians. Now Reed told the *Washington Times* that, "when 'faithful, frequently Mass-attending Roman Catholics' are added in, conservative religious voters will likely total close to 40% of the electorate—larger than the Hispanic, black and union votes combined." The article closed with a comment from E.W. Jackson, a Virginia pastor and a member of the CNP. "Yeah, I know he's not perfect, but here again: It's not Donald Trump or Jesus," he stated. "It's really Donald Trump or the devil in a way, if you know what I mean."

WHAT WOULD THE American pluto-theocracy look like? For a glimpse into the future, one can consider Oklahoma. The state government has long been heavily dependent on tax revenues from the oil and gas industry. In 2014, then governor Mary Fallin slashed the oil and natural gas gross production tax to 2 percent from its customary 7 percent.[47] By 2017 the tax breaks were costing the state nearly $400 million a year.[48]

The first victim was public education. Oklahoma has cut general state funds for public schools by over 28 percent between 2008 and 2018, the largest drop in the nation.[49] Oklahoma teachers gained the title of lowest-paid in the country.[50] The results were tangible; I heard about them from friends and family every time I went home. In Tulsa a group of students from a well-regarded public high school told of walls with crumbling plaster that went untended for months. They studied from battered old textbooks with missing pages. A fifth of the school districts retreated to a four-day school week. A friend's daughter, a dedicated teacher, had to move out of state to make a living. That wasn't unusual; even Oklahoma's 2016 Teacher of the Year, Shawn Sheehan, moved to Texas for the same reason. Other teachers took second jobs to make ends meet and held bake sales to buy classroom materials.[51]

In 2017 the Oklahoma teachers staged a walkout, and the following year sixty-five educators ran for the state legislature. They met keen opposition from the American Federation for Children, which was chaired by Betsy DeVos before she became secretary of education. The AFC's mantra was "school choice," which translated to diverting resources from public schools to private and religious schools, and opposing candidates who called for tax increases to fund public education. The goals coincided with the Council for National Policy's position on public education, as expressed in a 2017 manifesto. The CNP's "Education Reform Report" called for minimizing the role of the federal government in education, supporting religious schools and homeschooling, and using "historic Judeo-Christian principles" as an educational foundation.[52]

DeVos's organization advanced the mission by supporting challengers to public school advocates in twelve states with money, ads, direct mail, and calls.[53] In Oklahoma that translated into almost $45,000 spent on direct mail to oppose the teachers—over one week alone.[54] Nonetheless, sixteen teachers, administrators, and support staff from the Oklahoma Education Association won seats in the legislature.[55]

Oklahoma's crisis extended far beyond education. The waiting list for disability services lengthened to roughly ten years. Public health indicators were an ongoing disaster, and a quarter of the state's children lived with hunger.[56] In the meantime, the oil and gas industry counted among the largest beneficiaries of President Trump's tax reform.[57]

AT THE SAME time these transformations were taking place, there were countercurrents—signs that some members of the Democratic fold were taking note of their deficits. In May 2019 Maggie Severns reported in *Politico* that the Democracy Alliance was shifting its strategy, cutting back on its funding for Washington-based organizations and directing new resources to grassroots organizations at the state level. *Politico* reported that the alliance had retained New Media Ventures to head its digital organizing, "spurred by concerns among Democrats that the GOP and Trump campaign deployed better digital advertising and organizing tactics in 2016 than they did."[58]

The sands were shifting in the Koch empire as well. In 2018 David Koch withdrew from Seminar Network activities and resigned as chairman of Americans for Prosperity, citing poor health. The Kochs, never fans of Donald Trump, parted ways with the administration on various issues, including immigration and criminal justice reform. On May 20, 2019, the *Washington Post* reported that there were big changes afoot at the Seminar Network meeting in Indian Wells, California. The leadership announced that the Seminar Network would henceforth operate under the name Stand Together. Freedom Partners, which formerly aired campaign commercials, would disappear, and Americans for Prosperity would take over all political and policy operations.[59]

The meeting followed on the January session, which stressed financial support for mainstream nonprofits and charities. The network declined to announce a target amount for spending in the 2020 elections, and only three politicians attended (all Republican, but stressing bipartisan credentials).[60]

But the Koch campaign was far from over. The report on the May meeting noted the Kochs' intention to pursue a "comprehensive approach" toward four institutions: "the education field, the business world, community organizations, and politics/policy-making." They were expanding their media portfolio as well. Following the 2016 elections, Koch organizations offered a number of grants to cash-starved journalism organizations, including the American Society of News Editors and the Newseum in Washington, D.C.[61]

In April 2019 the venerable Poynter Institute, a leader in the field of journalism development, announced a new partnership with the Charles Koch Institute to train young journalists and place them in the newsrooms of leading news organizations.[62] The grants provoked debate among the recipients, who noted the Kochs' attempts to discredit reporters who published critical accounts of their operations: the salient example was Jane Mayer, whose book *Dark Money* revealed the Kochs' disinformation campaigns on climate and environmental issues. The Kochs' increased investments in education and journalism posed troubling questions, but it was too soon to say where they would lead.

The situation of the National Rifle Association was more transparent. The NRA had long been a critical partner of the CNP, and a prominent client of the Kochs' i360 data platform. Between 2016 and 2017 the NRA's revenue dropped by tens of millions of dollars, forcing it to carry out drastic cutbacks. In 2019 it experienced a full meltdown. Russian operative Maria Butina was sentenced to eighteen months in prison for her role in infiltrating the NRA and brokering relations between its leadership and the Putin government. The association was named in a lawsuit filed against the Federal Election Commission for failing to respond to alleged campaign law infractions. The New York attorney general launched an investigation of the legitimacy of the NRA's nonprofit status.[63]

In April the NRA sued its Oklahoma City–based advertising agency of thirty-eight years, Ackerman McQueen, accusing it of withholding billing information and breach of contract. This action sparked an ongoing feud between NRA president Oliver North and executive vice president Wayne LaPierre—both members of the CNP. Much of the suit revolved around the agency's handling of NRATV video service and a multimillion-dollar contract with North to host a series. Then the *Wall Street Journal* revealed that North had accused LaPierre of receiving over $200,000 toward designer suits (reportedly from the Beverly Hills outlet for Ermenegildo Zegna), purchased through Ackerman McQueen. LaPierre was also accused of using Ackerman McQueen to charge another $240,000 for lavish trips to Hungary, Italy, the Bahamas, Palm Beach, and Reno.[64]

There were promises of more revelations to come. The NRA's annual convention in Indianapolis erupted as North tried to banish LaPierre. LaPierre fought back, winning reelection by the board, and North was informed that he would not be renominated as president.[65] The NRA tried to divert attention from the disaster by publicizing President Trump and Vice President Pence's presence at the convention. On April 29, North was replaced by CNP member Carolyn Meadows, and the saga continued.

AS AMERICANS LOOKED toward the 2020 elections, much of the debate centered around the question of impeaching Donald Trump. It's possible that impeachment held little terror for the CNP—its favored son, Mike Pence, was next in line. The news media made surprisingly little mention of Pence, who had an uncanny ability to fade into the woodwork. Few pundits listened to Pence on *Washington Watch*, or attended to his role in striking the fundamentalists' bargain with Trump in 2016. Pence had long-standing ties to Tony Perkins and the CNP's membership, and a far better working knowledge of Washington than Trump. It's easy to imagine that the CNP would prefer him as president; an impeachment might work to their advantage. Trump provided the fire, the fury, and the spectacle, but impeaching him could improve their situation.

It was time to step back and take a hard look at the fault lines of the American political process. The ties that once connected the nation had frayed, including journalism. National news organizations parachuted reporters into communities to report on catastrophes or curiosities; in 2017, for example, the *Huffington Post* embarked on a million-dollar "Listen to America" project, which sent staffers on a bus tour across America to record interviews and produce reports in partnership with local news media.[66] But this was a profoundly different process from sharing a community's life and representing its interests. In the meantime, the colony collapse of the noncoastal news media has continued. In October 2018 the University of North Carolina released a new study reporting that about 1,300 U.S. communities had totally lost news coverage.[67]

The perspective of Middle America wasn't reaching the coasts. Coastal Americans who knew every European port of call were often curiously ignorant of their own country. Not everyone in Iowa grows corn; not everyone in Oklahoma herds cows. Our lesser-known states boast brilliant scientists and inventors, artists and musicians, entrepreneurs and scholars, but they often remain in obscurity.

The bias extends to religion. As I researched this book, when I told friends I was attending services at charismatic and fundamentalist churches, the reaction was often "They're all a bunch of racists." I found that some of the most racially integrated spaces I've experienced have been in nondenominational megachurches, whether in Oklahoma or Times Square. The Council for National Policy includes various African American pastors, and the Family Research Council promotes Martin Luther King Jr.'s niece Alveda as a spokeswoman.[68] It's complicated. The only useful response to oversimplification is inquiry.

But the 2016 election clearly demonstrated how the mechanics of democracy could be manipulated to produce antidemocratic results. The choice of America's evangelical population as the lever for power is telling. According to a 2014 study by Pew Research, evangelicals are 76 percent white and 84 percent third-generation American or higher, leaving them susceptible to fears of immigration. Seventy-eight percent don't have college degrees, and 57 percent have household incomes under $49,000 a year.[69] They take pride in their family farms and factory jobs, and those are disappearing. An entire way of life is eroding, and there's no solution on the horizon. They are ripe for manipulation, even if the end result is detrimental to their health, their well-being, and the future of their children.

The CNP and its partners have spent over four decades studying their audience and mastering the written and unwritten rules of American politics. Its moralists have little regard for the rights of minorities; its financiers lack concern for social welfare; and its strategists have no respect for majority rule. If it is fully realized, their combination of theocracy and plutocracy could result in a dystopia for those who fall outside their circle.

History teaches us that a nation neglects its democratic institutions at its peril. The "associations" lauded by Alexis de Tocqueville require constant renewal. The challenge of modernity is to use technology and organizations not to exploit divisions, but to seek common ground.

EPILOGUE

In the beginning there were the Southern Baptists. The architects of the Conservative Resurgence, pastor Paige Patterson and judge Paul Pressler, had developed tactics to take over the denomination and purge moderates, which would then be adopted, refreshed, and perfected by the Council for National Policy to apply to wider targets. If the CNP was a tree and each new partner a branch, the Southern Baptists were the core.

Over the ensuing four decades, Patterson and Pressler thrived, and pursued their campaign to roll back the clock. They inhabited the upper echelons of the Southern Baptist Convention, which accommodated their vision. In 1988 it passed a resolution calling homosexuality "a manifestation of a depraved nature" and "a deviant behavior that has wrought havoc in the lives of millions," resolving that it is therefore "a perversion of divine standards" and an "abomination before the eyes of God."[1] Even after the 2003 Supreme Court decision in *Lawrence v. Texas* struck down sodomy laws in Texas, invalidated similar laws in thirteen states, and helped pave the way for marriage equality, the convention held fast to its doctrine. Some fundamentalist leaders sought to have homosexuality recriminalized; others focused on promoting conversion therapy.

All the while, Judge Pressler's influence continued to grow. He and his wife, Nancy, were prominent members of the First Baptist Church in

Houston, where Pressler served as deacon, messenger, and head of the pastoral search committee. In 2002 his protégé and fellow Princeton graduate Richard Land had nominated him as first vice president of the convention. He won without opposition.

Pressler and Patterson entered the realm of legend. In 2013 Pressler's wife, Nancy, decided that Paige Patterson should pay special homage to giants of the Conservative Resurgence. A series of stained-glass windows was commissioned to honor Patterson, Pressler, their wives, and a gallery of other movement leaders, rimming the immersion baptismal basin outside the massive MacGorman Chapel. Their images loomed before a field of cobalt blue, adorned with Bible verses. The CNP was well represented, with Jerry Falwell and Richard Land as well as Pressler and Patterson. Also present was Ronnie Floyd, who would join Land on Donald Trump's future evangelical advisory council. Patterson's window included his dog.

But another drama unfolded in Houston. Almost four decades earlier, Paul Pressler had met a boy named Duane Rollins from the Bible class at his church. According to a lawsuit Rollins filed in 2018, Pressler told the fourteen-year-old's mother that her son was a "special student" and instructed her to deliver him to Pressler's sprawling ranch house a few times a month. There, sometimes with his wife present under the same roof, he allegedly sexually assaulted Rollins. For years the youth numbed himself with alcohol and drugs, and he was repeatedly imprisoned for drunk driving and burglary. The ordeal, he said, went on for thirty-five years.

Pressler had maintained an image of respectability over that period—with some lapses. In 1989—as Pressler was midway through his term as president of the Council for National Policy—George Bush tapped him as head of the Office on Government Ethics, but his name was withdrawn following an FBI background check. (The results were not published; a senior official would only tell the *Washington Post*, "Information was uncovered that we felt was disqualifying.")

Rollins's lawsuit revealed that Pressler had previously agreed to pay Rollins hush money, but eventually Pressler stopped making the payments.[2] The new complaint added codefendants for their role in the cover-up: among them Pressler's wife, Nancy, his Baptist church, and the pastor Paige Patterson.

The defendants denied the charges, but the lawsuit moved forward. In 2018 three more men filed affidavits accusing Pressler of molesting them over the same forty-year period. Duane Rollins's attorney called Pressler's abuses "the worst-kept secret in Houston." In 2019 a Houston judge dismissed the sexual assault charges against Pressler, saying they were too old to pursue in court, but he upheld several charges based on the 2004 hush money for sexual misconduct.[3]

The #MeToo movement came for the Southern Baptists. In May 2018 Paige Patterson (who had taken to signing his letters "The Red Bishop") was fired as head of the Southwestern Baptist Theological Seminary, charged with lying to the trustees about a student rape case. It got worse. On February 10, 2019, the *Houston Chronicle* published an exposé headlined "Abuse of Faith—20 Years, 700 Victims: Southern Baptist Sexual Abuse Spreads as Leaders Resist Reforms."[4] These events signaled the end of the Patterson-Pressler era, but the wounds would take years to heal.

At the same time, there were signs that the Southern Baptist Convention itself was in trouble. In 2019 the church press reported that while giving had risen to $11.8 billion, membership had fallen to its lowest level in thirty years, and that only half the children raised Southern Baptist remained in the church.

Perhaps they found the convention out of step with the times. But other changes were in the air. When Vice President Pence was invited to speak at the Southern Baptist Convention, a number of members objected. The new president, J. D. Greear, upheld the convention's positions on same-sex marriage and abortion, but he promised to improve the standing of women in the church and steer the denomination away from partisan politics. "I never want us to endorse candidates, whether overtly or implicitly."[5]

It wasn't clear what effect the troubles would have on the Council for National Policy's political strategy in the future. Much would depend on their opponents' ability to learn from the past. It was a daunting challenge. Republican strategist Kevin Phillips foresaw the implications of the CNP-Koch alliance in his 2006 book *American Theocracy*: "The Republican party has slowly become the vehicle of . . . a fusion of petroleum-defined national security; a crusading, simplistic Christianity; and a reckless credit-feeding financial complex." He added, "No leading world power in modern memory has become a captive, even a partial captive, of the sort of biblical inerrancy . . . that dismisses modern knowledge and science."[6] But not even Phillips could predict the momentum this movement would acquire—or its opponents' resolve to prevent the coalition's takeover of the American political system.

At the Southwestern Baptist Theological Seminary, the problem of the stained-glass windows remained. Medieval princes and patrons often ordered artisans to place their glowing images next to saints and angels, but this went out of fashion in the modern world, colored with vainglory, now tinted with shame.

In April 2019 the Southwestern Seminary announced that it had removed the windows of Pressler, Patterson, and the other Conservative Resurgence leaders, for transport to a new site not yet determined. Thomas Wright, an alumnus from Alabama, dryly commented, "Perhaps some of the window subjects illustrate why institutes tend to memorialize those whom history has confirmed finished well."[7]

In Fort Worth, the stained-glass pastors were replaced by clear windowpanes. On sunny days, the gallery is flooded with bright Texas light.

ACKNOWLEDGMENTS

As Suzanne Spaak, the heroine of my last book, said, "Something must be done." I unexpectedly undertook this project as something I could do to address our national crisis.

This book deals with a complex topic. If it "takes a village" to raise a child, the same was true of producing this work. It has benefited from the experiences of a lifetime. I can start with my deepening appreciation for my public school teachers in Oklahoma and Nebraska. I add the towering historians who shaped my thought in college, Edmund Morgan, David Brion Davis, and Sydney Ahlstrom. I also acknowledge my former students and valued colleagues from the Columbia School of Journalism, who sharpened my understanding of the practice and the business of journalism, and, in the case of James Carey and Tony Lewis, its role in public life. I thank my students and colleagues at the Columbia School of International and Public Affairs for accompanying me on a deep dive into digital platforms and assessing the impact they've had on society, for good and for ill.

I have continued to benefit from the intellectual community at Columbia SIPA, where President Lee Bollinger and Dean Merit Janow promote freedom of thought, human rights, and a culture of tolerance. Several of my Columbia colleagues have informed my research. Stuart Gottlieb illuminated some Byzantine policy byways, and Jack Snyder has long inspired and challenged me with his insights on media and politics. Volker Berghahn provides a model for the practice of writing history from a humane perspective.

Ken Anderson of American University helped me parse the mechanics of judicial appointments, and Jonathan Winer helped to decode Washington. Michelle Ferrier of Florida A&M shared her essential research on America's media deserts. All of the above deserve credit for whatever is good in this book; any flaws are regrettably my own.

Three young research assistants have made an immeasurable contribution to this work. In the initial stage, Avery Curran's research helped to frame the core of the book, as she populated huge sheets of paper with names and organograms until surprising patterns emerged. Midway, Colin Everett explored obscure digital realms with the zest of a spelunker. In the last lap, Eleanor Zafft appeared to offer her fine talents in research, production and design to help bring the book to completion. I offer all three my warmest thanks; their excellence inspires hope for the future.

I have been fortunate in my colleagues in this effort, beginning with Ethan Bassoff at Massie McQuilkin, who is everything an agent should be. My editor at Bloomsbury, Ben Hyman, has shepherded the project with sensitivity and wit, and Bloomsbury's excellent production team has been a joy to work with. The intrepid fact-checker Ben Kalin tackled the manuscript with exemplary rigor and speed.

Then there are those friends, family and fellows who have sustained me, body and soul, as I made my way down this arduous path. I thank Haney Armstrong; Sidney Babcock and José Romeu; George, David, and Julia Black; Harold Cardenas; Taralynn Dixon; Carole and C.J. Everett; Cathy Gay; Ingrid Gerstman; Martha Greenough; Donald Hamilton; Sharon Isbin; Larry Lee; Kati Marton; Cary McClelland; Kenneth Nelson; Tom Reston; Jay Shanker and Sara Jane Rose; D. Sharp; K. and L. Silverman; and the inimitable Jean-Marie Simon. I thank Rudy and Amber Rickner and the Saturday Squad for their insight and hospitality, and the Twelfth Night Players for making me smile.

Finally, I am grateful to my parents, Ted and Gerada Nelson, who grew up on Nebraska farms during the Depression. They taught us that truth matters and that American ideals are worth fighting for. I hope this book lives up to their example.

APPENDIX: SELECT ORGANIZATIONS

MAJOR GROUPS RUN BY MEMBERS OF THE COUNCIL FOR NATIONAL POLICY

Family Research Council
Focus on the Family
American Family Association
Concerned Women for America
Susan B. Anthony List
Students for Life of America
Live Action
Faith & Freedom Coalition
United in Purpose
National Religious Broadcasters
Alliance Defending Freedom
Leadership Institute
Federalist Society
American Center for Law & Justice
Heritage Foundation
Tea Party Patriots
State Policy Network
National Rifle Association

ORGANIZATIONS CONNECTED TO THE KOCH NETWORK

Americans for Prosperity
Grassroots Leadership Academy
Freedom Partners/Freedom Partners Shared Services/Freedom Partners Chamber of Commerce
Concerned Veterans for America
Libre Initiative
Generation Opportunity

DONOR NETWORKS

Koch Donor Network/Seminar Network (Koch brothers)
DonorsTrust/Donors Capital Fund (backers include the Koch brothers and the DeVos family)
National Christian Foundation (evangelical donor-advised fund)
Democracy Alliance (Democratic donor network)

STRATEGY AND TECH COMPANIES

uCampaign and RumbleUp (apps used by some groups run by CNP members and Republican clients)
i360 (data platform launched with Koch brothers funding)
Themis Trust (i360's original parent company)
Data Trust (Republican National Committee database)
WPA Intelligence (research and analytics firm for Ted Cruz and other Republican clients)
Barna Group (evangelical polling firm)
Catalist / Data Warehouse (database serving Democratic candidates and organizations)

NOTES

PROLOGUE

1. Robert Leonard, "Want to Get Rid of Trump? Only Fox News Can Do It," *New York Times*, July 5, 2017, https://www.nytimes.com/2017/07/05/opinion/trump-fox-news-media.html.

2. Emily Nussbaum, "The TV that Created Donald Trump," *New Yorker*, July 24, 2017, https://www.newyorker.com/magazine/2017/07/31/the-tv-that-created-donald-trump.

3. Rob Faris et al., "Partisanship, Propaganda, and Disinformation: Online Media and the 2016 U.S. Presidential Election," *Berkman Klein Center*, August 16, 2017, https://cyber.harvard.edu/publications/2017/08/mediacloud.

4. David Daley, *Ratf**ked: Why Your Vote Doesn't Count* (New York: W. W. Norton, 2017), 215.

5. Allan Lichtman, *White Protestant Nation* (New York: Atlantic Monthly Press, 2007).

6. "The Patriot WDTK," *Salem Media Group*, accessed July 16, 2019, http://salemmedia.com/radio-stations/newstalk1400-wdtk-the-patriot/.

7. "FaithTalk 99.5 FM KDIS," *Salem Media Group*, accessed July 16, 2019, http://salemmedia.com/radio-stations/faithtalk-99-5-fm-kdis/.

8. "On Homosexuality, Moore Running with God, the Founders, George Washington, Antonin Scalia, Sam Alito, and Clarence," *AFR Focal Point*, September 22, 2017, https://afr.net/podcasts/focal-point/2017/september/on

-homosexuality-moore-running-with-god-the-founders-george-washington -antonin-scalia-sam-alito-and-clarence/.

9. Richard Kelsey, "Watch Your Language: Progressivism is Not Progress," *Committed Conservative*, February 6, 2017, http://committedconservative.com /2017/02/06/watch-language-progressivism-not-progress/?v=iLY4uls76aE%3 B%20https%3A%2F%2F.

CHAPTER 1: IN THE BEGINNING

1. Rachel Siegel, "The Gripping Sermon that Got 'Under G-d' Added to the Pledge of Allegiance on Flag Day," *Washington Post*, June 14, 2018, https://www .washingtonpost.com/news/retropolis/wp/2018/06/14/the-gripping-sermon -that-got-under-god-added-to-the-pledge-of-allegiance-on-flag-day/?utm _term=.7dc7ec921249.
2. "Urban and Rural Population for the U.S. and All States: 1900–2000," *Iowa Data Center*, accessed July 16, 2019, https://www.iowadatacenter.org/data tables/UnitedStates/urusstpop19002000.pdf.
3. Laurie Goodstein, "Percentage of Protestant American is in Steep Decline, Study Finds" *New York Times*, October 9, 2012, https://www.nytimes.com/2012/10/10/us /study-finds-that-percentage-of-protestant-americans-is-declining.html.
4. "Strict Construction," *Cornell Law School*, accessed July 16, 2019, https:// www.law.cornell.edu/wex/strict_construction.
5. M. F. Fiegel, "The Baptist Church and the Confederate Cause," in *Proceedings of the Oklahoma Academy of Sciences* 47 (1967): 314.
6. Samuel Boykin, "Southern Baptist Convention Resolutions at the Beginning of the American Civil War—1861," *Baptist History Homepage*, accessed July 16, 2019, http://baptisthistoryhomepage.com/sbc.resolution.civil.war.html.
7. John W. Storey, *Texas Baptist Leadership and Social Christianity, 1900–1980* (College Station: Texas A&M University Press, 1986).
8. "Southern Baptist Convention States," *Association of Religious Data Archives*, accessed July 16, 2019, http://www.thearda.com/ql2010/QL_S_ALL_2_1168c.asp.
9. Glenna Whitley, "Baptist Holy War," *D Magazine*, January 1991, https://www .dmagazine.com/publications/d-magazine/1991/january/baptist-holy-war/.

10. Jeff Robinson, "Pressler: SBC Conservative Resurgence was Grassroots Movement," *Southern Baptist Theological Seminary*, March 30, 2004, http://news.sbts.edu/2004/03/30/pressler-sbc-conservative-resurgence-was-grassroots-movement/. See also Michael Foust, "25 Years Ago, Conservative Resurgence Got Its Start," *Baptist Press*, June 15, 2004, http://www.bpnews.net/18486/25-years-ago-conservative-resurgence-got-its-start.

11. Will Campbell, "When History Is All We Have," *Christianity and Crisis*, September 4, 1990, https://www.religion-online.org/article/when-history-is-all-we-have/.

12. Michael Erard, "Don't Stop Believing: Renegade Bloggers Besiege the Southern Baptist Convention," *Texas Observer*, July 13, 2007, https://www.texasobserver.org/2547-dont-stop-believing-renegade-bloggers-besiege-the-southern-baptist-convention/.

13. George Grant, *The Changing of the Guard* (Fort Worth: Dominion Press, 1987), 50, https://www.garynorth.com/freebooks/docs/pdf/the_changing_of _the_guard.pdf.

14. "The Seven Mountains of Societal Influence," *Generals International*, accessed July 16, 2019, https://www.generals.org/rpn/the-seven-mountains/.

15. Glenn H. Utter and John Woodrow Storey, *The Religious Right: A Reference Handbook* (Santa Barbara: ABC-CLIO, 2001), 122.

16. Christopher Ingraham, "Union Membership Remained Steady in 2017. The Trend May Not Hold," *Washington Post*, January 19, 2018, https://www.washingtonpost.com/news/wonk/wp/2018/01/19/union-membership-remained-steady-in-2017-the-trend-may-not-hold.

17. David Grann, "Robespierre of the Right," *New Republic*, October 27, 1997, https://newrepublic.com/article/61338/robespierre-the-right.

18. Molly Jackman, "ALEC's Influence over Lawmaking in State Legislatures," *Brookings*, December 6, 2013, https://www.brookings.edu/articles/alecs-influence-over-lawmaking-in-state-legislatures/.

19. Daniel K. Williams, *God's Own Party: The Making of the Christian Right* (New York: Oxford University Press, 2010), 183.

20. Another eighty-four stations nationwide continued to carry Robison's program.

21. Kathy Sawyer, "Linking Religion and Politics," *Washington Post*, August 24, 1980, https://www.washingtonpost.com/archive/politics/1980/08/24/linking-religion-and-politics/3d68ea8c-ed85-4d5d-94da-8b429f911a96.

22. Sidney M. Milkis and Daniel J. Tichenor, *Rivalry and Reform* (Chicago: University of Chicago Press, 2018), 229.

23. W. Scott Lamb, "35th Anniversary of Reagan's 'I Know You Can't Endorse Me. But I Endorse You," *Washington Times*, August 21, 2015, https://www.washingtontimes.com/news/2015/aug/21/w-scott-lamb-this-day-in-us-history-reagans-endors/.

24. W. Scott Lamb, *Mike Huckabee: The Authorized Biography* (Nashville: Thomas Nelson, 2015), 142.

25. Lamb, "35th Anniversary."

26. Holly Bailey, "Meet Rafael Cruz: Ted Cruz's Secret Evangelical Weapon," *Yahoo News*, October 27, 2015, https://news.yahoo.com/meet-rafael-cruz-ted-cruz-128667192104558.html.

27. "Taking Over the Republican Party," *Theocracy Watch*, last updated February 2005, accessed July 16, 2019, http://www.theocracywatch.org/taking_over.htm. See also "Life and Liberty for All Who Believe," *Theocracy Watch*, accessed July 16, 2019, http://www.theocracywatch.org/audio-video.htm.

28. "Ronald Reagan: National Affairs Campaign Address on Religious Liberty (Abridged)," *American Rhetoric Online Speech Bank* transcript, accessed July 16, 2019, https://americanrhetoric.com/speeches/ronaldreaganreligiousliberty.htm.

29. Dan Gilgoff, *The Jesus Machine: How James Dobson, Focus on the Family, and Evangelical America Are Winning the Culture War* (New York: St. Martin's Press, 2007), 80.

30. Ibid.

31. James C. Haley, *The Truth in Crisis* (Hannibal, MO: Hannibal Books, 1988), 210, https://billmoyers.com/content/battle-bible.

32. "Life and Liberty for All Who Believe," *Theocracy Watch*.

33. Paul Pressler, *A Hill on Which to Die: One Southern Baptist's Journey* (Nashville, TN: Broadman & Holman, 2002), 247.

34. Ibid., 247–48.

35. Ibid., 248.

36. Pressler was thoroughly enmeshed in Republican politics, but he came late to the party. He spent the first half of his life as a conservative Democrat, "believing some hope for the party still existed." It was only in 1988 that he changed his affiliation.

37. Mike Anglin, "The 'Baker vs. Wade' Litigation," *Dallas Way*, November 23, 2017, http://www.thedallasway.org/stories/written/2017/11/23/baker-vs-wade.

38. Gilgoff, *Jesus Machine*, 72.

39. Ibid., 82.

CHAPTER 2: THE BIRTH OF THE CNP

1. William Gilbert, *Renaissance and Reformation* (Lawrence, KS: Carrie, 1998), ch. 14, http://vlib.iue.it/carrie/texts/carrie_books/gilbert/14.html.

2. Wallace M. Alston Jr., *The Church of the Living God* (Louisville, KY: Westminster John Knox Press, 2002), 45. See for priests as intermediaries, a concept basic to religious history. Also Thomas Davis, ed., *John Calvin's American Legacy* (New York: Oxford University Press, 2010), 70. See for the role of elders.

3. Lorraine Boettner, *The Reformed Doctrine of Predestination* (Woodstock, Ontario: Devoted Publishing, 2017), 166.

4. Alexis de Toqueville, *Democracy in America* (Chicago: University of Chicago Press, 2012), 421.

5. "Book TV: Richard Viguerie, 'Takeover,'" YouTube video, 10:00, BookTV, August 5, 2014, https://www.youtube.com/watch?v=I7VtuqPpsTQ. See 4:34.

6. "Strom Thurmond's Dixiecrat Days: Newsreel," YouTube video, 9:20, tsgvideoplace, July 19, 2011, https://www.youtube.com/watch?v=TbUolXeJbi4. See 00:50.

7. "Platform of the States Rights Democratic Party," *American Presidency Project*, August 14, 1948, https://www.presidency.ucsb.edu/documents/platform-the-states-rights-democratic-party.

8. J. R. Moeringher, "Amid Uproar, Bob Jones U. Keeps the Faith," *Los Angeles Times*, February 27, 2000, https://www.latimes.com/archives/la-xpm-2000

-feb-27-mn-3089-story.html. See also Justin Taylor, "Is Segregation Scriptural? A Radio Address from Bob Jones on Easter 1960," *Gospel Coalition*, July 26, 2016, https://www.thegospelcoalition.org/blogs/evangelical-history/is-segregation-scriptural-a-radio-address-from-bob-jones-on-easter-of-1960.

9. Randall Balmer, "The Real Origins of the Religious Right," *Politico Magazine*, May 27, 2014, https://www.politico.com/magazine/story/2014/05/religious-right-real-origins-107133.

10. Taylor, "Is Segregation Scriptural?"

11. Sidney M. Milkis and Daniel J. Tichenor, "Rivalry and Reform: Building a Movement Party," University of Virginia Miller Center, accessed July 16, 2019. https://millercenter.org/rivalry-and-reform/building-movement-party.

12. Bob Jones Sr., "Is Segregation Scriptural?," transcript, April 17, 1960, 13–15, https://docs.google.com/file/d/0B6A7PtfmRgT7Q1kzZEVxUThMLWc/edit.

13. Frances FitzGerald, "The Triumphs of the New Right," *New York Review of Books*, November 19, 1981, https://www.nybooks.com/articles/1981/11/19/the-triumphs-of-the-new-right.

14. Lee Roy Chapman, "The Strange Love of Dr. Billy James Hargis," *This Land Press*, November 2, 2012, http://thislandpress.com/2012/11/02/the-strange-love-of-dr-billy-james-hargis.

15. Adam Bernstein, "Evangelist Billy James Hargis Dies; Spread Anti-Communist Message," *Washington Post*, November 30, 2004, http://www.washingtonpost.com/wp-dyn/articles/A20975-2004Nov29.html.

16. "Obituary: Billy James Hargis," *Economist*, December 16, 2004, https://www.economist.com/obituary/2004/12/16/billy-james-hargis.

17. Richard Viguerie, *Takeover: The 100-Year War for the Soul of the GOP and How Conservatives Can Finally Win It* (New York: WND, 2014), xvi, 16.

18. Ibid.

19. Ibid., 18.

20. *People* Staff, "Richard Viguerie," *People*, December 28, 1981, https://people.com/archive/richard-viguerie-vol-16-no-26.

21. "Blackwell, Morton C.: Files, 1981–1984," *Reagan Library*, accessed July 16, 2019, https://www.reaganlibrary.gov/sites/default/files/archives/textual/smof/blackwell.pdf. See also "Morton Blackwell—Staff and Faculty at the Leadership Institute," *Leadership Institute*, June 4, 2019, https://www.leadershipinstitute.org/training/contact.cfm?FacultyID=7159.

22. "CPAC: A Detailed History of the First 30 Years," *American Conservative Union*, accessed July 16, 2019, https://conservative.org/article/cpac-detailed-history-first-30-years. See also Morton C. Blackwell, "A Tribute to Paul Weyrich," *Leadership Institute*, October 6, 2015, https://www.leadershipinstitute.org/writings/?ID=1.

23. Viguerie, *Takeover*, 43–44. See also Morton C. Blackwell, "The Real Nature of Politics," *Leadership Institute News*, August 6, 2012, https://www.leadershipinstitute.org/news/?NR=8425.

24. Blackwell, "Real Nature of Politics."

25. Ibid.

26. Richard J. Meagher, "Political Strategy and the Building of the GOP Coalition," *Political Research Associates*, June 10, 2009, https://www.politicalresearch.org/2009/06/10/remembering-the-new-right-political-strategy-and-the-building-of-the-gop-coalition.

27. "CPAC: A Detailed History of the First 30 Years," *American Conservative Union*, accessed July 16, 2019, https://conservative.org/article/cpac-detailed-history-first-30-years. See also Blackwell, "A Tribute to Paul Weyrich."

28. "Reagan at the first CPAC, 'We Will be a City Upon a Hill,'" *Frontiers of Freedom*, March 12, 2013, https://www.ff.org/reagan-at-the-first-cpac-we-will-be-a-city-upon-a-hill.

29. Meagher, "Political Strategy."

30. Alex Jones, *Losing the News: The Future of the News That Feeds Democracy* (New York: Oxford University Press, 2009), 37.

31. Phyllis Schlafly, "ERA Would Affect Social Security for Stay-at-Home Moms and Widows," *Illinois Review*, February 28, 2008, https://www.illinoisreview.com/illinoisreview/2008/02/era-would-affec.html. See also Robert. J. Gray, "'An Amendment that Requires Both Sexes to be Treated Equally:' A Men's

Rights Activist Voices Support for the ERA," *History Matters*, accessed July 16, 2019, http://historymatters.gmu.edu/d/7028.

32. Richard A. Ostling, "Jerry Falwell's Crusade," *Time* 126 (September 2, 1985): 50.

33. Mary T. Schmich, "A Spokeslady of the Right," *Chicago Tribune*, March 23, 1986, https://www.chicagotribune.com/news/ct-xpm-1986-03-23-8601210901-story.html.

34. BookTV, "Book TV: Richard Vigeruie, 'Takeover.'" See 5:19.

35. Gray, "'An Amendment that Requires Both Sexes to be Treated Equally.'"

36. Blackwell, "Real Nature of Politics."

37. Viguerie, *Takeover*, 49.

38. Adam Clymer, "Conservatives Gather in Umbrella Council for a National Policy," New York Times, May 20, 1981, https://www.nytimes.com/1981/05/20/us/conservatives-gather-in-umbrella-council-for-a-national-policy.html.

39. Viguerie, *Takeover*, 44.

40. Ibid., 44, 49.

41. Adam Clymer, "Conservatives Gather in Umbrella Council."

42. Alissa Wilkinson, "The 'Left Behind' Series was just the Latest Way America Prepared for the Rapture," *Washington Post*, July 13, 2016, https://www.washingtonpost.com/news/act-four/wp/2016/07/13/the-left-behind-series-was-just-the-latest-way-america-prepared-for-the-rapture.

43. Great Oaks is at 910 North Foster Drive. Jenkins lived just down the road at 912. Four years into his tenure, Jenkins urged the CNP to buy Great Oaks, but Paul Weyrich decided the organization should move to Washington. Jenkins resigned and stayed in Baton Rouge, remaining a long-term member. He bought Great Oaks in 1984 as a home base for his various media and business enterprises.

44. Russ Bellant, *The Coors Connection* (Boston: South End Press, 1999), 38. See also "Illinois Sues Former KKK Member, others, who Sought Money for AIDS Victims," *United Press International Archives*, January 26, 1990, https://www.upi.com/Archives/1990/01/26/Illinois-sues-former-KKK-member-others-who-sought-money-for-AIDS-victims/8604633330000.

45. Baton Rouge *State-Times*, "Powerful Conservative Organization Formed to Influence Congress, Impact Foreign Policy," *People for the American Way*, January 8, 1987, http://media.pfaw.org/Right/CNP-IRAN.txt.

46. "Nicaragua and Iran Timeline," Brown University, accessed July 16, 2019, https://www.brown.edu/Research/Understanding_the_Iran_Contra_Affair/timeline-n-i.php.

47. Janet Cawley and Nathaniel Sheppard Jr., "Contributors Tell of '1-2 Punch' for Contra Aid," *Chicago Tribune*, May 22, 1987, https://www.chicagotribune.com/news/ct-xpm-1987-05-22-8702070939-story.html.

48. Baton Rouge *State-Times*, "Powerful Conservative Organization Formed."

49. Guy Gugliotta, "D'Aubuisson Kept U.S. on its Guard," *Washington Post*, January 4, 1994, https://www.washingtonpost.com/archive/politics/1994/01/04/daubuisson-kept-us-on-its-guard/c2ede026-fb05-49e7-80f2-12b568eb023b/?utm_term=.a5add721b58c.

50. Joanne Omang, "D'Aubuisson Honored by Conservatives at Capitol Hill Dinner," *Washington Post*, December 5, 1984, https://www.washingtonpost.com/archive/politics/1984/12/05/daubuisson-honored-by-conservatives-at-capitol-hill-dinner/f14ae112-2599-420d-aa9c-233aafac103c/?utm_term=.24c9bab9e424.

51. David Johnston, "Judge in Iran-Contra Trial Drops Case Against North After Prosecutor Gives Up," *New York Times*, September 17, 1991, https://www.nytimes.com/1991/09/17/us/judge-in-iran-contra-trial-drops-case-against-north-after-prosecutor-gives-up.html.

52. Baton Rouge *State-Times*, "North Was Member of Private group Once Based in BR," *People for the American Way*, January 8, 1978, http://media.pfaw.org/Right/CNP-IRAN.txt.

53. Clymer, "Conservatives Gather in Umbrella Council."

54. Robert M. Penna, "The Johnson Amendment: Fact-Checking the Narrative," *Stanford Social Innovation Review*, August 24, 2018, https://ssir.org/articles/entry/the_johnson_amendment_fact_checking_the_narrative#.

55. Internal Revenue Code. See also Penna, "The Johnson Amendment."

56. C. Eugene Emery Jr., "Donald Trump Correct—Lyndon Johnson Passed Legislation Limiting Political Activity of Churches," *PolitiFact*, July 22, 2016,

https://www.politifact.com/truth-o-meter/statements/2016/jul/22/donald-trump/donald-trump-correct-lyndon-johnson-passed-legisla.

57. I have been a member of the Council on Foreign Relations since 1994.

58. Jack Anderson and Michael Binstein, "For IRS, a Junket Takes on New Meaning," *Washington Post*, May 21, 1992, https://www.washingtonpost.com/archive/sports/1992/05/21/for-irs-a-junket-takes-on-new-meaning/1578edeb-b804-480e-a3ce-21d5befa1bc3.

CHAPTER 3: LORDS OF THE AIR

1. Viguerie, *Takeover*, 21.

2. *People* Staff, "Richard Viguerie."

3. "VVS 2017: Honoring Stu Eperson," YouTube video, 1:57:27, "FRC Action," October 18, 2017, https://www.youtube.com/watch?v=XuMQjdAAYBs. (See 5:55)

4. "Johnson's Radio Visitor," KMMJ Clay Center, September, 1929, accessed July 16, 2019, https://www.americanradiohistory.com/Archive-Station-Albums/KMMJ-Clay-Center-1929.pdf.

5. FRC Action, "VVS 2017." See 1:00:00, 36:15.

6. *Time* Staff, "Influential Evangelicals: Stuart Epperson," *Time*, February 7, 2005, http://content.time.com/time/specials/packages/article/0,28804,1993235_1993243_1993268,00.html. See also Eddie Huffman, "Radio Station WPAQ Celebrates 70 Years of Regional Americana," *Winston-Salem Journal*, January 24, 2018, https://www.journalnow.com/entertainment/music/radio-station-wpaq-celebrates-years-of-regional-americana/article_85c3b2f0-7432-58bd-9430-53f877a1cbbd.html.

7. FRC Action, "VVS 2017." See 1:11:30.

8. "Humble Beginnings to National Radio Network—Stu Epperson," *Wise Counsel*, accessed July 16, 2019, http://askwisecounsel.com/stu-epperson.

9. Michael Freedman, "Articles of Faith," *Forbes*, December 27, 1999, https://www.forbes.com/forbes/1999/1227/6415281a.html#2969a9452ac5.

10. Adam Piore, "A Higher Frequency," *Mother Jones*, December 2005, https://www.motherjones.com/politics/2005/12/higher-frequency.

11. FRC Action, "VVS 2017."

12. Alan Greenblatt and Tracie Powell, "Rise of Megachurches," *CQ Researcher*, September 21, 2007, https://library.cqpress.com/cqresearcher/document.php?id=cqresrre2007092100.

13. Sarah Burns, "25 Largest Churches in America," *24/7 Wall St.*, October 11, 2017, https://247wallst.com/special-report/2017/10/11/25-largest-churches-in-america/6.

14. Greenblatt and Powell, "Rise of Megachurches." James Twitchell quoted.

15. Viguerie, *Takeover*, 22.

16. Freedman, "Articles of Faith."

17. James Dobson, "The New Hide and Seek: What's the Cause of Homosexuality?" *Dobson Digital Library*, accessed July 16, 2019, https://www.dobsonlibrary.com/resource/article/0f184113-ff27-42d0-824c-4792ae56931a.

18. James Dobson, "The Woman's Role in Marriage," *OnePlace*, August 12, 2013, https://www.oneplace.com/ministries/family-talk/listen/the-womans-role-in-marriage-357741.html. See 15:16.

19. Gilgoff, *Jesus Machine*, 24.

20. "Letter from Jerry Falwell on Keeping Old Time Gospel Hour on Air," *Portal to Texas History*, accessed July 16, 2019, https://texashistory.unt.edu/ark:/67531/metadc177440/m1/1.

21. "Network Evening News Ratings," *Pew Research Center*, March 13, 2006, https://www.journalism.org/numbers/network-evening-news-ratings.

22. Viguerie, *Takeover*, 68.

23. Richard M. Harley, "The Evangelical Vote and the Presidency," *Christian Science Monitor*, June 25, 1980, https://www.csmonitor.com/1980/0625/062555.html.

24. Jason. C. Bivins, "Tracing the Rise of Christian Media in American Political Discourse," *Pacific Standard*, May 30, 2018, https://psmag.com/news/the-rise-of-the-christian-media.

25. Joel Achenbach, "Did the News Media, Led by Walter Cronkite, Lose the War in Vietnam?" *Washington Post*, May 25, 2018, https://www.washingtonpost

.com/national/did-the-news-media-led-by-walter-cronkite-lose-the-war-in-vietnam/2018/05/25/a5b3e098-495e-11e8-827e-190efaf1f1ee_story.html.

26. Piore, "A Higher Frequency."

27. Kent Demaret, "Methodist Pastor Don Wildmon Leads a Holy War Against Sex, Violence and Booze on TV," *People*, November 27, 1978, https://people.com/archive/methodist-pastor-don-wildmon-leads-a-holy-war-against-sex-violence-and-booze-on-tv-vol-10-no-22.

28. As of 2018, American Family Radio's stars include Wildmon's son Tim, who inherited his father's mission; Bryan Fischer; Abraham Hamilton III; Dr. Robert Jeffress, pastor of the First Baptist Church of Dallas; David Barton, the fundamentalist historical revisionist; Trump's attorney Jay Sekulow; and fundamentalist financial advisor Dan Celia.

29. David Craig, "The Rev. Jerry Falwell, Returning to Heritage USA to . . . ," *United Press International Archives*, October 9, 1987, https://www.upi.com/Archives/1987/10/09/The-Rev-Jerry-Falwell-returning-to-Heritage-USA-to/8017560750400.

CHAPTER 4: THE NEWS HOLE IN THE HEART OF AMERICA

1. This assessment would have surprised many leftists, who regarded "legacy media" as conservative.

2. Alabama Public Radio, "How the Media Covered the Civil Rights Movement: the Children's March," *Alabama Public Radio*, April 25, 2013, https://www.apr.org/post/how-media-covered-civil-rights-movement-childrens-march#stream/0.

3. James D. Squires, *Read All About It: The Corporate Takeover of America's Newspapers* (New York: Times Books, 1994), 223–24.

4. Blackwell, "The Real Nature of Politics."

5. Phillip Knightley, *The First Casualty: The War Correspondent as Hero and Myth-Maker, from the Crimea to Iraq* (Baltimore: Johns Hopkins University Press, 2004), 21–25.

6. Squires, *Read All About It*, 10.

7. Matthew Baum, "Soft News and Foreign Policy: How Expanding the Audience Changes the Policies," *Research Gate*, April 2007, https://www

.researchgate.net/publication/231980745_Soft_News_and_Foreign_Policy_How_Expanding_the_Audience_Changes_the_Policies.

8. "Number of U.S. Daily Newspapers, 5-Year Increments," *Pew Research Center*, March 12, 2007, https://www.journalism.org/numbers/number-of-u-s-daily-newspapers-5-year-increments. See also Squires, *Read All About It*, 208.

9. "Newspapers Fact Sheet," *Pew Research Center*, July 9, 2019, https://www.journalism.org/fact-sheet/newspapers. See also Erin Duffin, "Number of Households in the U.S. from 1960 to 2018," *Statista*, last edited April 29, 2019, https://www-statista-com.ezp-prod1.hul.harvard.edu/statistics/183635/number-of-households-in-the-us. See also "U.S. Daily Newspaper Circulation Versus Number of Households," *Pew Research Center*, March 13, 2006, https://www.journalism.org/numbers/u-s-daily-newspaper-circulation-versus-number-of-households.

10. Marc Gunther, "The Transformation of Network News," *Nieman Reports*, June 15, 1999, https://niemanreports.org/articles/the-transformation-of-network-news.

11. Lou Ureneck, "Newspapers Arrive at Economic Crossroads," *Neiman Reports*, June 15, 1999, https://niemanreports.org/articles/newspapers-arrive-at-economic-crossroads.

12. Squires, *Read All About It*, 208.

13. Derek Thompson, "The Print Apocalypse and How to Survive It," *Atlantic*, November 3, 2016, https://www.theatlantic.com/business/archive/2016/11/the-print-apocalypse-and-how-to-survive-it/506429.

14. Penelope Muse Abernathy, *The Expanding News Desert* (Chapel Hill: Center for Innovation and Sustainability in Local Media, University of North Carolina, 2018).

15. Angel Au-Yeung, "Why Billionaire Craig of Craigslist is Giving Millions to Journalism and Education," *Forbes*, August 13, 2018, https://www.forbes.com/sites/angelauyeung/2018/08/13/why-billionaire-craig-of-craigslist-is-giving-millions-to-journalism-and-education/#586536437942.

16. Katerina Eva Matsa and Jan Lauren Boyles, "America's Shifting Statehouse Press," *Pew Research Center*, July 10, 2014, https://www.journalism.org/2014/07/10/americas-shifting-statehouse-press.

17. "Who We Are," *American Family Radio*, accessed July 26, 2019, https://afr.net/who-we-are.

18. "History," *Bott Radio Network*, accessed July 16, 2019, https://bottradionetwork.com/about/history.

19. "Broadcast Listing," *Bott Radio Network*, accessed July 16, 2019, https://bottradionetwork.com/broadcasts.

20. "Infanticide Adopted by Democrats," *American Family Radio*, February 2, 2019, https://afr.net/podcasts/exposing-washington/2019/february/infanticide-adopted-by-democrats. See also: Life & Liberty Minute, "Homosexuality is the Dividing Line Between Light and Darkness," *American Family Radio*, December 4, 2018, https://afr.net/podcasts/life-liberty-minute/2018/december/homosexuality-is-the-dividing-line-between-light-and-darkness.

21. Life & Liberty Minute, "Muslim Call to Prayer in New Zealand—What Should Christians Do?," *American Family Radio*, March 25, 2019, https://afr.net/podcasts/life-liberty-minute/2019/march/muslim-call-to-prayer-in-new-zealand-what-should-christians-do.

22. Piore, "A Higher Frequency."

23. Freedman, "Articles of Faith."

24. "Find NPR Member Stations and Donate," *National Public Radio*, accessed July 16, 2019, https://www.npr.org/stations. See also "Find Your Local AFR Station," *American Family Radio*, accessed July 16, 2019, https://afr.net/station-finder. See also "Station List," *Bott Radio Network*, accessed July 16, 2019, https://bottradionetwork.com/stations.

25. "Salem Radio Businesses," *Salem Media Group*, accessed July 16, 2019, https://salemmedia.com/radio-main-page.

26. "SRN News," *Salem Radio Network*, accessed July 16, 2019, http://www.srnonline.com/news.

27. Michael Hiltzik, "Column: Orrin Hatch is Leaving the Senate, but his Deadliest Law Will Live On," *Los Angeles Times*, January 5, 2018, https://www.latimes.com/business/hiltzik/la-fi-hiltzik-hatch-20180105-story.html.

28. Tim Murphy, "How This Company—and Mike Huckabee—Cashed in by Scaring Conservatives," *Mother Jones*, December 2015, https://www

.motherjones.com/politics/2015/12/agora-huckabee-conservative-bible-cures. See also Alex Kasprak, "'Sour Honey' is a Cure for Cancer?," *Snopes*, April 10, 2017, https://www.snopes.com/fact-check/sour-honey-cure-cancer.

29. "The Patriot WDTK," *Salem Media Group*, accessed July 16, 2019, https://salemmedia.com/radio-stations/newstalk1400-wdtk-the-patriot/.

30. Piore, "A Higher Frequency."

31. "State Policy Network," *Conservative Transparency*, accessed July 16, 2019, http://conservativetransparency.org/org/state-policy-network/?order_by=year%20DESC&opptax=recipient. See also Andy Kroll, "Exposed: The Dark-Money ATM of the Conservative Movement," *Mother Jones*, February 5, 2013, https://www.motherjones.com/politics/2013/02/donors-trust-donor-capital-fund-dark-money-koch-bradley-devos/.

32. Will Drabold, "Here's What Mike Pence Said on LGBT Issues Over the Years," *Time*, July 15, 2016, http://time.com/4406337/mike-pence-gay-rights-lgbt-religious-freedom/. See also Jessie Hellmann, "Pence: Abortion Will End in U.S. 'in Our Time,'" *Hill*, February 27, 2018, https://thehill.com/policy/healthcare/375852-pence-says-abortion-will-end-in-us-in-our-time.

33. R. D. Ray, "Military Necessity and Homosexuality," *Indiana Policy Review*, August 1993, http://files.pfaw.org/pfaw_files/images/4335_001.pdf?_ga=1.263053636.952385%20322.1475090377. See also "The Pink Newsroom," *Indiana Policy Review*, December 1993, http://files.pfaw.org/pfaw_files/images/4336_001.pdf?_ga=1%20.234380446.161301739.1469202878.

34. "1998 Membership by State," *Public Eye*, accessed July 16, 2019, http://www.publiceye.org/ifas/cnp/state98.html

35. FRC Action, "VVS 2017." See 5:55.

36. "A Response to False Claims Made by The Nation," *Family Research Council*, June 15, 2005, https://www.frc.org/response-to-false-claims-made-by-the-nation.

37. "Council of Conservative Citizens," *Southern Poverty Law Center*, accessed July 16, 2019, https://www.splcenter.org/fighting-hate/extremist-files/group/council-conservative-citizens.

38. "Opposition to Gay Marriage Links Members of Arlington Group," *Religion News Service*, May 16, 2006, https://religionnews.com/2006/05/16/opposition

-to-gay-marriage-links-members-of-arlington-group. See also "Pro-Family Groups Unite to Promote 'Marriage Protection Week,'" *American Family Association Journal*, October 2003, https://afajournal.org/past-issues/2003/october/pro-family-groups-unite-to-promote-marriage-protection-week. See also George Barna, *The Day Christians Changed America* (Ventura, CA: Metaformation, 2017). See also Gilgoff, *Jesus Machine*, 156–58.

39. "American Family Association," *Charity Navigator*, accessed July 16, 2019, https://www.charitynavigator.org/index.cfm?bay=search.irs&ein=640607275.

CHAPTER 5: MONEY PEOPLE

1. "Nomination Process," *Public Eye Archives*, accessed July 17, 2019, https://web.archive.org/web/20051028104448/http://www.publiceye.org/ifas/cnp/nomination.html.

2. Heidi Beirich and Mark Potok, "The Council for National Policy: Behind the Curtain," *Southern Poverty Law Center*, https://www.splcenter.org/hatewatch/2016/05/17/council-national-policy-behind-curtain.

3. Baton Rouge *State-Times*, "Powerful Conservative Organization Formed to Influence Congress, Impact Foreign Policy."

4. "Nomination Process," *Public Eye Archives*.

5. Jim Dwyer, "Remembering a City Where the Smog Could Kill," *New York Times*, February 28, 2017, https://www.nytimes.com/2017/02/28/nyregion/new-york-city-smog.html.

6. Christine Mai-Duc, "The 1969 Santa Barbara Oil Spill that Changed Oil and Gas Forever," *Los Angeles Times*, May 20, 2015, https://www.latimes.com/local/lanow/la-me-ln-santa-barbara-oil-spill-1969-20150520-htmlstory.html.

7. Michael Rotman, "Cuyahoga River Fire," *Cleveland Historical*, accessed July 17, 2019, https://clevelandhistorical.org/items/show/63.

8. Jim Malewitz, "Abandoned Texas Oil Wells Seen as 'Ticking Time Bombs' of Contamination," *Texas Tribune*, December 21, 2016, https://www.texastribune.org/2016/12/21/texas-abandoned-oil-wells-seen-ticking-time-bombs-. See also Russel Lawson, "Orphaned Oil Wells," *Oklahoma Magazine*, September 25, 2018, https://www.okmag.com/blog/2018/09/25/orphaned-oil-wells.

9. Rebecca Hersher, "After Decades of Air Pollution, A Louisiana Town Rebels Against a Chemical Giant," *National Public Radio*, March 6, 2018, https://www.npr.org/sections/health-shots/2018/03/06/583973428/after-decades-of-air-pollution-a-louisiana-town-rebels-against-a-chemical-giant.

10. Lawrence L. Hewitt and Arthur W. Bergeron, eds., *Louisianans in the Civil War* (Columbia, MO: University of Missouri Press, 2002), 2–3.

11. SCVOK, "Sons of Confederate Veterans Oklahoma Division," Facebook page, accessed July 17, 2019, https://www.facebook.com/SCVOK.

12. "About Us," *Heartland Institute*, accessed July 17, 2019, https://www.heartland.org/about-us/index.html.

13. "Videos—Heartland Liberty Prize: Morton Blackwell," *Heartland Institute*, accessed July 17, 2019, https://www.heartland.org/multimedia/videos/heartland-liberty-prize-morton-blackwell.

14. "The Foster Friess Story—the American Dream," *Foster's Outriders*, accessed July 17, 2019, https://www.fosterfriess.com/about.

15. Andrew Graham, "Friess Gives, Forgives, and Gets Returns from Faith, Donations," *WyoFile*, August 10, 2018, https://www.wyofile.com/friess-gives-forgives-and-gets-returns-from-faith-donations. See also "Lynn & Foster Friess Family Foundation," *Conservative Transparency*, accessed July 17, 2019, http://conservativetransparency.org/donor/lynn-foster-friess-family-foundation.

16. Adam Berstein, "Joseph Coors Sr., 85, Dies," *Washington Post*, accessed July 17, 2019, https://www.washingtonpost.com/archive/local/2003/03/18/joseph-coors-sr-85-dies/fc026a48-3ae3-479d-8e4c-d5ecdbe7c808.

17. "Evangelist James Robinson and Millionaire T. Cullen Davis Last . . . ," *United Press International Archives*, January 11, 1983, https://www.upi.com/Archives/1983/01/11/Evangelist-James-Robison-and-millionaire-T-Cullen-Davis-last/1963411109200.

18. Gary Cartwright, "How Cullen Davis Beat the Rap," *Texas Monthly*, May 1979, https://www.texasmonthly.com/articles/how-cullen-davis-beat-the-rap-2. See also Maureen Maher, "Did a Texas Millionaire get Away with a Brutal Double Murder?," *CBS News*, January 23, 2018, https://www.cbsnews.com

/news/48-hours-cullen-davis-case-mansion-murders-did-a-texas-millionaire-get-away-with-brutal-double-killing.

19. Matt Schudel, "Nelson Bunker Hunt, Texas Oil Baron who Lost Much of his Fortune, Dies at 88," *Washington Post*, October 22, 2014, https://www.washingtonpost.com/business/nelson-bunker-hunt-texas-oil-baron-who-lost-much-of-his-fortune-dies-at-88/2014/10/22/81739876-5a02-11e4-8264-deed989ae9a2_story.html.

20. "1998 Membership by State," *Public Eye*.

21. Mark Ellis, "One of the Richest Men in the World Ensured Bankruptcy, but One Investment Brought Eternal Rewards," *GodReports*, November 13, 2014, https://blog.godreports.com/2014/11/one-of-the-richest-men-in-the-world-forced-into-bankruptcy-but-one-investment-brought-eternal-rewards.

22. Richard DeVos, *Simply Rich* (New York: Simon & Schuster, 2016), 11. Richard DeVos Sr. wrote in his autobiography that he grew up in the even more severe Protestant Reformed Church, which splintered from the Christian Reformed Church.

23. Kristina Rizga, "Betsy DeVos Wants to Use America's Schools to Build 'God's Kingdom,'" *Mother Jones*, March/April 2017, https://www.motherjones.com/politics/2017/01/betsy-devos-christian-schools-vouchers-charter-education-secretary.

24. "History," *Christian Reformed Church*, accessed July 17, 2019, https://www.crcna.org/welcome/history.

25. Ibid.

26. "Christian Reformed Church in North America (CRCNA)," *Christ Community Church*, accessed July 17, 2019, http://www.christcommunitysheboygan.org/about/christian-reformed-church-in-north-america-crcna.

27. Greg Chandler, "Holland Leaders Tighten Rules Against Loud Noises, Put Curfew on Yelling, Whistling," *MLive*, February 2, 2012, https://www.mlive.com/news/grand-rapids/index.ssf/2012/02/holland_leaders_tighten_rules.html.

28. "LGBT+ Students and Homosexuality FAQ," *Calvin University*, accessed July 17, 2019, https://calvin.edu/events/sexuality-series/lgbt-homosexuality-faq.html.

29. Rizga, "Betsy DeVos."

30. Debra A. Valentine, "International Monetary Funds Seminar on Current Legal Issues Affecting Central Banks," *Federal Trade Commission*, May 13, 1998, https://www.ftc.gov/public-statements/1998/05/pyramid-schemes.

31. L. Lee, email to author, January 30, 2019.

32. Charles Stanley, *Success God's Way: Achieving True Contentment and Purpose* (Nashville: Thomas Stanley, 2000).

33. "Amway," *Consumer Affairs*, accessed July 17, 2019, https://www.consumeraffairs.com/online/amway.htm. See also Stephen Butterfield, *Amway: The Cult of Free Enterprise* (Boston: South End Press, 1985). See also Eric Scheibeler, *Merchants of Deception* (Scotts Valley, CA: CreateSpace, 2009).

34. Rizga, "Betsy DeVos."

35. Ibid.

36. DeVos, *Simply Rich*, 198–99.

37. Gary L. Bauer, "Letter," *Internet Christian Library*, April 13, 1995, https://www.iclnet.org/pub/resources/text/frc/frc-msn.9504.txt.

38. David Johnston and John M. Broder, "F.B.I. Says Guards Killed 14 Iraqis Without Cause," *New York Times*, November 14, 2007, https://www.nytimes.com/2007/11/14/world/middleeast/14blackwater.html. See also Eileen Sullivan, "Blackwater Security Contractor Found Guilty, Again, in Deadly 2007 Iraq Shooting," *New York Times*, December 19, 2018, https://www.nytimes.com/2018/12/19/us/politics/blackwater-security-contractor-iraq-shooting.html.

39. Blackwater was sold and renamed several times, most recently as Academi.

40. Stephanie Henderson, "Betsy DeVos and the Twilight of Public Education," *Detroit Free Press*, December 3, 2016, https://www.freep.com/story/opinion/columnists/stephen-henderson/2016/12/03/betsy-devos-education-donald-trump/94728574. See also Kate Wells, "Three Detroit Charter Schools Closing this Year," *Michigan Radio*, June 28, 2016, https://www.michiganradio.org/post/three-detroit-charter-schools-closing-year. See also Valerie Strauss, "A Sobering Look at What Betsy DeVos Did to Education in Michigan and What she Might do as Secretary of Education," *Washington Post*, December 8,

2016, https://www.washingtonpost.com/news/answer-sheet/wp/2016/12/08/a-sobering-look-at-what-betsy-devos-did-to-education-in-michigan-and-what-she-might-do-as-secretary-of-education.

41. "Background on Betsy DeVos From the ACLU of Michigan," *ACLU*, accessed July 17, 2019, https://www.aclu.org/other/background-betsy-devos-aclu-michigan.

42. "2019 Venue: Dallas at Las Colinas," *Gathering*, accessed July 19, 2019, https://thegathering.com/event/venue. As of 2019.

43. Betsy DeVos and Dick DeVos, "Betsy and Dick DeVos Talk About Reforming Education at a Gathering of Wealthy Christians in 2001," *Politico* video, 54:55, December 2, 2016, https://www.politico.com/video/2016/12/betsy-and-dick-devos-talk-about-reforming-education-at-a-gathering-of-wealthy-christians-in-2001-061697. See 38:00.

44. Ibid., from 38:00 to 50:00.

45. Andy Kroll, "Meet the New Kochs: The DeVos Clan's Plan to Defund the Left," *Mother Jones*, January/February 2014, https://www.motherjones.com/politics/2014/01/devos-michigan-labor-politics-gop/2.

46. "Union Membership Historical Table for Michigan," *Bureau of Labor Statistics*, accessed July 17, 2019, https://www.bls.gov/regions/midwest/data/unionmembershiphistorical_michigan_table.htm.

47. Drew DeSilver, "American Unions Membership Declines as Public Support Fluctuates," *Pew Research Center*, February 20, 2014, https://www.pewresearch.org/fact-tank/2014/02/20/for-american-unions-membership-trails-far-behind-public-support.

48. James Feigenbaum, Alexander Hertel-Fernandez, and Vanessa Williamson, "From the Bargaining Table to the Ballot Box: Political Effects of Right to Work Laws," *National Bureau of Economic* Research, January 20, 2018, https://jamesfeigenbaum.github.io/research/pdf/fhw_rtw_jan2018.pdf.

49. "The Public-Union Ascendancy," *Wall St. Journal*, last updated February 3, 2010, https://www.wsj.com/articles/SB10001424052748703837004575013424060649464.

50. "2004 United States Presidential Election," *Wikipedia*, accessed July 17, 2019, https://en.wikipedia.org/wiki/2004_United_States_presidential_election.

CHAPTER 6: FISHERS OF MEN

1. Joan Boudreau, "A Civil War Press Pass for William Conant Church," *American Printing History Association*, January 26, 2015, https://printinghistory.org/civil-war-press-pass-william-conant-church. See also "William Conant Church," *Century Association Archives*, accessed July 17, 2018, http://centuryarchives.org/caba/bio.php?PersonID=272. See also "A Brief History of the NRA," *National Rifle Association*, accessed July 17, 2018, https://home.nra.org/about-the-nra. See also Joe Sommerlad, "How was the NRA Founded and How did a Gun Lobby Become so Influential in American Politics?," *Independent*, April 26, 2019, https://www.independent.co.uk/news/world/americas/us-politics/nra-national-rifle-association-history-gun-control-second-amendment-oliver-north-a8887286.html.

2. Author, "Meeting of the National Rifle Association Election of Officers," *New York Times Archive*, November 25, 1871, https://www.nytimes.com/1871/11/25/archives/meeting-of-the-national-rifle-association-election-of-officers. See also E.B. Solomont, "ASB to pay Thor $90M for Dolce & Gabbana's Soho Home," *Real Deal*, June 24, 2016, https://therealdeal.com/2016/06/24/asb-to-pay-thor-90m-for-dolce-gabbanas-soho-home. See also Christopher Gray, "New Bells and Whistles at the Old Firehouse," *New York Times*, May 11, 2013, https://www.nytimes.com/2013/05/12/realestate/new-bells-and-whistles-for-an-old-firehouse.html.

3. "A Brief History of the NRA," *National Rifle Association*.

4. Lauren-Brooke Eisen and Oliver Roeder, "America's Faulty Perception of Crime Rates," *Brennan Center for Justice*, March 16, 2015, https://www.brennancenter.org/blog/americans-faulty-perception-crime-rates.

5. Arica L. Coleman, "When the NRA Supported Gun Control," *Time*, July 29, 2016, https://time.com/4431356/nra-gun-control-history.

6. Ibid.

7. Joel Achenbach, Scott Higham, and Sari Horwitz, "How NRA's True Believers Converted a Marksmanship Group into a Mighty Gun Lobby," *Washington Post*, January 12, 2013, https://www.washingtonpost.com/politics/how-nras-true-believers-converted-a-marksmanship-group-into-a-mighty-gun-lobby/2013/01/12/51c62288-59b9-11e2-88d0-c4cf65c3ad15_story.html.

8. Jeff Suess, "NRA: 'Revolt at Cincinnati' Molded National Rifle Association," *Cincinnati Enquirer*, March 8, 2018, https://www.cincinnati.com/story/news/politics/2018/03/08/revolt-cincinnati-molded-nra-did-you-know-jeff-suess-schism-within-national-rifle-association-led/404628002.

9. John M. Crewdson, "Hard-Line Opponent of Gun Laws Wins New Term at Helm of Rifle," *New York Times Archive*, May 4, 1981, https://www.nytimes.com/1981/05/04/us/hard-line-opponent-of-gun-laws-wins-new-term-at-helm-of-rifle.html.

10. Laura Smith, "The Man Responsible for the Modern NRA Killed a Hispanic Teenager, Before Becoming a Border Agent," *Timeline*, July 6, 2017, https://timeline.com/harlon-carter-nra-murder-2f8227f2434f.

11. Jeffery A. Sierpien, "Frontline Strategies of the National Rifle Association," *Naval Postgraduate School*, March 2006, https://calhoun.nps.edu/bitstream/handle/10945/2949/06Mar_Sierpien.pdf, 4.

12. "Neal Knox," *NRA On the Record*, accessed July 17, 2019, http://nraontherecord.org/neal-knox.

13. Howard Kohn, "Inside the Gun Lobby," *Rolling Stone*, May 14, 1981, https://www.rollingstone.com/politics/politics-news/inside-the-gun-lobby-112530.

14. Sierpien, "Frontline Strategies," 7.

15. Kelly Phillips Erb, "Ask the Taxgirl: is the NRA a Charity?," *Forbes*, March 8, 2018, https://www.forbes.com/sites/kellyphillipserb/2018/03/08/ask-the-taxgirl-is-the-nra-a-charity/#783c688d17df.

16. Sierpien, "Frontline Strategies."

17. "California Proposition 15, Handgun Registration Initiative (1982)," *Ballotpedia*, accessed July 17, 2019, https://ballotpedia.org/California_Proposition_15,_Handgun_Registration_Initiative_(1982).

18. Sierpien, "Frontline Strategies."

19. Robert Lindsey, "Bradley Loses Close Contest on Coast," *New York Times Archive*, November 4, 1982, https://www.nytimes.com/1982/11/04/us/bradley-loses-close-contest-on-coast.html.

20. Josh Kovensky, "History Repeats Itself: How Corruption Nearly Killed the NRA Twice," *Talking Points Memo*, April 26, 2019, https://talkingpointsmemo.com/muckraker/nra-lawsuit-new-financial-troubles-wayne-lapierre. See also Brad Tuttle, "Wayne LaPierre Has Made a Fortune as CEO of the NRA. Here's What We Know About His Money," *Money*, February 28, 2018, http://money.com/money/5178193/wayne-lapierre-net-worth-nra-money-salary.

21. Katherine Q. Seelye, "Staying on Sidelines in Presidential Race, N.R.A. Snubs Dole," *New York Times Archive*, September 18, 1996, https://www.nytimes.com/1996/09/18/us/staying-on-sidelines-in-presidential-race-nra-snubs-dole.html.

22. Kovensky, "History Repeats Itself." See also "2000.07.26 NRA Convention—Charlton Heston—From My Cold, Dead Hands!," YouTube video, 1:25, Jared Law, May 12, 2012, https://www.youtube.com/watch?v=ORYVCML8xeE.

23. Joel Achenbach, Scott Higham, and Sari Horwitz, "How NRA's True Believers Converted a Marksmanship Group into a Mighty Gun Lobby."

24. Judy Sarasohn, "Fortune: NRA Lobby is No. 1 on Capitol Hill," *Washington Post*, May 17, 2001, https://www.washingtonpost.com/archive/politics/2001/05/17/fortune-nra-lobby-is-no-1-on-capitol-hill/8019e21d-766e-47ab-acaf-d43fcfe2adcd.

25. Andy Kiersz and Brett LoGiurato, "Here's Where You're Most Likely to Own a Gun," *Business Insider*, July 3, 2015, https://www.businessinsider.com/gun-ownership-by-state-2015-7. See also Charlie Mahtesian, "What are the Swing States in 2016?," *Politico*, June 15, 2016, https://www.politico.com/blogs/swing-states-2016-election/2016/06/what-are-the-swing-states-in-2016-list-224327.

26. Josh Harkinson, "Does the NRA Really Have 4 Million Members?," *Mother Jones*, January 14, 2013, https://www.motherjones.com/crime-justice/2013/01/nra-membership-numbers.

27. Kim Parker et al., "The Demographics of Gun Ownership," *Pew Research Center*, June 22, 2017, https://www.pewsocialtrends.org/2017/06/22/the-demographics-of-gun-ownership.

28. Sarah Eekhoff Zylstra, "Praise the Lord and Pass the Ammunition, Quantified," *Christianity Today*, July 24, 2017, https://www.christianitytoday

.com/news/2017/july/praise-lord-pass-ammunition-who-loves-god-guns-pew.html.

29. Mark Silk, "When George H. W. Bush Played the Religion Card," *Religion News Service*, December 2, 2018, https://religionnews.com/2018/12/02/when-george-h-w-bush-played-the-religion-card.

30. "Basic Beliefs," *Southern Baptist Convention*, accessed July 17, 2019, http://www.sbc.net/aboutus/basicbeliefs.asp.

31. "Interview: Doug Wead," *Frontline*, November 18, 2003, https://www.pbs.org/wgbh/pages/frontline/shows/jesus/interviews/wead.html.

32. See also Bradley Wright, "How Many Americans are Evangelical Christians? Born-Again Christians?," *Patheos*, March 28, 2013, https://www.patheos.com/blogs/blackwhiteandgray/2013/03/how-many-americans-are-evangelical-christians-born-again-christians. See also Daniel Schlozman, "How the Christian Right Ended Up Transforming American Politics," *Talking Points Memo*, August 25, 2015, https://talkingpointsmemo.com/cafe/brief-history-of-the-christian-right.

33. Eric Levitz, "Democrats Paid a Huge Price for Letting Unions Die," *Intelligencer*, January 26, 2018, http://nymag.com/intelligencer/2018/01/democrats-paid-a-huge-price-for-letting-unions-die.html.

34. "Interview: Doug Wead," *Frontline*.

35. Viguerie, *Takeover*, 247–48.

36. Blackwell, "Real Nature of Politics."

37. Concerned Women for America, *The Homosexual Deception: Making Sin a Civil Right* (Washington, D.C.: Concerned Women for America, 1992.)

38. "State Family Policy Councils," Family Research Council, accessed July 17, 2019, https://www.frc.org/state-policy-organizations.

39. "About Us," *Florida Family Action*, accessed July 17, 2019, https://floridafamilyaction.org/about-us.

40. Harper D. Ward, "Misrepresenting Susan B. Anthony on Abortion," *Susan B. Anthony Museum and House*, 2018, accessed July 17, 2019, https://susanbanthonyhouse.org/blog/misrepresenting-susan-b-anthony-on-abortion.

41. Kate Sheppard, "Susan B. Anthony List Founder: Republicans Hijacked my PAC!" *Mother Jones*, February 22, 2012, https://www.motherjones.com/politics/2012/02/susan-b-anthony-list-sharp-right-turn-rachel-macnair.

42. "Who We Are," *Girl Scouts*, accessed July 17, 2019, https://www.girlscouts.org/en/about-girl-scouts/who-we-are.html.

43. Bill Federer, "Forget the Girl Scouts, Try American Heritage Girls," *WorldNetDaily*, March 11, 2018, https://www.wnd.com/2018/03/forget-the-girl-scouts-try-american-heritage-girls.

44. Sarah Gulseth, "The Coffee Hour—American Heritage Girls March for Life," *KFUO Radio*, February 1, 2019, https://www.kfuo.org/2019/02/01/ch-020119-american-heritage-girls-march-for-life.

45. Dr. Susan Berry, "American Heritage Girls Introduces 'Respect Life' Patch for Pro-Life Service," *Breitbart*, February 15, 2014, https://www.breitbart.com/politics/2014/02/15/american-heritage-girls-introduces-respect-life-patch-for-pro-life-service.

46. Committee on Adolescence, "Homosexuality and Adolescence," *Pediatrics* 72, no. 2 (August 1983), https://pediatrics-aappublications-org.ezp-prod1.hul.harvard.edu/content/72/2/249.

47. "SBA List Honored as 'Grassroots Organization of the Year,'" *Susan B. Anthony List*, March 14, 2013, https://www.sba-list.org/suzy-b-blog/sba-list-honored-grassroots-organization-year.

48. Morton C. Blackwell, "A Movement Conservative Perspective," *Leadership Institute News*, September 17, 2012, https://leadershipinstitute.org/News/?NR=8737.

49. Ibid. See also Marc J. Ambinder, "Inside the Council for National Policy," *ABC News* via *Bishop Accountability*, March 20, 2007, http://www.bishop-accountability.org/news2007/03_04/2007_03_20_Ambinder_InsideThe.htm.

50. Robert Arnakis, "The Real Nature of Politics," *Family Research Council Action* webcast, July 12, 2017, https://blog.frcaction.org/2017/07/real-nature-politics; at 26:00.

51. Ibid., at 43:00-44:50.

52. Julie Rovner, "'Partial-Birth Abortion:' Separating Fact from Spin," *National Public Radio*, February 21, 2006, https://www.npr.org/2006/02/21/5168163/partial-birth-abortion-separating-fact-from-spin.

53. "Darla St. Martin," Political Research, accessed July 17, 2019, http://www.politicalresearch.org/ifas/cnp/bios/stmda.html.

54. Oklahoma City, October 3, 2017.

55. "Leadership Institute Grassroots Training," YouTube video, 3:16, Robert Arnakis, February 8, 2018, https://www.youtube.com/watch?v=j__JI1GSUgw; at 2:26.

56. Ibid., at 2:30–2:40.

57. "About the Leadership Institute," *Leadership Institute*, accessed July 17, 2019, https://www.leadershipinstitute.org/aboutus.

58. "What is Barna?," *Barna*, accessed July 17, 2019, https://www.barna.com/about.

59. Tim Stafford, "The Third Coming of George Barna," *Christianity Today*, August 5, 2002, https://www.christianitytoday.com/ct/2002/august5/third-coming-of-george-barna.html.

60. Ibid.

61. Michael Patrick Leahy, "George Barna: 8 Nov. 16—the Day Christians Changed America," *Breitbart*, December 24, 2017, https://www.breitbart.com/politics/2017/12/24/barna-8-nov-16-the-day-christians-changed-america.

62. Barna, *Day Christians Changed America*, 126–27.

63. Sean Flynn, "The Sins of Ralph Reed," *GQ*, July 12, 2006, https://www.gq.com/story/ralph-reed-gop-lobbyist-jack-abramoff.

64. Jeff Horwitz, "My Right-Wing Degree," *Salon*, May 25, 2005, https://www.salon.com/2005/05/25/blackwell_9. See also "Ralph Reed—Former Guest Speaker at the Leadership Institute," *Leadership Institute*, accessed July 17, 2019, https://www.leadershipinstitute.org/training/contact.cfm?FacultyID=140273.

65. Gilgoff, *Jesus Machine*, 96.

66. "1998 Membership by State," *Public Eye*.

67. Beirich and Potok, "The Council for National Policy: Behind the Curtain."

68. Richard L. Berke, "Lawsuit Says Christian Coalition Gave Illegal Help to Candidates," *New York Times Archive*, July 31, 1996, https://www.nytimes.com/1996/07/31/us/lawsuit-says-christian-coalition-gave-illegal-help-to-candidates.html.

69. Sam Fulwood III, "Christian Coalition Denied Tax-Exempt Status by IRS," *Los Angeles Times Archive*, June 11, 1999, https://www.latimes.com/archives/la-xpm-1999-jun-11-mn-45397-story.html.

70. Berke, "Lawsuit Says Christian Coalition Gave Illegal Help to Candidates."

71. Bill Miller and Susan B. Glasser, "A Victory for Christian Coalition," *Washington Post*, August 3, 1999, https://www.washingtonpost.com/wp-srv/politics/daily/aug99/fec3.htm.

72. Ralph Reed Jr., "Casting a Wider Net," *Policy Review* 65 (Summer 1993): 31–35.

73. Frances FitzGerald, *The Evangelicals: The Struggle to Shape America* (New York: Simon & Schuster, 2017), 423–24.

74. Alex Henderson, "10 Past Republicans Who'd Never Make It in Today's Crazy GOP," *Salon*, October 3, 2013, https://www.salon.com/2013/10/03/10_past_republicans_whod_never_make_it_in_todays_crazy_gop_partner.

75. Max Blumenthal, "The Man Who Helped Drive Powell Away From His Party," *Daily Beast*, July 14, 2017, https://www.thedailybeast.com/the-man-who-helped-drive-powell-away-from-his-party.

76. Gilgoff, *Jesus Machine*, 112.

77. Nathan L. Gonzalez, "The Stunningly Static White Evangelical Vote," *Roll Call*, November 17, 2014, https://www.rollcall.com/news/elections-2014-exit-polls-white-evangelical-vote.

78. Benjamin Domenech, "Dobson's Choice," *Washington Post*, April 19, 1998, https://www.washingtonpost.com/archive/opinions/1998/04/19/dobsons-choice/d4f44419-87b0-47fc-bd47-94ceae7e4e16.

79. "Network Evening News Shows Buck Decade-Long Trend, Grow Audience," *Marketing Charts*, March 19, 2012, https://www.marketingcharts.com/television-21536.

80. Max Blumenthal, *Republican Gomorrah: Inside the Movement that Shattered the Party* (New York: Bold Type Books, 2010), 116.

81. Benjamin Domenech, "Dobson's Choice."

82. James Carney, "The G.O.P. Mantra: Keep Dobson Happy," CNN All Politics, May 11, 1998, http://www.cnn.com/ALLPOLITICS/1998/05/04/time/dobson.html.

83. Gilgoff, *Jesus Machine*, 112–14.

84. "A Dozen Major Groups Help Drive the Religious Right's Anti-Gay Crusade," *Southern Poverty Law Center Intelligence Report*, April 28, 2005, https://www.splcenter.org/fighting-hate/intelligence-report/2005/dozen-major-groups-help-drive-religious-right%E2%80%99s-anti-gay-crusade.

85. Jim Yardley, "THE 2000 CAMPAIGN: THE GOVERNOR'S SPEECH; Bush's Words to Conservative Group Remain a Mystery," *New York Times*, May 19, 2000, https://www.nytimes.com/2000/05/19/us/2000-campaign-governor-s-speech-bush-s-words-conservative-group-remain-mystery.html.

86. "The Leadership Institute," *SourceWatch*, accessed July 17, 2019, https://www.sourcewatch.org/index.php/The_Leadership_Institute. See also FitzGerald, *Evangelicals*, 437.

87. Eric Heubeck, "The Integration of Theory and Practice: A Program for the New Traditionalist Movement," *Free Congress Foundation Archive*, 2001, accessed July 17, 2019, http://web.archive.org/web/20010713152425/www.freecongress.org/centers/conservatism/traditionalist.htm.

88. Bertolt Brecht, "Die Lösung," *Die Welt*, 1959.

89. "Arlington Group," *Ballotpedia*, accessed July 17, 2019, https://ballotpedia.org/Arlington_Group. See also "1998 Membership by State," *Public Eye*.

90. Gilgoff, *Jesus Machine*, 175. See also Associated Press, "Kerry's Positions on Gay Marriage," *NBC News*, last updated December 2, 2004, http://www.nbcnews.com/id/4245324/ns/politics/t/kerrys-positions-gay-marriage/#.XTCID5NKjOQ.

91. David D. Kirkpatrick, "THE 2004 CAMPAIGN: the Conservatives; Club of the Most Powerful Gathers in Strictest Privacy," *New York Times Archive*,

August 28, 2004, https://www.nytimes.com/2004/08/28/us/2004-campaign-conservatives-club-most-powerful-gathers-strictest-privacy.html.

92. FitzGerald, *Evangelicals*, 491.

93. Piore, "A Higher Frequency."

94. James Dao, "Same-Sex Marriage Issue Key to Some G.O.P. Races," *New York Times*, November 4, 2004, https://www.nytimes.com/2004/11/04/politics/campaign/samesex-marriage-issue-key-to-some-gop-races.html?mtrref=www.google.com&gwh=BB2178E5577C387179F1B6938C554F64&gwt=pay. See also Albert Salvato, "Ohio Recount Gives a Smaller Margin to Bush," *New York Times*, December 29, 2004, https://www.nytimes.com/2004/12/29/politics/ohio-recount-gives-a-smaller-margin-to-bush.html.

95. Gilgoff, *Jesus Machine*, 194.

96. Morton C. Blackwell, "Advice to a Just-Elected Conservative Friend," *Leadership Institute*, November 13, 1998, https://www.leadershipinstitute.org/writings/?ID=4.

CHAPTER 7: IDEOLOGY 101

1. "Race, Immigration, Same-Sex Marriage, Abortion, Global Warming, Gun Policy, Marijuana Legalization," *Pew Research Center*, March 1, 2018, https://www.people-press.org/2018/03/01/4-race-immigration-same-sex-marriage-abortion-global-warming-gun-policy-marijuana-legalization.

2. "Conservative Activist Paul Weyrich Dead at 66," *NBC News*, December 18, 2008, http://www.nbcnews.com/id/28299805/ns/politics/t/conservative-activist-paul-weyrich-dead.

3. Heubeck, "The Integration of Theory and Practice."

4. Ibid.

5. "Hillsdale College," *U.S. News and World Report*, accessed July 17, 2019, https://www.usnews.com/best-colleges/hillsdale-college-2272. See also "College Profile," *Hillsdale College*, accessed July 17, 2019, https://www.hillsdale.edu/about/college-profile. See also Cal Abbo "Private Colleges Struggle with Enrollment, Hillsdale Defies the Trend," *Hillsdale Collegian*, March 21, 2019,

http://hillsdalecollegian.com/2019/03/private-colleges-struggle-enrollment-hillsdale-defies-trend.

6. "Top Colleges Doing the Most for the American Dream," *New York Times Sunday Review*, May 25, 2017, https://www.nytimes.com/interactive/2017/05/25/sunday-review/opinion-pell-table.html.

7. Gary Bauer, "Who Counts the Most Important Things of All?," *Imprimis* 23, no. 7 (July 1994), https://imprimis.hillsdale.edu/wp-content/uploads/2016/11/Who-Counts-the-Most-Important-Things-of-All-July-1994.pdf. See also Roy Moore, "Putting God Back in the Public Square," *Imprimis* 28, no. 8 (August 1999), accessed through https://imprimis.hillsdale.edu/wp-content/uploads/2016/10/Imprimis-Putting-God-Back-in-the-Public-Square-Aug-1999.pdf.

8. Nathan Prigmore, "Erik Prince," *Hillsdale College*, accessed July 17, 2019, https://www.hillsdale.edu/hillsdale-blog/launch/erik-prince.

9. "History of Family Research Council," *Family Research Council*, accessed July 17, 2019, https://www.frc.org/historymission. See also Sam Tanenhaus, "'I'm Tired of America Wasting Our Blood and Treasure': The Strange Ascent of Betsy DeVos and Erik Prince," *Vanity Fair*, October 2018, https://www.vanityfair.com/news/2018/09/the-strange-ascent-of-betsy-devos-and-erik-prince.

10. Prigmore, "Erik Prince." See also Tanenhaus, "The Strange Ascent."

11. Robyn Meredith, "Scandal Rocks a Conservative Campus," *New York Times Archive*, November 15, 1999, https://www.nytimes.com/1999/11/15/us/scandal-rocks-a-conservative-campus.html. See also "Reconciled Father and Son Heal a Wound at Hillsdale," *Washington Times*, April 4, 2005, https://www.washingtontimes.com/news/2005/apr/4/20050404-124035-3518r.

12. "Q&A with Larry Arnn," *C-SPAN*, June 4, 2009, https://www.c-span.org/video/transcript/?id=8181.

13. "Federalist Society," *Hillsdale College*, accessed July 17, 2019, https://www.hillsdale.edu/campus-life/clubs-intramurals/federalist-society.

14. "U.S. Voting Rights Timeline," *Northern California Citizenship Project*, accessed July 17, 2019, https://a.s.kqed.net/pdf/education/digitalmedia/us-voting-rights-timeline.pdf.

15. "National Leadership Seminar: Principle and Politics," *Hillsdale College*, accessed July 17, 2019, https://www.hillsdale.edu/event/principles-and-politics-2019.

16. William L. Walton et al., "Letter to President Donald Trump," *Politico*, April 6, 2018, https://www.politico.com/f/?id=00000162-9c7a-d2e5-ade3-dd7e92e60000. CNP Action sent a letter of support of Scott Pruitt when he was under fire at the EPA. See also "Council for National Policy," *SourceWatch*, accessed July 17, 2019, https://www.sourcewatch.org/index.php/Council_for_National_Policy#People_Who_Have_Addressed_CNP. John Bolton addressed the CNP's 2006 meeting.

17. Scott Pruitt, "The Next Supreme Court Justice," *Imprimis* 45, no. 7/8 (July/August 2016), accessed through https://imprimis.hillsdale.edu/next-supreme-court-justice/3.

18. "Mission," *Hillsdale College*, accessed July 17, 2019, https://www.hillsdale.edu/about/mission.

19. Paul Kane, "Democrats say GOP Tax Cut Perk Aimed at Helping One Influential Conservative College," *Washington Post*, December 1, 2017, https://www.washingtonpost.com/powerpost/democrats-say-gop-tax-perk-aimed-at-helping-one-influential-conservative-college/2017/12/01/19f6c8c2-d6fe-11e7-a986-d0a9770d9a3e_story.html.

20. Thomas Novelly, "Hillsdale Alumni Take Over Trump's Administration," *Hillsdale Collegian*, February 9, 2017, http://hillsdalecollegian.com/2017/02/hillsdale-alumni-take-trumps-administration.

21. "Hillsdale College," Conservative Transparency, accessed July 17, 2019, http://conservativetransparency.org/recipient/hillsdale-college/?og_tot=254&order_by=&adv=friess&min=&max=&yr=&yr1=&yr2=&submit=.

22. "Capitol Hill Staff Training School 2018," *Leadership Institute*, accessed July 17, 2019, https://www.leadershipinstitute.org/Training/agenda/school/38150/Capitol%20Hill%20Staff%20Training%20School%202018.pdf.

23. "Intro to Fundraising Workshop," *Leadership Institute*, accessed July 17, 2019, https://www.leadershipinstitute.org/Training/agendas/school/36026/sample.pdf.

24. "Boyle Radio Studio Dedication at Hillsdale College's Kirby Center," YouTube video, 30:33, Hillsdale College, November 12, 2015, https://www.youtube.com/watch?v=5JZGt6kjWwo.

25. Breana Noble, "To the News (Max)," *Hillsdale College*, accessed July 17, 2019, https://www.hillsdale.edu/hillsdale-blog/launch/to-the-news-max.

26. "State of the Media: Audio Today—How America Listens," *Nielson Company*, March 5, 2015, https://www.nielsen.com/us/en/insights/reports/2015/state-of-the-media-audio-today-how-america-listens.html.

27. "Boyle Radio Studio Dedication," Hillsdale College. See 7:35.

28. Hillsdale College, "Implications of the Kavanaugh SCOTUS Confirmation and Originalism," *Hillsdale Dialogues* (blog), July 13, 2018, http://blog.hillsdale.edu/online-courses/implications-kavanaugh-scotus-confirmation-originalism.

29. "About Us," *Daily Caller*, accessed July 17, 2019, https://dailycaller.com/about-us. See also "About Us," *Daily Caller News Foundation*, accessed July 17, 2019, http://dailycallernewsfoundation.org/about-us.

30. Rachel Stoltzfoos, "Trump Considering Hillsdale's Larry Arnn for Secretary of Education," *NewBostonPost*, November 17, 2016, https://newbostonpost.com/2016/11/17/trump-considering-hillsdales-larry-arnn-for-secretary-of-education. See also "The Daily Caller Interviews Hillsdale College President Larry Arnn," *American National Militia*, accessed July 17, 2019, https://americannationalmilitia.com/the-daily-caller-interviews-hillsdale-college-president-larry-arnn.

31. "National Leadership Seminar," *Hillsdale College*.

32. "Tim Pearce," Twitter profile, accessed July 17, 2019, https://twitter.com/timbpearce. See also "Thomas Phippen," LinkedIn profile, accessed July 17, 2019, https://www.linkedin.com/in/thomasphippen. See also "Anders Hagstrom," LinkedIn profile, accessed July 17, 2019, https://www.linkedin.com/in/anders-hagstrom-35a501122.

33. Ginni Thomas, "Here's the List of Conservative Leaders who Impacted American Culture in 2017," *Daily Caller* video, December 30, 2017, https://dailycaller.com/2017/12/30/heres-the-list-of-conservative-leaders-who-impacted-american-culture-in-2017-video.

34. "Hillsdale College Free Online Courses," *Hillsdale College*, accessed July 17, 2019, https://www.hillsdale.edu/academics/free-online-courses. See also

"Constitution 201: The Progressive Rejection of the Founding and the Rise of Bureaucratic Despotism," *Hillsdale College*, accessed July 17, 2019, https://online.hillsdale.edu/page.aspx?pid=1185.

35. Erik Eckholm, "In Hillsdale College, a 'Shining City on a Hill' for Conservatives," *New York Times*, February 1, 2017, https://www.nytimes.com/2017/02/01/education/edlife/hillsdale-college-great-books-constitution-conservatives.html.

36. "Imprimis," *Twitter* profile, accessed July 17, 2019, https://twitter.com/HCimprimis?ref_src=twsrc%5Egoogle%7Ctwcamp%5Eserp%7Ctwgr%5Eauthor. See also "Imprimis, a Production of Hillsdale College," Facebook profile, accessed July 17, 2019, https://www.facebook.com/imprimis.

37. Nick Anderson, "Virginia's Liberty Transforms into Evangelical Mega-University," *Washington Post*, March 4, 2013, https://www.washingtonpost.com/local/education/virginias-liberty-transforms-into-evangelical-mega-university/2013/03/04/931cb116-7d09-11e2-9a75-dab0201670da_story.html. See also Alex MacGillis, "Billion-Dollar Blessings," *Pro Publica*, April 17, 2018, https://www.propublica.org/article/liberty-university-online-jerry-falwell-jr.

38. Alex MacGillis, "How Liberty University Built a Billion-Dollar Empire Online," *New York Times*, April 17, 2018, https://www.nytimes.com/2018/04/17/magazine/how-liberty-university-built-a-billion-dollar-empire-online.html.

39. "Fear God, not Man, says Tony Perkins," *Liberty University News Service*, October 31, 2016, http://www.liberty.edu/news/index.cfm?PID=18495&MID=212183.

40. Will Young, "Liberty Leaders, Faculty, and Students Meet with U.S. policymakers in D.C.," *Liberty University News Service*, April 12, 2018, https://www.liberty.edu/news/index.cfm?PID=18495&MID=270266.

41. "Leadership Institute Expands Partnership with Liberty University and Trains over 130 in Campaign School," *Leadership Institute*, September 21, 2009, https://www.leadershipinstitute.org/news/?NR=1561.

42. Paul Fain, "Title IX Enforcement and LGBT Students," *Inside Higher Ed*, February 27, 2017, https://www.insidehighered.com/news/2017/02/27/liberty-and-bob-jones-universities-may-run-afoul-obama-title-ix-protections-lgbt.

43. Ibid.

44. "Oklahoma Wesleyan University," *U.S. News and World Report*, accessed July 17, 2019, https://www.usnews.com/best-colleges/oklahoma-wesleyan-3151.

45. "OKWU Partners with Family Research Council," *Oklahoma Wesleyan University*, accessed July 17, 2019, https://www.okwu.edu/blog/2016/07/okwu-partners-family-research-council.

46. Lee Fang, "At Secretive Retreat, Evangelicals Celebrate Brett Kavanaugh's Confirmation," *Intercept*, October 7, 2018, https://theintercept.com/2018/10/07/brett-kavanaugh-evangelicals-council-for-national-policy.

47. Mary Margaret Olohan, "5 Books To Send Your Collegiate Off To School With," *Daily Caller*, August 29, 2018, https://dailycaller.com/2018/08/29/five-books-collegiate-school.

48. "Pat Robertson," *SourceWatch*, accessed July 17, 2019, https://www.sourcewatch.org/index.php?title=Pat_Robertson.

49. "About OKWU," *Oklahoma Wesleyan University*, accessed July 17, 2019, https://www.okwu.edu/about.

50. Dawn Ennis, "Oklahoma Wesleyan University President's Anti-Trans Policy Denounced as 'Despicable,'" *Advocate*, January 6, 2016, https://www.advocate.com/transgender/2016/1/06/oklahoma-wesleyan-presidents-anti-trans-policy-denounced-despicable-hrc.

51. Everett Piper, "Conversations about Sex," *Washington Time*s, March 4, 2018, https://www.washingtontimes.com/news/2018/mar/4/why-sexual-immorality-should-be-repudiated-rather-.

52. "Everett Piper," *Omics International*, accessed July 17, 2019, http://research.omicsgroup.org/index.php/Everett_Piper.

53. Max Brantley, "State to seek repayment from Ecclesia College. At last," *Arkansas Times* (blog), September 14, 2018, https://arktimes.com/arkansas-blog/2018/09/14/state-to-seek-repayment-from-ecclesia-college-at-last.

54. "Ecclesia College," *UnivStats*, accessed July 17, 2019, https://www.univstats.com/colleges/ecclesia-college.

55. Max Brantley, "Indictment Charges Former Sen. Jon Woods, College President and Pal in Kickback Scheme," *Arkansas Times* (blog), March 3, 2017, https://arktimes.com/arkansas-blog/2017/03/03/indictment-charges-former

-sen-jon-woods-college-president-and-pal-in-kickback-scheme. See also Rick Seltzer, "The President's Indictment," *Inside Higher Ed*, March 6, 2017, https://www.insidehighered.com/news/2017/03/06/indictment-reveals-details-alleged-ecclesia-kickback-scheme.

56. Deni Kamper, "Former Ecclesia College President Sentenced to Three Years in Federal Prison," *NWA*, September 12, 2018, https://www.nwahomepage.com/news/former-ecclesia-college-president-sentenced-to-three-years-in-federal-prison.

57. "Ginni Thomas," *Turning Point USA*, accessed July 17, 2019, https://www.tpusa.com/aboutus/advisory-council/ginni-thomas.

58. Alex Kotch, "Who Funds Conservative Campus Group Turning Point USA? Donors Revealed," *International Business Times*, November 28, 2017, https://www.ibtimes.com/political-capital/who-funds-conservative-campus-group-turning-point-usa-donors-revealed-2620325. See also Alyson Klein, "Betsy DeVos to Conservative High Schoolers: Are You 'Bored' in School?," *Education Week* (blog), July 25, 2018, http://blogs.edweek.org/edweek/campaign-k-12/2018/07/betsy_devos_turning_point_conservative.html.

59. "conservativememes.com," *Who Is*, accessed July 17, 2019, https://www.whois.com/whois/conservativememes.com. "NRA Hero," *Conservative Memes* image, accessed July 17, 2019, https://conservativememes.com/i/nra-hero-the-hero-who-shot-the-texas-church-shooter-20859080. See also "NRA Hero," *me.me*, accessed July 17, 2019, https://me.me/i/nra-hero-turning-point-usa-the-hero-who-shot-the-19346451.

60. "NRA Hero," *me.me*. See also Nicholas Confessore and Daisuke Wakabayashi, "How Russia Harvested American Rage to Reshape U.S. Politics," *New York Times*, October 9, 2017, https://www.nytimes.com/2017/10/09/technology/russia-election-facebook-ads-rage.html. See also Kevin Poulsen et al., "Exclusive: Russians Appear to Use Facebook to Push Trump Rallies in 17 U.S. Cities," *Daily Beast*, September 20, 2017, https://www.thedailybeast.com/russians-appear-to-use-facebook-to-push-pro-trump-flash-mobs-in-florida.

61. David McCabe, "Senate-commissioned reports show scale of Russian misinformation campaign," *Axios*, December 17, 2018, https://www.axios.com/senate-reports-russian-interference-2016-election-9d0daca6-1e2d-4617-9295-f8eec61c1719.html. See also John Haltiwanger, "Meet Charlie Kirk, the 25-year-old self-declared free speech absolutist and BFF to Trump Jr. who's

rapidly taking over the conservative movement," *Business Insider*, Jan. 5, 2019, https://www.businessinsider.com/turning-point-usa-charlie-kirk-free-speech-russia-trumpism-2018-12.

62. Jane Mayer, "A Conservative Nonprofit That Seeks to Transform College Campuses Faces Allegations of Racial Bias and Illegal Campaign Activity," *New Yorker*, December 21, 2017, https://www.newyorker.com/news/news-desk/a-conservative-nonprofit-that-seeks-to-transform-college-campuses-faces-allegations-of-racial-bias-and-illegal-campaign-activity. See also "Charlie Kirk: 19 Years Old and Already Making a Difference," *Illinois Review*, April 29, 2013, https://www.illinoisreview.com/illinoisreview/2013/04/charlie-kirk-19-years-old-and-already-making-a-difference-.html.

63. Mayer, "A Conservative Nonprofit That Seeks to Transform College Campuses."

64. "Student Movement for Free Markets and Limited Government," *Turning Point USA*, accessed July 17, 2019, https://www.tpusa.com.

65. "Request an Activism Grant," *Turning Point USA*, accessed July 17, 2019, https://www.tpusa.com/resources/activismgrants.

66. Joseph Guinto, "Trump's Man on Campus," *Politico Magazine*, April 6, 2018, https://www.politico.com/magazine/story/2018/04/06/trump-young-conservatives-college-charlie-kirk-turning-point-usa-217829.

67. "About," *Campus Reform*, accessed July 17, 2019, https://www.campusreform.org/about.

68. "LI Regional Field Coordinator Map," *Leadership Institute*, accessed July 17, 2019, https://www.leadershipinstitute.org/campus/map.cfm.

69. "Balance in the Media Grant Form," *Leadership Institute*, accessed July 17, 2019, https://www.leadershipinstitute.org/balanceinmedia.

70. Mayer, "A Conservative Nonprofit That Seeks to Transform College Campuses."

71. Guinto, "Trump's Man on Campus."

72. "Generation Next: A White House Forum Charlie Kirk interviews President Donald Trump," YouTube video, 20:02, Turning Point News, March 22, 2018, https://www.youtube.com/watch?v=XCOjvUmNq24&t=15s.

73. "Charlie Kirk," *Daily Caller*, accessed July 19, 2019, https://dailycaller.com/buzz/charlie-kirk.

74. "CNP Action, Inc.," *Council for National Policy*, accessed July 17, 2019, https://cfnp.org/cnp-action-inc. See also "Policy Council: May 2019 Policy Council Speeches," *Council for National Policy*, accessed July 17, 2019, https://cfnp.org/policy-counsel/may-2019.

75. Joel Shannon, "After Backlash, Conservative Pundit Candace Owens Clarifies Viral Hitler Comment," *USA Today*, February 8, 2019, https://www.usatoday.com/story/news/politics/2019/02/08/candace-owens-clarifies-hitler-nationalism-remark-after-backlash/2818679002.

76. John Bonazzo, "Trump Surrogate Regrets Nazis Didn't 'Keep F***ing Going' in Snapchat Clip," *Observer*, May 11, 2018, https://observer.com/2018/05/juan-pablo-andrade-nazis-turning-point-usa.

77. Jill Jacobs, "Your Tax Dollars Are Propping Up the Intellectual Heirs to an Israeli Terrorist," *Washington Post*, January 11, 2019, https://www.washingtonpost.com/outlook/your-tax-dollars-are-propping-up-the-intellectual-heirs-to-an-israeli-terrorist/2019/01/10/3683c6e0-0efa-11e9-8938-5898adc28fa2_story.html.

78. "Hoboken GOP and Hudson County Young Republicans Celebrate Successful Training," *Insider NJ*, April 2, 2019, https://www.insidernj.com/press-release/hoboken-gop-hudson-county-young-republicans-celebrate-successful-training.

79. Emily Shugerman, "Turning Point USA: How One Student in a Diaper Caused an Eruption in the Conservative Youth Organization," *Independent*, February 26, 2018, https://www.independent.co.uk/news/world/americas/diaper-turning-point-usa-kent-state-student-conservative-youth-repulican-kaitlin-bennett-a8230021.html.

80. Armonie Mendez, "Student Disrupts Free Speech Demonstration by Stabbing Giant Beach Ball, Is Questioned by Police," *Guardian*, October 9, 2017, http://ucsdguardian.org/2017/10/09/student-disrupts-free-speech-demonstration-by-stabbing-giant-beach-ball-is-questioned-by-police.

81. Deidre Olsen, "How a 'Diaper Protest' Imploded a Conservative Student Group," *Salon*, March 25, 2018, https://www.salon.com/2018/03/25/how-a

-diaper-protest-led-to-the-implosion-of-a-conservative-student-group. See also Robby Soave, "U. of Delaware Students Drew a Penis on a Free Speech Ball. Cops Made Them Censor It," *Reason*, April 15, 2016, https://reason.com/2016/04/15/u-of-delaware-students-drew-a-penis-on-a.

82. "Turning Point USA NFP," *Pro Publica*, accessed July 17, 2019, https://projects.propublica.org/nonprofits/organizations/800835023. See also Mayer, "A Conservative Nonprofit That Seeks to Transform College Campuses."

83. Guinto, "Trump's Man on Campus."

84. "Students for Life of America," *Charity Navigator*, accessed July 17, 2019, https://www.charitynavigator.org/index.cfm?bay=search.summary&orgid=16015. Charity Navigator gives the organization a dismal two-star rating, noting that in 2016 41 percent of its budget was spent on fund-raising activities.

85. "Homepage: Students for Life," *Students for Life*, accessed July 17, 2019, https://studentsforlife.org.

86. "Training," *Students for Life*, accessed July 17, 2019,, https://studentsforlife.org/college/training. See also "2020 Schedule," *Students for Life*, accessed July 17, 2019, https://sflalive.org/schedule. See also "Save the Date: 2017-2018 Leadership Workshops," *Students for Life*, September 20, 2017, https://studentsforlife.org/2017/09/20/save-the-date-2017-2018-leadership-workshops. See also "Students for Life Leadership Summits," *Students for Life*, accessed July 17, 2019, https://studentsforlife.org/high-school/students-for-life-regional-conferences.

87. "FAQs about Students for Life," *Students for Life*, accessed July 17, 2019, https://studentsforlife.org/about/donorfaq.

88. "The Planned Parenthood Project," *Students for Life*, accessed July 17, 2019, https://studentsforlife.org/plannedparenthood.

89. "Cemetery of the Innocents," Students for Life, accessed July 17, 2019, https://studentsforlife.org/cemetery-of-the-innocents.

90. Council for National Policy, "Letter to Donald Trump," *Amazon Web Services*, March 1, 2017, https://s3.amazonaws.com/lifesite/CNP_Letter_to_Pres_Trump_3-1-17.pdf

91. Dana Ford, "Josh Duggar after Ashley Madison Hack: 'I Have Been the Biggest Hypocrite Ever,'" *CNN*, August 21, 2015, https://www.cnn.com/2015/08/20/us/josh-duggar-ashley-madison/index.html.

92. Samuel Smith, "FRC President Tony Perkins Says Josh Duggar's Conduct 'Harms the Cause He Has Publicly Espoused,'" *Christian Post*, August 20, 2015, https://www.christianpost.com/news/frc-president-tony-perkins-says-josh-duggars-conduct-harms-the-cause-he-has-publicly-espoused.html.

93. "Wes Goodman's Campaign Finances," *Vote Smart*, accessed July 17, 2019, https://votesmart.org/candidate/campaign-finance/166898/wes-goodman#.xHHBYy2ZN04.

94. Kimberly Kindy and Elise Viebeck, "How a Conservative Group Dealt with a Fondling Charge against a Rising GOP Star," *Washington Post*, November 17, 2017, https://www.washingtonpost.com/politics/how-a-conservative-group-dealt-with-a-fondling-charge-against-a-rising-gop-star/2017/11/17/b3b4b8da-c956-11e7-b0cf-7689a9f2d84e_story.html.

95. Ibid.

96. Rod Dreher, "More Wes Goodman Fallout," *American Conservative*, November 20, 2017, https://www.theamericanconservative.com/dreher/wes-goodman-fallout-tony-perkins.

97. Caleb Hull, "EXCLUSIVE: 30 Sources Expose Sexually Explicit Evidence of Harassment by Ohio GOP Rep. Wes Goodman," *Independent Journal Review*, November 20, 2017, https://ijr.com/exclusive-30-sources-expose-sexually-explicit-evidence-harassment-ohio-gop-rep-wes-goodman.

CHAPTER 8: KOCH, DEVOS, SOROS

1. Sara Fischer, "David Koch is Pro-Choice, Supports Gay Rights; Just Not Democrats," *CNN Politics*, December 15, 2014, https://www.cnn.com/2014/12/14/politics/david-koch-gay-rights-abortion-democrats/index.html.

2. Ibid.

3. Matt Schudel, "Richard DeVos, Billionaire Co-Founder of Amway and GOP Financial Supporter, Dies at 92," *Washington Post*, September 6, 2018, https://www.washingtonpost.com/local/obituaries/richard-devos-billionaire-co-founder-of-amway-and-gop-financial-supporter-dies-at-92/2018/09/06/3fdefb24-b1e9-11e8-aed9-001309990777_story.html. See also Tim Dickinson, "Inside the Koch Brothers' Toxic Empire," *Rolling Stone*, September 24, 2014, https://www.rollingstone.com/politics/politics-news/inside-the-koch-brothers-toxic-empire-164403.

4. Nicholas Confessore, "Quixotic '80 Campaign Gave Birth to Kochs' Powerful Network," *New York Times*, May 17, 2004, https://www.nytimes.com/2014/05/18/us/politics/quixotic-80-campaign-gave-birth-to-kochs-powerful-network.html.

5. Ibid.

6. Te-Ping Chen, "Behind the Climate Skepticism Curtain: the Koch Family and the Cato Institute," *Center for Public Integrity*, last updated May 19, 2014, https://publicintegrity.org/environment/behind-the-climate-skepticism-curtain-the-koch-family-and-the-cato-institute.

7. Confessore, "Quixotic '80 Campaign."

8. "National Platform 1980," *LPedia*, accessed July 17, 2019, http://www.lpedia.org/1980_National_Platform#3._Victimless_Crimes.

9. Confessore, "Quixotic '80 Campaign."

10. Daniel Schulman, *Sons of Wichita* (New York: Grand Central, 2014), 7.

11. "Spindletop launches Modern Petroleum Industry," American Oil and Gas History Society, accessed July 17, 2019, https://aoghs.org/petroleum-pioneers/spindletop-launches-modern-oil-industry.

12. "'Hidden History' of Koch Brothers Traces Their Childhood and Political Rise," *National Public Radio* audio segment, 38:57, January 19, 2016, https://www.npr.org/2016/01/19/463565987/hidden-history-of-koch-brothers-traces-their-childhood-and-political-rise.

13. Thomas C. Frohlich and Bill Friedricks, "The 10 Largest Privately Held Companies in America," *Microsoft Network*, May 8, 2015, https://www.msn.com/en-us/money/companies/the-10-largest-privately-held-companies-in-america/ss-BBiKtaL.

14. Daniel Schulman, "Koch vs. Koch: The Brutal Battle That Tore Apart America's Most Powerful Family," *Mother Jones*, May 20, 2014, https://www.motherjones.com/politics/2014/05/koch-brothers-family-history-sons-of-wichita.

15. Carl Hulse, "In Wichita, Koch Influence Is Revered and Reviled," *New York Times*, June 17, 2014, https://www.google.com/search?q=koch+brothers+dona

te+heavily+in+kansas&oq=koch+brothers+donate+heavily+in+kansas&aqs=chrome..69i57j33.7156j0j9&sourceid=chrome&ie=UTF-8.

16. Dan Voorhis, "What It's Like to Grow up a Koch," *Wichita Eagle*, November 7, 2016, https://www.kansas.com/news/business/article113168633.html.

17. Luisa Kroll and Kerry A. Dolan, "The Definitive Ranking of the Wealthiest Americans," *Forbes*, October 3, 2018, https://www.forbes.com/forbes-400/#692d8d0d7e2f.

18. Elizabeth Bumiller, "Woman Ascending a Marble Staircase," *New York Times Magazine Archive*, January 11, 1998, https://www.nytimes.com/1998/01/11/magazine/woman-ascending-a-marble-staircase.html.

19. Mike Janssen, "Activists Turn Up Heat on WGBH over Role of David Koch," *Current*, April 8, 2014, https://current.org/2014/04/activists-turn-up-heat-on-wgbh-over-role-of-david-koch.

20. Frank Holmes, "6 Reasons Why Texas Trumps All Other U.S. Economies," *Forbes*, October 23, 2018, https://www.forbes.com/sites/greatspeculations/2018/10/23/6-reasons-why-texas-trumps-all-other-u-s-economies/#710d5bd58be8.

21. Matt Phillips, "It's Texas versus New York. And Texas Is Winning," *Quartz*, June 10, 2015, https://qz.com/424775/its-texas-versus-new-york-and-texas-is-winning.

22. Deena Zaidi, "Here Are the 5 Industries Spending the Most on Political Donations," *Street*, August 15, 2016, https://www.thestreet.com/story/13667209/1/here-are-the-5-industries-spending-the-most-on-political-donations.html. See also "Oil and Gas: Top Contributors," *Open Secrets*, accessed July 17, 2019, https://www.opensecrets.org/industries/indus.php?ind=E01.

23. "Leadership Institute," *Conservative Transparency*, accessed July 17, 2019, http://conservativetransparency.org/recipient/leadership-institute.

24. Rich Fink, "The Structure Of Social Change Liberty Guide," *Liberty Guide Archive*, October 18, 2012, https://archive.org/stream/TheStructureOfSocialChangeLibertyGuideRichardFinkKoch; see page 4. See also George Monbiot, "How US Billionaires Are Fuelling the Hard-Right Cause in Britain," *Guardian*, December 7, 2018, https://www.theguardian.com/commentisfree/2018/dec/07/us-billionaires-hard-right-britain-spiked-magazine-charles-david-koch-foundation.

25. United States Environmental Protection Agency, "Koch Industries to Pay Record Fine for Oil Spills in Six States," *Department of Justice*, January 13, 2000, https://www.justice.gov/archive/opa/pr/2000/January/019enrd.htm.

26. Kevin Bogardus, "Koch's Low Profile Belies Political Power," *Center for Public Integrity*, updated May 19, 2014, https://publicintegrity.org/environment/kochs-low-profile-belies-political-power.

27. Jane Mayer, *Dark Money: The Hidden History of the Billionaires behind the Rise of the Radical Right* (New York: Anchor, 2016), 180.

28. "Philanthropy Roundtable," *Conservative Transparency*, accessed July 17, 2019, http://conservativetransparency.org/org/philanthropy-roundtable/?order_by=year%20DESC.

29. "Overview," *Donors Capital Fund*, accessed July 17, 2019, http://donorscapitalfund.org/AboutUs/Overview.aspx.

30. Lee Fang, *The Machine: A Field Guide to the Resurgent Right* (New York: New Press, 2013), 120.

31. Jessica Reaves, "Counting the Lost Votes of Election 2000," *Time*, July 17, 2001, http://content.time.com/time/nation/article/0,8599,167906,00.html.

32. Alexander Hertel-Fernandez, Theda Skocpol, and Jason Sclar, "When Political Mega-Donors Join Forces: How the Koch Network and the Democracy Alliance Influence Organized U.S. Politics on the Right and Left," *Studies in American Political Development* 32, no. 2 (October 2018): 11, https://scholar.harvard.edu/files/ahertel/files/when_political_megadonors_join_forces_how_the_koch_network_and_the_democracy_alliance_influence_organized_us_politics_on_the_right_and_left.pdf.

33. Bill Wilson and Roy Wenzl, "The Kochs' Quest to Save America," *Wichita Eagle*, October 13, 2012. See also Roy Wenzl, "How to Change a Company and a Country," *Wichita Eagle*, October 31, 2015. Quoted in Hertel-Fernandez, Skocpol, and Sclar, "Political Mega-Donors," 6.

34. Gavin Aronsen, "Exclusive: The Koch Brothers' Million-Dollar Donor Club," *Mother Jones*, September 6, 2011, https://www.motherjones.com/politics/2011/09/koch-brothers-million-dollar-donor-club.

35. "Astroturf," *Urban Dictionary*, accessed July 17, 2019, https://www.urbandictionary.com/define.php?term=astroturf.

36. Gavin Aronsen, "How Dark-Money Groups Sneak By the Taxman," *Mother Jones*, June 13, 2012, https://www.motherjones.com/politics/2012/06/dark-money-501c4-irs-social-welfare.

37. "FreedomWorks Foundation," *Conservative Transparency*, accessed July 17, 2019, http://conservativetransparency.org/recipient/freedomworks-foundation/page/3/?order_by=year%20DESC.

38. Fang, *The Machine*, 23.

39. Hertel-Fernandez, Skocpol, and Sclar, "Political Mega-Donors," 11.

40. "1998 Membership by State," *Public Eye*, accessed July 17, 2019, http://www.publiceye.org/ifas/cnp/state98.html. See also Felicia Sonmez, "Who is 'Americans for Prosperity'?," *Public Eye*, August 26, 2010, http://www.publiceye.org/ifas/cnp/state98.html.

41. Hertel-Fernandez, Skocpol, and Sclar, "Political Mega-Donors," 11.

42. "Americans for Prosperity," *Americans for Prosperity*, accessed March 4, 2019, https://americansforprosperity.org.

43. "Top Beneficiaries of DonorsTrust," *Conservative Transparency*, accessed July 17, 2019, http://conservativetransparency.org/top/?donor=3184&yr=&yr1=&yr2=&submit=.

44. Ibid.

45. Eli Clifton, "Who Else Is in the Koch Brothers Billionaire Donor Club?" *Nation*, November 3, 2014, https://www.thenation.com/article/who-else-koch-brothers-billionaire-donor-club. See also Kroll, "Exposed."

46. "Top Supporters of Leadership Institute," *Conservative Transparency*, accessed July 17, 2019, http://conservativetransparency.org/top/?recipient=29140&yr=&yr1=&yr2%20=&submit=.

47. "Careers," Americans for Prosperity, accessed July 17, 2019, https://americansforprosperity.org/careers.

48. Philip Rojc, "Path to Power: Who Funds the Religious Right?," *Inside Philanthropy*, January 17, 2017, https://www.insidephilanthropy.com/home/2017/1/17/giving-to-glorify-god-who-funds-the-religious-right. See also Philip Rojc, "Big Money, Quiet Power: A Look at the National Christian Foundation,"

Inside Philanthropy, October 3, 2015, https://www.insidephilanthropy.com/economic-policy-research/2016/10/3/big-money-quiet-power-a-look-at-the-national-christian-found.html.

49. "Fidelity Charitable Tops List of Largest Charities in 2016," *Philanthropy News Digest*, November 2, 2017, https://philanthropynewsdigest.org/news/fidelity-charitable-tops-list-of-largest-charities-in-2016.

50. Lauren Debter, "How George Soros Became One Of America's Biggest Philanthropists And A Right-Wing Target," *Forbes*, October 23, 2018, https://www.forbes.com/sites/laurengensler/2018/10/23/how-george-soros-became-one-of-americas-biggest-philanthropists-and-a-right-wing-target/#1d04aa7b39ba.

51. Hertel-Fernandez, Skocpol, and Sclar, "Political Mega-Donors," 13.

52. "#1175 Peter Lewis," *Forbes*, last updated March 26, 2013, https://www.forbes.com/profile/peter-lewis/#533828e2178a.

53. Andrew Prokop, "The Democracy Alliance: How a secretive group of donors helps set the progressive agenda," *Vox*, November 24, 2014, https://www.vox.com/2014/11/24/7274819/democracy-alliance.

54. Hertel-Fernandez, Skocpol, and Sclar, "Political Mega-Donors," 18.

55. Ibid., 20.

56. Ibid., 38.

57. Ibid., 3.

58. Rachel Chason, "A Short History of Roy Moore's Controversial Interpretations of the Bible," *Washington Post*, September 27, 2017, https://www.washingtonpost.com/news/acts-of-faith/wp/2017/09/27/a-short-history-of-roy-moores-controversial-interpretations-of-the-bible.

59. "Home," *Family Research Council*, accessed March 10, 2019, https://www.frc.org/wotwwebsite/north-carolina-pastors-briefing.

60. "FREE Tools for your Sanctity of Human Life Sunday," *Family Research Council*, January 14, 2014, https://www.frc.org/watchmenonthewall/free-tools-for-your-sanctity-of-human-life-sunday.

61. "Watchmen on the Wall Regional Events," *Watchmen on the Wall*, accessed July 17, 2019, http://www.watchmenpastors.org/events.

62. "Stay on Your Knees and Roll up Your Sleeves!," Tony Perkins's *Washington Update Archive*, March 10, 2017, https://web.archive.org/web/20170610172622/https://www.frc.org/updatearticle/20170310/stay-knees-roll-sleeves.

63. "Watchmen on the Wall National Briefing FAQs," *Watchmen on the Wall*, accessed July 17, 2019, http://www.watchmenpastors.org/national-event-faq.

64. "Watchmen on the Wall 2015," *Family Research Council*, accessed July 17, 2019, https://downloads.frc.org/EF/EF15E106.pdf.

65. Ibid.

66. "Kenyn Cureton," *Family Research Council*, accessed July 17, 2019, https://www.frc.org/content/kenyn-cureton-vice-president-for-church-ministries.

67. "Pushing the Envelope? The Political Activities of Religious Organizations in Campaign 2004," *Pew Research Center* transcript, September 28, 2004, https://www.pewforum.org/2004/09/28/pushing-the-envelope-the-political-activities-of-religious-organizations-in-campaign-2004.

68. "2016 Values Voter Presidential Voter Guide," *Family Research Council*, accessed July 17, 2019, https://downloads.frc.org/EF/EF16J17.pdf.

69. "Kenyn Cureton," *Family Research Council*.

70. "Pastors Network," *Watchmen on the Wall* map, accessed July 17, 2019, http://www.watchmenpastors.org/pastors-network-map.

71. "VVS19: About VVS," *Values Voter Summit*, accessed July 17, 2019, http://www.valuesvotersummit.org/about.

72. Ibid.

73. "VVS18: Breakout Sessions," *Values Voter Summit*, accessed July 17, 2019, http://www.valuesvotersummit.org/breakout-2015. See also "VVS19: Schedule," *Values Voter Summit*, accessed July 17, 2019, http://www.valuesvotersummit.org/schedule.

74. Author attended, September 21–22, 2018.

75. "Graduated Persecution against America's VP," Tony Perkins's *Washington Update via Family Research Council*, May 14, 2019, https://www.frc.org/updatearticle/20190514/graduated-persecution.

CHAPTER 9: THE OBAMA CHALLENGE

1. Lisa Cannon Green, "ACP: Worship Attendance Rises, Baptisms Decline," *Baptist Press*, June 1, 2018, http://www.bpnews.net/51000/acp-worship-attendance-rises-baptisms-decline.

2. Daniel Cox and Robert P. Jones, "America's Changing Religious Identity," *Public Religion Research Institute*, September 6, 2017, https://www.prri.org/research/american-religious-landscape-christian-religiously-unaffiliated.

3. Thom File, "Voting in America: A Look at the 2016 Presidential Election," *United States Census Bureau*, May 10, 2017, https://www.census.gov/newsroom/blogs/random-samplings/2017/05/voting_in_america.html.

4. "Our Leadership Team," *Alliance Defending Freedom*, accessed July 18, 2019, https://www.adflegal.org/about-us/leadership.

5. "Who We Are," *Alliance Defending Freedom*, accessed July 18, 2019, http://www.adflegal.org/about-us/who-we-are. See also "No One Should Be Forced to Pay for Another Person's Abortion," *Alliance Defending Freedom*, accessed July 18, 2019, http://www.adflegal.org/issues/sanctity-of-life/defending-those-who-defend-life/key-issues/obamacare/hhs-obamacare.

6. Erik Eckholm, "Legal Alliance Gains Host of Court Victories for Conservative Christian Movement," *New York Times*, May 11, 2014, https://www.nytimes.com/2014/05/12/us/legal-alliance-gains-host-of-court-victories-for-conservative-christian-movement.html. See also "990 Form," *Alliance Defending Freedom*, July 1, 2015, https://adflegal.blob.core.windows.net/web-content-dev/docs/default-source/documents/resources/about-us-resources/financials/990-public-adf-june-2016.pdf.

7. "Who We Are," *Alliance Defending Freedom*.

8. "Family Research Council," *Alliance Defending Freedom*, accessed July 18, 2019, http://www.adflegal.org/about-us/allies/family-research-council. See also "Donate Now," *Alliance Defending Freedom*, accessed July 18, 2019, https://www.adflegal.org/donate.

9. "Blackstone Legal Fellowship," *Blackstone*, accessed July 18, 2019, http://www.blackstonelegalfellowship.org.

10. "History," *Alliance Defending Freedom*, accessed July 18, 2019, http://www.adflegal.org/about-us/who-we-are/history.

11. "Alliance Defending Freedom," *Southern Poverty Law Center*, accessed July 18, 2019, https://www.splcenter.org/fighting-hate/extremist-files/group/alliance-defending-freedom.

12. "Alliance Defending Freedom," *Conservative Transparency*, accessed July 18, 2019, http://conservativetransparency.org/recipient/alliance-defending-freedom.

13. Rojc, "Path to Power: Who Funds the Religious Right?"

14. "Marriage is the Future," *Alliance Defending Freedom*, accessed July 18, 2019, http://www.adflegal.org/issues/marriage/redefining-marriage/key-issues/other-relationships-v-marriage.

15. Dale Carpenter, "A 'Reality Check' for the Regnerus Study on Gay Parenting," *Washington Post*, May 10, 2015, https://www.washingtonpost.com/news/volokh-conspiracy/wp/2015/05/10/new-criticism-of-regnerus-study-on-parenting-study.

16. Carpenter, "A 'Reality Check.'" See also Tom Bartlett, "U. of Texas Finds No Scientific Misconduct by Author of Gay-Parenting Study," *Chronicle of Higher Education*, August 29, 2012, https://www-chronicle-com.ezp-prod1.hul.harvard.edu/blogs/percolator/university-of-texas-finds-no-scientific-misconduct-by-gay-parenting-study-author/30594. Following the critiques of his method, the University of Texas launched an inquiry on Regnerus's scholarship. It found "no evidence of scientific misconduct," but specified that this did not mean the study wasn't "seriously flawed." See Glenn Stanton, "Key Findings of Mark Regnerus' New Family Structure Study," *Focus on the Family*, accessed July 18, 2019, https://www.focusonthefamily.com/about/focus-findings/family-formation-trends/regnerus-family-structures-study. The Alliance Defending Freedom removed most citations of his work from its websites, but citations of his "New Family Structures Study" remained on the sites of organizations headed by CNP members, including the Heritage Foundation and Focus on the Family.

17. Ben Leubsorf, "City Wins Church Tax Fight," *Concord Monitor*, May 23, 2012, https://www.concordmonitor.com/Archive/2012/05/999668595-999668596-1205-CM.

18. "Lawyer Accused of Being Sexual Predator of 14-Year-Old Girl," *WMUR*, January 9, 2013, https://www.wmur.com/article/lawyer-accused-of-being-sexual-predator-of-14-year-old-girl/5178804.

19. Jeremy Blackman, "Former Manchester Lawyer Sentenced to 40 Years for Producing Child Pornography," *Concord Monitor*, May 24, 2013, https://www.concordmonitor.com/Archive/2013/05/LisaBironSentence-CM-052413.

20. "Find Top Donors and Beneficiaries," *Conservative Transparency*, accessed July 18, 2019, http://conservativetransparency.org/top.

21. Brendan Joel Kelley, "Turning Point USA Accused of 'Boosting Their Numbers with Racists' by Long-Established Conservative student Group," *Southern Poverty Law Center*, June 15, 2018, https://www.splcenter.org/hatewatch/2018/06/15/turning-point-usa-accused-%E2%80%98boosting-their-numbers-racists%E2%80%99-long-established-conservative. See also "Allies," *Alliance Defending Freedom*, accessed https://www.adflegal.org/about-us/allies.

22. In actuality, many judges choose to step down for higher-paying pursuits.

23. "About Federal Judges," United States Courts, accessed July 18, 2019, https://www.uscourts.gov/judges-judgeships/about-federal-judges.

24. John Gramlich, "Federal Judicial Picks Have Become More Contentious, and Trump's Are No Exception," *Fact Tank*, March 7, 2018, https://www.pewresearch.org/fact-tank/2018/03/07/federal-judicial-picks-have-become-more-contentious-and-trumps-are-no-exception.

25. Lee Rawls, "Its Ratings System Under Fire, ABA Stresses Importance of Federal Judicial Candidate Evaluations," *American Bar Association*, January 1, 2018, http://www.abajournal.com/magazine/article/federal_judicial_candidate_evaluations.

26. "Five Ways the White House and Senate Have Broken the Judicial Confirmation Process," *American Constitution Society*, October 15, 2018, https://www.acslaw.org/inbrief/broken-process-an-unprecedented-senate-judicial-nomination-hearing.

27. Patrick L. Gregory, "Trump Picks More 'Not Qualified' Judges," *Bloomberg Law*, last updated December 19, 2018, https://news.bloomberglaw.com/us-law-week/trump-picks-more-not-qualified-judges-1.

28. Michael Avery and Danielle McLaughlin, "How Conservatives Captured the Law," *Chronicle of Higher Education*, April 15, 2013, https://www.chronicle.com/article/How-Conservatives-Captured-the/138461.

29. "Roger Severino," U.S. Department of Health and Human Services, last modified July 2, 2019, www.hhs.gov/about/leadership/roger-severino/index.html.

30. Anya Kamenetz, "DeVos Family Money Is All Over The News Right Now," *National Public Radio*, August 2, 2018, https://www.npr.org/2018/08/02/630112697/devos-family-money-is-all-over-the-news-right-now. See also "Federalist Society," *Conservative Transparency*, accessed July 18, 2019, http://conservativetransparency.org/basic-search/1/?q=federalist%20society&order_t=year%20DESC&sf%5B0%5D=transaction. See also Michael Reynolds, "Rendering Unto God," *Mother Jones*, December 2005, https://www.motherjones.com/politics/2005/12/rendering-unto-god.

31. Noah Feldman, "Democrats Can't Stop Brett Kavanaugh's Confirmation," *Bloomberg*, September 4, 2018, https://www.bloomberg.com/opinion/articles/2018-09-04/kavanaugh-hearings-federalist-society-is-so-close-to-victory.

32. Phone interview by author, May 25, 2019.

33. Jay Sekulow, "Jay Sekulow: How a Jewish Lawyer from Brooklyn Came to Believe in Jesus," *Jews for Jesus*, January 1, 2005, https://jewsforjesus.org/our-stories/jay-sekulow-how-a-jewish-lawyer-from-brooklyn-came-to-believe-in-jesus.

34. Olivia Nuzzi, "How to Get Rich Suing For Jesus," *Daily Beast*, last updated April 14, 2017, https://www.thedailybeast.com/how-to-get-rich-suing-for-jesus. See also "About Jay Sekulow," *Jay Sekulow*, accessed July 18, 2019, http://jaysekulow.com.

35. Jon Swaine, "Trump Lawyer's Firm Steered Millions in Donations to Family Members, Files Show," *Guardian*, June 27, 2017, https://www.theguardian.com/us-news/2017/jun/27/trump-lawyer-jay-sekulow-donations#img-2; see image #2.

36. "About Jay Sekulow," *American Center for Law and Justice*, accessed July 18, 2019, https://aclj.org/jay-sekulow.

37. "Christian Conservatives Name the Most Effective Cultural Change Organization," *American Culture and Faith Institute Archive*, May 16, 2017,

https://web.archive.org/web/20170518211951/https://www.culturefaith.com/christian-conservatives-name-the-most-effective-cultural-change-organizations.

38. Linda Greenhouse, "Opinion: How the G.O.P. Outsourced the Judicial Nomination Process," *New York Times*, July 21, 2016, https://www.nytimes.com/2016/07/21/opinion/how-the-gop-outsourced-the-judicial-nomination-process.html.

39. "Help Prevent Merrick Garland's Confirmation to the U.S. Supreme Court!," YouTube video, 2:51, NRA, April 29, 2016, https://www.youtube.com/watch?v=kSEn24QU-AU.

40. "McConnell: Senate Won't Vote on Garland Because NRA Opposes Him," YouTube video, 00:50, Igor Volsky, March 20, 2016, https://www.youtube.com/watch?v=ix7lQLplA_E.

41. "Newspapers Fact Sheet," *Pew Research Center*, July 9, 2019, https://www.journalism.org/fact-sheet/newspapers.

42. Piore, "A Higher Frequency."

43. "Member Voices: Stuart W. Epperson Sr., Salem Media Group, Inc.," *National Religious Broadcasters*, August 31, 2017, http://nrb.org/news-room/articles/nrbt/member-voices-stuart-w-epperson-sr-salem-media-group-inc.

44. "Salem Hires Dr. Frank Wright as Its President and COO," *National Religious Broadcasters*, December 17, 2013, http://nrb.org/news-room/media_source1/nrb-members/salem-hires-dr.-frank-wright-as-its-president-and-coo.

45. "Salem Communications Corporation," *SourceWatch*, accessed July 18, 2019, https://www.sourcewatch.org/index.php/Salem_Communications_Corporation.

46. Piore, "A Higher Frequency."

47. "About the Show," *Salem Radio Network*, accessed July 18, 2019, http://www.srnonline.com/show/srn-news.

48. Gilgoff, *Jesus Machine*, 6–7.

49. Omotayo Banjo and Kesha Morant Williams, eds., *Contemporary Christian Culture: Messages, Missions, and Dilemmas* (Lanham, MD: Lexington Books, 2017), 32.

50. Kirkpatrick, "THE 2004 CAMPAIGN: the Conservatives; Club of the Most Powerful Gathers in Strictest Privacy."

51. Piore, "A Higher Frequency."

52. Joseph Carrol, "Economy, Terrorism Top Issues in 2004 Election Vote," *Gallup*, September 25, 2003, https://news-gallup-com/poll/9337/economy-terrorism-top-issues-2004%20-election-vote.aspx.

53. Thomas Roberts and Sean Gibbons, "Same-Sex Marriage Bans Winning on State Ballots," *CNN*, November 3, 2004, http://www.cnn.com/2004/ALLPOLITICS/11/02/ballot.samesex.marriage.

54. "Ohio Definition of Marriage, Amendment 1 (2004)," *Ballotpedia*, accessed July 18, 2019, https://ballotpedia.org/Ohio_Definition_of_Marriage,_Amendment_1_(2004).

55. Andrew R. Flores and Scoot Barclay, "Trends in Public Support for Marriage for Same-Sex Couples by State," *Williams Institute*, April 2015, https://williamsinstitute.law.ucla.edu/wp-content/uploads/Trends-in-Public-Support-for-Same-Sex-Marriage-2004-2014.pdf.

56. Reid J. Epstein, "John Kerry Backs Gay Marriage," *Politico*, July 22, 2011, https://www.politico.com/story/2011/07/john-kerry-backs-gay-marriage-059643.

57. Gilgoff, *Jesus Machine*, 174.

58. "Our Story," *Citizens for Community Values*, accessed July 18, 2019, http://www.ccv.org/about/our-story. Ohio Definition of Marriage, Amendment 1 (2004)," *Ballotpedia*.

59. Gilgoff, *Jesus Machine*, 179.

60. Ibid., 181.

61. Office of Congressman Mike Pence, "File: Mike Pence with Tony Perkins," *Wikimedia* image, 2004, https://en.m.wikipedia.org/wiki/File:Mike_Pence_with_Tony_Perkins.png.

62. Gilgoff, *Jesus Machine*, 182.

63. Rob Boston, "The Religious Right And Election 2004," *Americans United*, December 2004, https://www.au.org/church-state/december-2004-church-state/featured/the-religious-right-and-election-2004.

64. "Former Ohio Elections Chief Blackwell Brings a Troubled Record on Elections to Fraud Commission," *Brennan Center for Justice*, accessed July 18, 2019, https://www.brennancenter.org/sites/default/files/analysis/Ken_Blackwell.pdf.

65. "Playing with the Election Rules," *New York Times*, September 30, 2004, https://www.nytimes.com/2004/09/30/opinion/playing-with-the-election-rules.html.

66. Isaac Stanley-Becker, "Jerome Corsi is a Harvard-Trained Conspiracy Kingpin. But Is He the Link between WikiLeaks and the Trump Campaign?," *Washington Post*, November 28, 2018, https://www.washingtonpost.com/nation/2018/11/28/jerome-corsi-is-harvard-trained-conspiracy-kingpin-is-he-link-between-wikileaks-trump-campaign.

67. John Kenneth Blackwell and Jerome R. Corsi, "Rebuilding America: A Prescription for Creating Strong Families, Building the Wealth of Working People, and Ending Welfare," *Amazon*, accessed July 18, 2019, https://www.amazon.com/Rebuilding-America-Prescription-Creating-Families/dp/1581825013.

68. Salvato, "Ohio Recount Gives a Smaller Margin to Bush."

69. Gilgoff, *Jesus Machine*, 174.

70. Ibid., 190.

71. Ibid., 190–91.

72. Piore, "A Higher Frequency."

73. Gilgoff, *Jesus Machine*, 125.

74. Carl Hulse, "On Wave of Voter Unrest, Democrats Take Control of House," *New York Times*, November 8, 2006, https://www.nytimes.com/2006/11/08/us/politics/08house.html. See also "Democrats win majority of governorships," *CNN*, November 8, 2006, http://www.cnn.com/2006/POLITICS/11/07/election.governors/index.html.

75. Jonathan Martin, "NRA Plans $40M Fall Blitz Targeting Obama," *Politico*, June 30, 2008, https://www.politico.com/story/2008/06/nra-plans-40m-fall-blitz-targeting-obama-011452.

76. Michael McNutt, "Amid Controversy, Kern Gets Support," *Oklahoman*, April 3, 2008, https://oklahoman.com/article/3224704/amid-controversy-kern-gets-support.

77. Lisa Leff, "Money Pouring In for Both Sides in California's Prop. 8 Fight," *Deseret News*, October 27, 2008, https://www.deseretnews.com/article/705258280/Money-pouring-in-for-both-sides-in-Californias-Prop-8-fight.html.

78. "Sen. McCain's Agents of Intolerance," *New York Times*, May 24, 2008, https://www.nytimes.com/2008/05/24/opinion/24sat2.html.

79. Max Blumenthal, "The Council For National Policy Meets In Minn, Vets Palin," *Talk to Action*, September 1, 2008, http://www.talk2action.org/story/2008/9/1/24846/28141/Front_Page/The_Council_For_National_Policy_Meets_In_Minn_Vets_Palin. See also Morgan Gstalter, "McCain says he regrets picking Palin as running mate," *Hill*, May 5, 2018, https://thehill.com/homenews/news/386392-mccain-i-regret-picking-palin-as-my-vice-presidential-nominee.

80. "Election Results 2008," *New York Times*, last updated December 9, 2008, https://www.nytimes.com/elections/2008/results/president/votes.html.

81. "Party Affiliation among Voters: 1992–2016," *Pew Research Center*, September 13, 2016, https://www.people-press.org/2016/09/13/2-party-affiliation-among-voters-1992-2016.

82. "Election 2008: Party Platforms," *New York Times*, May 23, 2012, https://www.nytimes.com/elections/2008/president/issues/party-platforms/index.html.

83. "Crude Oil Prices—70 Year Historical Chart," *Macrotrends*, accessed July 18, 2019, https://www.macrotrends.net/1369/crude-oil-price-history-chart.

84. "Q&A with Paul Weyrich," *C-SPAN* transcript, March 22, 2005, https://www.c-span.org/video/transcript/?id=7958.

85. "Welcome to the Weyrich Lunch," *Weyrich Lunch*, accessed July 18, 2019, https://www.weyrichlunch.com.

86. Katherine Stewart, "What Was Maria Butina Doing at the National Prayer Breakfast?," *New York Times*, July 18, 2018, https://www.nytimes.com/2018/07/18/opinion/maria-butina-putin-infiltration.html.

87. Bruce Weber, "Paul Weyrich, 66, a Conservative Strategist, Dies," *New York Times*, December 18, 2008, https://www.nytimes.com/2008/12/19/us/politics/19weyrich.html.

88. Fang, *The Machine*, 51–53.

89. Hertel-Fernandez, Skocpol, and Sclar, "Political Mega-Donors," 30.

90. Mayer, *Dark Money*, 309.

91. Byron York, "Same Old Party: Tranquility in the Ranks," *World Affairs Journal*, accessed July 18, 2019, http://www.worldaffairsjournal.org/article/same-old-party-tranquility-ranks.

92. Fang, *The Machine*, 54–55.

93. Reihan Salam, "The Santelli Conspiracy?*," *Atlantic*, March 2, 2009, https://www.theatlantic.com/politics/archive/2009/03/the-santelli-conspiracy/1099.

94. "Tea Party Patriots," *SourceWatch*, accessed July 18, 2019, https://www.sourcewatch.org/index.php?title=Tea_Party_Patriots.

95. Fang, *The Machine*, 111.

96. Martha Shanahan, "5 Memorable Moments When Town Hall Meetings Turned To Rage," *National Public Radio*, August 7, 2013, https://www.npr.org/sections/itsallpolitics/2013/08/07/209919206/5-memorable-moments-when-town-hall-meetings-turned-to-rage.

97. Katie Connolly, "What exactly is the Tea Party?," *British Broadcasting Corporation*, September 16, 2010, https://www.bbc.com/news/world-us-canada-11317202.

98. Sarah Posner, "Will Ralph Reed's New Venture Wed Religious Right to Tea Partiers?," *Religion Dispatches*, March 13, 2010, http://religiondispatches.org/will-ralph-reeds-new-venture-wed-religious-right-to-tea-partiers.

99. Sarah Posner, "Ralph Reed's Synergy with the Religious Right," *Religion Dispatches*, September 13, 2010, http://religiondispatches.org/ralph-reeds-synergy-with-the-religious-right.

100. Posner, "Will Ralph Reed's New Venture Wed Religious Right to Tea Partiers?."

101. Stephanie Mencimer, "Tea Party Courts GOP's Evangelical Wing," *Mother Jones*, October 6, 2010, https://www.motherjones.com/politics/2010/10/tea-party-patriots-tim-lahaye-evangelicals.

102. Fang, *The Machine*, 11.

103. Mencimer, "Tea Party Courts GOP's Evangelical Wing."

104. Fang, *The Machine*, 60.

105. "990 Form," *Faith and Freedom Coalition*, accessed July 18, 2019, https://pdf.guidestar.org/PDF_Images/2015/270/182/2015-270182697-0d4d2b24-9O.pdf.

106. "Conservative and Tea Party Leaders to Gather at Election Night Victory Party," *Christian News Wire*, accessed July 18, 2019, http://www.christiannewswire.com/news/2863515225.html.

107. Viguerie, *Takeover*, xix–xx.

108. "Americans for Prosperity Foundation," *Conservative Transparency*, accessed July 18, 2019, http://conservativetransparency.org/recipient/americans-for-prosperity-foundation/page/2/?order_by=year%20DESC.

109. Matea Gold, "Tea Party PACs reap money for midterms, but spend little on candidates," *Washington Post*, April 26, 2014, https://www.washingtonpost.com/politics/tea-party-pacs-reap-money-for-midterms-but-spend-little-on-candidates/2014/04/26/0e52919a-cbd6-11e3-a75e-463587891b57_story.html

110. "Americans for Prosperity Foundation," *Conservative Transparency*.

111. "Claude R. Lambe Charitable Foundation," *Conservative Transparency*, accessed July 18, 2019, http://conservativetransparency.org/org/claude-r-lambe-charitable-foundation.

112. "Mercer Family Foundation," *Conservative Transparency*, accessed July 18, 2019, http://conservativetransparency.org/donor/mercer-family-foundation.

113. Brian Kaylor, "Conservative Christian Group Seeks New Reagan," *Ethics Daily*, June 23, 2011, https://ethicsdaily.com/conservative-christian-group-seeks-new-reagan-cms-18098.

114. Francesca Jones, "Broadcasting the Bible: Life.Church Broadcasts High-Tech Worship in Rogers," *Arkansas Democrat Gazette*, September 8, 2018,

https://www.arkansasonline.com/news/2018/sep/08/broadcasting-the-bible-20180908. See also "2020 CoMo Christian Men's Conference," *Brown Paper Tickets*, accessed July 18, 2019, https://www.brownpapertickets.com/event/4231662.

115. Brian Kaylor, "Conservative Christian Leaders Plot to Replace Obama," *Ethics Daily*, November 15, 2010, https://ethicsdaily.com/conservative-christian-leaders-plot-to-replace-obama-cms-17004.

116. Kaylor, "Conservative Christian Group Seeks New Reagan."

117. Ibid.

118. "A Chesterfield Advertisement with Ronald Reagan," Getty image, accessed July 18, 2019, https://www.gettyimages.com/detail/news-photo/chesterfield-advertisement-with-ronald-reagan-news-photo/595717876.

119. Jim Romenesko, "Associated Press profit and revenue slide in 2009," *Poynter*, April 29, 2010, https://www.poynter.org/reporting-editing/2010/associated-press-profit-and-revenue-slide-in-2009.

120. Rick Edmonds, "Curley: Newspapers Now Provide Only 20 Percent of AP Revenue," *Poynter*, October 26, 2010, https://www.poynter.org/reporting-editing/2010/curley-newspapers-now-provide-only-20-percent-of-ap-revenue.

121. Gillian Reagan, "Chart of the Day: How Fox Conquered Cable News," *Business Insider*, January 11, 2010, https://www.businessinsider.com/chart-of-the-day-fox-cnn-msnbc-ratings-2010-1. See also Paul Farri, Jack Gillum and Chris Alcantara, "In this Town, you can Flip all the Channels you want—TV News is Often the Same," *Washington Post*, May 15, 2018, https://www.washingtonpost.com/graphics/2018/lifestyle/sinclair-broadcasting.

122. Daniel C. Vock, "How Political Donors Are Changing Statehouse News Reporting," *Governing*, November 2014, https://www.governing.com/topics/politics/gov-political-donors-statehouse-news.html.

123. Paul Abowd, "Donors Use Charity to Push Free-Market Policies in States," *Center for Public Integrity*, last updated January 10, 2015, https://publicintegrity.org/federal-politics/donors-use-charity-to-push-free-market-policies-in-states.

124. "Franklin Center for Government & Public Integrity," *Conservative Transparency*, accessed July 18, 2019, http://conservativetransparency.org/recipient/franklin-center-for-government-public-integrity.

125. Vock, "How Political Donors Are Changing Statehouse News Reporting." See also "Franklin Center for Government & Public Integrity," *Conservative Transparency*.

126. "Franklin Center for Government and Public Integrity," *Instant Car Donation*, accessed July 18, 2019, https://instantcardonation.org/charity-information/franklin-center-for-government-and-public-integrity.

127. Lachlan Markay, "Heritage to Co-Host 'Breitbart Awards' at Future of Journalism Summit," *Daily Signal*, June 6, 2012, https://www.dailysignal.com/2012/06/06/heritage-to-co-host-breitbart-awards-at-future-of-journalism-summit.

128. Mark Jurkowitz, Amy Mitchell, and Monica Anderson, "Nonprofit Journalism: A Growing but Fragile Part of the U.S. News System," *Pew Research Center*, June 10, 2013, http://www.journalism.org/2013/06/10/nonprofit-journalism.

129. "Franklin Center for Government and Public Integrity," *SourceWatch*, accessed July 18, 2019, https://www.sourcewatch.org/index.php/Franklin_Center_for_Government_and_Public_Integrity.

130. Patrick B. McGuigan, "Neither Weiners nor whiners here—AFP-OK and A. G. Pruitt rebuff EPA's shaft job," *Capitol Beat OK*, July 29, 2013, https://capitolbeatok.worldsecuresystems.com/reports/neither-weiners-nor-whiners-here-afp-ok-and-a-g-pruitt-rebuff-epa-s-shaft-job.

CHAPTER 10: DATA WARS

1. Miles Benson, "Here Come Demzilla and Voter Vault/Democrats and the GOP are snooping on you," *SF Gate*, August 3, 2003, https://www.sfgate.com/opinion/article/PRIVACY-Here-Come-Demzilla-and-Voter-Vault-2575339.php.

2. Ibid.

3. "GOP Data Center (formerly Voter Vault)," *FILPAC*, accessed July 18, 2019, http://www.filpac.com/votervault.htm.

4. Brian Reich, "Please Standby . . . the DNC is Still Experiencing Technical Difficulties," *Personal Democracy Media*, April 18, 2004, https://personaldemocracy.com/blogs/brian-reich.

5. Fredreka Schouten, "Liberal Donors Gear Up to Fund New State-Level Agenda," *USA Today*, April 12, 2015, https://www.usatoday.com/story/news/politics/elections/2016/2015/04/12/democracy-alliance-to-direct-millions-to-30-liberal-groups/25672531.

6. *The Economist*, "Politics by the Numbers," *Catalist*, March 23, 2016, https://www.catalist.us/news-innovation/2016-news/politics-the-numbers-the-economist.

7. Sue Halpern, "How Campaigns Are Using Marketing, Manipulation, and 'Psychographic Targeting' to Win Elections—and Weaken Democracy," *New Republic*, October 18, 2018, https://newrepublic.com/article/151548/political-campaigns-big-data-manipulate-elections-weaken-democracy.

8. Leslie Wayne, "Clinton Aide's Databank Venture Breaks Ground in Politicking," *New York Times*, April 12, 2008, https://www.nytimes.com/2008/04/12/us/politics/12vote.html.

9. Ibid.

10. Scott Walter, "The State of the Left: Technological Revolutions," *Capital Research Center*, April 12, 2019, https://capitalresearch.org/article/the-state-of-the-left-part-4.

11. Wayne, "Clinton Aide's Databank Venture." For MoveOn and the tech industry, see Chris Carr, "Internet Anti-Impeachment Drive Yields Big Pledges of Money, Time," *Washington Post*, February 7, 1999, https://www.washingtonpost.com/wp-srv/politics/special/clinton/stories/moveon020799.htm.

12. Leslie Wayne, "Democrats Take Page From Their Rival's Playbook," *New York Times*, October 31, 2008, https://www.nytimes.com/2008/11/01/us/politics/01target.html.

13. "Voter Activation Network and NGP Software to Merge," *NGP Van* (blog), January 1, 2011, https://blog.ngpvan.com/news/voter-activation-network-and-ngp-software-merge.

14. Wayne, "Clinton Aide's Databank Venture."

15. Sasha Isenberg, "Obama Does it Better," *Slate*, October 29, 2012, https://slate.com/news-and-politics/2012/10/obamas-secret-weapon-democrats-have-a-massive-advantage-in-targeting-and-persuading-voters.html. See also Marc Ambinder, "Exclusive: How Democrats Won The Data War In 2008," *Atlantic*, October 5, 2009, https://www.theatlantic.com/politics/archive/2009/10/exclusive-how-democrats-won-the-data-war-in-2008/27647.

16. "Data Integrations," *Catalist*, accessed July 18, 2019, https://www.catalist.us/products/data-integrations.

17. Toby Harnden, "John McCain 'Technology Illiterate' Doesn't Email or Use Internet," *Telegraph*, July 13, 2008, https://www.telegraph.co.uk/news/news topics/uselection2008/johnmccain/2403704/John-McCain-technology-illiterate-doesnt-email-or-use-internet.html.

18. David Carr, "How Obama Tapped into Social Networks' Power," *New York Times,* November 9, 2008, https://www.nytimes.com/2008/11/10/business/media/10carr.html.

19. Ambinder, "Exclusive: How Democrats Won the Data War in 2008."

20. Robert Draper, "A Post-Obama Democratic Party in Search of Itself," *New York Times* Magazine, November 1, 2017, https://www.nytimes.com/2017/11/01/magazine/a-post-obama-democratic-party-in-search-of-itself.html.

21. "TC4 Trust," *SourceWatch*, accessed July 18, 2019, https://www.sourcewatch.org/index.php/TC4_Trust.

22. Peter Henderson, "Kochs help Republicans catch up on technology," *Reuters*, May 17, 2012, https://www.reuters.com/article/us-usa-politics-kochs/kochs-help-republicans-catch-up-on-technology-idUSBRE84G0E820120517.

23. Viveca Novak, Robert Maguire and Russ Choma, "Exclusive: Nonprofit Funneled Money to Kochs' Voter Database Effort, Other Conservative Groups," *Open Secrets*, December 21, 2012, https://www.opensecrets.org/news/2012/12/nonprofit-funneled-money-to-kochs-voter-database-effort-other-conservative-groups.

24. Kenneth P. Vogel and Maggie Haberman, "The GOP's Data Dogfight," *Politico*, April 22, 2013, https://www.politico.com/story/2013/04/karl-rove-koch-brothers-control-republican-data-090385.

25. Matt Mayer, "How the Electoral College Favors Democrats and Why Republicans Must Change it," *Washington Examiner*, June 8, 2014, https://www.washingtonexaminer.com/how-the-electoral-college-favors-democrats-and-why-republicans-must-change-it.

26. Mark S. Granovetter, "The Strength of Weak Ties," *American Journal of Sociology* 78, no. 6 (May 1973): 1360-1380, https://www.jstor.org/stable/2776392.

27. Lauren Markoe, "5 Faith Facts about Scott Walker: Son of a Preacher Man," *Washington Post*, July 13, 2015, https://www.washingtonpost.com/national/religion/5-faith-facts-about-scott-walker-son-of-a-preacher-man/2015/07/13/1e0152f2-2990-11e5-960f-22c4ba982ed4_story.html.

28. Andy Kroll, "'He Lied to the People of Wisconsin,'" *Mother Jones*, April 9, 2012, https://www.motherjones.com/politics/2012/04/scott-walker-recall-wisconsin-democrat-union.

29. Derek Willis, "To Understand Scott Walker's Strength, Look at His Donors," *New York Times*, February 11, 2015, https://www.nytimes.com/2015/02/12/upshot/to-understand-scott-walkers-strength-look-at-his-donors.html.

30. Peter Dreier, "Why Was Obama Missing-in-Action in Wisconsin?," *HuffPost*, August 11, 2011, https://www.huffpost.com/entry/obama-mia-wisconsin_b_924045.

31. Gavin Aronsen, "The Dark Money Behind the Wisconsin Recall," *Mother Jones*, June 5, 2012, https://www.motherjones.com/politics/2012/06/wisconsin-walker-recall-money-stats.

32. Amy Sherman, "Obama never marched with union picketers," *PolitiFact*, December 14, 2016, https://www.politifact.com/truth-o-meter/promises/obameter/promise/896/walk-picketers-when-collective-bargaining-rights-a.

33. Dreier, "Why Was Obama Missing-in-Action in Wisconsin?."

34. Matt Pressman, "What ever happened to Air America," *Vanity Fair*, March 12, 2009, https://www.vanityfair.com/news/2009/03/what-ever-happened-to-air-america. See also Brian Stelter, "Air America, the Talk Radio Network, Will Go Off the Air," *New York Times*, January 21, 2010, https://www.nytimes.com/2010/01/22/business/media/22radio.html.

35. Charles G. Koch, "Letter," *American Progress Association*, accessed July 18, 2019, https://images2.americanprogressaction.org/ThinkProgress/secretkoch meeting.pdf.

36. "990 Form," United in Purpose via *GuideStar*, accessed July 18, 2019, https://www.guidestar.org/FinDocuments/2016/262/495/2016-262495973 -0ece8ee1-9O.pdf.

37. "Mission," *United in Purpose Archive*, accessed July 18, 2019, https://web.archive .org/web/20160317145633/http://unitedinpurpose.org/about/mission.

38. Joel Roberts and Beth Lester, "Democrats Show Rare Unity," *CBS News*, May 28, 2004, https://www.cbsnews.com/news/democrats-show-rare-unity.

39. "Bill Dallas, Lessons from San Quentin," YouTube video, 4:39, Tyndale House Publishers, February 15, 2010, https://www.youtube.com/watch ?v=9r623BwCIII.

40. Thomas Brewster, "Right-Wing Company of Convicted Embezzler Turned Christian Linked to Huge Leaks of US Voter Records," *Forbes*, January 4, 2016, https://www.forbes.com/sites/thomasbrewster/2016/01/04/191-million -leak-bill-dallas-christian-anti-abortion/#5c5802d278f7.

41. Author was present.

42. Brian Kaylor, "Conservative Christian Leaders Plot to Replace Obama."

43. Michael Gryboski, "Life.Church Has Grown to 30 Campuses and 85,000 Attendees," *Christian Post*, September 12, 2018, https://www.christianpost.com /news/life-church-has-grown-to-30-campuses-and-85000-attendees.html.

44. Life.Church service, Oklahoma, October 1, 2017.

45. Interviews by author: Florida, Texas, and Oklahoma.

46. "CCN – Church Communication Network," YouTube video, 8:20, Dereck Packard, February 14, 2009, https://www.youtube.com/watch?v=2r3YA HsDRlc.

47. Mia Evans-Saracual, "Bill Dallas: Sanctified at San Quentin," *Christian Broadcasting Network*, accessed July 18, 2019, http://www.cbn.com/700club /guests/interviews/bill_dallas102308.aspx.

48. Jim Way, "Watchmen on the Wall Report," *Capernaum Inn*, accessed July 18, 2019, https://capernauminn.com/watchmen-on-the-wall-report.

49. Matea Gold and Tom Hamburger, "Silicon Valley Gives Conservative Christians a Boost," *Los Angeles Times*, September 15, 2011, http://articles.latimes.com/2011/sep/15/nation/la-na-evangelical-outreach-20110916.

50. Kyle Mantyla, "AFA Using Perry's Prayer Rally Mailing List To Mobilize Christian Voters," *Right Wing Watch*, August 18, 2011, http://www.rightwingwatch.org/post/afa-using-perrys-prayer-rally-mailing-list-to-mobilize-christian-voters.

51. Barbara Bradley Hagerty, "To Get Out the Vote, Evangelicals Try Data Mining," *National Public Radio*, February 27, 2012, https://www.npr.org/2012/02/27/147504999/to-get-out-the-vote-evangelicals-try-data-mining.

52. Barna, *Day Christians Changed America*, 147, 151.

53. Ibid., 54.

54. Ibid., 54–55.

55. Ibid., 60–61.

56. Brad Friedman, "Exclusive Audio: Inside the Koch Brothers' Secret Seminar," *Mother Jones*, September 6, 2011, https://www.motherjones.com/politics/2011/09/exclusive-audio-koch-brothers-seminar-tapes.

57. Ibid.

58. "Foster Friess," *Notable Names Database*, accessed July 18, 2019, https://www.nndb.com/people/114/000353052.

59. "Transcript: Inside the Koch Brothers' 2011 Summer Seminar," *Brad Blog*, accessed July 18, 2019, http://www.bradblog.com/?page_id=8700. See also Brad Friedman, "Inside the Koch Brothers' Secret Seminar."

60. Robert Maguire and Viveca Novak, "Koch Group's IRS Report Unlocks A Few Mysteries," *Open Secrets*, September 18, 2013, https://www.opensecrets.org/news/2013/09/koch-groups-irs-report-unlocks-mysteries-details-giant-trade-group.

61. "Freedom Partners: Grant Stipulations," *Document Cloud*, accessed July 18, 2019, https://www.documentcloud.org/documents/798004-freedom-partners-990-2012#document/p28/a144787.

62. Maguire and Novak, "Koch Group's IRS Report Unlocks A Few Mysteries."

63. "Freedom Partners," *SourceWatch*, accessed July 18, 2019, https://www.sourcewatch.org/index.php/Freedom_Partners. See also Mike Allen and Jim Vandehei, "The Koch Brothers' Secret Bank," *Politico*, September 11, 2013, https://www.politico.com/story/2013/09/behind-the-curtain-exclusive-the-koch-brothers-secret-bank-096669.

64. Jesse Marx, "Koch Brothers, Donors to Hold Desert Gathering Next Weekend," *Desert Sun*, January 22, 2016, https://www.desertsun.com/story/news/2016/01/22/koch-brothers-donors-hold-desert-gathering-next-weekend/78817052.

65. Nicholas Confessore, "Koch Political Group Spent $400 Million in 2015, Officials Say," *New York Times*, February 1, 2016, https://www.nytimes.com/politics/first-draft/2016/01/31/koch-political-group-spent-400-million-in-2015-officials-say. See also Kenneth P. Vogel, "Koch Brothers Summon Bush, Cruz, Walker, Rubio to SoCal Confab," *Politico*, July 27, 2015, https://www.politico.com/story/2015/07/koch-brothers-wealthy-donors-gop-2016-freedom-partners-seminar-california-120663.

66. "Freedom Partners Shared Services," *SourceWatch*, accessed July 18, 2019, https://www.sourcewatch.org/index.php?title=Freedom_Partners_Shared_Services.

67. Mark E. Benbow, "Holding The Line," *Arlington Magazine*, October 21, 2013, https://www.arlingtonmagazine.com/holding-the-line.

68. Viveca Novak, "GenOpp, Too: Another Group Almost Wholly Funded by Koch Network," *OpenSecrets*, May 13, 2014, https://www.opensecrets.org/news/2014/05/genopp-too-another-group-almost-wholly-funded-by-koch-network.

69. Matea Gold, "The players in the Koch-backed $400 million political donor network," *Washington Post*, January 5, 2014, https://www.washingtonpost.com/politics/the-players-in-the-koch-backed-400-million-political-donor-network/2014/01/05/714451a8-74b5-11e3-8b3f-b1666705ca3b_story.html.

70. "990 Form," Evanghr4 Trust vs *PR Watch*, accessed July 18, 2019, https://www.prwatch.org/files/45-2324423_9900_2013051.pdf.

71. Gold, "The Players in the Koch-Backed $400 Million Political Donor Network."

72. *Hatewatch* Staff, "Trump Administration Taps Long-Time Anti-Feminist and Anti-Choice Activist for Global Women's Issues Position," *Southern Poverty Law Center*, November 8, 2017, https://www.splcenter.org/hatewatch/2017/11/08/trump-administration-taps-long-time-anti-feminist-and-anti-choice-activist-global-women's.

73. "Leadership Institute," *Conservative Transparency*.

74. Hagerty, "To Get Out the Vote, Evangelicals Try Data Mining."

75. Matthew Haag, "Robert Jeffress, Pastor Who Said Jews Are Going to Hell, Led Prayer at Jerusalem Embassy," *New York Times*, May 14, 2018, https://www.nytimes.com/2018/05/14/world/middleeast/robert-jeffress-embassy-jerusalem-us.html.

76. Richard A. Oppel and Erik Eckholm, "Prominent Pastor Calls Romney's Church a Cult," *New York Times*, October 7, 2011, https://www.nytimes.com/2011/10/08/us/politics/prominent-pastor-calls-romneys-church-a-cult.html.

77. Viguerie, *Takeover*, xxiii.

78. NRB Staff, "Vice President Mike Pence Speaks at Focus on the Family's 40th Anniversary Celebration," *National Religious Broadcasting*, accessed July 18, 2019, http://nrb.org/news-room/articles/nrbt/vice-president-mike-pence-speaks-focus-familys-40th-anniversary-celebration.

79. Ashley Parker, "Pence Is Values Voters' Choice for President . . . and Vice President," *Caucus* (blog) *New York Times*, September 18, 2010, https://thecaucus.blogs.nytimes.com/2010/09/18/pence-is-values-voters-choice-for-president-and-vice-president.

80. Michael A. Memoli, "GOP Rep. Mike Pence Gets Nod for 2012 Presidential Run," *Los Angeles Times*, September 19, 2010, http://articles.latimes.com/2010/sep/19/nation/la-na-values-voter-20100919.

81. McKay Coppins, "God's Plan for Mike Pence," *Atlantic*, January/February, 2018, https://www.theatlantic.com/magazine/archive/2018/01/gods-plan-for-mike-pence/546569.

82. Erik Eckholm, "A Political Revival for Ralph Reed," *New York Times*, May 31, 2011, https://www.nytimes.com/2011/06/01/us/politics/01reed.html.

83. Nancy Scola, "Democrats Push Obama Quality Digital Tools All the Way Down to State House Races," *Washington Post*, October 13, 2014, https://www.washingtonpost.com/news/the-switch/wp/2014/10/13/democrats-push-obama-quality-digital-tools-all-the-way-down-to-state-house-races.

84. Justin Rubio, "Obama for America iOS App Launches in Preparation for Election Season," *Verge*, July 31, 2012, https://www.theverge.com/2012/7/31/3206276/obama-for-america-ios-app. See also Ari Melber, "How the Obama Campaign's New iPhone App Really Works," *Nation*, July 31, 2012, https://www.thenation.com/article/how-obama-campaigns-new-iphone-app-really-works.

85. Alex Fitzpatrick, "Meet the Romney Campaign's Official iPhone App [EXCLUSIVE]," *Mashable*, May 29, 2012, https://mashable.com/2012/05/29/romney-official-app/#HzDf_rVGHuqH.

86. John Ekdahl, "The Unmitigated Disaster Known as Project ORCA," *Ace of Spades HQ*, November 8, 2012, http://ace.mu.nu/archives/334783.php.

87. "2012 Election Results," *New York Times* map, last updated November 29, 2012, https://www.nytimes.com/elections/2012/results/president.html. See also Robert Schlesinger, "Conservatives Can't Win at the Negotiating Table What They Lost at the Ballot Box," *U.S. News and World Report*, January 4, 2013, https://www.usnews.com/opinion/blogs/robert-schlesinger/2013/01/04/the-final-2012-presidential-election-results-arent-close.

88. Scola, "Democrats Push Obama Quality Digital Tools."

89. W. Gardner Shelby, "Republicans Won More House Seats than More Popular Democrats, though Not Entirely because of How Districts Were Drawn," *PolitiFact*, November 26, 2013, https://www.politifact.com/texas/statements/2013/nov/26/lloyd-doggett/democrats-outpolled-republicans-who-landed-33-seat. See also Sam Wang, "The Great Gerrymander of 2012," *New York Times*, February 2, 2013, https://www.nytimes.com/2013/02/03/opinion/sunday/the-great-gerrymander-of-2012.html.

90. Amber Phillips, "These 3 Maps Show Just How Dominant Republicans Are in America," *Washington Post*, November 12, 2016, https://www.washingtonpost.com/news/the-fix/wp/2016/11/12/these-3-maps-show-just-how-dominant-republicans-are-in-america-after-tuesday.

91. Theresa Riley, "How Michigan's Right-To-Work Law Came to Be," *Moyers*, December 11, 2012, https://billmoyers.com/2012/12/11/how-michigans-right-to-work-law-came-to-be.

92. Feigenbaum, Hertel-Fernandez, and Williamson, "Bargaining Table to the Ballot Box."

93. Matt Mayer, "How the Electoral College Favors Democrats."

94. David M. Drucker, "Data Trust Hires Ex-Boehner Aide Johnny DeStefano to Run GOP Technology Effort," *Washington Examiner*, July 29, 2013, https://www.washingtonexaminer.com/data-trust-hires-ex-boehner-aide-johnny-destefano-to-run-gop-technology-effort.

95. Barna, *Day Christians Changed America*, 157.

96. Ibid., 7.

97. Paige Lavender, "Koch Brothers Postpone Post-Election Meeting," *HuffPost*, December 12, 2012, https://www.huffpost.com/entry/koch-brothers_n_2277700.

98. Hertel-Fernandez, Skocpol, and Sclar, "Political Mega-Donors." See also Jason Sclar, Alexander Hertel-Fernandez, Theda Skocpol, and Vanessa Williamson, "Donor Consortia on the Left and Right: Comparing the Membership, Activities, and Impact of the Democracy Alliance and the Koch Seminars," *Scholar*, prepared for April 8, 2016, accessed July 18, 2019, https://scholars.org/sites/scholars/files/mpsa_donor_consortia.pdf.

99. "Generation Opportunity," *SourceWatch*, accessed July 18, 2019, https://www.sourcewatch.org/index.php?title=Generation_Opportunity. S section 3.1, "Creepy" Uncle Sam TV Ads."

100. Brendan Fischer, "Kochs' Freedom Partners Spent $129M in 2014, Invested Massively in Voter Data Lists," *PR Watch*, November 18, 2015, https://www.prwatch.org/news/2015/11/12979/freedom-partners.

101. Fang, *The Machine*, 54–55.

102. Jeff Muskus, "Gay GOP Group To Republican Homophobes: 'Who's The Pansy?,'" *HuffPost*, May 25, 2011, https://www.huffpost.com/entry/gay-gop-group-to-republic_n_469410.

103. Fang, *The Machine*, 57.

104. Kevin Robillard, "FRC's Perkins: Stop Giving to GOP," *Politico*, April 12, 2013, https://www.politico.com/story/2013/04/frc-tony-perkins-gop-gay-marriage-089989.

105. "Mike Mears," LinkedIn profile, accessed July 18, 2019, https://www.linkedin.com/in/mike-mears-48635559.

106. Tal Kopan, "FRC Chief: Cruz Leader of the GOP," *Politico*, October 11, 2013, https://www.politico.com/story/2013/10/family-research-council-tony-perkins-ted-cruz-098178.

107. Matt Bai, "Obama vs. Boehner: Who Killed the Debt Deal?," *New York Times*, March 28, 2012, https://www.nytimes.com/2012/04/01/magazine/obama-vs-boehner-who-killed-the-debt-deal.html.

108. Paul Kane, "House GOP leader Steve Scalise Fires Top Aide, Paul Teller, citing breach of trust," *Washington Post*, December 11, 2013, https://www.washingtonpost.com/politics/house-gop-leader-steve-scalise-fires-top-aide-paul-teller-citing-breach-of-trust/2013/12/11/5bee749e-62a1-11e3-a373-0f9f2d1c2b61_story.html.

109. Rob Bluey, "Conservative Leaders Voice Outrage at Firing of RSC Executive Director," *Daily Signal*, December 12, 2013, https://www.dailysignal.com/2013/12/12/conservative-leaders-voice-outrage-firing-rsc-executive-director.

110. Anna Giartelli, "Trump Hires Former Cruz Chief of Staff for White House Role," *Washington Examiner*, January 26, 2017, https://www.washingtonexaminer.com/trump-hires-former-cruz-chief-of-staff-for-white-house-role.

111. John Fea, "Ted Cruz's Campaign Is Fueled by a Dominionist Vision for America," *Washington Post*, February 4, 2016, https://www.washingtonpost.com/national/religion/ted-cruzs-campaign-is-fueled-by-a-dominionist-vision-for-america-commentary/2016/02/04/86373158-cb6a-11e5-b9ab-26591104bb19_story.html.

112. "United in Purpose," *Political Research Associates*, September 25, 2014, http://www.politicalresearch.org/tag/united-in-purpose/#sthash.RNlvO8Cy.dpbs.

113. Elizabeth Dias, "Ted Cruz Courts Conservative Pastors at Private Gathering," *Time*, May 21, 2015, http://time.com/3892493/ted-cruz-watchmen-wall.

114. Elizabeth Dias, "Watchmen on the Wall: Pastors Prepare to Take Back America," *Time*, May 30, 2014, https://time.com/138134/watchmen-on-the-wall-pastors-prepare-to-take-back-america.

115. Ibid.

116. Tim Alberta, "Inside the Secret Meeting Where Ted Cruz Trounced His Rivals," *National Journal*, June 5, 2015, https://www.nationaljournal.com/s/26227.

117. Noah Rayman, "Ted Cruz Dominates Republican Straw Poll," *Time*, October 13, 2013, http://swampland.time.com/2013/10/13/ted-cruz-dominates-republican-straw-poll.

118. Eli Yokley, "Ted Cruz Wins Values Voter Summit Straw Poll Again," *Roll Call*, September 26, 2015, https://www.rollcall.com/news/ted-cruz-wins-values-voter-summit-straw-poll.

119. Elizabeth Dias, "Tony Perkins Endorses Ted Cruz for President," *Time*, January 27, 2016, https://time.com/4195258/tony-perkins-ted-cruz-endorsement.

120. Rachel Weiner, "Who Is Ted Cruz?," *Washington Post*, August 1, 2012, https://www.washingtonpost.com/blogs/the-fix/post/who-is-ted-cruz/2012/08/01/gJQAqql8OX_blog.html.

121. "Council for National Policy Meets in Virginia," *Political Research Associates*, accessed July 18, 2019, http://www.politicalresearch.org/ifas/cnp/tysons.html.

122. Jesse Witt, "Ted Cruz Is Still Using a Blacklisted Cambridge Analytica App Developer," *Fast Company*, November 6, 2018, https://www.fastcompany.com/90262252/ted-cruz-still-using-blacklisted-cambridge-analytica-app-developer-aggregateiq.

123. Ibid.

124. Andy Kroll, "Cloak and Data: The Real Story Behind Cambridge Analytica's Rise and Fall," *Mother Jones*, May/June 2018, https://www.motherjones.com/politics/2018/03/cloak-and-data-cambridge-analytica-robert-mercer.

125. Jane Mayer, "The Reclusive Hedge-Fund Tycoon Behind the Trump Presidency," *New Yorker*, March 27, 2017, https://www.newyorker.com/magazine/2017/03/27/the-reclusive-hedge-fund-tycoon-behind-the-trump-presidency.

126. Jose A. DelReal, "Hedge Fund Magnate Donates $11 Million to Cruz Super PAC," *Washington Post*, July 31, 2015, https://www.washingtonpost.com/news/post-politics/wp/2015/07/31/hedge-fund-magnate-donates-11-million-to-cruz-super-pac/.

127. Tom Hamburger, "Cruz Campaign Credits Psychological Data and Analytics for Its Rising Success," *Washington Post*, December 13, 2015, https://www.washingtonpost.com/politics/cruz-campaign-credits-psychological-data-and-analytics-for-its-rising-success/2015/12/13/4cb0baf8-9dc5-11e5-bce4-708fe33e3288_story.html.

128. Mike Allen and Kenneth P. Vogel, "Inside the Koch Data Mine," *Politico*, December 8, 2014, https://www.politico.com/story/2014/12/koch-brothers-rnc-113359.html.

129. Ibid.

130. Thomas Peters, "We Are the Stealth Startup that Helped Ted Cruz Win Iowa," *Medium*, February 4, 2016, https://medium.com/@uCampaignCEO/meet-the-stealth-startup-that-helped-ted-cruz-win-iowa-fea6745b8a6d.

131. "Thomas Peters," *CatholicVote*, accessed July 18, 2019, https://www.catholicvote.org/author/thomas-peters.

132. Joshua Green, "The NRA Has a Secret Weapon to Fight Gun Control," *Bloomberg News*, March 1, 2018, https://www.bloomberg.com/news/articles/2018-03-01/the-nra-has-a-secret-weapon-to-fight-gun-control-a-powerful-app.

133. Hillary Mast, "Do You Stand with Thomas Peters?," *Catholic News Agency* (blog), November 14, 2013, https://www.catholicnewsagency.com/blog/do-you-stand-with-thomas-peters. See also Tim Stanley, "Thomas Peters: 'The Course of My Life has Changed Forever,'" *Catholic Herald*, December 11, 2014, https://catholicherald.co.uk/issues/december-12th-2014/thomas-peters-its-amazing-what-i-can-still-do.

134. Natasha Singer and Nicholas Confessore, "Republicans Find a Facebook Workaround: Their Own Apps," *New York Times*, October 20, 2018, https://www.nytimes.com/2018/10/20/technology/politics-apps-conservative-republican.html.

135. "The Issue of Data Targeting, Based around the Facebook, GSR and Cambridge Analytica Allegations," *UK Parliament*, accessed July 18, 2019,

https://publications.parliament.uk/pa/cm201719/cmselect/cmcumeds/363/36306.htm.

136. "Vlad Seryakov's Email," *Rocket Reach*, accessed July 18, 2019, https://rocketreach.co/vlad-seryakov-email_4819040.

137. Chris Vickery, Twitter post, December 2, 2018, https://twitter.com/VickerySec/status/1069473792106221568. White-hat hacker Chris Vickery also tweeted that some of the code for the Cruz Crew app was written by a Russian named Yaroslav Leontenko, giving him live access to the RNC Data Trust database. See also Chris Vickery, *Twitter* post, December 10, 2018, https://twitter.com/vickerysec/status/1072181769716215808.

138. Witt, "Ted Cruz is still using a blacklisted Cambridge Analytica app developer."

139. Peters, "We Are the Stealth Startup."

140. Ibid.

141. "Ted Cruz's Official "Cruz Crew" Campaign App Tops 2016 Field," *Press 2016*, October 14, 2015, http://www.p2016.org/cruz/cruz101415prapp.html.

142. Peters, "We Are the Stealth Startup."

143. Ibid.

144. Ibid.

145. Matea Gold, "Koch Network Strikes New Deal to Share Voter Data with RNC-Aligned Firm," *Washington Post*, July 29, 2015, https://www.washingtonpost.com/news/post-politics/wp/2015/07/29/koch-network-strikes-new-deal-to-share-voter-data-with-rnc-aligned-firm.

146. American Bridge 21st Century, "With Nowhere to Go on Voter Data, RNC Folds, Returning to the Kochs' Warm Embrace," *Press 2016*, July 29, 2015, http://www.p2016.org/parties/datatrust0715.html.

147. "Get Involved as We Gear Up for 2017 Elections," *NRA Political Victory Fund*, accessed July 18, 2019, https://www.nrapvf.org/take-action.

148. Tyler Fisher, Sarah Frostenson, and Lily Mihalik, "The Gun Lobby: See How Much Your Representative Gets," *Politico*, February 21, 2018, https://www.politico.com/interactives/2017/gun-lobbying-spending-in-america-congress.

149. Mike Weiss, "How Many Members Does The NRA Really Have?," *HuffPost*, July 11, 2017, https://www.huffpost.com/entry/how-many-members-does-the-nra-really-have_b_59651114e4b005b0fdc8fe90.

150. Daniel Terrill, "NRA Releases Financial Statement Showing Revenue, Expenses for 2016," *Guns*, May 5, 2017, https://www.guns.com/news/2017/05/05/nra-revenue-expenses-in-2016.

151. Peter Stone, "Inside the NRA's Koch-Funded Dark-Money Campaign," *Mother Jones*, April 2, 2013, https://www.motherjones.com/politics/2013/04/nra-koch-brothers-karl-rove.

152. "990 Form," Freedom Partners *Chamber of Commerce* via *Huffington Post*, accessed July 18, 2019, http://big.assets.huffingtonpost.com/FreedomPartners2014990Form.pdf.

153. "Our Mission," *Trigger the Vote,* accessed July 18, 2019, https://triggerthevote.org.

154. Steve Friess, "How The NRA Built a Massive Secret Database of Gun Owners," *Buzzfeed News*, August 20, 2013, https://www.buzzfeednews.com/article/stevefriess/how-the-nra-built-a-massive-secret-database-of-gun-owners.

155. Mayer, "The Reclusive Hedge-Fund Tycoon Behind the Trump Presidency."

156. Peter Stone, "NRA to Spend $15m on Ads to Defeat Hillary Clinton in Key States," *Guardian*, September 16, 2016, https://www.theguardian.com/us-news/2016/sep/16/nra-hillary-clinton-donald-trump-gun-control.

157. Ibid.

158. "National Rifle Association Disbursements," *Federal Election Commission*, accessed July 18, 2019, https://www.fec.gov/data/disbursements/?two_year_transaction_period=2016&data_type=processed&committee_id=C00053553&recipient_name=i360&min_date=01%2F01%2F2015&max_date=12%2F31%2F2016.

159. Ibid.

160. Ibid.

161. Andrew Dolkart and Matthew A. Postal, *Guide to New York City Landmarks* (New York: Wiley, 2009), 85. In 2007 Trinity sounded a note of

historical irony by acquiring New York studios operating out of the old Century Association building on East Fifteenth Street, which had served as William Conant Church's clubhouse when he co-founded the National Rifle Association.

162. Peters, "We Are the Stealth Startup."

163. Ibid.

164. "Elections 2016: Iowa," *CNN*, accessed July 18, 2019, https://edition.cnn.com/election/2016/primaries/states/ia.

165. "New Mobile App: Keep Tabs on Washington on the Go," *Family Research Council*, accessed July 18, 2019, https://www.frc.org/alert/new-mobile-app-keep-tabs-on-washington-on-the-go.

166. Chris Cillizza, "Winners and Losers from the Iowa Caucuses," *Washington Post*, February 2, 2016, https://www.washingtonpost.com/news/the-fix/wp/2016/02/02/winners-and-losers-from-the-iowa-caucuses.

167. Kenneth P. Vogel and Cate Martel, "The Kochs Freeze Out Trump," *Politico*, July 29, 2015, https://www.politico.com/story/2015/07/kochs-freeze-out-trump-120752.

168. "Vendor/Recipient: i360," *OpenSecrets*, accessed July 18, 2019, https://www.opensecrets.org/expends/vendor.php?year=2016&vendor=i360.

169. "2015 Values Voter Summit, Donald Trump," *C-SPAN* video, 27:54, September 25, 2015, https://www.c-span.org/video/?328352-13/2015-values-voter-summit-donald-trump. Bible at 5:09, "nice person" at 18:45. Text included on site.

170. Leada Gore, "Southern Baptist Leader: Donald Trump Is not Our Friend," *AL*, September 27, 2015, https://www.al.com/news/2015/09/southern_baptist_leader_donald.html.

171. CP Editors, "Donald Trump Is a Scam. Evangelical Voters Should Back Away (CP Editorial)," *Christian Post*, February 29, 2016, https://www.christianpost.com/news/donald-trump-scam-evangelical-voters-back-away-cp-editorial-158813.

172. "Ted Cruz: Donald Trump is a 'Pathological liar,'" YouTube video, 4:28, CNN, May 3, 2016, https://www.youtube.com/watch?v=Bz44wKKQJho.

173. Issie Laowsky, "Trump's Big Win is a Giant Setback for Data Crunchers," *Wired*, May 4, 2016, https://www.wired.com/2016/05/one-step-trump-one-giant-setback-data-crunchers.

CHAPTER 11: THE ART OF THE DEAL

1. See chapter 10.

2. "Pro-Life Women Sound the Alarm: Donald Trump is Unacceptable," *Susan B. Anthony List*, January 16, 2016, https://www.sba-list.org/home/pro-life-women-sound-the-alarmdonald-trump-is-unacceptable.

3. Matt Wilstein, "Donald Trump 'Fine' With Same-Sex Marriage," *Daily Beast*, last updated April 13, 2017, https://www.thedailybeast.com/donald-trump-fine-with-same-sex-marriage. See also Philip Bump, "Donald Trump Took 5 Different Positions on Abortion in 3 Days," *Washington Post*, April 3, 2016, https://www.washingtonpost.com/news/the-fix/wp/2016/04/03/donald-trumps-ever-shifting-positions-on-abortion.

4. Daniel Burke, "The Guilt-Free Gospel of Donald Trump," *CNN*, October 24, 2016, https://www.cnn.com/2016/10/21/politics/trump-religion-gospel/index.html.

5. I was there. See also Adele M. Stan, "White Nationalism and Christian Right Unite at Values Voter Summit," *Moyers*, October 17, 2017, https://billmoyers.com/story/white-nationalism-values-voter-summit.

6. Author was present at Values Voter Summit, Washington, September 2018.

7. Stephen Collins, "Republicans Seize Senate, Gaining Full Control of Congress," *CNN*, November 5, 2014, https://www.cnn.com/2014/11/04/politics/election-day-story/index.html.

8. Tim Reid, "Democrats Face 'Almost Impossible Map' to Retake U.S. Senate," *Reuters*, August 24, 2018, https://www.reuters.com/article/us-usa-election-democrats-explainer/democrats-face-almost-impossible-map-to-retake-u-s-senate-idUSKCN1L920M. See also Manas Sharma et al., "Here's What the 2020 Senate Map Looks Like," *Washington Post*, November 21, 2018, https://www.washingtonpost.com/graphics/2018/politics/2020-senate.

9. Scott Clement, "Another Bad Night for Political Polls? Not Really, Despite Criticism on Cable TV," *Washington Post*, November 7, 2018, https://www

.washingtonpost.com/politics/another-bad-night-for-political-polls-not-really-despite-criticism-on-cable-tv/2018/11/07/20eea090-e252-11e8-b759-3d88a5ce9e19_story.html.

10. Sarah Eekhoff Zylstra, "The Season of Adventists: Can Ben Carson's Church Stay Separatist amid Booming Growth?," *Christianity Today*, January 22, 2015, https://www.christianitytoday.com/ct/2015/januaryfebruary/season-of-adventists-can-ben-carson-church-stay-separatist.html. See also Adele M. Banks, "5 Faith Facts about Mike Huckabee, Southern Baptist Pastor-Turned-Politician," *Washington Post*, May 5, 2015, https://www.washingtonpost.com/national/religion/5-faith-facts-about-mike-huckabee-southern-baptist-pastor-turned-politician/2015/05/05/fe2fb192-f34a-11e4-bca5-21b51bbdf93e_story.html. See also Sarah Pulliam Bailey, "Here's What We Know about the Faith of Sen. Cruz, Who's Set to Announce his 2016 bid at Liberty University," *Washington Post*, March 22, 2015, https://www.washingtonpost.com/news/acts-of-faith/wp/2015/03/22/heres-what-we-know-about-the-faith-of-sen-ted-cruz-whos-set-to-announce-his-2016-bid-at-liberty-university. See also Michael Kruse, "Marco Rubio's Crisis of Faith," *Politico Magazine*, January 22, 2016, https://www.politico.com/magazine/story/2016/01/marco-rubios-crisis-of-faith-213553.

11. Gabriel Sherman, "Inside Operation Trump, the Most Unorthodox Campaign in Political History," *Intelligencer*, April 3, 2016, http://nymag.com/intelligencer/2016/04/inside-the-donald-trump-presidential-campaign.html.

12. Martha Gajanan, "Hillary Clinton Leads Donald Trump by 14 Points Nationally in New Poll," *Time*, October 26, 2016, http://time.com/4546942/hillary-clinton-donald-trump-lead-poll.

13. Elizabeth Dias, "Exclusive: Evangelical Leaders Plan Meeting to Test Donald Trump's Values," *Time*, May 20, 2016, http://time.com/4343321/donald-trump-evangelical-social-conservative-meeting.

14. Jessica Taylor, "Citing 'Two Corinthians,' Trump Struggles to Make the Sale to Evangelicals," *National Public Radio*, January 18, 2016, https://www.npr.org/2016/01/18/463528847/citing-two-corinthians-trump-struggles-to-make-the-sale-to-evangelicals.

15. Ibid.

16. Eric Bradner, "Trump Blames Tony Perkins for '2 Corinthians,'" *CNN*, January 21, 2016, https://www.cnn.com/2016/01/20/politics/donald-trump-tony-perkins-sarah-palin.

17. Eugene Scott, "In Addition to a Rare Church Visit, Trump Spent Most of His Sunday Blasting Critics on Twitter," *Washington Post*, March 18, 2019, https://www.washingtonpost.com/politics/2019/03/18/addition-rare-church-visit-trump-spent-most-his-sunday-blasting-critics-twitter. See also Neelesh Moorthy, "What Do We Know about Hillary Clinton's Religion? A Lot, Actually," *PolitiFact*, June 24, 2016, https://www.politifact.com/truth-o-meter/statements/2016/jun/24/donald-trump/what-do-we-know-about-hillary-clintons-religion-lo.

18. Nolan D. McCaskill, "Trump's Favorite Bible Verse: 'Eye for an Eye,'" *Politico*, April 14, 2016, https://www.politico.com/blogs/2016-gop-primary-live-updates-and-results/2016/04/trump-favorite-bible-verse-221954.

19. Jason Russell, "Michigan Mega-Donor: Trump Doesn't Represent GOP," *Washington Examiner*, March 7, 2016, https://www.washingtonexaminer.com/michigan-mega-donor-trump-doesnt-represent-gop.

20. Melissa Chan, "Charles Koch Says It's 'Possible' Hillary Clinton Is Better Choice Than Republicans," *Time*, April 24, 2016, https://time.com/4305927/charles-koch-hillary-clinton-republicans.

21. Theodore Schleifer, "Clinton burying Trump: $42 million to $1.3 million," *CNN*, June 21, 2016, https://www.cnn.com/2016/06/20/politics/republicans-cash-crunch-donald-trump/index.html.

22. Matea Gold and Anu Narayanswamy, "Trump Entered June with Just $1.3 million in the Bank, while Clinton Sat on $42 Million War Chest," *Washington Post*, June 20, 2016, https://www.washingtonpost.com/news/post-politics/wp/2016/06/20/trump-entered-june-with-just-1-3-million-in-the-bank-while-clinton-sat-on-42-million-war-chest.

23. Matea Gold, "Here's Why the RNC Needs Donald Trump to Step Up His Fundraising Game," *Washington Post*, June 20, 2016, https://www.washingtonpost.com/news/post-politics/wp/2016/06/20/heres-why-the-rnc-needs-donald-trump-to-step-up-his-fundraising-game.

24. Barna, *Day Christians Changed America*, 73.

25. Ibid., 76. See also Elizabeth Dias, "How Evangelicals Helped Donald Trump Win," *Time*, November 9, 2016, http://time.com/4565010/donald-trump-evangelicals-win.

26. Dias, "Exclusive: Evangelical Leaders Plan Meeting."

27. "Donald Trump Remarks at Faith and Freedom Coalition Conference," *C-SPAN* video, 29:30, June 10, 2016, https://www.c-span.org/video/?410912-4/donald-trump-addresses-faith-freedom-coalition-conference. See 00:24–01:10.

28. "Richard Lee," *There's Hope America*, accessed July 18, 2019, https://www.thereshope.org/about-dr-lee. See also Ken Stone, "Jim Garlow Quitting Skyline Megachurch, Moving to Washington Ministry," *Times of San Diego*, September 12, 2018, https://timesofsandiego.com/life/2018/09/12/jim-garlow-quitting-skyline-megachurch-moving-to-washington-ministry. See also "Fr. Frank A. Pavone," *Priests for Life*, accessed July 18, 2019, https://www.priestsforlife.org/frpavonebio.aspx.

29. Barna, *Day Christians Changed America*, 78.

30. Ibid., 87. See also Kelsey Snell, "Clinton: We are going to win back the House and the Senate," *Washington Post*, June 22, 2016, https://www.washingtonpost.com/news/powerpost/wp/2016/06/22/hillary-clinton-to-meet-wednesday-with-house-democrats.

31. "Join the Movement," *MyFaithVotes*, accessed July 18, 2019, https://www.myfaithvotes.org. See also "United in Purpose & My Faith Votes Organize A Conversation with Donald Trump and Ben Carson," *PR Newswire*, May 25, 2016, https://www.prnewswire.com/news-releases/united-in-purpose—my-faith-votes-organize-a-conversation-with-donald-trump-and-ben-carson-300274757.html.

32. "My Faith Votes: Mission," *GuideStar*, accessed July 18, 2019, https://www.guidestar.org/profile/48-6393123. See also "990 Form," *Vision Charitable Trust* via *GuideStar*, accessed July 18, 2019, https://pdf.guidestar.org/PDF_Images/2016/486/393/2016-486393123-0e552255-9.pdf.

33. Todd Starnes, "Conservatives Call on Trump to Protect Religious Liberty," *Todd Starnes*, March 1, 2017, https://www.toddstarnes.com/uncategorized/conservatives-call-on-trump-to-protect-religious-liberty.

34. Todd Starnes, "Mega-Christian Leaders Having Private Meeting With Donald Trump," *American Dispatch*, May 23, 2016, https://www.charismanews.com/opinion/american-dispatch/57341-mega-christian-leaders-having-private-merting-with-donald-trump. See also Kindly and Viebeck, "How a Conservative Group Dealt with a Fondling Charge."

35. Barna, *Day Christians Changed America*, 79.

36. Tony Perkins and Huckabee are Southern Baptist pastors. Ben Carson is a Seventh Day Adventist, and James Dobson is Nazarene.

37. Barna, *Day Christians Changed America*, 79. For the Marriott ballroom, see "New York Marquis Meetings," *Mariott Marquis New York*, accessed July 18, 2019, http://www.meetings.nymarriottmarquis.com/new-york-city-meetings-group-events-hotel-nycmq/Photo-Galleries-43.html.

38. Barna, *Day Christians Changed America*, 81.

39. "Samaritan's Purse," *Charity Navigator*, accessed July 18, 2019, https://www.charitynavigator.org/index.cfm?bay=search.summary&orgid=4423.

40. Barna, *Day Christians Changed America*, 83.

41. Maggie Haberman, Alexander Burns, and Ashley Parker, "Donald Trump Fires Corey Lewandowski, His Campaign Manager," *New York Times*, June 20, 2016, https://www.nytimes.com/2016/06/21/us/politics/corey-lewandowski-donald-trump.html.

42. Sarah McCammon, "Inside Trump's Closed-Door Meeting, Held To Reassure 'the Evangelicals,'" *National Public Radio*, June 21, 2016, https://www.npr.org/2016/06/21/483018976/inside-trumps-closed-door-meeting-held-to-reassures-the-evangelicals.

43. Shane Goldmacher, Eliana Johnson, and Josh Gerstein, "How Trump Got to Yes on Gorsuch," *Politico*, January 31, 2017, https://www.politico.com/story/2017/01/trump-supreme-court-gorsuch-234474.

44. Bob Woodward, Robert Costa, "In a Revealing Interview, Trump Predicts a 'Massive Recession' but Intends to Eliminate the National Debt in 8 Years," *Washington Post*, April 2, 2016, https://www.washingtonpost.com/politics/in-turmoil-or-triumph-donald-trump-stands-alone/2016/04/02/8c0619b6-f8d6-11e5-a3ce-f06b5ba21f33_story.html.

45. Billye Brim, "A Conversation with Donald Trump," *Eagle Mountain International Church* (blog), June 23, 2016, https://www.emic.org/blog/conversation-donald-trump.

46. Tim Alberta, "Trump Struggles to Close the Deal with Evangelicals," *National Review*, June 22, 2016, https://www.nationalreview.com/2016/06/donald-trump-evangelical-leaders-new-york-meeting-recap.

47. Jon Ward, "Transcript: Donald Trump's closed-door meeting with evangelical leaders," *Yahoo News*, June 22, 2016, https://www.yahoo.com/news/transcript-donald-trumps-closed-door-meeting-with-evangelical-leaders-195810824.html.

48. Barna, *Day Christians changed America*, 89–90.

49. Alberta, "Trump Struggles to Close the Deal with Evangelicals."

50. Tom Gjelten, "As Trump Defies Expectations of Faith, Might We Be Entering a New Era?," *National Public Radio*, June 26, 2016, https://www.npr.org/2016/06/26/483506379/as-trump-defies-expectations-of-faith-might-we-be-entering-a-new-era.

51. Jill Colvin, Katherine Creag, and Adam Warner, "Protests in Times Square as Donald Trump Meets With Hundreds of Christian Leaders," *NBC New York*, last updated June 22, 2016, https://www.nbcnewyork.com/news/local/NYC-Trump-Carson-Meet-Christian-Leaders-Midtown-Hotel-Protests-Vigils-383745171.html.

52. Jonathan Merritt, "How Todd Starnes Is Compromising Fox News's Credibility," *Atlantic*, September 14, 2015, https://www.theatlantic.com/politics/archive/2015/09/how-todd-starnes-is-compromising-fox-news-credibility/405118.

53. Todd Starnes, Twitter post, June 21, 2016, https://twitter.com/toddstarnes/status/745296092246347776.

54. "Heard around the Hill," *CNP Action*, Inc., July 2016, https://myemail.constantcontact.com/Heard-Around-the-Hill.html?soid=1103333458754&aid=Sa7-DDBPzcU.

55. Nick Gass, "Trump's Evangelical Advisory Board Features Bachmann, Falwell," *Politico*, June 21, 2016, https://www.politico.com/story/2016/06/trump-evangelical-advisory-board-224612.

56. "President Obama's Advisory Council on Faith-Based and Neighborhood Partnerships," *Pew Research Center*, last updated September 9, 2009, https://www.pewforum.org/2009/08/18/president-obamas-advisory-council-on-faith-based-and-neighborhood-partnerships.

57. Gass, "Trump's Evangelical Advisory Board."

58. Ruth Graham, "Church of The Donald," *Politico*, May/June 2018, https://www.politico.com/magazine/story/2018/04/22/trump-christian-evangelical-conservatives-television-tbn-cbn-218008. See also "Protesters Rally Outside Times Square Hotel as Trump Seeks Support from Evangelical Leaders," *CBS New York*, June 21, 2016, https://newyork.cbslocal.com/2016/06/21/protest-trump-evangelicals.

59. "Mike Salisbury Joins Industry Leading Literary Agency Yates & Yates," *FrontGate*, April 21, 2014, https://www.frontgatemedia.com/mike-salisbury-joins-industry-leading-literary-agency-yates-yates.

60. "My Faith Votes Chairman Sealy Yates Releases Statement after Praying for President Trump in the Oval Office," *MyFaithVotes*, July 13, 2017, https://www.myfaithvotes.org/statements/my-faith-votes-chairman-sealy-yates-releases-statement-after-praying-for-president-trump-in-the-oval-office.

61. Barna, *Day Christians Changed America*, 103–4.

62. Jacqueline Alemany, "Donald Trump Offered Chris Christie vice President Role before Mike Pence, sources say," *CBS News*, October 30, 2016, https://www.cbsnews.com/news/donald-trump-offered-chris-christie-vice-president-role-before-mike-pence. See also Alexander Burns and Maggie Haberman, "Chris Christie Becomes Powerful Figure in Trump Campaign," *New York Times*, June 30, 2016, https://www.nytimes.com/2016/07/01/us/politics/chris-christie-donald-trump.html.

63. Kimberly Winston, "5 Faith Facts about Chris Christie: Cradle Catholic and Member of the Church of Bruce," *Washington Post*, June 30, 2015, https://www.washingtonpost.com/national/religion/5-faith-facts-about-chris-christie-cradle-catholic-and-member-of-the-church-of-bruce/2015/06/30/c244e872-1f42-11e5-a135-935065bc30d0_story.html.

64. Barna, *Day Christians Changed America*, 104–5.

65. Ibid.

66. Liam Stack, "Trump Victory Alarms Gay and Transgender Groups," *New York Times*, November 10, 2016, https://www.nytimes.com/2016/11/11/us/politics/trump-victory-alarms-gay-and-transgender-groups.html. See also Maggie Haberman, "Donald Trump's More Accepting Views on Gay Issues Set Him Apart in G.O.P.," *New York Times*, April 22, 2016, https://www.nytimes.com/2016/04/23/us/politics/donald-trump-gay-rights.html.

67. Katie Shepherd and Alan Rappeport, "How Mike Pence and Donald Trump Compare on the Issues," *New York Times*, July 15, 2016, https://www.nytimes.com/2016/07/16/us/politics/mike-pence-issues.html.

68. Alemany, "Donald Trump offered Chris Christie Vice President Role."

69. Ibid.

70. Barna, *Day Christians Changed America*, 121–22.

71. "Mike Mears," LinkedIn profile.

72. Barna, *Day Christians Changed America*, 107.

73. Matthew Yglesias, "Draft Republican Platform Calls for Auditing the Fed, Bathroom Bills, and Action on EMPs," *Vox*, July 11, 2016, https://www.vox.com/2016/7/11/12148806/draft-republican-platform-gop.

74. Zeke J. Miller, "GOP Platform Contemplates Anti-Porn Provision, Embrace of 'Conversion Therapy,'" *Time*, July 11, 2016, https://time.com/4401600/gop-platform-contemplates-anti-porn-provision-embrace-of-conversion-therapy.

75. "Republican Platform 2016," *Republican Party*, accessed July 18, 2019, http://files.ctctcdn.com/2438cc3e001/5de6ec65-ba1f-4142-8d67-81e977047304.pdf.

76. Jeremy W. Peters, "Emerging Republican Platform Goes Far to the Right," *New York Times*, July 12, 2016, https://www.nytimes.com/2016/07/13/us/politics/republican-convention-issues.html.

77. Theodore Schleifer and Stephen Collinson, "Defiant Ted Cruz Stands by Refusal to Endorse Trump after Being booed During Convention Speech," *CNN*, July 22, 2016, https://www.cnn.com/2016/07/20/politics/ted-cruz-republican-convention-moment/index.html.

78. "Full Speech: Tony Perkins – Republican National Convention," YouTube video, 3:19, ABC15 Arizona, July 21, 2016, https://www.youtube.com/watch?v=SN74taRE5hc.

79. Barna, *Day Christians Changed America*, 80.

80. Ibid., 85.

81. Theodore Schleifer, "Bernie Sanders: Hillary Clinton Is not 'Qualified' to Be President," *CNN*, April 7, 2016, https://www.cnn.com/2016/04/06/politics/bernie-sanders-hillary-clinton-qualified/index.html.

82. Hannah Fingerhut, "About Seven-in-Ten Americans Oppose Overturning Roe v. Wade," *Pew Research Center*, January 3, 2017, https://www.pewresearch.org/fact-tank/2017/01/03/about-seven-in-ten-americans-oppose-overturning-roe-v-wade.

83. Justin McCarthy, "Americans' Support for Gay Marriage Remains High, at 61%," *Gallup*, May 19, 2016, https://news.gallup.com/poll/191645/americans-support-gay-marriage-remains-high.aspx. See also Jennifer Agiesta and Tom LoBianco, "Poll: Gun control support spikes after shooting," *CNN*, June 20, 2016, https://www.cnn.com/2016/06/20/politics/cnn-gun-poll/index.html.

84. Barna, *Day Christians Changed America*, 183.

85. Ibid., 128, 135.

CHAPTER 12: "THE MIRACLE"

1. Christopher Ingraham, "Somebody Just Put a Price Tag on the 2016 Election. It's a Doozy," *Washington Post*, April 14, 2017, https://www.washingtonpost.com/news/wonk/wp/2017/04/14/somebody-just-put-a-price-tag-on-the-2016-election-its-a-doozy.

2. Hamburger, "Cruz Campaign Credits Psychological Data and Analytics."

3. Ibid.

4. Daniel White, "Database Leak Exposes 191 Million Voters on Internet," *Time*, December 28, 2015, http://time.com/4162696/database-leak-exposes-191-million-voters. See also G.W. Schulz, "Are Christian Conservatives behind Breach of 18 Million Voter Records?," *Reveal News*, March 2, 2016, https://www

.revealnews.org/article/are-christian-conservatives-behind-breach-of-18-million-voter-records.

5. Ibid.

6. Barna, *Day Christians Changed America*, 152–53.

7. Ibid., 147.

8. Ibid., 150.

9. Ibid., 157.

10. Ibid., 119–20.

11. "Todd Starnes, Tony Perkins," *American Family Radio*, accessed August 22, 2016, https://afr.net/podcasts/washington-watch/2016/august/todd-starnes-tony-perkins; at 00:18.

12. "About," *Dana Loesch Radio*, accessed July 18, 2019, http://www.danaloeschradio.com/page/about.

13. "E. W. Jackson's New Video Urges Black Voters to Abandon Democrat Party, Vote for Trump," *Urban Family video*, 4:03, October 25, 2016, https://urbanfamilytalk.com/articles/politics/2016/october/25/ew-jacksons-new-video-urges-black-voters-to-abandon-democrat-party-vote-for-trump. See 2:05.

14. Bob Eschliman, "Tony Perkins: FRC to Encourage Evangelical Voters in 20 States," *Charisma Caucus*, September 12, 2016, https://www.charismanews.com/politics/press-releases/59834-tony-perkins-frc-to-encourage-evangelical-voters-in-20-states.

15. Washington Watch, "Roger Severino, Tony Perkins, Gary McCaleb, Joe Digenova," *American Family Radio* podcast, 54:03, November 2, 2016, https://afr.net/podcasts/washington-watch/2016/november/roger-severino-tony-perkins-gary-mccaleb-joe-digenova/?p=25.

16. Barna, *Day Christians Changed America*, 160.

17. Ibid., 157.

18. "NPR Ratings at All-Time High," *National Public Radio*, March 15, 2017, https://www.npr.org/about-npr/520273005/npr-ratings-at-all-time-high.

19. Barna, *Day Christians Changed America*, 158.

20. "CWA Values Bus Tour," Concerned Women for America," *Concerned Women for America,* accessed July 18, 2019, https://concernedwomen.org/cwa-values-bus-tour. See also "FRC Action's Values Bus Tour comes to OKWU," *Bartlesville Examiner-Enterprise*, last updated September 20, 2016, https://www.examiner-enterprise.com/news/20160920/frc-action8217s-values-bus-tour-comes-to-okwu.

21. Barna, *Day Christians Changed America*, 161.

22. Ibid.

23. Eric Levitz, "Donald Trump's Great White Hope Is Fading Fast," *Intelligencer*, August 23, 2016, http://nymag.com/intelligencer/2016/08/donald-trumps-great-white-hope-is-fading-fast.html.

24. "Trump endorses 'Protect Life and Marriage Marriage Oklahoma' Drive," *Capitol Beat OK*, January 13, 2016, https://capitolbeatok.worldsecuresystems.com/reports/trump-endorses-protect-life-and-marriage-marriage-oklahoma-drive.

25. Fairview Baptist Church service, February 11, 2018. See also Emma Green, "The New Abortion Bills Are a Dare," *Atlantic*, May 15, 2019, https://www.theatlantic.com/politics/archive/2019/05/alabama-georgia-abortion-bills/589504. In 2019 other fundamentalists raised the estimate to fifty million babies.

26. "Abortion Procedures," *LiveAction*, accessed July 18, 2019, https://www.liveaction.org.

27. "Susan B. Anthony List TV Ad: Micah," YouTube video, 1:00, Susan B. Anthony List, August 2, 2016, https://www.youtube.com/watch?v=fw7bMhkguGM.

28. Ibid., 00:47.

29. "Induced Abortions in the United States," *Guttmacher Institute*, January 2018, https://www.guttmacher.org/fact-sheet/induced-abortion-united-states. See also Ariana Eunjung Chen, "What Are Late-Term Abortions and Who Gets Them?," *Washington Post*, February 6, 2019, https://www.washingtonpost.com/us-policy/2019/02/06/tough-questions-answers-late-term-abortions-law-women-who-get-them.

30. Linda Qiu, "Marco Rubio says Hillary Clinton Supports Abortions 'Even on the Due Date,'" *PolitiFact*, February 10, 2016, https://www.politifact.com/truth

-o-meter/statements/2016/feb/10/marco-rubio/marco-rubio-says-hillary-clinton-supports-abortion.

31. "One on One with Ted Cruz," YouTube video, 59:23, *Texas Tribune*, September 25, 2016, https://www.youtube.com/watch?v=LLCxVfKkFNg. See 52:00.

32. Qiu, "Marco Rubio says Hillary Clinton Supports Abortions 'Even on the Due Date.'"

33. Olga Khazan, "Why Christians Overwhelmingly Backed Trump," *Atlantic*, November 9, 2016, https://www.theatlantic.com/health/archive/2016/11/why-women-and-christians-backed-trump/507176.

34. Christopher Heine, "Trump's Campaign Just Quietly Launched a Mobile App Called 'America First,'" *AdWeek*, August 18, 2016, https://www.adweek.com/digital/trumps-campaign-just-quietly-launched-mobile-app-called-america-first-173044. See also "Download the Official NRA-ILA App!," *National Rifle Association Institute for Legislative Action*, July 8, 2016, https://www.nraila.org/articles/20160708/download-the-official-nra-ila-app.

35. Thomas Peters, "Brexit? There Was an App for That," *Medium*, June 24, 2016, https://medium.com/@uCampaignCEO/brexit-there-was-an-app-for-that-57d1d658b4f1.

36. Daniel Dunford and Ashley Kirk, "How Right or Wrong Were the Polls about the EU Referendum?," *Telegraph*, June 27, 2016, https://www.telegraph.co.uk/news/2016/06/24/eu-referendum-how-right-or-wrong-were-the-polls. See also Sascha O. Becker, Thiemo Fetzer, Dennis Novy, "Who voted for Brexit? A Comprehensive District-Level Analysis," *Economic Policy* 32, no. 92 (October 2017), https://academic-oup-com.ezp-prod1.hul.harvard.edu/economicpolicy/article/32/92/601/4459491. See also Atif Shafique, "Brexit Was Driven by Places 'Left Behind,'" *RSA*, August 30, 2016, https://www.thersa.org/discover/publications-and-articles/rsa-blogs/2016/08/brexit-was-driven-by-places-left-behind.

37. Thomas Peters, "Trump and Brexit used a new digital organizing tool to help achieve their surprise victories," *Medium*, December 20, 2016, https://medium.com/@uCampaignCEO/how-trump-and-brexit-used-a-new-digital-organizing-tool-to-win-their-surprise-victories-ceca7c720b3.

38. Becker, Fetzer, and Novy, "Who Voted for Brexit?," 601–50.

39. "Vote Leave Fined and Referred to the Police for Breaking Electoral Law," *Electoral Commission*, July 17, 2018, https://www.electoralcommission.org.uk/i-am-a/journalist/electoral-commission-media-centre/party-and-election-finance-to-keep/vote-leave-fined-and-referred-to-the-police-for-breaking-electoral-law. See also "Media Statement: Vote Leave," *Electoral Commission*, March 29, 2019, https://www.electoralcommission.org.uk/i-am-a/journalist/electoral-commission-media-centre/referendums-to-keep/media-statement-vote-leave. See also Natasha Lomas, "It's Official: Brexit Campaign Broke the Law—with Social Media's Help," *Tech Crunch*, July 17, 2018, https://techcrunch.com/2018/07/17/its-official-brexit-campaign-broke-the-law-with-social-medias-help.

40. Stephen Castle, "Having Won, Some 'Brexit' Campaigners Begin Backpedaling," *New York Times*, June 26, 2016, https://www.nytimes.com/2016/06/27/world/europe/having-won-some-brexit-campaigners-begin-backpedaling.html.

41. Lomas, "It's official: Brexit Campaign Broke the Law."

42. "Robust Mobile Apps Changing Political and Advocacy Campaigns with Thomas Peters uCampaign," *Karen Jagoda* interview, 16:56, November 12, 2017, http://digitalpoliticsradio.com/robust-mobile-apps-changing-political-and-advocacy-campaigns-with-thomas-peters-ucampaign.

43. Ibid., at 6:50 and 8:40.

44. Issie Lapowsky, "Clinton's App Is Trouncing Trump's in Pretty Much Every Way," *Wired*, September 21, 2016, https://www.wired.com/2016/09/clintons-app-trouncing-trumps-pretty-much-every-way.

45. "Robust Mobile Apps Changing Political and Advocacy Campaigns," *Karen Jagoda* interview.

46. Nicole Karlis, "How the NRA Uses an App to Organize Opposition to Gun Control," *Salon*, February 25, 2018, https://www.salon.com/2018/02/25/how-the-nra-uses-an-app-to-organize-opposition-to-gun-control.

47. "2018 TED-Style Talks," YouTube video, 1:22:37, TheAAPC1969, April 27, 2018, https://www.youtube.com/watch?v=oEoaitWArGU&feature=youtu.be+&t=29m5s.

48. Peters, "Trump and Brexit Used a New Digital Organizing Tool to Help Achieve Their Surprise Victories."

49. Allen and Vogel, "Inside the Koch Data Mine."

50. Ibid.

51. John Frank, "The Koch Brothers Plot a Conservative Resistance Movement in Colorado Springs Strategy Session," *Denver Post*," June 25, 2017, https://www.denverpost.com/2017/06/25/koch-brothers-colorado-springs-conservative-resistance-movement-2018-election.

52. Kyle Cheney and Matthew Nussbaum, "Donald Trump's Man on the Hill," *Politico*, January 18, 2017, https://www.politico.com/story/2017/01/who-is-marc-short-trump-legislative-liaison-233710.

53. "Freedom Partners Shared Services Recruiting—Guest Speaker at the Leadership Institute," *Leadership Institute*, accessed July 18, 2019, https://www.leadershipinstitute.org/training/contact.cfm?FacultyID=718481.

54. Allen and Vogel, "Inside the Koch Data Mine."

55. Matea Gold, "Koch Network Seeks to Defuse Donor Frustration over Trump Rebuff," *Washington Post*, August 1, 2016, https://www.washingtonpost.com/politics/koch-network-seeks-to-defuse-donor-frustration-over-trump-rebuff/2016/08/01/7247b8c2-579a-11e6-831d-0324760ca856_story.html.

56. Barna, *Day Christians Changed America*, 63.

57. Ibid., 128.

58. Ibid., 182.

59. Jonathan Allen and Amie Parnes, *Shattered: Inside Hillary Clinton's Doomed Campaign* (New York: Crown, 2017), 25.

60. Alexander Hertel-Fernandez, Caroline Tervo, and Theda Skocpol, "How the Koch Brothers Built the Most Powerful Rightwing Group You've Never Heard of," September 26, 2018, *Guardian*, https://www.theguardian.com/us-news/2018/sep/26/koch-brothers-americans-for-prosperity-rightwing-political-group.

61. Allen and Parnes, *Shattered*, 368.

62. "About Us," *Libre Initiative*, accessed July 18, 2019, http://thelibreinitiative.com/about-us.

63. Allen and Parnes, *Shattered*, 229.

64. Harry Enten, "Registered Voters Who Stayed Home Probably Cost Clinton the Election," *FiveThirtyEight*, January 5, 2018, https://fivethirtyeight.com/features/registered-voters-who-stayed-home-probably-cost-clinton-the-election.

65. Khazan, "Why Christians Overwhelmingly Backed Trump."

66. Tony Perkins, Twitter post, November 8, 2016, https://twitter.com/tperkins/status/796225023304486912.

67. File, "Voting in America: A Look at the 2016 Presidential Election."

68. Sarah Pulliam Bailey, "White Evangelicals Voted Overwhelmingly for Donald Trump, Exit Polls show," *Washington Post*, November 9, 2018, https://www.washingtonpost.com/news/acts-of-faith/wp/2016/11/09/exit-polls-show-white-evangelicals-voted-overwhelmingly-for-donald-trump. See also Tara Isabella Burton, "Poll: White Evangelical Support for Trump Is at an All-Time High," *Vox*, April 20, 2018, https://www.vox.com/identities/2018/4/20/17261726/poll-prri-white-evangelical-support-for-trump-is-at-an-all-time-high.

69. Barna, *Day Christians Changed America*, 135.

70. Sarah Pulliam Bailey and Julie Zauzmer, "Trump to the National Prayer Breakfast: 'I Will Never Let You Down. I Can Say That. Never,'" *Washington Post*, February 7, 2019, https://www.washingtonpost.com/religion/2019/02/06/national-prayer-breakfast-trump-is-likely-play-white-evangelicals-fears.

71. "Marc Short," *Ballotpedia*, accessed July 19, 2019, https://ballotpedia.org/Marc_Short. See also "Marc Short to Serve as Vice President Pence's Chief of Staff as White House Gears Up for 2020 Campaign," *Washington Post*, February 19, 2019, https://www.washingtonpost.com/politics/marc-short-to-return-to-white-house-and-serve-as-vice-president-pences-chief-of-staff/2019/02/19/d4f928a4-345e-11e9-af5b-b51b7ff322e9_story.html.

72. "CNP: William F. Buckley Jr. Council – November 2016," *Soundcloud* audio file, November 2016, https://soundcloud.com/cnp-786867471/william-f-buckley-jr-council-november-2016.

73. Ben White, "Meet Bill Walton," *Politico*, November 23, 2016, https://www.politico.com/tipsheets/morning-money/2016/11/meet-bill-walton-217544. See also Max Abelson, "After Fraud Case with SEC, Former Allied Capital Head Bill Walton Makes a Comeback with Trump Role," *St. Louis Post Dispatch*, November 29, 2016, https://www.stltoday.com/business/local/after-fraud-case-with-sec-former-allied-capital-head-bill/article_563286bc-ebcc-5770-b37e-ed6a3279b6e4.html.

74. Adelle M. Banks, "The Key Evangelical Players on Trump's Advisory Board," *National Catholic Reporter*, September 5, 2017, https://www.ncronline.org/news/politics/key-evangelical-players-trumps-advisory-board.

75. Ana Santos, "What Donald Trump Said during Atlanta's NRA Convention: 'No Longer Will Federal Agencies Be Coming After Law-Abiding Gun Owners,'" *AJC*, October 2, 2017, https://www.ajc.com/news/national-govt—politics/what-donald-trump-said-during-atlanta-nra-convention-longer-will-federal-agencies-coming-after-law-abiding-gun-owners/4jYnq5j1WacCVjBcUVJi2N.

76. Jessica Taylor, "Trump to Values Voters: In America 'We Don't Worship Government, We Worship God,'" *National Public Radio*, October 13, 2017, https://www.npr.org/2017/10/13/557459193/trump-set-to-address-values-voter-summit-for-first-time-as-president.

77. Jeremy W. Peters, "Trump Keeps His Conservative Movement Allies Closest," *New York Times*, August 2, 2017, https://www.nytimes.com/2017/08/02/us/politics/trump-conservative-republicans.html.

78. "CNP: William F. Buckley Jr. Council – November 2016," *Soundcloud* audio file. See HAH file 3.

79. "Remarks by President Trump in Meeting with SCOTUS Groups," *White-House.gov* transcript, February 1, 2017, https://www.whitehouse.gov/briefings-statements/remarks-president-trump-meeting-scotus-groups.

80. Ibid.

81. Heather Sells, "Faith Leaders Pray for Trump in Oval Office, Enjoy 'Open Door' at White House," *Christian Broadcasting Network*, July 12, 2017, http://www1.cbn.com/cbnnews/us/2017/july/faith-leaders-enjoy-open-door-at-white-house.

82. Mark Joseph Stern, "Trump's Trans Troops Ban Will Never Take Effect," *Slate*, March 24, 2018, https://slate.com/news-and-politics/2018/03/trumps-new-trans-troops-ban-is-still-unconstitutional.html.

83. Graham, "Church of The Donald."

84. "The 115th Congress Is among the Oldest in History," *Quorum*, accessed July 19, 2019, https://www.quorum.us/data-driven-insights/the-115th-congress-is-among-the-oldest-in-history/175.

85. Philip Rucker and Robert Barnes, "Trump to Inherit More than 100 Court Vacancies, Plans to Reshape Judiciary," *Washington Post*, December 25, 2016, https://www.washingtonpost.com/politics/trump-to-inherit-more-than-100-court-vacancies-plans-to-reshape-judiciary/2016/12/25/d190dd18-c928-11e6-85b5-76616a33048d_story.html.

86. Lee Fang, "Koch Document Reveals Laundry List of Policy Victories Extracted from the Trump Administration," *Intercept*, February 25, 2018, https://theintercept.com/2018/02/25/koch-brothers-trump-administration. See also "Network by the Numbers," *Document Cloud*, accessed July 18, 2019, https://www.documentcloud.org/documents/4364735-Koch-by-the-Numbers.html.

87. "Corporate Tax Cuts Mainly Benefit Shareholders and CEOs, Not Workers," *Center on Budget and Policy Priorities*, last updated October 11, 2017, https://www.cbpp.org/research/federal-tax/corporate-tax-cuts-mainly-benefit-shareholders-and-ceos-not-workers.

88. Josh Israel, "Trump's Tax Cuts for Betsy DeVos and the Very Rich Are being Paid for by Education Cuts," *Think Progress*, April 10, 2019, https://thinkprogress.org/betsy-devos-benefits-from-trump-tax-bill-pay-for-education-cuts-260654117eb2.

89. Kayla Kitson, "The Koch Brothers' Best Investment," *American Prospect*, June 28, 2018, https://prospect.org/article/koch-brothers-best-investment.

90. Ian Salisbury, "President Trump's New Budget Would Slash These 10 Federal Programs. Here's What They Cost (and Actually Do)," *Money*, February 12, 2018, http://money.com/money/5153676/trump-budget-targets.

91. Teresa Ghilarducci, "Senate Republicans Set Sights On Cutting Social Security," *Forbes*, October 16, 2018, https://www.forbes.com/sites/teresaghilarducci

/2018/10/16/senate-republicans-set-sights-on-cutting-social-security/#39b6b2045da1.

CHAPTER 13: MIDTERMS

1. Matthew Haag, "Robert Jeffress, Pastor Who Said Jews Are Going to Hell, Led Prayer at Jerusalem Embassy," *New York Times*, May 14, 2018.
2. "Executive Order on the Establishment of a White House Faith and Opportunity Initiative," *WhiteHouse.gov*, May 3, 2018, https://www.whitehouse.gov/presidential-actions/executive-order-establishment-white-house-faith-opportunity-initiative.
3. "President Trump Hosts Faith Leaders at the White House," *WhiteHouse.gov*, May 4, 2017, https://www.whitehouse.gov/articles/president-trump-hosts-faith-leaders-white-house.
4. Elizabeth Dias, "Inside Evangelical Leaders' Private White House Dinner," *Time*, May 4, 2017.
5. Mike Pence, Twitter post, May 19, 2017, https://twitter.com/vp/status/865670477460656130
6. Elizabeth Dias, "President Trump Lost a Fight to Allow Churches to Get More Involved in Politics," *Time*, December 15, 2017.
7. Paul Kane, "Democrats Say GOP Tax Perk Aimed at Helping One Influential Conservative College," *Washington Post*, December 1, 2017.
8. Alice Lloyd, "The College That Wants to Take Over Washington," *Politico*, May 12, 2018, https://www.politico.com/magazine/story/2018/05/12/hillsdale-college-trump-pence-218362. See also "Remarks by Vice President Pence at the Hillsdale College 166th Commencement Ceremony, *WhiteHouse.gov*, May 12, 2018, https://www.whitehouse.gov/briefings-statements/remarks-vice-president-pence-hillsdale-college-166th-commencement-ceremony.
9. *Washington Watch*, September 21, 2015.
10. "Watchmen on the Wall 2015: Championing Pastors to Transform America" *WatchmenPastors.org*, accessed July 18, 2019, https://downloads.frc.org/EF/EF15E106.pdf.
11. "Watchmen on the Wall 2017 Video Archive," *Watchmen on the Wall,* accessed July 18, 2019, http://www.watchmenpastors.org/archive-2017.

12. Ibid., Craig at 8:15, French at 15:25, and Church closing remarks at 16:25.

13. Ibid.

14. "James Robison Honored at Watchmen on the Wall," Facebook Live, Family Research Council, May 25, 2017, https://www.facebook.com/familyresearchcouncil/videos/10155302623262442.

15. Ibid., at 18:00.

16. Jess Witt, "Ted Cruz Is Still Using a Blacklisted Cambridge Analytica App Developer," *Fast Company*, November 6, 2018, https://www.fastcompany.com/90262252/ted-cruz-still-using-blacklisted-cambridge-analytica-app-developer-aggregateiq. See also Christopher Heine, "Trump's Campaign Just Launched a Mobile App."

17. Patrick O'Keefe, "How P2P Texting is Revolutionizing Politics," August 26, 2018, *Medium*, https://medium.com/political-moneyball/how-p2p-texting-is-revolutionizing-politics-bfe697c2abb8.

18. "2018 TED-Style Talks," YouTube video, 1:22:37, TheAAPC1969, April 27, 2018, https://www.youtube.com/watch?v=oEoaitWArGU&feature=youtu.be&t=29m5s.

19. "While It Is Day . . . Engage" session, chaired by Todd Starnes, *Watchmen on the Wall 2018 Video Archive*, http://watchmenpastors.org/archive-2018. See 3:14.

20. Associated Press, "Hobby Lobby Fined $3 Million for Smuggling Iraqi Religious Artifacts," *Fortune*, July 6, 2017, https://fortune.com/2017/07/06/hobby-lobby-bible-museum-smuggling-artifacts-iraq

21. Museum of the Bible, "Museum of the Bible Releases Research Findings on Fragments in Its Dead Sea Scrolls Collection," *Museum of the Bible* press release, October 22, 2018, https://www.museumofthebible.org/press/press-releases/museum-of-the-bible-releases-research-findings-on-fragments-in-its-dead-sea-scrolls-collection.

22. Philip Rojc, "Path to Power: Who Funds the Religious Right?," *Inside Philanthropy*, January 17, 2017, https://www.insidephilanthropy.com/home/2017/1/17/giving-to-glorify-god-who-funds-the-religious-right.

23. Photo of wall.

24. Adam Cancryn, "Back Home, Freedom Caucus' Meadows Hailed as Anti-Obamacare Hero," *Politico*, March 27, 2017, https://www.politico.com/story/2017/03/mark-meadows-obamacare-carolina-236525.

25. "Watchmen on the Wall 2018 Video Archive," *Watchmen on the Wall*, accessed July 19, 2019, http://www.watchmenpastors.org/archive-2018?videoId=5786063310001. See "big brother" comment at 1:00.

26. Alliance Defense Fund, "FRC Honors ADF Attorney Mike Johnson with 'Family, Faith and Freedom Award,'" *Alliance Defense Fund* press release, March 17, 2005, https://www.adflegal.org/detailspages/press-release-details/frc-honors-adf-attorney-mike-johnson-with—family—faith—and-freedom-award-.

27. Marc J. Franklin, "Inside Broadway's Mark Hellinger Theatre," *Playbill*, February 6, 2019, http://www.playbill.com/article/step-inside-broadways-mark-hellinger-theatre.

28. "WOTW 2018 Pastor Carter Conlon," *Carter Conlon* video, June 21, 2018, http://carterconlon.com/watchmen-conference-2018.

29. "Watchmen: Standing on the Wall and in the Gap,"Tony Perkins's *Washington Update*, May 25, 2018, https://web.archive.org/web/20180914173423/https://www.frc.org/updatearticle/20180525/standing-wall-gap. Accessed Wayback Machine for September 14, 2018.

30. Ibid.

31. Katherine Stewart, "The Christian Right Adopts a 50-State Strategy," *New York Times*, June 20, 2018.

32. Susie Hawkins, "Becoming Winsome in Ministry," *Susie Hawkins* Blog, April 24, 2018, https://www.namb.net/resource-blog/becoming-winsome-in-ministry.

33. Ann E. Marimow, "Two Years In, Trump's Appeals Court Confirmations at a Historic High Point," *Washington Post*, February 4, 2019.

34. See "McConnell's Laser Focus on Transforming the Judiciary," *Politico*, October 17, 2018, https://www.politico.com/story/2018/10/17/senate-gop-judges-911935.

35. Liz Moyer, "As Funds Invoke Bible Values, Others See Intolerance," *New York Times*, February 28, 2017.

36. Edward Wong, "The Rapture and the Real World: Mike Pompeo Blends Beliefs and Policy," *New York Times*, March 30, 2019. See also "Summit Church [Kansas] God and Country Rally with U.S. Congressman Mike Pompeo," YouTube video, 42:37, Summit Church Kansas, June 28, 2015, https://www.youtube.com/watch?v=sOoopXYM52w.

37. Values Voter Summit, Washington, September 21–23, 2018. "Values Bus Tour Stops," *Values Bus Tour*, accessed July 18, 2019, http://www.valuesbustour.com/tour. "Values Bus Media," *Values Bus Tour*, accessed July 18, 2019, http://www.valuesbustour.com/media. See also FRC Action, "Family Research Action's Values Bus Tour Heads to Indiana," *FRCAction* press release, October 17, 2018, https://www.frcaction.org/get.cfm?i=PR18J13.

38. Michelle Moons, "Mike Pence to Rally for Hawley, Koback, Other Republicans in Kansas City," *Breitbart*, October 30, 2018, https://www.breitbart.com/midterm-election/2018/10/30/mike-pence-rally-hawley-kobach-republicans-kansas-city.

39. "Values Bus Tour Stops," *Values Bus Tour*.

40. WPA Intelligence, "Our Team: Chris Wilson," *WPA Intelligence*, accessed July 18, 2019, http://wpaintel.com/team/chris-wilson.

41. "Glen Caroline, "Volunteer Faculty at the Leadership Institute," *Leadership Institute*, accessed July 18, 2019, https://www.leadershipinstitute.org/training/contact.cfm?FacultyID=14734.

42. Author screenshots.

43. John McCormick, "Koch Network Plans to Spend $400 Million in U.S. Midterm Cycle," *Bloomberg*, January 27, 2018, https://www.bloomberg.com/news/articles/2018-01-28/koch-network-plans-to-spend-400-million-in-u-s-midterm-cycle.

44. James Hohmann, "Daily 202: Koch Network Laying Groundwork to Fundamentally Transform America's Education System," *Washington Post*, January 30, 2018, https://www.bloomberg.com/news/articles/2018-01-28/koch-network-plans-to-spend-400-million-in-u-s-midterm-cycle.

45. James Hohmann, "Koch Network Identifies Top 2018 Targets and Outlines Plans for Heavy Early Spending," *Washington Post*, January 29, 2018, https://www.washingtonpost.com/news/powerpost/wp/2018/01/29/koch-network-identifies-top-2018-targets-and-outlines-plans-for-heavy-early-spending/?utm_term=.e4adf4319a27.

46. "Join Our Team to Change America," *Americans for Prosperity*, accessed July 18, 2019, https://americansforprosperity.org/careers.

47. Hiroko Tabuchi, "How the Koch Brothers Are Killing Public Transit Projects Around the Country," *New York Times*, June 19, 2018, https://www.nytimes.com/2018/06/19/climate/koch-brothers-public-transit.html.

48. "SBA List 2018 Election Report," *Susan B. Anthony List*, accessed July 18, 2019, https://www.sba-list.org/2018-election-report. See also "Mobilizing the Pro-Life Vote to Win a Pro-Life Senate Majority," *Susan B. Anthony List*, accessed July 18, 2019, https://s27319.pcdn.co/wp-content/uploads/2018/12/12.07.18-2018-Election-SBA-List-By-the-Numbers.pdf.

49. Christopher Hooks and Mike Spies, "Documents Show NRA and Republican Candidates Coordinated Ads in Key Senate Races," *Mother Jones*, January 11, 2019, https://www.motherjones.com/politics/2019/01/nra-republicans-campaign-ads-senate-josh-hawley.

50. "Disbursements for i360, 2017-2018," *Federal Election Commission*, July 18, 2019, https://www.fec.gov/data/disbursements/?data_type=processed&recipient_name=i360&two_year_transaction_period=2018&min_date=01%2F01%2F2017&max_date=10%2F14%2F2018.

51. Calvin Sloan, "Koch Brothers Are Watching You: And New Documents Reveal Just How Much They Know," *Salon*, November 5, 2018, https://www.fec.gov/data/disbursements/?data_type=processed&recipient_name=i360&two_year_transaction_period=2018&min_date=01%2F01%2F2017&max_date=10%2F14%2F2018.

52. "The Event," *Truth and Liberty*, accessed July 18, 2019, https://truthandliberty.net/episode/the-event-2018.

53. Jordan Misra, "Behind the 2018 U.S. Midterm Election Turnout," *United States Census Bureau*, April 23, 2019, https://www.census.gov/library/stories/2019/04/behind-2018-united-states-midterm-election-turnout.html.

54. "Our Team, Chris Wilson," *WPA Intelligence*, accessed June 18, 2019, http://wpaintel.com/team/chris-wilson/

CHAPTER 14: "DEMOCRACY IN AMERICA"

1. Family Research Council, "A Look Back on 2018," Facebook Live, posted December 19, 2018, https://www.facebook.com/FRCAction/videos/215127782739315.
2. Debbie Elliot, "Alabama Lawmakers Move to Outlaw Abortion in Challenge to Roe v. Wade," *National Public Radio*, May 1, 2019, https://www.npr.org/2019/05/01/719096129/alabama-lawmakers-move-to-outlaw-abortion-in-challenge-to-roe-v-wade.
3. "Dare to Ask: What Do You Mean by Choice?," Suzy B Blog, *Susan B. Anthony List*, January 21, 2012, https://www.sba-list.org/suzy-b-blog/dare-ask-what-do-you-mean-choice.
4. "Emergency Contraception: Another PP Way of Supporting Taxpayer-Funded Abortion," Suzy B Blog, *Susan B. Anthony List*, April 8, 2011, https://www.sba-list.org/suzy-b-blog/emergency-contraception-another-pp-way-supporting-taxpayer-funded-abortion; Julie Rovner, "Morning-After Pills Don't Cause Abortion, Studies Say," *National Public Radio*, February 21, 2013, https://www.npr.org/sections/health-shots/2013/02/22/172595689/morning-after-pills-dont-cause-abortion-studies-say.
5. Family Research Council, "Plan B No Substitute for Plan A: Abstinence!," *Family Research Council*, May 1, 2019, https://www.frc.org/get.cfm?i=WA15G45
6. W. Gardner Selby, "Ted Cruz Claim that Hillary Clinton Backs 'Unlimited Abortion' to Moment of Birth," *PolitiFact*, October 9, 2016, https://www.politifact.com/texas/statements/2016/oct/09/ted-cruz/false-ted-cruz-claim-hillary-clinton-backs-unlimit.
7. Susan B. Anthony List, "SBA List Urges Senate Passage of Born-Alive Legislation," *Susan B. Anthony List* press release, February 1, 2019, https://www.sba-list.org/newsroom/press-releases/sba-list-urges-senate-passage-born-alive-legislation.
8. "Reproductive Health," *Centers for Disease Control and Prevention*, accessed May 1, 2019, https://www.cdc.gov/reproductivehealth/data_stats/abortion.htm.

9. Petula Dvorak, "A Local Landlord Turns the Tables on Anti-Abortion Protesters," *Washington Post*, March 20, 2012.

10. Reggie Ugwu, "With 'Unplanned,' Abortion Opponents Turn Toward Hollywood," *New York Times*, April 8, 2019.

11. Jordan Hoffman, "Unplanned Review—Anti-Abortion Propaganda is a Gory Mess," *Guardian*, March 28, 2019.

12. Susan B. Anthony List, "Unplanned" Facebook post, March 30, 2019, https://www.facebook.com/SusanBAnthonyList/posts/10156081878976370. See also Molly Jong-Fast, "I Saw Unplanned, the Pro-Life Movie Beloved of Mike Pence and Donald Trump Jr. It Painfully Aborted Two Hours of my Life," *Independent*, April 4, 2019. Tony Perkins's *Washington Update*, "The *Unplanned* Censorship of the Abby Johnson Story," *Family Research Council*, April 1, 2019, https://www.frc.org/updatearticle/20190401/unplanned-censorship.

13. "Hundreds Needed for Faith-Based Movie Filming in Stillwater," *Stillwater News-Press*, May 3, 2018.

14. Ben Protess, Danielle Ivory and Steve Eder, "Where Trump's Hands-Off Approach to Governing Does Not Apply," *New York Times*, September 10, 2017.

15. John Wright, "Anti-LGBT Lawmakers Unveil Slew of 'Religious Freedom' Bills Despite Business Concerns, *Texas Observer,* accessed July 18, 2019, https://www.texasobserver.org/anti-lgbt-lawmakers-unveil-slew-of-religious-freedom-bills-despite-business-concerns.

16. Nsikan Akpan, Gretchen Frazee, and Courtney Norris, "What the New Religious Exemptions Law Means for Your Health Care," *PBS NewsHour*, May 3, 2019, https://www.pbs.org/newshour/health/what-the-new-religious-exemptions-law-means-for-your-health-care.

17. Peter Sprigg, "The Hidden Truth About Changing Sexual Orientation: Ten Ways Pro-LGBT Sources Undermine the Case for Therapy Bans," *Family Research Council*, accessed July 18, 2019, https://downloads.frc.org/EF/EF18E83.PDF.

18. Family Research Council, "Family Research Council Files Amicus Brief in US Supreme Court Marriage Case," *Family Research Council* press release, April 8, 2015, https://www.frc.org/pressrelease/family-research-council-files-amicus-brief-in-us-supreme-court-marriage-case.

19. Molly Ball, "America is Ready for Gay Marriage," *Atlantic*, April 28, 2015, https://www.theatlantic.com/politics/archive/2015/04/america-is-ready-for-gay-marriage/391643. Tom Jacobs, "Legalizing Gay Marriage Reduced Homophobia," *Pacific Standard*, April 15, 2019, https://psmag.com/news/legalizing-gay-marriage-reduced-homophobia-per-new-research.

20. Dhruv Khullar, MD, "Stigma Against Gay People Can Be Deadly," *New York Times*, October 9, 2018, https://www.nytimes.com/2018/10/09/well/live/gay-lesbian-lgbt-health-stigma-laws.html.

21. Jeffrey Toobin, "Harry Reid's Enduring Gift to Barack Obama," *New Yorker*, November 1, 2018, https://www.newyorker.com/news/daily-comment/harry-reids-enduring-gift-to-barack-obama.

22. Justin McCarthy, "Two in Three Americans Support Same-Sex Marriage," *Gallup News*, May 23, 2018, https://news.gallup.com/poll/234866/two-three-americans-support-sex-marriage.aspx; "Public Opinion on Abortion, *Pew Forum*, October 15, 2018, https://www.pewforum.org/fact-sheet/public-opinion-on-abortion.

23. Isaac Stanley-Becker, "Trump Administration Asks Court to Completely Invalidate Obama's Affordable Care Act," *Washington Post*, March 26, 2019, https://www.washingtonpost.com/nation/2019/03/26/trump-administration-asks-court-totally-repeal-obamas-affordable-care-act.

24. Melissa Quinn, "Senate Confirms Trump's 100th Judicial Nominee," *Washington Examiner*, May 2, 2019. Jordain Carney, "Senate Confirms Trump's 100th Judicial Nominee," *Hill*, May 3, 2019, https://thehill.com/blogs/floor-action/senate/442089-senate-confirms-trumps-100th-judicial-nominee.

25. Ben Feuer, "Thanks to Trump, the Liberal 9th Circuit Is No Longer Liberal," *Washington Post*, February 28, 2019, https://www.washingtonpost.com/outlook/2019/02/28/thanks-trump-liberal-ninth-circuit-is-no-longer-liberal.

26. Eli Rosenberg and Deanna Paul, "Senate Just Confirmed a Judge Who Interned at an Anti-LBTQ Group. She'll Serve for Life," *Washington Post*, March 6, 2019, https://www.washingtonpost.com/dc-md-va/2019/03/06/senate-just-confirmed-judge-who-interned-an-anti-lgbtq-group-shell-serve-life.

27. "Trump Picks More 'Not Qualified' Judges," *Bloomberg Law*, December 19, 2018, https://news.bloomberglaw.com/us-law-week/trump-picks-more-not-qualified-judges-1.

28. Lisa Rein, "'I've Never Seen These Positions Politicized': White House Rejection of Veterans Judges Raises Concerns of Partisanship," *Washington Post*, October 23, 2018, https://www.washingtonpost.com/politics/ive-never-seen-these-positions-politicized-white-house-rejection-of-veterans-judges-raises-concerns-of-partisanship/2018/10/23/f488046a-ce51-11e8-920f-dd52e1ae4570_story.html.

29. Drew DeSilver, "Trump's Victory Another Example of How Electoral College Wins Are Bigger Than Popular Vote Ones," *Pew Research Center*, December 20, 2016, https://www.pewresearch.org/fact-tank/2016/12/20/why-electoral-college-landslides-are-easier-to-win-than-popular-vote-ones/.

30. Eric W. Orts, "The Path to Give California 12 Senators, and Vermont Just One," *Atlantic*, January 2, 2019, https://www.theatlantic.com/ideas/archive/2019/01/heres-how-fix-senate/579172.

31. Mark Joyella, "CNN Drops 26% in Prime Time as Fox News Dominates April Cable Ratings," *Forbes*, April 30, 2019, https://www.forbes.com/sites/markjoyella/2019/04/30/cnn-drops-26-percent-in-prime-time-as-fox-news-dominates-april-cable-ratings/#424505453c59.

32. "Stations List," *Bott Radio Network*, accessed July 18, 2019, https://bottradionetwork.com/stations/#.

33. "NPR Stations," *National Public Radio,* accessed July 18, 2019, https://www.npr.org/stations/pdf/nprstations.pdf.

34. "Top 10 Missouri Daily Newspapers," *Cision*, accessed July 18, 2019, https://www.cision.com/us/2013/01/top-10-missouri-daily-newspapers.

35. "McCaskill Tapes: For Your Lies Only," *FRC Action*, October 18, 2018, https://www.frcaction.org/updatearticle/20181018/mccaskill-tapes.

36. "Pastors Network," *Watchmen on the Wall* map. See also "iVoter Guide: The Most Comprehensive and Easy-to-Use Voter Guide," *iVoter Guide*, accessed July 18, 2019, http://home.ivoterguide.com/?doing_wp_cron=1563471680.6732900142669677734375.

37. Kenneth P. Vogel, "James O'Keefe, Practitioner of the Sting, Has an Ally in Trump," *New York Times*, December 7, 2017, https://www.nytimes.com/2017/12/07/us/politics/james-okeefe-project-veritas-trump.html. Kenneth P. Vogel, "O'Keefe Crew's Conservative Training," *Politico*, January 28, 2010,

https://www.politico.com/story/2010/01/okeefe-crews-conservative-training-032138.

38. NRA-ILA app, September 2018.

39. Susan B. Anthony List, "SBA List Visits 310,000+ Missouri Voters to Elect Josh Hawley & Defeat Senator Claire McCaskill," *Susan B. Anthony List* press release, November 6, 2018, https://www.sba-list.org/newsroom/press-releases/sba-list-visits-310000-missouri-voters-elect-josh-hawley-defeat-senator-claire-mccaskill.

40. Americans for Prosperity, "Americans for Prosperity Launches New TV Ad on Sen. McCaskill's Double-Talk on Tax Reform," *Americans for Prosperity* press release, July 18, 2018, https://americansforprosperity.org/americans-for-prosperity-launches-new-tv-ad-on-sen-mccaskills-double-talk-on-tax-reform.

41. Will Lennon, "An Introduction to the Koch Digital Media Network," *Open Secrets*, October 9, 2018, https://www.opensecrets.org/news/2018/10/intro-to-koch-brothers-digital.

42. Ronald Brownstein, "How the Rustbelt Paved Trump's Road to Victory," *Atlantic,* November 10, 2016, https://www.theatlantic.com/politics/archive/2016/11/trumps-road-to-victory/507203.

43. Josh Pacewitz, "Here's the Real Reason Rust Belt Cities and Towns Voted for Trump," *Washington Post*, December 20, 2016, https://www.washingtonpost.com/news/monkey-cage/wp/2016/12/20/heres-the-real-reason-rust-belt-cities-and-towns-voted-for-trump/?utm_term=.88b6dd81b190.

44. Heather Long, "Tax Day 2019: Did the GOP Tax Bill Live Up to its Promises?," *Washington Post*, April 15, 2019.

45. Kate Rabinowitz and Kevin Uhrmacher, "What Trump Proposed in his 2020 Budget," *Washington Post*, updated March 12, 2019, https://www.washingtonpost.com/graphics/2019/politics/trump-budget-2020/?utm_term=.ce6282a3b6d9.

46. Ken Cuccinelli, "Here's How Trump Can be Even More Aggressive in Protecting Our Border," *Washington Examiner*, December 4, 2018.

47. David Sherfinski, "Enthusiastic Evangelicals Mobilize to Multiply Votes for Trump, *Washington Times*, June 16, 2019.

48. Adam Wilmoth, "Oklahoma Sets Oil Production Tax at 2 Percent," Tribune News Service, *Governing*, May 29, 2014, https://www.governing.com/news/headlines/ok-sets-oil-production-tax-at-2-percent.html.

49. David Blatt, "Cost of Oil and Gas Tax Breaks Continues to Approach $400 Million," *Ok Policy*, December 21, 2017, https://okpolicy.org/cost-oil-gas-tax-breaks-continues-approach-400-million.

50. "What's the Matter with Oklahoma?," *Economist*, January 30, 2018.

51. Abigail Hess, "In Oklahoma You Can Make More Money Working at a Gas Station Than as a Teacher," *CNBC*, March 7, 2018, https://www.cnbc.com/2018/03/07/many-oklahoma-teachers-earn-less-than-gas-station-workers.html.

52. Liz Farmer, "Nation's Least-Funded Schools Get What They Pay For," *Governing*, June 2017, https://www.governing.com/topics/education/gov-oklahoma-states-education-funding.html.

53. Emma Brown, "Influential Conservative Group: DeVos Should Dismantle Education Department and Bring God into Classrooms," *Washington Post*, February 15, 2017.

54. "Progress: American Federation for Children 2018 Legislative Impact Report," *American Federal for Children*, accessed July 18, 2019, http://www.federationforchildren.org/wp-content/uploads/2018/08/AFC_LIR_2018_digital2_spreads.pdf

55. Ben Felder, "National School Choice Group Opposing Teacher Candidates, Teacher Pay Raise Supporters," *Oklahoman*, August 25, 2018.

56. David William, "16 Oklahoma Educators Elected to Office on Tuesday," *CNN*, November 7, 2018, https://www.cnn.com/2018/11/07/politics/oklahoma-teachers-election-trnd.

57. Russell Cobb, "Oklahoma Isn't Working. Can Anyone Fix This Failing American State?," *Guardian*, August 29, 2017, https://www.theguardian.com/us-news/2017/aug/29/oklahoma-education-system-four-day-school-weeks-poor.

58. Antonia Juhasz, "Inside the Tax Bill's $25 Billion Oil Company Bonanza," *Pacific Standard*, March 27, 2018, https://psmag.com/economics/tax-bill-oil-company-bonanza.

59. Maggie Severns, "Liberal Megadonors Plan $100 Million Swing-State Blitz to Beat Trump," *Politico*, updated March 6, 2019, https://www.politico.com/story/2019/05/05/liberal-donors-trump-2020-1301639.

60. James Hohmann, "The Daily 202: The Koch Network Is Reorganizing Under a New Name and with New Priorities," *Washington Post,* May 20, 2019, https://www.washingtonpost.com/news/powerpost/paloma/daily-202/2019/05/20/daily-202-the-koch-network-is-reorganizing-under-a-new-name-and-with-new-priorities/5ce1a94fa7a0a435cff8c0d3/?utm_term=.c4c795fd27f6.

61. James Hohmann, "The Daily 202: The Koch Network Donor Retreat Turns Touchy-Feely," *Washington Post,* January 28, 2019, https://www.washingtonpost.com/news/powerpost/paloma/daily-202/2019/01/28/daily-202-the-koch-network-donor-retreat-turns-touchy-feely/5c4e843a1b326b29c3778ce2/.

62. James Hohmann, "The Daily 202: The Koch Network Is Reorganizing Under a New Name and with New Priorities," *Washington Post,* May 20, 2019, https://www.washingtonpost.com/news/powerpost/paloma/daily-202/2019/05/20/daily-202-the-koch-network-is-reorganizing-under-a-new-name-and-with-new-priorities/5ce1a94fa7a0a435cff8c0d3/. See also Paul Farhi, "Charles Koch, Champion of Free Speech? His Grants to the News Media Accelerate," *Washington Post,* July 5, 2018.

63. Dina Dyakon, "Poynter Announces Nine Schools Selected for the 2018-2019 College Media Project," *Poynter Institute* press release, September 17, 2018, https://www.poynter.org/educators-students/2018/poynter-announces-nine-schools-selected-for-the-2018-19-college-media-project.

64. Mark Follman, "Why the National Rifle Association Is Under Fire Like Never Before," *Mother Jones*, March 27, 2019, https://www.motherjones.com/politics/2019/03/nra-russia-butina-torshin-trump-investigations.

65. Mark Maremont, "NRA Chief Wayne LaPierre Questioned on Travel Expenses," *Wall Street Journal*, May 2, 2019, https://www.wsj.com/articles/nra-chief-wayne-lapierre-questioned-on-travel-expenses-11556834268.

66. Tim Dickinson and Andy Kroll, "WTF Is Happening at the NRA, Explained," *Rolling Stone*, May 3, 2019, https://www.rollingstone.com/politics/politics-features/wtf-nra-scandals-explainer-830567.

67. Kevin Bohn and Eli Watkins, "Oliver North: 'Informed' I Will Not Be Renominated NRA President," *CNN*, April 27, 2019, https://www.cnn.com/2019/04/27/politics/oliver-north-nra/index.html.

68. Tom Stites, "About 1,300 U.S. Communities Have Totally Lost News Coverage, UNC News Desert Study Finds," *Poynter Institute*, https://www.poynter.org/business-work/2018/about-1300-u-s-communities-have-totally-lost-news-coverage-unc-news-desert-study-finds.

69. Tony Perkins's *Washington Update*, "When Freedom Was King," Family Research Council, January 15, 2018, http://www.frc.org/updatearticle/20180115/freedom-king. Wayback Machine, archived February 19, 2018.

70. "Evangelical Protestants," *Pew Research Center*, 2019, https://www.pewforum.org/religious-landscape-study/religious-tradition/evangelical-protestant.

EPILOGUE

1. Southern Baptist Convention, "Resolution on Homosexuality," San Antonio, June 1988.

2. Bob Allen, "Pressler Abuse Lawsuit Turns Attention to Confidential Settlement of Earlier Case in 2004," *Baptist News*, February 19, 2018, https://baptistnews.com/article/pressler-abuse-lawsuit-turns-attention-confidential-settlement-earlier-case-2004.

3. Robert Downen, "Lawsuit Against Ex-Judge, Southern Baptist Churches, Drawing to a Close," *Houston Chronicle*, February 6, 2019, https://www.houstonchronicle.com/news/houston-texas/houston/article/Lawsuit-against-ex-judge-Southern-Baptist-13596126.php.

4. Robert Downen, Lise Olsen, and John Tedesco, "Abuse of Faith: 20 Years, 700 Victims, Southern Baptist Abuse Spreads as Leaders Resist Reforms," *Houston Chronicle*, February 10, 2019, https://www.houstonchronicle.com/news/investigations/article/Southern-Baptist-sexual-abuse-spreads-as-leaders-13588038.php.

5. Hannah Long, "J. D. Greear and the Rejection of Partisanship, but not Politics," *Weekly Standard*, July 18, 2018, https://www.weeklystandard.com/hannah-long/j-d-greear-tries-to-distance-southern-baptist-convention-from-partisan-politics.

6. Kevin Phillips, *American Theocracy: The Peril and Politics of Radical Religion, Oil, and Borrowed Money in the 21st Century* (New York: Viking, 2006), ix, xiii.

7. Carrie Brown McWhorter, "Southwestern Seminary Removes Stained Glass Windows Depicting Patterson, Other SBC Leaders," *Alabama Baptist*, April 11, 2019, https://www.thealabamabaptist.org/southwestern-seminary-removes-stained-glass-windows-depicting-patterson-other-sbc-leaders.

RECOMMENDED READING

HISTORY

Ahlstrom, Sydney. *A Religious History of the American People*. Yale University Press: New Haven, 1972.

Baird, W. David, and Danney Goble. *Oklahoma: A History*. University of Oklahoma Press: Norman, 2011.

Davis, David Brion. *The Problem of Slavery in the Age of Emancipation*. Alfred A. Knopf: New York, 2014.

FitzGerald, Frances. *Evangelicals: The Struggle to Shape America*. Simon & Schuster: New York, 2017.

Foner, Eric. *Reconstruction: America's Unfinished Revolution*. Harper Perennial Modern Classics: New York, 2014.

Isenberg, Nancy. *White Trash: The 400-Year Untold History of Class in America*. Penguin Books: New York, 2016.

LePore, Jill. *These Truths*. W.W. Norton: New York, 2018.

MacLean, Nancy. *Democracy in Chains: The Deep History of the Radical Right's Stealth Plan for America*. Penguin Books: New York, 2017.

Monter, E. William. *Calvin's Geneva*. Wipf & Stock: Eugene, OR, 2012.

Morgan, Edmund. *Visible Saints: The History of a Puritan Idea*. Cornell University Press: Ithaca, 1965.

CURRENT EVENTS

Allen, Jonathan, and Amie Parnes. *Shattered: Inside Hillary Clinton's Doomed Campaign*. Crown: New York, 2017.

Blumenthal, Max. *Republican Gomorrah: Inside the Movement that Shattered the Party*. Nation Books: New York, 2009.

Fang, Lee. *The Machine: A Field Guide to the Resurgent Right*. The New Press: New York, 2013.

Frank, Thomas. *What's the Matter with Kansas?: How Conservatives Won the Heart of America*. Metropolitan Books: New York, 2004.

Gilgoff, Dan. *The Jesus Machine: How James Dobson, Focus on the Family, and Evangelical America are Winning the Culture War*. St. Martin's Griffin: New York, 2008.

Mayer, Jane. *Dark Money: The Hidden History of the Billionaires Behind the Rise of the Radical Right*. Anchor Books: New York, 2017.

Oreskes, Naomi, and Erik M. Conway. *Merchants of Doubt: How a Handful of Scientists Obscured the Truth on Issues from Tobacco Smoke to Global Warming*. Bloomsbury Publishing: New York, 2011.

Phillips, Kevin. *American Theocracy: The Peril and Politics of Radical Religion, Oil, and Borrowed Money in the 21st Century*. Viking Press: New York, 2006.

Sharlat, Jeff. *The Family: The Secret Fundamentalism at the Heart of American Power*. Harper Perennial: New York, 2009.

——— *C Street: The Fundamentalist Threat to American Democracy*. Back Bay Books: New York, 2010.

Stewart, Katherine. *The Good News Club: The Religious Right's Stealth Assault on America's Children*. PublicAffairs: New York, 2012.

MOVEMENT WRITINGS

Arnn, Larry. *Liberty and Learning: The Evolution of American Education*. Hillsdale College Press: Hillsdale, MI, 2010.

Barna, George. *The Day Christians Changed America: How Christian Conservatives Put Trump in the White House and Redirected America's Future*. Metaformation: Ventura, 2017.

Dobson, James. *Love Must Be Tough*. Word Publishing: Dallas, 1996.

Jeffress, Robert. *Twilight's Last Gleaming: How America's Last Days Can Be Your Best Days*. Worthy Publishing: Brentwood, TN, 2011.

Johnson, Clint. *The Politically Incorrect Guide to the South (and Why It Will Rise Again)*. Regnery Publishing: Washington, D.C., 2006.

LaHaye, Tim, and Craig Parshall. *Brink of Chaos*. Zondervan: Grand Rapids, 2012.

Loesch, Dana. *Flyover Nation: You Can't Run a Country You've Never Been To.* Sentinel Books: New York, 2016.

Nance, Penny. *Feisty & Feminine: A Rallying Cry for Conservative Women.* Zondervan: Grand Rapids, 2016.

Pressler, Paul. *A Hill on Which to Die: One Southern Baptist's Journey.* Broadman & Holman Publishers: Nashville, 2002.

Sekulow, Jay. *Undemocratic: Rogue, Reckless and Renegade: How the Government is Stealing Democracy One Agency at a Time.* Howard Books: New York, 2014.

Viguerie, Richard. *Takeover: The 100-Year War for the Soul of the GOP and How Conservatives Can Finally Win It.* WND Books: Washington, D.C., 2014.

Wallnau, Lance. *God's Chaos Candidate: Donald J. Trump and the American Unraveling.* Killer Sheep Media: Keller, TX, 2016.

INDEX

A NOTE ON THE AUTHOR

ANNE NELSON has received a Livingston Award for her journalism and a Guggenheim Fellowship for her historical research. A graduate of Yale University, she has taught at Columbia University for more than two decades, first at the School of Journalism and then at the School of International and Public Affairs. She is a member of the New York Council on the Humanities. Her previous books include *Red Orchestra*, a *New York Times Book Review* Editors' Choice, and *Suzanne's Children*, a finalist for the National Jewish Book Award. A native of Oklahoma, she lives in New York City.